PageMaker®
for Windows™
Illustrated

PageMaker® 5
for Windows™
Illustrated

Kevin G. Proot
St. Louis University

Thomas J. Fischer

Course Technology

Course Technology, Inc. One Main Street, Cambridge, MA 02142
An International Thomson Publishing Company

I(T)P

Albany • Bonn • Boston • Cincinnati • London • Madrid • Melbourne • Mexico City
New York • Paris • San Francisco • Singapore • Tokyo • Toronto • Washington

PageMaker 5 for Windows — Illustrated is published by Course Technology, Inc.

Managing Editor:	Marjorie Hunt
Product Manager:	Nicole Jones Pinard
Production Editor:	Roxanne Alexander
Text Designer:	Leslie Hartwell
Cover Designer:	John Gamache

For more information contact:
Course Technology, Inc.
One Main Street
Cambridge, MA 02142

International Thomson Publishing Europe
Berkshire House 168-173
High Holborn
London WCIV 7AA
England

Thomas Nelson Australia
102 Dodds Street
South Melbourne, 3205
Victoria, Australia

Nelson Canada
1120 Birchmount Road
Scarborough, Ontario
Canada M1K 5G4

International Thomson Editores
Campos Eliseos 385, Piso 7
Col. Polanco
11560 Mexico D.F. Mexico

International Thomson Publishing GmbH
Königswinterer Strasse 418
53227 Bonn
Germany

International Thomson Publishing Asia
211 Henderson Road
#05-10 Henderson Building
Singapore 0315

International Thomson Publishing Japan
Hirakawacho Kyowa Building, 3F
2-2-1 Hirakawacho
Chiyoda-ku, Tokyo 102
Japan

Trademarks

Disclaimer

ISBN 1-56527-281-1

Printed in the United States of America

10 9 8 7 6 5 4 3 2 1

From the Publisher

At Course Technology, Inc., we believe that technology will transform the way that people teach and learn. We are very excited about bringing you, instructors and students, the most practical and affordable technology-related products available.

The Course Technology Development Process

Our development process is unparalleled in the educational publishing industry. Every product we create goes through an exacting process of design, development, review, and testing.

Reviewers give us direction and insight that shape our manuscripts and bring them up to the latest standards. Every manuscript is quality tested. Students whose background matches the intended audience work through every keystroke, carefully checking for clarity and pointing out errors in logic and sequence. Together with our technical reviewers, these testers help us ensure that everything that carries our name is as error-free and easy to use as possible.

Course Technology Products

We show both *how* and *why* technology is critical to solving problems in the classroom and in whatever field you choose to teach or pursue. Our time-tested, step-by-step instructions provide unparalleled clarity. Examples and applications are chosen and crafted to motivate students.

The Course Technology Team

This book will suit your needs because it was delivered quickly, efficiently, and affordably. In every aspect of business, we rely on a commitment to quality and the use of technology. Every employee contributes to this process. The names of all our employees are listed below: Diana Armington, Tim Ashe, Sara Ballestero, Debora Barrow, Stephen M. Bayle, Ann Marie Buconjic, Jody Buttafoco, Kerry Cannell, Jei Lee Chong, Jim Chrysikos, Barbara Clemens, Susan Collins, John M. Connolly, Stephanie Crayton, Myrna D'Addario, Lisa D'Alessandro, Jodi Davis, Howard S. Diamond, Kathryn Dinovo, Joseph B. Dougherty, Jennifer Dolan, Patti Dowley, Laurie Duncan, Karen Dwyer, MaryJane Dwyer, Kristin Dyer, Chris Elkhill, Don Fabricant, Ronan Fagen, Dean Fossella, Jane Fraser, Viktor Frengut, Jeff Goding, Laurie Gomes, Eileen Gorham, Chris Greacen, Catherine Griffin, Jamie Harper, Roslyn Hooley, Marjorie Hunt, Nicole Jones Pinard, Matt Kenslea, Marybeth LaFauci, Susannah Lean, Brian Leussler, Kim Mai, Margaret Makowski, Tammy Marciano, Elizabeth Martinez, Debbie Masi, Don Maynard, Kathleen McCann, Sarah McLean, Jay McNamara, Mac Mendelsohn, Karla Mitchell, Kim Munsell, Michael Ormsby, Debbie Parlee, Kristin Patrick, Charlie Patsios, Darren Perl, Kevin Phaneuf, George J. Pilla, Nancy Ray, Brian Romer, Laura Sacks, Carla Sharpe, Deborah Shute, Roger Skilling, Jennifer Slivinski, Christine Spillett, Audrey Tortolani, Michelle Tucker, David Upton, Jim Valente, Mark Valentine, Karen Wadsworth, Renee Walkup, Tracy Wells, Donna Whiting, Rob Williams, Janet Wilson, Lisa Yameen.

Preface

Course Technology, Inc. is proud to present this new book in its Illustrated Series. *PageMaker 5 for Windows — Illustrated* provides a highly visual, hands-on introduction to PageMaker. The book is designed as a learning tool for PageMaker novices but will also be useful as a source for future reference.

Organization and Coverage

PageMaker 5 for Windows — Illustrated contains a Windows overview and nine units that cover basic PageMaker skills. In these units students learn how to plan, design, build, edit, and enhance PageMaker publications. In Unit 10, students apply these skills as they work on additional PageMaker projects.

Approach

PageMaker 5 for Windows — Illustrated distinguishes itself from other textbooks with its highly visual approach to computer instruction.

Lessons: Information Displays

The basic lesson format of this text is the "information display," a two-page lesson that is sharply focused on a specific task. This sharp focus and the precise beginning and end of a lesson make it easy for students to study specific material. Modular lessons are less overwhelming for students, and they provide instructors with more flexibility in planning classes and assigning specific work. The units are modular as well and can be presented in any order.

Each lesson, or "information display," contains the following elements:

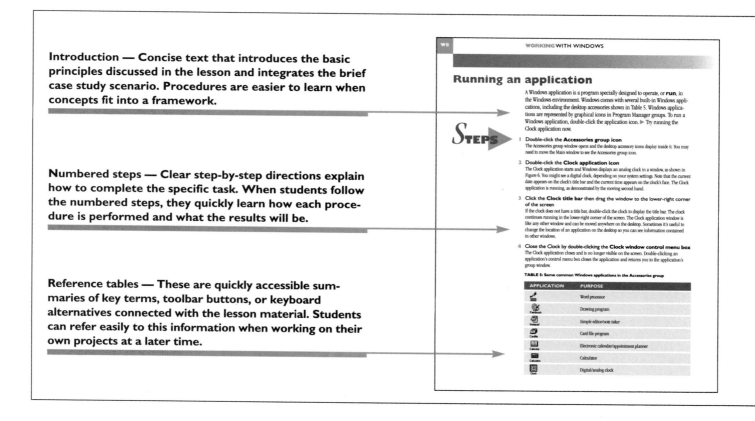

Introduction — Concise text that introduces the basic principles discussed in the lesson and integrates the brief case study scenario. Procedures are easier to learn when concepts fit into a framework.

Numbered steps — Clear step-by-step directions explain how to complete the specific task. When students follow the numbered steps, they quickly learn how each procedure is performed and what the results will be.

Reference tables — These are quickly accessible summaries of key terms, toolbar buttons, or keyboard alternatives connected with the lesson material. Students can refer easily to this information when working on their own projects at a later time.

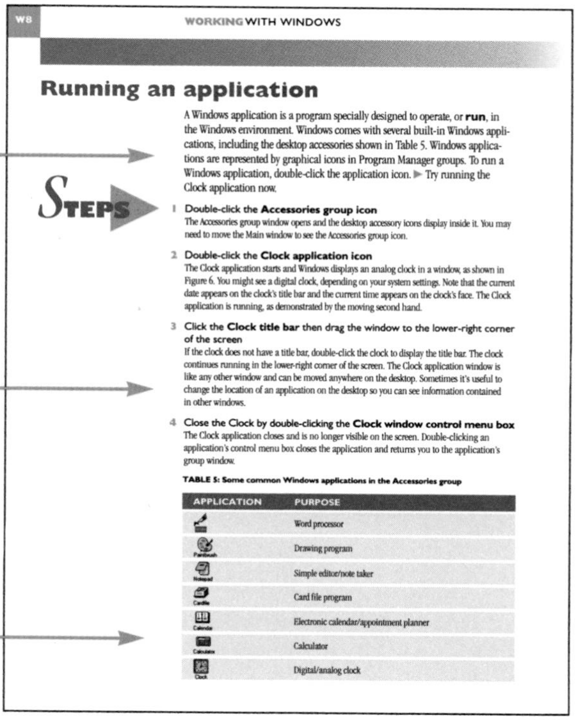

W8 WORKING WITH WINDOWS

Running an application

A Windows application is a program specially designed to operate, or **run**, in the Windows environment. Windows comes with several built-in Windows applications, including the desktop accessories shown in Table 5. Windows applications are represented by graphical icons in Program Manager groups. To run a Windows application, double-click the application icon. ▶ Try running the Clock application now.

STEPS

1 Double-click the **Accessories group icon**
The Accessories group window opens and the desktop accessory icons display inside it. You may need to move the Main window to see the Accessories group icon.

2 Double-click the **Clock application icon**
The Clock application starts and Windows displays an analog clock in a window, as shown in Figure 6. You might see a digital clock, depending on your system settings. Note that the current date appears on the clock's title bar and the current time appears on the clock's face. The Clock application is running, as demonstrated by the moving second hand.

3 Click the **Clock title bar** then drag the window to the lower-right corner of the screen
If the clock does not have a title bar, double-click the clock to display the title bar. The clock continues running in the lower-right corner of the screen. The Clock application window is like any other window and can be moved anywhere on the desktop. Sometimes it's useful to change the location of an application on the desktop so you can see information contained in other windows.

4 Close the Clock by double-clicking the **Clock window control menu box**
The Clock application closes and is no longer visible on the screen. Double-clicking an application's control menu box closes the application and returns you to the application's group window.

TABLE 5: Some common Windows applications in the Accessories group

APPLICATION	PURPOSE
	Word processor
Paintbrush	Drawing program
Notepad	Simple editor/note taker
Cardfile	Card file program
Calendar	Electronic calendar/appointment planner
Calculator	Calculator
Clock	Digital/analog clock

Features

PageMaker 5 for Windows — Illustrated is an exceptional textbook because it contains the following features:

- "Read This Before You Begin..." Pages — These pages, one for the Windows section and one before Unit 1, provide essential information that both students and instructors need to know before they begin working through the units.
- Windows Overview — The "Microsoft Windows 3.1" section provides an overview so students can begin working in the Windows environment right away.
- Real-World Case — The case study used throughout the text book is designed to be "real-world" in nature and representative of the kinds of activities that students will encounter when working with desktop publishing software. With a real-world case, the process of learning skills will be more meaningful to students.
- Design Workshop — At the end of Units 2-9 students are asked to critique the design of the PageMaker publication they created in that unit. Students develop critical thinking skills as they evaluate whether their publication is effective as well as visually pleasing.
- End-of-Unit Material — Each unit concludes with a meaningful Concepts Review that tests students' understanding of what they learned in the unit. The Concepts Review is followed by an Applications Review, which provides students with additional hands-on practice of the skills they learned in the unit. The Applications Review is followed by Independent Challenges, which pose case problems for students to solve. The Independent Challenges allow students to learn by exploring and develop critical thinking skills.

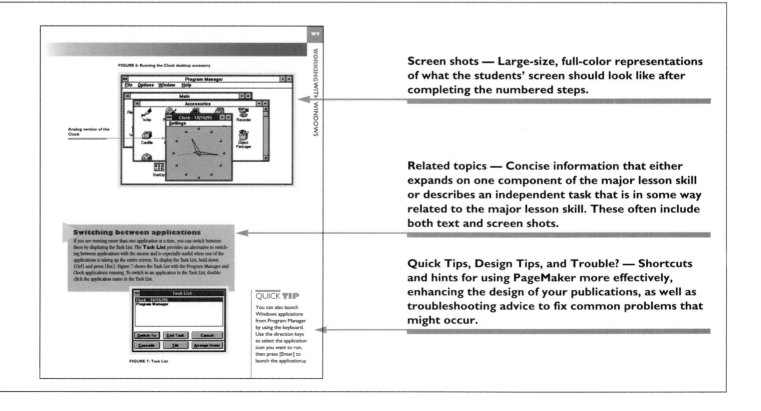

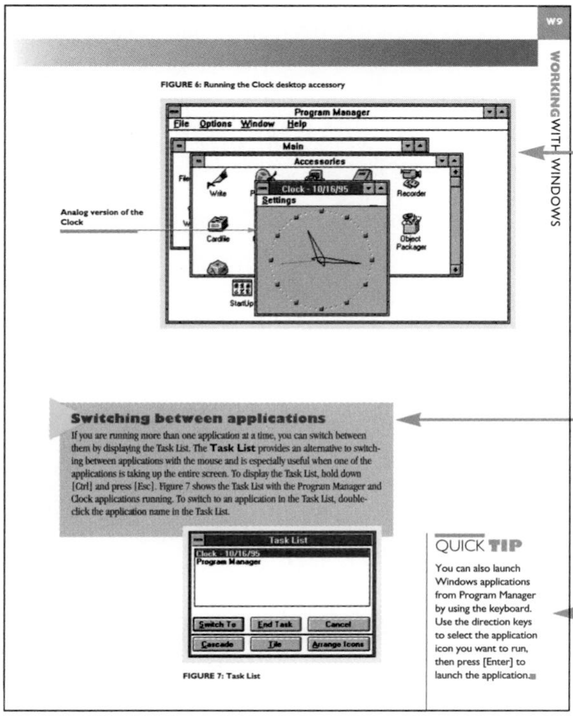

Screen shots — Large-size, full-color representations of what the students' screen should look like after completing the numbered steps.

Related topics — Concise information that either expands on one component of the major lesson skill or describes an independent task that is in some way related to the major lesson skill. These often include both text and screen shots.

Quick Tips, Design Tips, and Trouble? — Shortcuts and hints for using PageMaker more effectively, enhancing the design of your publications, as well as troubleshooting advice to fix common problems that might occur.

Student Disks

The CTI WinApps Setup Disk bundled with the instructor's copy of this book contains an innovative Student Disk generating program designed to save instructors time. Once this software is installed on a network or standalone workstation, students can double-click the "Make PageMaker 5 Illust Student Disks" icon in the CTI WinApps group window. Double-clicking this icon transfers all the data files students need to complete the lessons, Application Reviews, and Independent Challenges to eight high-density disks in drive A or B. The lesson entitled, "Creating your Students Disks" in Unit 1 provides complete step-by-step instructions for making the Student Disks.

Adopters of this text are granted the right to post the Student Disks on any standalone computer or network used by students who have purchased this product.

For more information on the Student Disks, see the page in this book called "Read This Before You Begin PageMaker 5 for Windows."

The Supplements

Instructor's Manual — The Instructor's Manual is quality-assurance tested. It includes:

- Solutions to all lessons, Concept Reviews, Application Reviews, and Independent Challenges
- A disk containing solutions to all of the lessons, Concept Reviews, Application Reviews, and Independent Challenges
- Unit notes containing tips from the authors about the instructional progression of each lesson
- Extra problems for every unit
- Transparency masters of key concepts

Test Bank — The Test Bank contains approximately 50 questions per unit in true/false, multiple choice, and fill-in-the-blanks formats, plus two essay questions. Each question has been quality-assurance tested by students to achieve clarity and accuracy.

Electronic Test Bank — The Electronic Test Bank allows instructors to edit individual test questions, select questions individually or at random, and print out scrambled versions of the same test to any supported printer.

Acknowledgments

We would like to thank the many people who contributed to this book. First, we thank the reviewers for their feedback and thoughtful insights. Producing this book was a team effort and we would like share our gratitude to our teammates at Course Technology. We would like to thank our product development team, Majorie Hunt, Nicole Jones Pinard, Katherine Pinard, Rachel Bunin, and Ann Marie Buconjic. We would also like to thank our production team, Roxanne Alexander, Cynthia Anderson, Jane Pedicini, Jenny Kilgore, and Nancy Ray, our desktop publishing and design team, Debbie Masi and Gex, Inc., Jeff Goding, our quality-assurance manager; and the author of the additional projects, David Beskeen.

We would like to thank Joe Dougherty and Marjorie Hunt who gave us the opportunity to write this book and we are especially grateful to Nicole Jones Pinard for her constant patience, direction and support throughout the entire project.

We would like to give special thanks to our family and friends who have given us constant support and encouragement. In addition we would like to thank Joyelle Proot and John Reiker for providing photographs used in the student exercises. We are especially grateful to Jason Devine, Bob Figliola and Brian Schlueter who chipped in to give us help during the deadline crunch times. Finally we would like to thank you the reader. We hope this book meets your needs in learning a great software application, PageMaker. Happy desktop publishing!

Kevin G. Proot
Thomas J. Fischer

Photography Credits

Unit 1: Eiffel Tower photo, Joyelle Proot, page 7; Beach photo, Thomas J. Fischer, page 11; Big Ben photo, John Reiker, page 11; Unit 3: Eiffel Tower Far, Joyelle Proot, page 57; St. Peter's Square, Joyelle Proot, page 11; Caribbean bay photo, Thomas J. Fischer, page 97; Unit 5: New York Skyline, Kevin G. Proot, page 117; Unit 6: The Needle, Kevin G. Proot, page 135; Airplane, Kevin G. Proot, 135; St. Louis, Gateway Arch, Kevin G. Proot, page 137; Unit 8: Times Square, Kevin G. Proot, page 191; Unit 9: Rome Arch, Joyelle Proot, page 213; St. Peter's Cathedral, Joyelle Proot, page 215.

Brief Contents

Contents

Microsoft® Windows™ 3.1

UNIT 1 Getting Started with Microsoft Windows 3.1

UNIT 2 Creating and Managing Files

Read This Before You Begin Microsoft Windows 3.1

To the Student

To complete some of the step-by-step lessons, Applications Reviews, and Independent Challenges in this book, you must have a Student Disk. You can use a blank, formatted disk or, if you are using another Illustrated book from Course Technology, Inc., *use the Student Disk that accompanies that book*. If you use a Student Disk from another Illustrated book, your instructor will do one of the following: 1) provide you with your own copy of the disk; 2) have you copy it from the network onto your own floppy disk; or 3) have you copy the lesson files from a network into your own subdirectory on the network. Always use your own copies of the lesson and exercise files. See your instructor or technical support person for further information.

Using Your Own Computer

If you are going to work through this book using your own computer, you need a computer system running Microsoft Windows 3.1 and a blank, formatted disk or a Student Disk. If you are using another Illustrated book, use the Student Disk that accompanies that book. If you are not using another Illustrated book, you can simply use a blank, formatted disk to work through these units. This blank, formatted disk becomes your Student Disk.

To the Instructor

This book does not come with a Student Disk. Students do not need any files to work through these units. However, students are asked to create a MY_FILES directory on their Student Disk that they will use to store the files they create and save.

If you have adopted another Illustrated book, instruct your students to use the Student Disk that accompanies that book as they work through these units. If you have adopted more than one Illustrated book, or if another Illustrated book has more than one Student Disk, instruct your students to create a MY_FILES directory on each Student Disk. If you are not using another Illustrated book, you can instruct your students to use a blank, formatted disk to work through these units. This blank, formatted disk becomes their Student Disk.

The instructions in this book assume that the students know which drive and directory contain the Student Disk, so it's important that you provide disk location information before the students start working through the units.

UNIT 1

OBJECTIVES

- Start Windows
- Use the mouse
- Use Program Manager groups
- Resize a window
- Use scroll bars
- Run an application
- Use menus
- Use dialog boxes
- Arrange windows and icons
- Exit Windows

Getting Started WITH MICROSOFT WINDOWS 3.1

Microsoft Windows 3.1 is the **graphical user interface** (GUI) that works hand in hand with MS-DOS to control the basic operation of your computer and the programs you run on it. Windows is a comprehensive control program that helps you run useful, task-oriented programs known as **applications**. ▶ This unit will introduce you to basic skills that you can use in all Windows applications. First you'll learn how to start Windows and how to use the mouse in the Windows environment. Next you'll get some hands-on experience with Program Manager, and you'll learn how to work with groups, resize a window, scroll a window, run an application, use menus and dialog boxes, and arrange windows and icons. Then you'll learn how to exit a Windows application and exit Windows itself. ▶

Starting Windows

Windows is started, or **launched**, from MS-DOS with the WIN command. Once started, Windows takes over most of the duties of MS-DOS and provides a graphical environment in which you run your applications. Windows has several advantages over MS-DOS. As a graphical interface, it uses meaningful pictures and symbols known as **icons** to replace hard-to-remember commands. Also, each application is represented in a rectangular space called a **window**. ▶ Once you launch Windows, you see the Windows desktop. The **desktop** is an electronic version of a desk that provides workspace for different computing tasks. Use Table 1-1 to identify the key elements of the desktop, referring to Figure 1-1 for their locations. Because the Windows desktop can be customized, your desktop might look slightly different. ▶ Try starting Windows now.

STEPS

1 **If your computer is not on, turn it on**
The computer displays some technical information as it starts up and tests its circuitry. MS-DOS starts automatically, then displays the **command prompt** (usually C:\>). The command prompt gives you access to MS-DOS commands and applications. If your computer is set up so that it automatically runs Windows when it starts, the command prompt will not appear. You can then skip Step 2.

2 **Type win then press [Enter]**
This command starts Windows. The screen momentarily goes blank while the computer starts Windows. An hourglass appears, indicating Windows is busy processing a command. Then the Program Manager appears on your screen, as shown in Figure 1. Your screen might look slightly different depending on which applications are installed on your computer.

FIGURE 1-1: Program Manager window

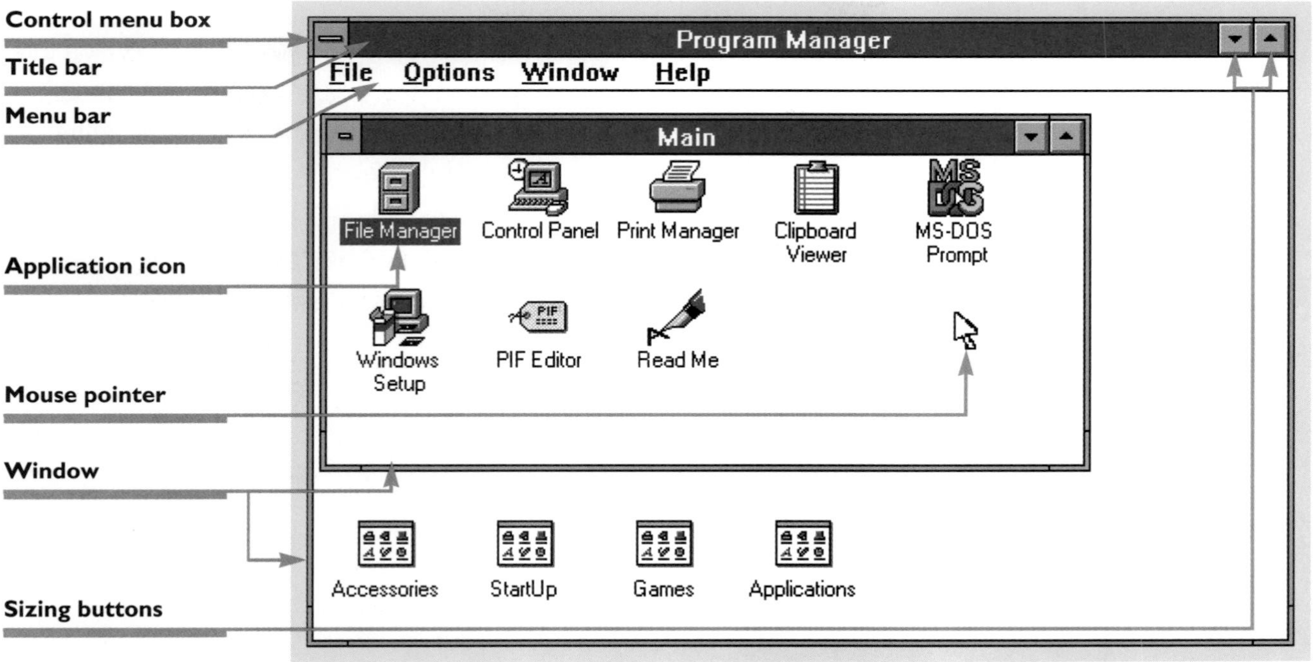

TABLE 1-1:
Elements of the Windows desktop

DESKTOP ELEMENT	DESCRIPTION
Program Manager	The main control program of Windows; all Windows applications are started from Program Manager
Window	A rectangular space framed by a double border on the screen; Program Manager is framed in a window
Application icon	The graphic representation of a Windows application
Title bar	The area directly below a window's top border that displays the name of a window or an application
Sizing buttons	Buttons in the upper-right corner of a window that you can use to minimize, maximize, or restore a window
Menu bar	The area under the title bar on a window that provides access to an application's commands
Control menu box	A box in the upper-left corner of each window that provides a menu used to resize, move, maximize, minimize, or close a window; double-clicking this box closes a window or an application
Mouse pointer	An arrow indicating the current location of the mouse on the desktop

Using the mouse

The **mouse** is a handheld input device that you roll on your desk to position the mouse pointer on the Windows desktop. When you move the mouse on your desk, the **mouse pointer** on the screen moves in the same direction. The buttons on the mouse, as shown in Figure 1-2, are used to select icons and commands, and to indicate the work to be done in applications. Table 1-2 lists the four basic mouse techniques. Table 1-3 shows some common mouse pointer shapes. ▶ Try using the mouse now.

STEPS

1 **Locate the mouse pointer on the Windows desktop and move the mouse across your desk**
Watch how the mouse pointer moves on the Windows desktop in response to your movements. Try moving the mouse pointer in circles, then back and forth in straight lines.

2 **Position the mouse pointer over the Control Panel application icon in the Main group window**
Positioning the mouse pointer over an icon is called **pointing**. The Control Panel icon is a graphical representation of the Control Panel application, a special program that controls the operation of the Windows environment. If the Control Panel application icon is not visible in the Main group window, point to any other icon. The Program Manager is customizable so the Control Panel could be hidden from view or in a different window.

3 **Press and release the left mouse button**
Unless otherwise indicated, you will use the left mouse button to perform all mouse operations. Pressing and releasing the mouse button is called **clicking**. When you position the mouse pointer on an icon in Program Manager then click, you **select** the icon. When the Control Panel icon is selected, its title is highlighted, as shown in Figure 1-3. If you clicked an icon that caused a menu to open, click the icon again to close the menu. You'll learn about menus later. Now practice a mouse skill called **dragging**.

4 **With the icon selected, press and hold the left mouse button, then move the mouse down and to the right and release the mouse button**
The icon changes from color to black and white and moves with the mouse pointer. When you release the mouse button, the icon relocates in the group window.

5 **Drag the Control Panel application icon back to its original position**

TABLE 1-2: Basic mouse techniques

TECHNIQUE	HOW TO DO IT
Pointing	Move the mouse pointer to position it over an item on the desktop
Clicking	Press and release the mouse button
Double-clicking	Press and release the mouse button twice quickly
Dragging	Point at an item, press and hold the mouse button, move the mouse to a new location, then release the mouse button

FIGURE 1-2: The mouse

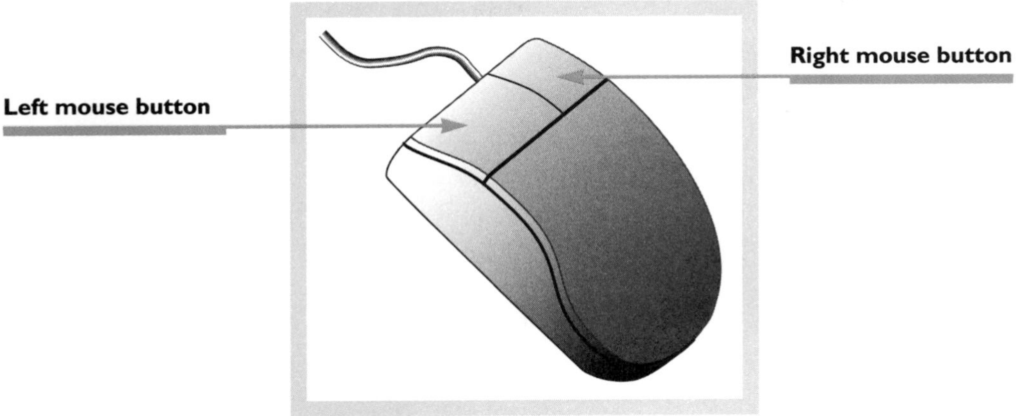

FIGURE 1-3: Selecting an icon

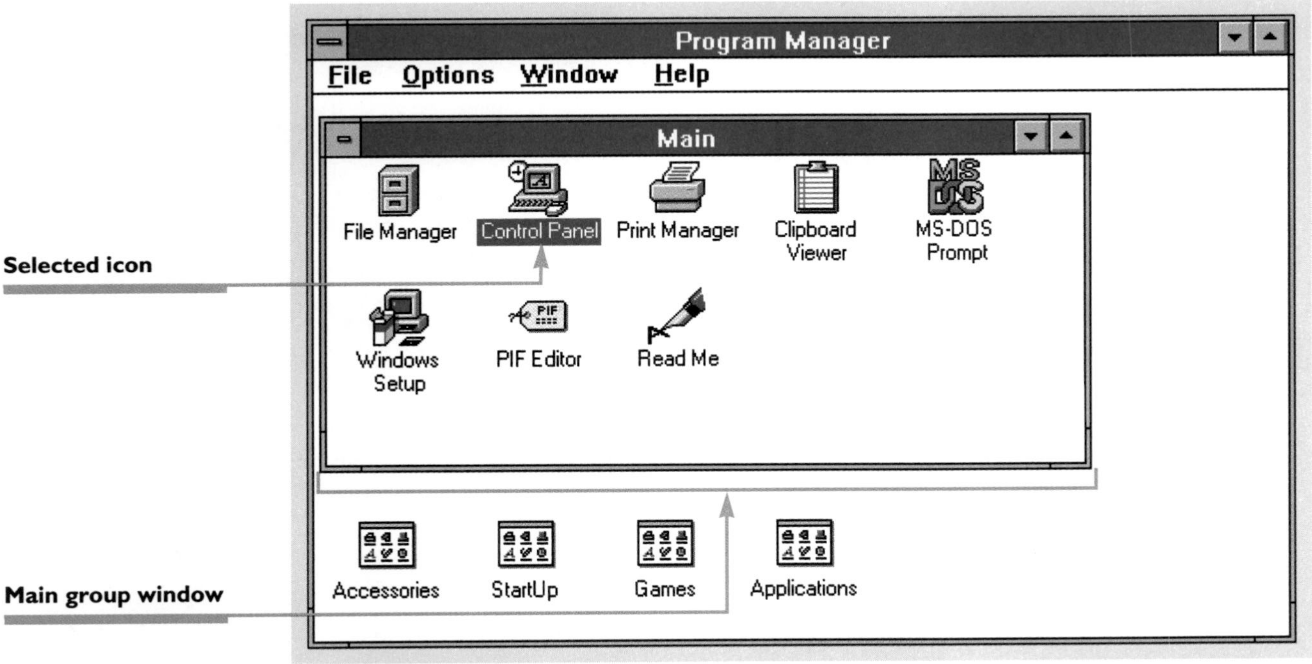

TABLE 1-3: Common mouse pointer shapes

SHAPE	USED TO
	Select items, choose commands, start applications, and work in applications
	Position mouse pointer for editing or inserting text; called the insertion point or cursor
	Indicate Windows is busy processing a command
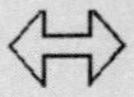	Change the size of a window; appears when mouse pointer is on the border of a window

QUICK TIP

Windows comes with a short tutorial about using the mouse and improving your hand-eye coordination. Press [Alt][H], then [W] and follow the instructions on the screen to run the tutorial.

Using Program Manager groups

In Program Manager, you start applications and organize your applications into windows called **groups**. A group can appear as an open window or as an icon in the Program Manager window. Each group has a name related to its contents, and you can reorganize the groups to suit your needs. The standard Windows groups are described in Table 1-4, but each can be customized to include additional applications. ▶ Try working with groups now.

STEPS

1 **If necessary, double-click the Main group icon to open the Main group window**
The Main group icon is usually located at the bottom of the Program Manager window.

2 **Double-click the Accessories group icon**
When you double-click the Accessories group icon, it expands into the Accessories group window, as shown in Figure 1-4. Your group window might contain different icons. Now move the Accessories group window to the right.

3 **Click the Accessories group window title bar, then drag the window to the right**
An outline of the window moves to the right with the mouse. When you release the mouse button, the Accessories group window moves to the location you've indicated. Moving a window lets you see what is beneath it. Any window in the Windows environment can be moved with this technique.

4 **Click the title bar of the Main group window**
The Main group window becomes the **active window**, the one you are currently working in. Other windows, including the Accessories group window, are considered background windows. Note that the active window has a highlighted title bar. Program Manager has a highlighted title bar because it is the **active application**.

5 **Activate the Accessories group window by clicking anywhere in that window**
The Accessories group window becomes the active window again. Now try closing the Accessories group window.

6 **Double-click the control menu box in the Accessories group window**
When you double-click this box, the Accessories group window shrinks to an icon and the Main group window becomes the active window, as shown in Figure 1-5. Double-clicking the control menu box is the easiest way to close a window or an application.

FIGURE 1-4: Accessories group expanded into a window

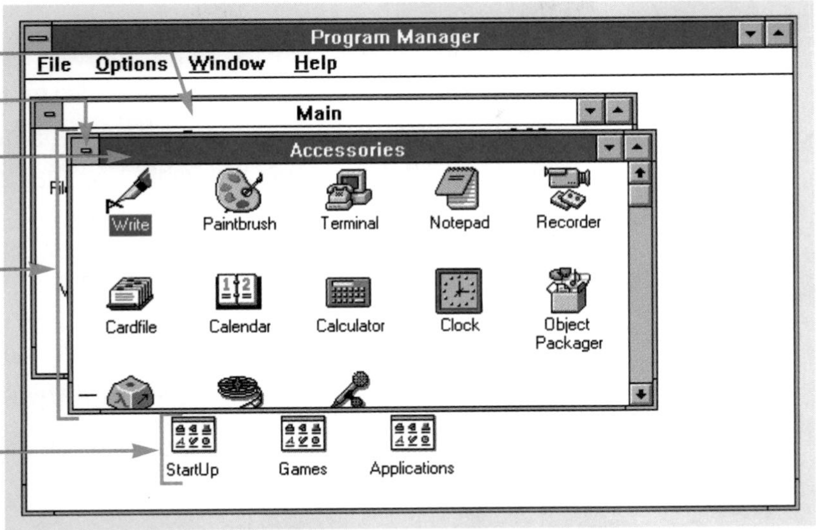

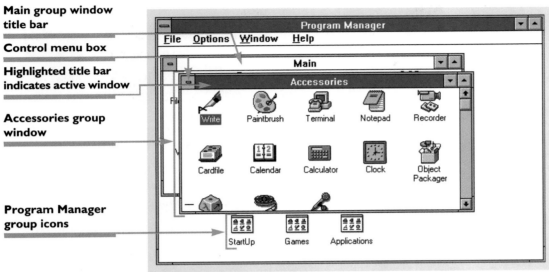

FIGURE 1-5: Closing the Accessories group window

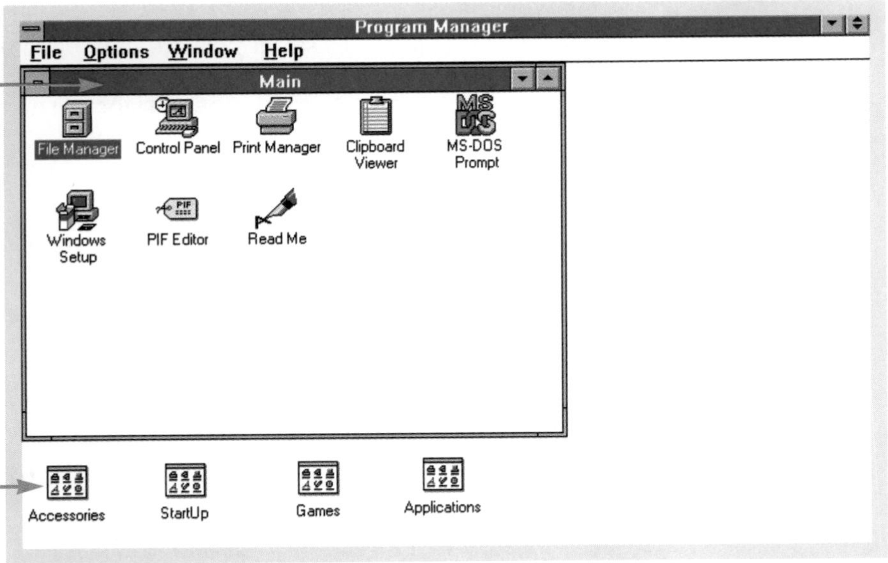

TABLE 1-4: Standard Windows groups

GROUP NAME	CONTENTS
Main	Applications that control how Windows works; the primary Windows group
Accessories	Useful desktop accessories for day-to-day tasks
StartUp	Applications that run automatically when Windows is started
Games	Game applications for Windows
Applications	Applications found on your hard disk

QUICK TIP

To switch between active windows using the keyboard, press [Ctrl][F6].

Resizing a window

The Windows desktop can get cluttered with icons and windows if you are working with several applications. Each window is surrounded by a standard border and sizing buttons that allow you to minimize, maximize, and restore windows as needed. The sizing buttons are shown in Table 1-5. They help you keep the desktop organized. ▶ Try sizing the Program Manager and Accessories group windows now.

STEPS

1. **Click the Minimize button in the upper-right corner of the Program Manager window**
   When you minimize a window, it shrinks to an icon at the bottom of the screen, as shown in Figure 1-6. Windows applications continue to run after you minimize them.

2. **Restore the Program Manager window to its previous size by double-clicking the Program Manager icon**
   The Program manager window returns to its previous size.

3. **Click the Maximize button in the upper-right corner of the Program Manager window**
   When you maximize a window, it takes up the whole screen, as shown in Figure 1-7.

4. **Click the Restore button in the upper-right corner of the Program Manager window**
   The Restore button, shown in Figure 1-7, appears *after* an application has been maximized. The Restore button returns an application to its original size. In addition to minimizing, maximizing, and restoring windows, you can also change the dimensions of any window. Open the Accessories group and change the dimensions of its window.

5. **Double-click the Accessories group icon, then position the mouse pointer on the right edge of the Accessories group window until the pointer changes to ⇔**

6. **Drag the Accessories window border to the right to increase the window's width**
   You can increase or decrease the size of a window, but its shape will always be a rectangle. Finally, decrease the width of the Accessories group window before proceeding to the next lesson.

7. **Drag the Accessories group window border to the left until it is the same size as in Figure 1-8**
   Continue with the next lesson.

TABLE 1-5: Buttons for managing windows

BUTTON	PURPOSE
▼	Minimizes an application to an icon on the bottom of the screen
▲	Maximizes an application to its largest possible size
⬍	Restores an application, returning it to its original size

FIGURE 1-6: Program Manager minimized

FIGURE 1-7: Program Manager maximized

Restore button

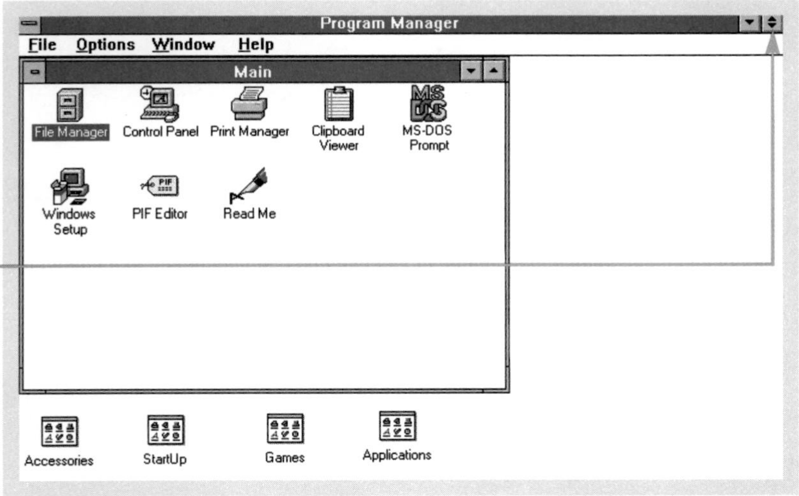

FIGURE 1-8: Accessories group window resized

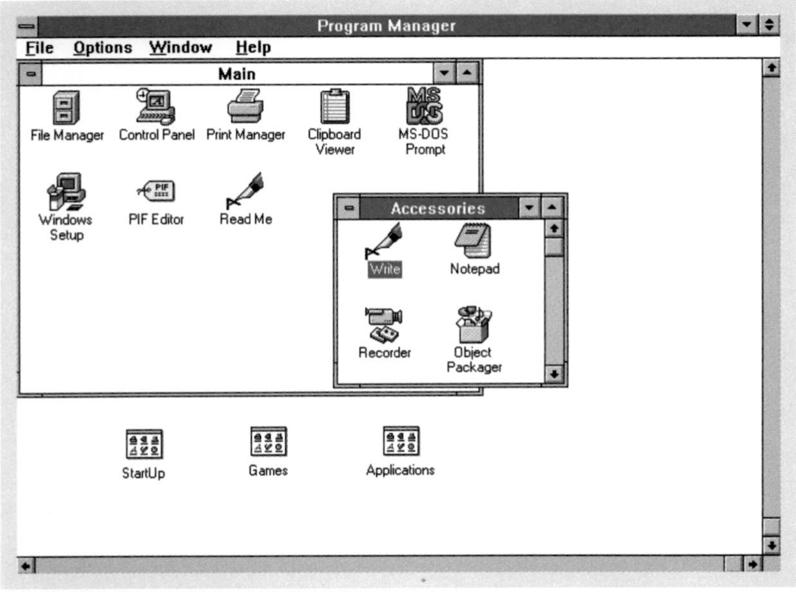

Using scroll bars

If a window contains more information than can be displayed at one time, **scroll bars** appear on the right and/or bottom edges of the window to give you access to that information. For example, when you resized the Accessories group window, scroll bars appeared on the right, as shown in Figure 1-9. Both the horizontal and vertical scroll bars have **scroll arrows** and **scroll boxes** that help you to move around the window. To move around the window, you click the vertical or horizontal arrows that point in the direction in which you want to move, or you can drag the scroll box along the scroll bar. ▶ Scroll through the Accessories group window to view the available applications.

STEPS

1. **Make sure your Accessories group window is open with the vertical scroll bar visible**

2. **Click the down scroll arrow on the vertical scroll bar once**
   Notice that the contents of the window and the vertical scroll box scroll up a small increment, as shown in Figure 1-9. This technique is useful when you only need to scroll a short distance. You can click the scroll arrows several times to move a greater distance or you can use the scroll box.

3. **Drag the scroll box down to the bottom of the vertical scroll bar**
   Use the scroll box if you want to move quickly from one end of a window to another. You can also click in the scroll bar, above or below the scroll box to scroll a window in larger increments. The horizontal scroll bar and scroll box works in the same way as the vertical scroll bar and scroll box, except the horizontal scroll bar moves the contents of a window left to right or right to left.

4. **Scroll the Accessories group window until the Clock application is visible**
   See Figure 1-10. In the next lesson, you will learn how to run the Clock application.

FIGURE 1-9: Window with vertical scroll bar

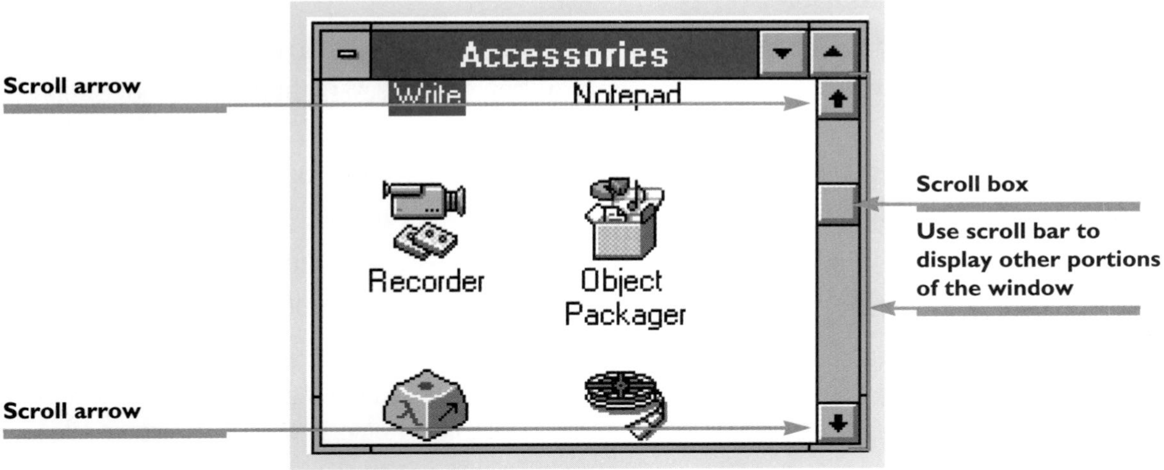

FIGURE 1-10: Scrolling the Accessories group window

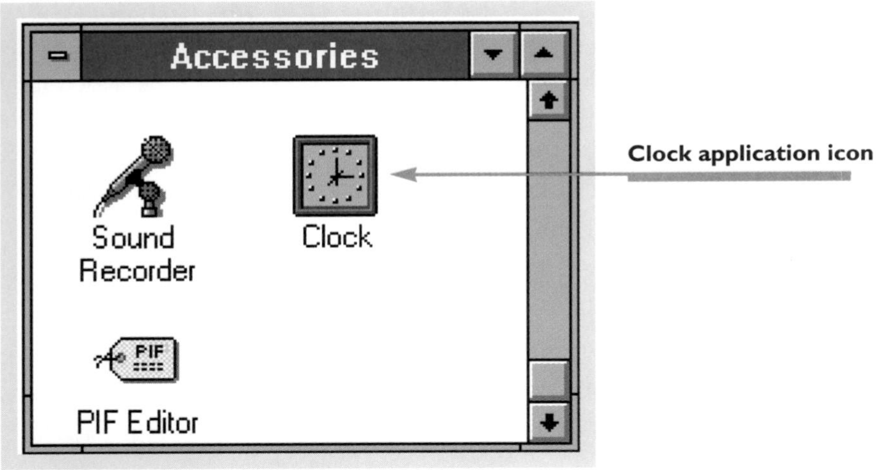

QUICK TIP

You can use direction keys on the keyboard to scroll the contents of an active window. (Remember that an active window is the window with the highlighted title bar.) To scroll vertically, press [↑] or [↓]. To scroll horizontally, press [←] or [→].

Running an application

A Windows application is a program specially designed to operate, or **run**, in the Windows environment. Windows comes with several built-in Windows applications, including the desktop accessories shown in Table 1-6. Windows applications are represented by icons in Program Manager groups. To run a Windows application, double-click the application icon. In Windows, you can run more than one application at a time. See the related topic "Switching between applications" for more information. ▶ Try running the Clock application now.

STEPS

1 Double-click the **Clock application icon** in the Accessories group window

The Clock application starts and displays an analog clock in a window, as shown in Figure 1-11. You might see a digital clock, depending on your system settings. Note that the current date appears on the clock's title bar and the current time appears on the clock's face. The Clock application is running, as demonstrated by the moving second hand.

2 Click the **Clock window title bar**, then drag the window to the lower-right corner of the screen

If the clock does not have a title bar, double-click the clock to display the title bar. The clock continues running in the lower-right corner of the screen. The Clock application window is like any other window and can be moved anywhere on the desktop. Sometimes it's useful to change the location of an application on the desktop so you can see information contained in other windows.

3 Double-click the **control menu box** on the Clock application window to close it

The Clock application closes and is no longer visible on the screen. Double-clicking an application's control menu box closes the application and returns you to the application's group window.

TABLE 1-6: Some common Windows applications in the Accessories group

APPLICATION	PURPOSE
 Write	Word processor
 Paintbrush	Drawing program
 Notepad	Simple editor/note taker
 Cardfile	Card file program
 Calendar	Calendar/appointment planner
 Calculator	Calculator
 Clock	Digital/analog clock

FIGURE 1-11: Running the Clock desktop accessory

Analog version of the clock

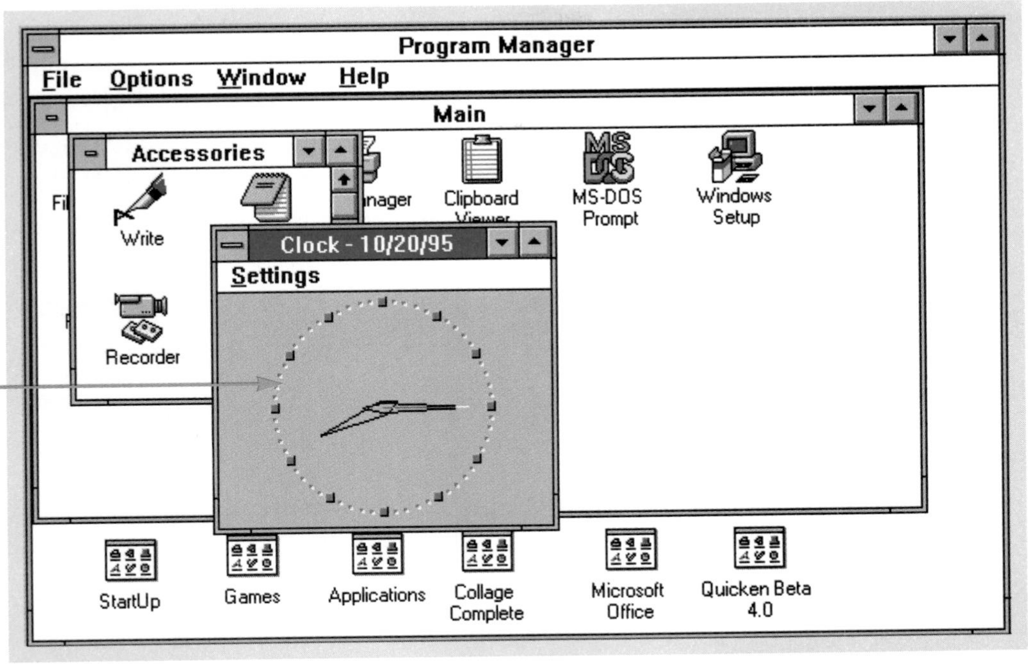

Switching between applications

Running more than one application at a time is called **multitasking**. This is useful if you want to share information between applications. When you have more than one application running, you can use the **Task List** to switch between applications. To display the Task List, press [Ctrl] [Esc]. Figure 1-12 shows the Task List with the Program Manager and Clock applications running. To switch to an application in the Task List, double-click the application name in the Task List.

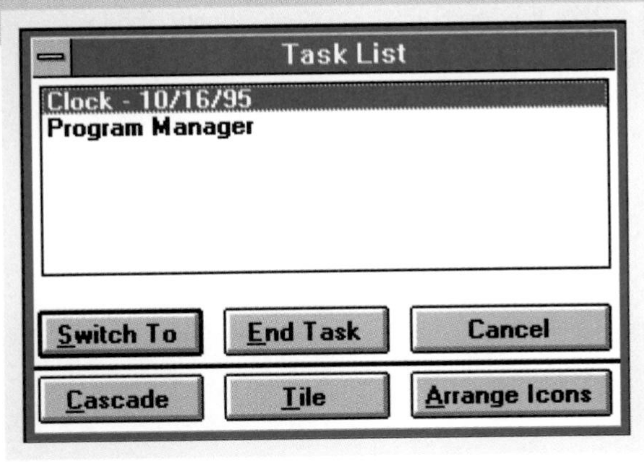

FIGURE 1-12: Task List

QUICK TIP

To switch quickly between several applications, press [Alt][Tab] until you see the application you want. Release [Alt] to switch to that application.

Using menus

A **menu** is a list of commands that you use to accomplish certain tasks. Each Windows application has its own set of menus, which are located on the **menu bar** along the top of the application window. The menus organize commands into groups of related operations. For example, the Help menu contains commands for accessing Windows' extensive on-line Help system. You can use both the mouse and the keyboard to access menu commands. See Table 1-7 for examples of what you might see on a typical menu. ▶ Use the Help menu to open Windows on-line Help.

STEPS

1. **Click Help on the Program Manager menu bar**
   The Help menu opens, as shown in Figure 1-13.

2. **Click Contents on the Help menu**
   The Program Manager Help window appears and displays its contents page.

3. **Position the pointer over the green underlined text Switch Between Applications until the pointer changes to**
   If you are using a monochrome monitor, this text is in black.

4. **Click the topic Switch Between Applications**
   Another Help window opens, giving you information on how to switch between applications. Read this information, using the scroll bars as necessary. It should reinforce what you learned in the "Running an application" lesson. You can use Program Manager Help to answer any questions that arise as you are working with Windows.

5. **Click Back to return to the contents page**
   You can also open menus by pressing the Alt key and then the underlined letter on the menu bar. Now use the keyboard, instead of the mouse, to exit Help.

6. **Press [Alt]**
   The File menu is selected as shown in Figure 1-14.

7. **Press [F] to open the File menu**
   You could also press [↓] or [Enter] to open the menu. The File menu opens. Notice that a letter in each command is underlined. You can access these commands by pressing the underlined letter. Notice also that the Open and Print Setup commands are followed by an ellipsis (...). An **ellipsis** indicates that a dialog box will open when you choose this command. You will learn about dialog boxes in the next lesson.

   Now you can exit Help.

8. **Press [X] to exit Help**

FIGURE 1-13: Help menu on Program Manager menu bar

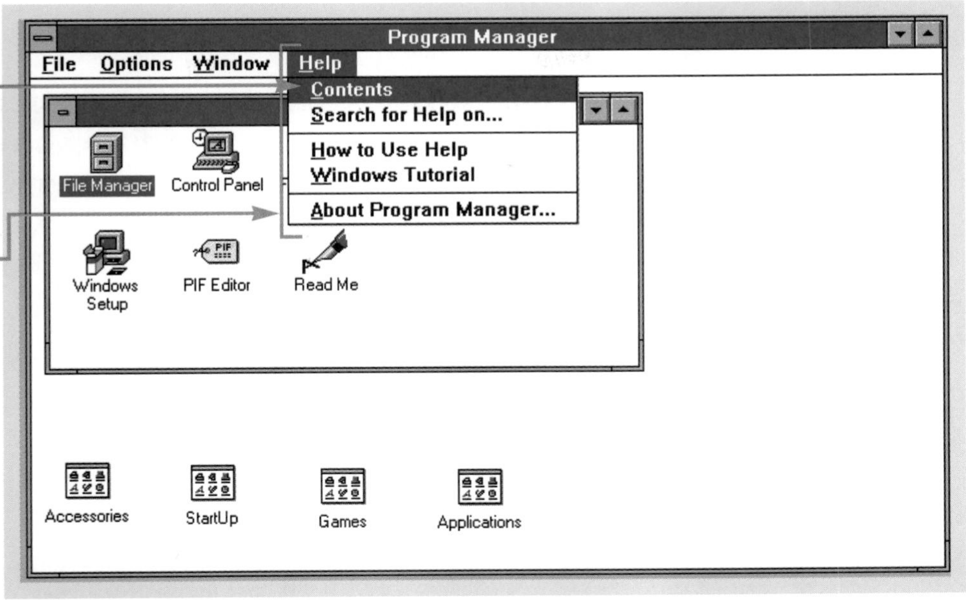

Highlighted command indicates it is selected

Help menu

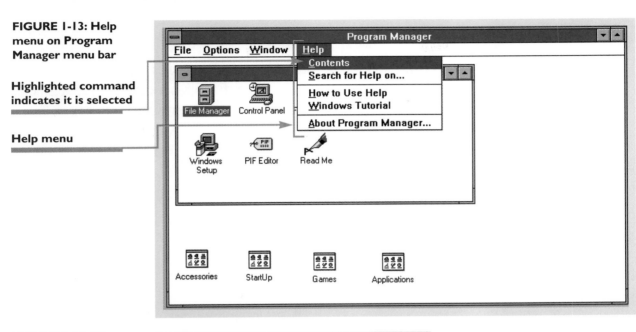

FIGURE 1-14: File highlighted on Help window menu bar

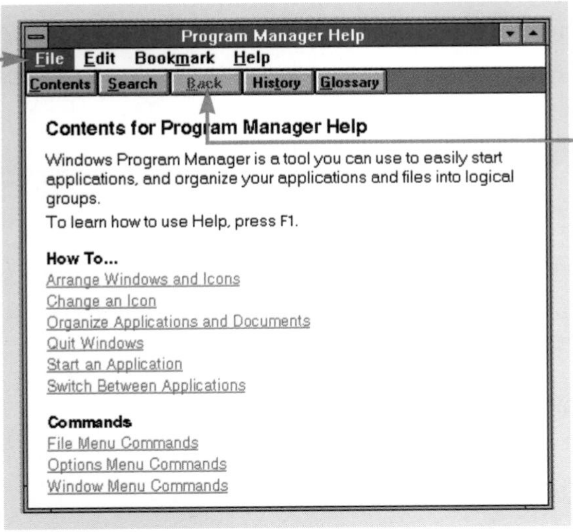

File menu selected

Click to return to previous screen

QUICK **TIP**

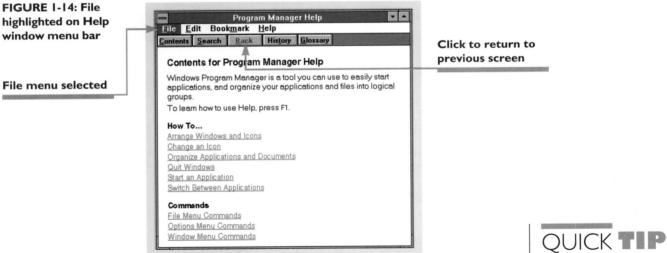

To learn how to use Help, press [F1].■

TABLE 1-7: Typical items on a menu

ITEM	DESCRIPTION	EXAMPLE
Dimmed command	A menu command that is not currently available	Undo
Ellipsis	Choosing this menu command opens a dialog box that asks for further information	Paste Special...
Triangle	Clicking this button opens a cascading menu containing an additional list of menu commands	Axis ▸
Keyboard shortcut	A keyboard alternative for executing a menu command	Cut Ctrl+X
Underlined letter	Pressing the underlined letter executes this menu command	Copy Right

Using dialog boxes

Sometimes when you select a command from a menu, the command needs more information before it can complete its task. A **dialog box** opens requesting more information. See Table 1-8 for some of the typical elements of a dialog box. ▶ Try using the Control Panel, which lets you customize your Windows desktop, to practice using dialog boxes.

STEPS

1 **Click the Main group window to make it active, then double-click the Control Panel application icon**
Drag other windows out of the way, if necessary. If the Control Panel application icon is not in the main group window, ask your technical support person for assistance. The Control Panel group window opens.

2 **Click Settings on the menu bar**
A menu appears listing all the commands that let you adjust different aspects of your desktop.

3 **Click Desktop to display the Desktop dialog box**
This dialog box provides options to customize your desktop. See Figure 1-15. Next, locate the Screen Saver section in the middle of the dialog box. A **screen saver** is a moving pattern that fills your screen after your computer has not been used for a specified amount of time.

4 **Click the Name list arrow in the Screen Saver section**
A list of available screen saver patterns appears.

5 **Click the screen saver pattern of your choice, then click Test**
The screen saver pattern you chose appears. It will remain on the screen until you move the mouse or press a key.

The Test button is a **command button**. The two most common command buttons are OK and Cancel, which you'll see in almost every dialog box.

6 **Move the mouse to exit the screen saver**
Next, you'll adjust the cursor blink rate in the Cursor Blink Rate section of the dialog box. The **cursor**, or in some applications called the insertion point, is the blinking vertical line that shows you where you are on the screen. See Figure 1-15.

7 **Drag the scroll box all the way to the right of the scroll bar, then click the left arrow in the scroll bar a few times**
By moving the scroll box between Slow and Fast on the scroll bar, you can adjust the cursor blink rate to suit your needs.

8 **Click OK to save your changes and close the dialog box**
Clicking OK accepts your changes; clicking Cancel rejects your changes. Now you can exit the Control Panel.

9 **Double-click the control menu box on the Control Panel window to close it**

FIGURE 1-15: Desktop dialog box

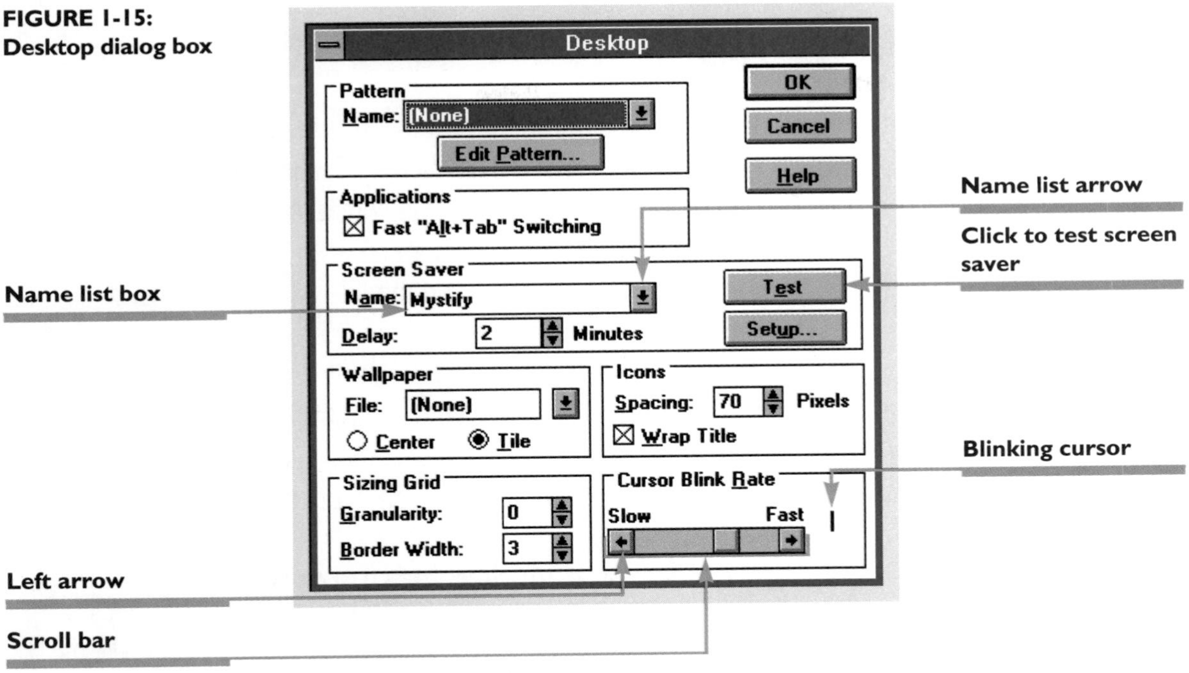

QUICK TIP

If you are in a computer lab, you should return the desktop settings you changed to their original state.

TABLE 1-8: Typical items in a dialog box

ITEM	DESCRIPTION	EXAMPLE
Check box	Clicking this square box turns a dialog box option on or off	☒ Wrap Title
Text box	A box in which you type text	tours.wk4
Radio button	Clicking this small circle selects a single dialog box option	◉ Tile
Command button	Clicking this button executes the dialog box command	OK
List box	A box containing a list of items; to choose an item, click the list arrow, then click the desired item	c: ms-dos_5

Arranging windows and icons

If your desktop contains many groups that you open regularly, you might find that the open windows clutter your desktop. The Tile and Cascade commands on the Window menu let you view all your open group windows at once in an organized arrangement. You can also use the Window menu to open all the program groups installed on your computer. ▶ Once you are comfortable working with Windows, you might decide to reorganize the icon in your group windows. You can easily move an icon from one group window to another by dragging it with the mouse. In the following steps, you'll drag the Clock application icon from the Accessories group window to the StartUp group window. The StartUp group window contains programs that automatically start running when you launch Windows.

STEPS

1. **Click the Program Manager window Maximize button to maximize this window, then click Window on the menu bar**

   The Window menu opens, as shown in Figure 1-16, displaying the commands Cascade, Tile, and Arrange Icons, followed by a numbered list of the program groups installed on your computer. You might see a check mark next to one of the items, indicating that this program group is the active one. Locate StartUp on the numbered list. If you don't see StartUp, see your instructor or technical support person for assistance.

2. **Click StartUp**

   The StartUp group window opens. Depending on how your computer is set up, you might see some program icons already in this window. At this point, your screen is getting cluttered with three program group windows open (Main, Accessories, and StartUp). Use the Cascade command to arrange them in an orderly way.

3. **Click Window on the menu bar, then click Cascade**

   The windows appear in a layered arrangement, with the title bars of each showing. This formation is neatly organized and shows all your open group windows, but it doesn't allow you to easily drag the Clock application icon from the Accessories group window to the StartUp group window. The Tile command arranges the windows so that the contents of all the open windows are visible.

4. **Click Window on the menu bar, then click Tile**

   The windows are now positioned in an ideal way to drag an icon from one window to another. Before continuing to Step 5, locate the Clock application icon in the Accessories group window. If you don't see the icon, use the scroll bar to bring it into view.

5. **Drag the Clock application icon from the Accessories group window to the StartUp group window**

   Your screen now looks like Figure 1-17. The Clock application will automatically start the next time Windows is launched. If you are working on your own computer and want to leave the Clock in the StartUp group, skip Step 6 and continue to the next lesson, "Exiting Windows." If you are working in a computer lab, move the Clock application icon back to its original location in the Accessories group window.

6. **Drag the Clock application icon from the StartUp group window to the Accessories group window**

   The Clock icon is now back in the Accessories group.

FIGURE 1-16: Window menu

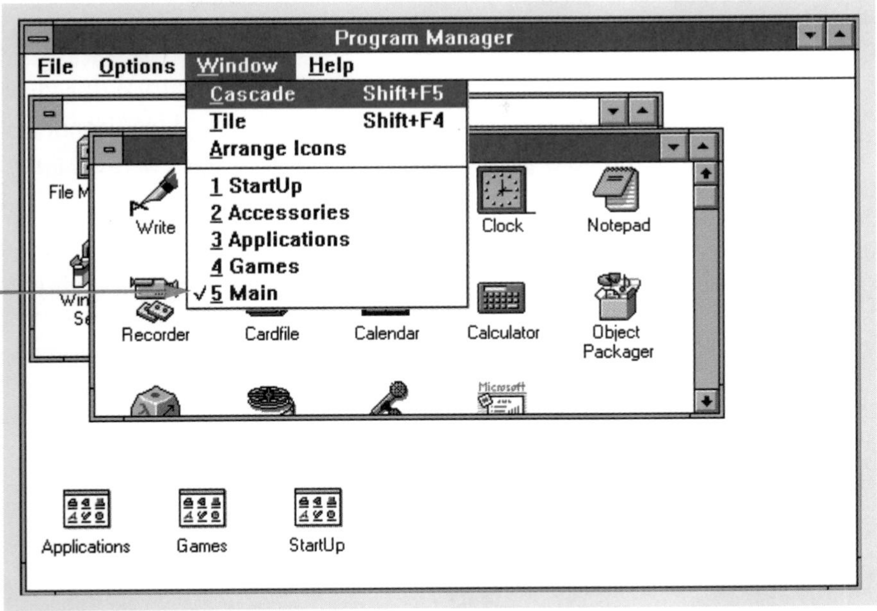

Check mark indicates the active program group

FIGURE 1-17: Tiled group windows

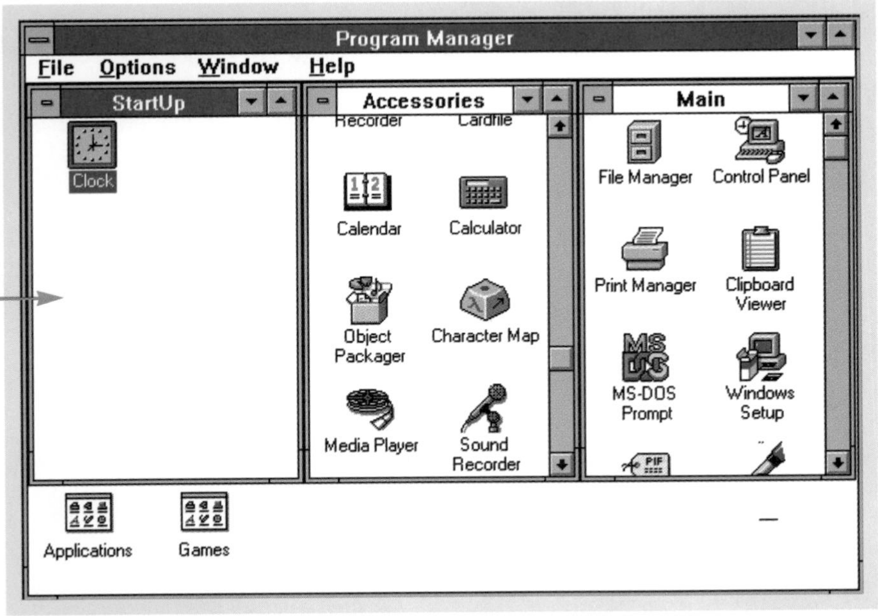

StartUp group window with Clock application icon

QUICK **TIP**

To move a copy of an icon from one group window to another, press and hold [Ctrl] as you drag the icon.

Exiting Windows

When you are finished working with Windows, close all the applications you are running and exit Windows from the Program Manager. Do not turn off the computer while Windows is running; you could lose important data if you turn off your computer too soon. For more information, see the related topic "Exiting Windows with the Program Manager control menu box." ▶ Now try closing all your active applications and exiting Windows.

STEPS

1. **Close any active applications or group windows by double-clicking the control menu boxes on the open windows, one at a time**
   The windows close. If you have any unsaved changes in your application, a dialog box opens, asking if you want to save them.

2. Click **File** on the Program Manager menu bar
   The File menu opens, as shown in Figure 1-18.

3. Click **Exit Windows**
   Program Manager displays the Exit Windows dialog box, as shown in Figure 1-19. You have two options at this point: click OK to exit Windows, or click Cancel to abort the Exit Windows command and return to the Program Manager.

4. Click **OK** to exit Windows
   Windows closes and the MS-DOS command prompt appears. You can now safely turn off the computer.

FIGURE 1-18: Exiting Windows using the File menu

Menu bar

Exit Windows command

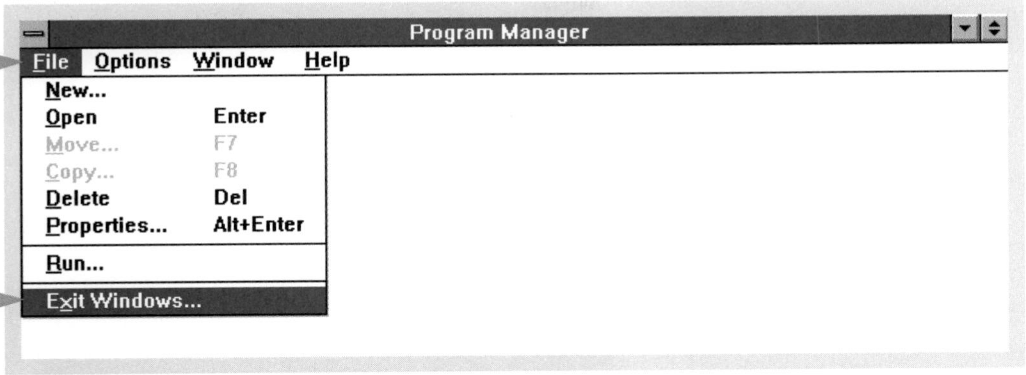

FIGURE 1-19: Exit Windows dialog box

Exiting Windows with the Program Manager control menu box

You can also exit Windows by double-clicking the control menu box in the upper-left corner of the Program Manager window, as shown in Figure 1-20. After you double-click the control menu box, you see the Exit Windows dialog box. Click OK to exit Windows.

Double-click the control menu box

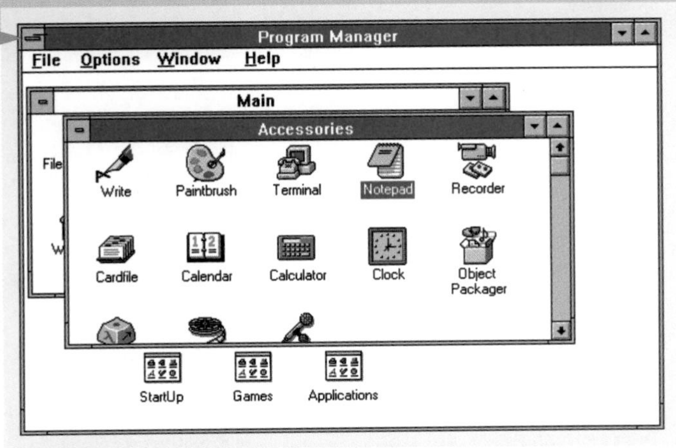

FIGURE 1-20: Exiting Windows with the Program Manager control menu box

TROUBLE?

If you do not exit from Windows before turning off the computer, you might lose data from the applications you used while you were running Windows. Always close your applications and exit from Windows before turning off your computer. Do not turn off the computer if you are in a computer lab.

CONCEPTS REVIEW

Label each of the elements of the Windows screen shown in Figure 1-21.

1 Size Buttons

2

3

4

5

6

7

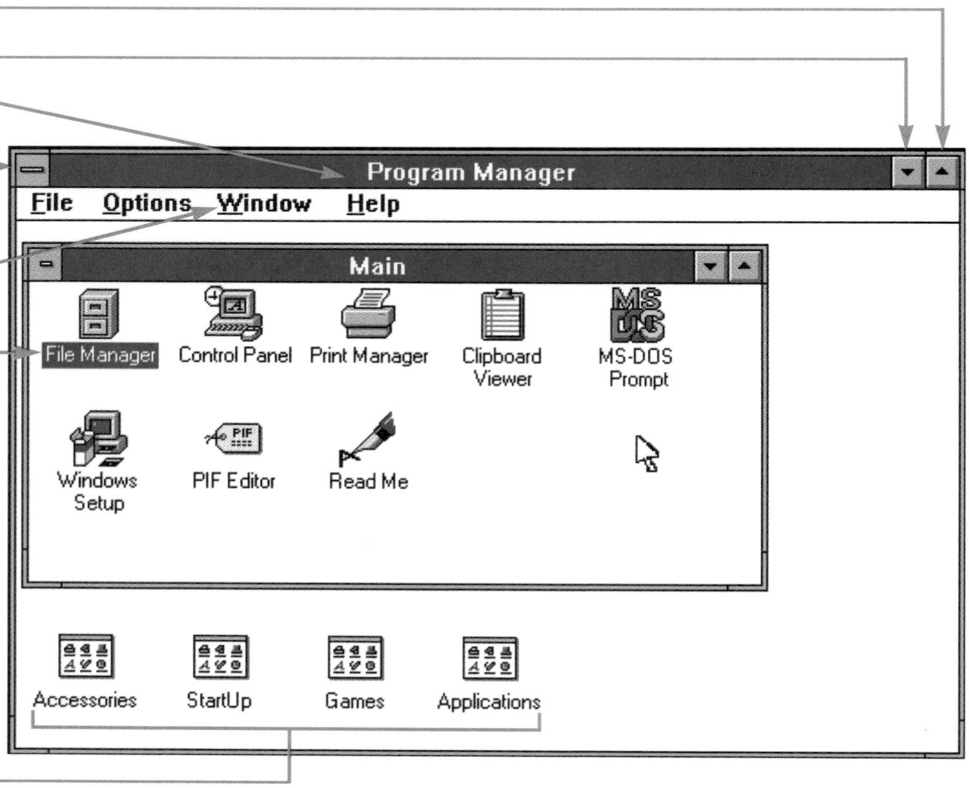

FIGURE 1-21

Match each of the statements with the term it describes.

8 Shrinks an application window to an icon

9 Displays the name of the window or application

10 Serves as a launching pad for all applications

11 Requests more information that you supply before executing command

12 Lets the user point at screen menus and icons

a. Program Manager
b. Dialog box
c. Mouse
d. Title bar
e. Minimize button

Select the best answer from the list of choices.

13 The acronym GUI means
- a. Grayed user information
- b. Group user icons
- c. Graphical user interface
- d. Group user interconnect

14 The term for starting Windows is
- a. Prompting
- b. Launching
- c. Applying
- d. Processing

15 The small pictures that represent items such as applications are called

a. Icons
b. Windows
c. Buttons
d. Pointers

16 All of the following are examples of using a mouse, EXCEPT:

a. Clicking the Maximize button
b. Pressing [Enter]
c. Pointing at the control menu box
d. Dragging the Games group icon

17 When Windows is busy performing a task, the mouse pointer changes to a(n)

a. Hand
b. Arrow
c Clock
d. Hourglass

18 The term for moving an item to a new location on the desktop is

a. Pointing
b. Clicking
c. Dragging
d. Restoring

19 The Clock, Notepad, and Calendar applications in Windows are known as

a. Menu commands
b. Control panels
c. Sizing buttons
d. Desktop accessories

20 The Maximize button is used to

a. Return a window to its original size
b. Expand a window to fill the computer screen
c. Scroll slowly through a window
d. Run programs from the main menu

21 What appears if a window contains more information than can be displayed in the window?

a. Program icon
b. Cascading menu
c. Scroll bars
d. Check box

22 A window is active when its title bar is

a. Highlighted
b. Dimmed
c. Checked
d. Underlined

23 What is the term for changing the dimensions of a window?

a. Selecting
b. Resizing
c. Navigating
d. Scrolling

24 The menu bar provides access to an application's functions through

a. Icons
b. Scroll bars
c. Commands
d. Control menu box

25 When your desktop is too cluttered, you can organize it by all the following methods, EXCEPT:

a. Double-clicking the control menu box to close unneeded windows
b. Using the Tile command to view all open group windows
c. Using the Cascade command to open group window title bars
d. Clicking File, clicking Exit Windows, then clicking OK

26 You can exit Windows by double-clicking the

a. Accessories group icon
b. Program Manager control menu box
c. Main window menu bar
d. Control Panel application

APPLICATIONS REVIEW

1 Start Windows and identify items on the screen.

a. Turn on the computer, if necessary.

b. At the command prompt, Launch Windows. After Windows loads and the Program Manager appears, try to identify as many items on the desktop as you can, without referring to the lesson material. Then compare your results with Figure 1-1.

2 Minimize and restore the Program Manager window.

a. Click the Minimize button. Notice that the Program Manager window shrinks to an icon at the bottom of the screen. Now try restoring the window.

b. Double-click the Program Manager icon. The Program Manager window opens.

c. Practice minimizing and restoring other windows on the desktop.

3 Resize and move the Program Manager window.

a. Activate the Program Manager window.

b. Resize the Program Manager window up and to the right until the Program Manager takes up the top third of your screen.

c. Drag the Program Manager title bar to reposition the window at the bottom of the screen.

4 Practice working with menus and dialog boxes.

a. Open the Accessories group.

b. Start the Calculator application.

c. Click numbers and operators as you would on a handheld calculator to perform some simple arithmetic operations.

d. Close the Calculator window when you are finished.

e. Start the Clock application.

f. Using the Settings menu on the Clock menu bar, change the display from digital to analog or analog to digital.

g. Change the settings back, then exit the Clock application.

5 Exit Windows.

a. Close any open applications.

b. Using the control menu box of the Program Manager window, exit Windows. The Exit Windows dialog box appears.

c. Click OK. Windows closes and the MS-DOS command prompt appears.

INDEPENDENT CHALLENGE

Microsoft Windows 3.1 provides an on-line tutorial that can help you master essential Windows controls and concepts. The tutorial features interactive lessons that teach you how to use Windows elements such as the mouse, Program Manager, menus, and icons. The tutorial also covers how to use Help.

The tutorial material you should use depends on your level of experience with Windows. Some users might want to review the basics of Windows. Others might want to explore additional and advanced Windows topics, such as managing files and customizing windows.

Ask your instructor or technical support person about how to use the Windows tutorial.

To complete this challenge:

1 Turn on the computer and start Windows if necessary.

2 Click Help on the Program Manager menu bar.

3 Click Windows Tutorial.

4 After the introductory screen, read the instructions that appear on the screen.

5 Continue through the tutorial.

6 You can press [Esc] at any time during the tutorial if you want to exit it.

7 Exit Windows when you complete the on-line tutorial.

UNIT 2

OBJECTIVES

- Create and save a Paintbrush file
- Start and view File Manager
- Create a directory
- Move, copy, and rename files
- Format and copy disks

Creating AND MANAGING FILES

Now that you have learned the basics of Microsoft Windows 3.1, you can explore its file management features. In this unit, you will create a file using **Paintbrush**, a drawing program that comes with Windows, then learn how File Manager can help you organize the files you create. Finally, you will learn how to copy and format disks. To complete this unit you will need a Student Disk. For more information on your Student Disk, refer to the page entitled "Read This Before You Begin Microsoft Windows 3.1" at the beginning of this book.

Creating and saving a Paintbrush file

Much of your work with Windows will involve creating and saving different types of files. The files you create using a computer are stored in the computer's random access memory (RAM). **RAM** is a temporary storage space that is erased when the computer is turned off. To store a file permanently, you need to save it to a disk. You can save your work to either a 3.5-inch or 5.25-inch disk, also known as a **floppy disk**, which you insert into the drive of your computer (i.e., drive A or drive B), or a hard disk, which is built into your computer (usually drive C). ▶ In this lesson you will create a file using Paintbrush, then you will save the Paintbrush file to your Student Disk.

STEPS

1. **Make sure your Student Disk is in the disk drive**
2. **In Program Manager double-click the Accessories group icon, then double-click the Paintbrush application icon to start Paintbrush**
   The Paintbrush window opens on your screen. Notice the title and menu bars across the top. Along the left side of the window is the Toolbox and Linesize box. The white rectangular area, called the **drawing area**, is where you draw. The **color palette**, which contains the colors you can use to paint with, are at the bottom of the window.
3. **Click the maximize button, if necessary, to maximize the window, then click the Brush tool**
   The Brush tool is a freehand drawing tool that you will control with your mouse. See Table 2-1 for a description of each of the Paintbrush tools.
4. **In the Linesize box, click the thickest line width**
   The selection arrow moves down to the left of the thickest line. Make sure the black colored box appears in the color selection area. See Figure 2-1. Now you are ready to create a simple picture.
5. **Move the mouse pointer onto the drawing area of the Paintbrush window, press and hold the left mouse button, drag the mouse in a large circle, then release the mouse button**
6. **Add eyes and a mouth inside the circle to create a smiling face**
   Next, you will add color to the image.
7. **Click the Paint Roller tool in the Toolbox, click the yellow box (top row, fourth from left), then point inside the smiling face and click**
   The Paint Roller fills the area with the currently selected color.

Turn to page W30 to compare your screen to Figure 2-2 and save this file to your Student Disk.

FIGURE 2-1: Maximized Paintbrush window

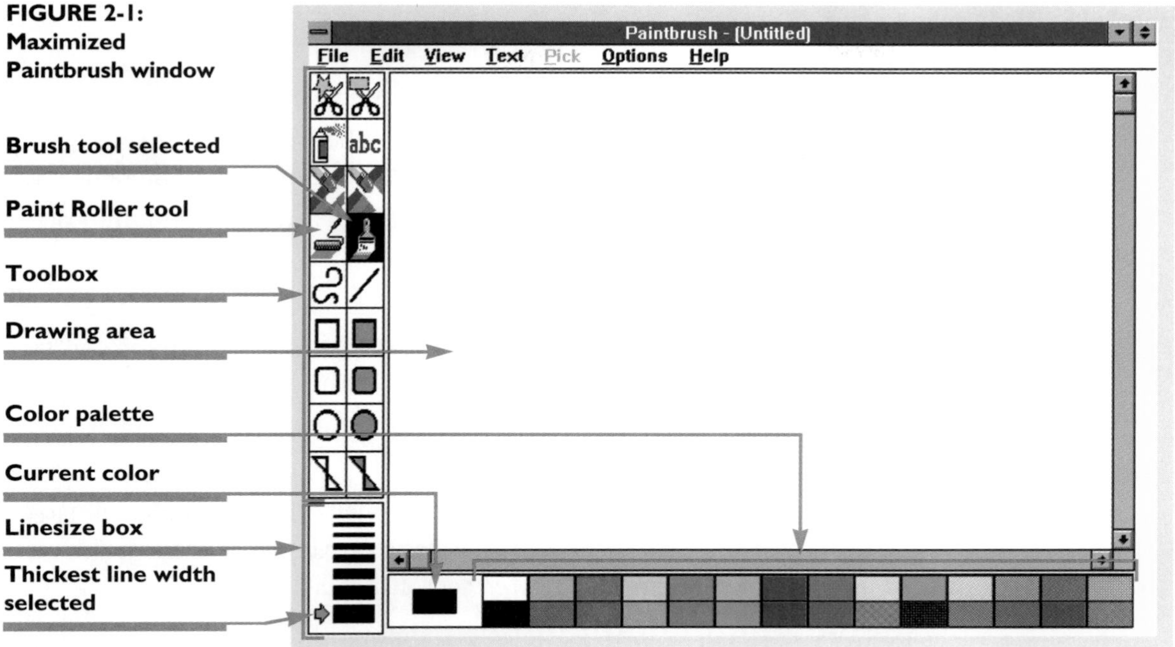

TABLE 2-1: Paintbrush Tools

TOOL	DESCRIPTION	TOOL	DESCRIPTION
	Use to define a free-form cutout		Use to define a rectangular cutout
	Use to produce a circular spray of dots	abc	Use to add text to your drawings
	Use to change the selected foreground color under the cursor to the selected background color or use to change every occurrence of one color in the drawing area to another color		Use to change all the foreground colors that it touches to the selected background color
	Use to fill any closed shape or area with the selected foreground color		Use to draw freehand shapes and lines in the selected foreground color and drawing width
	Use to draw curved lines in the selected foreground color and drawing width		Use to draw straight lines in the selected foreground color and drawing width
	Use to draw hollow squares or rectangles in the selected foreground color and drawing width		Use to draw squares or rectangles that are filled with the selected foreground color and bordered with the selected background color
	Use the same way as the box tool above; the difference is these boxes have rounded corners		Use the same way as the filled box tool above; the difference is these boxes have rounded corners
	Use to draw hollow circles or ellipses in the selected foreground color and drawing width		Use to draw circles or ellipses that are filled with the selected foreground color and bordered with the selected background color
	Use to draw polygons from connected straight-line segments in the selected foreground color and drawing width		Use to draw polygons that are filled with the selected foreground color and bordered by the selected background color

Creating and saving a Paintbrush file, continued

Compare the file you just created to Figure 2-2. Don't worry if your file looks slightly different from Figure 2-2. If you want to start over, see the TROUBLE? on the next page. Now, you need to save the Paintbrush file to your Student Disk. You will find the Save and Save As commands on the File menu in most Windows applications.

STEPS

8 Click **File** on the menu bar, then click **Save As**
The Save As dialog box opens, as shown in Figure 2-3. This dialog box allows you to choose a disk drive, directory, filename, and file type for your image.

9 Type **smile** in the File Name text box
Your entry replaces the highlighted (selected) *.bmp, which is the **file extension** that identifies the type of file you created. Paintbrush will automatically add this file extension when you click OK. Now you need to specify the drive where your Student Disk is located.

10 Click the **Drives list arrow** to display the drives on your computer, click **a:** or **b:** depending on which drive contains your Student Disk, then click **OK**
The Save As dialog box closes and SMILE.BMP is now saved to your Student Disk. Next, you'll exit Paintbrush.

11 Click **File** on the menu bar, then click **Exit**
The Paintbrush application window closes.

FIGURE 2-2: The Paintbrush window with smiling face

FIGURE 2-3: Save As dialog box

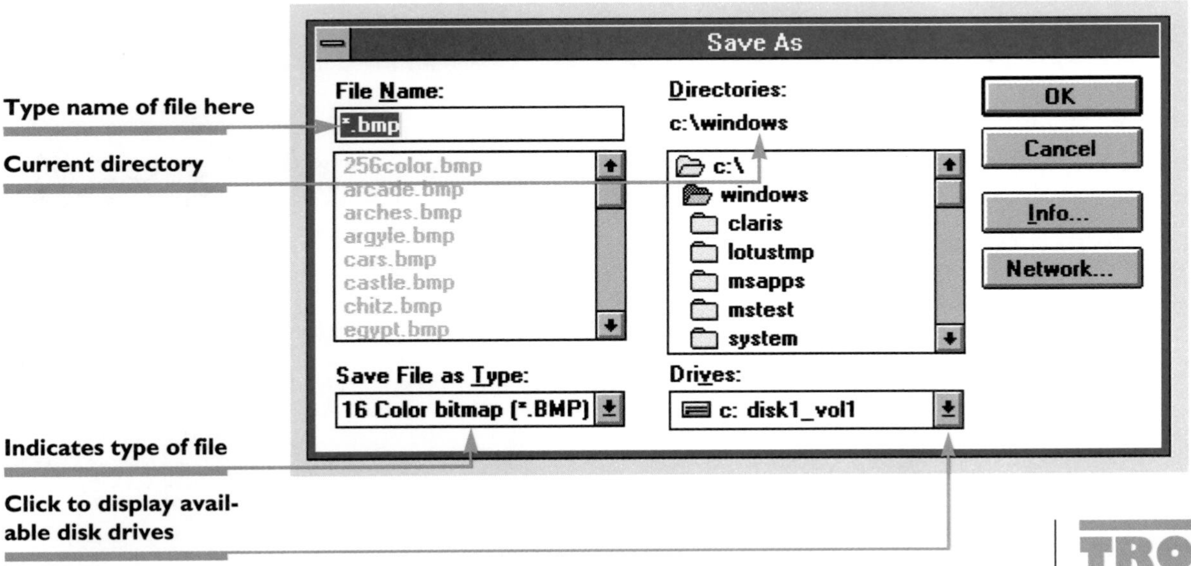

TROUBLE?

If you made a mistake while painting and want to start over, click File on the menu bar, click New, then click No when asked to save the previous image.

Starting and viewing File Manager

Windows comes with an application called **File Manager** that you can use to organize your files. Moving, copying, deleting, renaming, and searching for specific files are just some of the many tasks you can accomplish using File Manager. ▶ Use File Manager to view the contents of your Student Disk and become familiar with the various parts of the File Manager window.

STEPS

1. **In the Program Manager window, double-click the Main group icon, or if the window is already open, click the Main group window to activate it, then double-click the File Manager application icon**
   The File Manager window opens, as shown in Figure 2-4. Your File Manager will contain different drives and directories. The **directory window** is divided by the **split bar**. The left side of the directory window displays the structure of the current drive, which is drive C, or the **directory tree**. The right side of the directory window displays a list of files and subdirectories in the selected directory. See Table 2-2 for a description of the various icons used in the directory window. The status bar displays the information about the current drive and directory and other information to help you with file management tasks.
2. **Click the drive icon that corresponds to the drive containing your Student Disk**
   An hourglass icon appears as File Manager reads the drive containing your Student Disk. After a moment, File Manager displays the contents of your Student Disk. See Table 2-3 for a description of the various drive icons.
3. **Scroll, if necessary, to find SMILE.BMP, the file you created in the previous lesson**
   With File Manager open, continue to the next lesson where you'll create a directory on your Student Disk.

TABLE 2-2: Directory window icons

ICON	DESCRIPTION
	Displays the contents of a directory one level up in the directory tree
	Represents a directory
	Represents a directory that contains additional directories not displayed in the directory tree
	Represents a directory that contains additional directories that are displayed in the directory tree
	Represents an open directory; the files in this directory are listed in the right side of the directory window
	Represents an application file; these files start applications or start programs
	Represents a document file associated with an application; when you double-click this icon, the application that you used to create it starts
	Represents other document files
	Represents hidden, system, read-only files

FIGURE 2-4: File Manager window

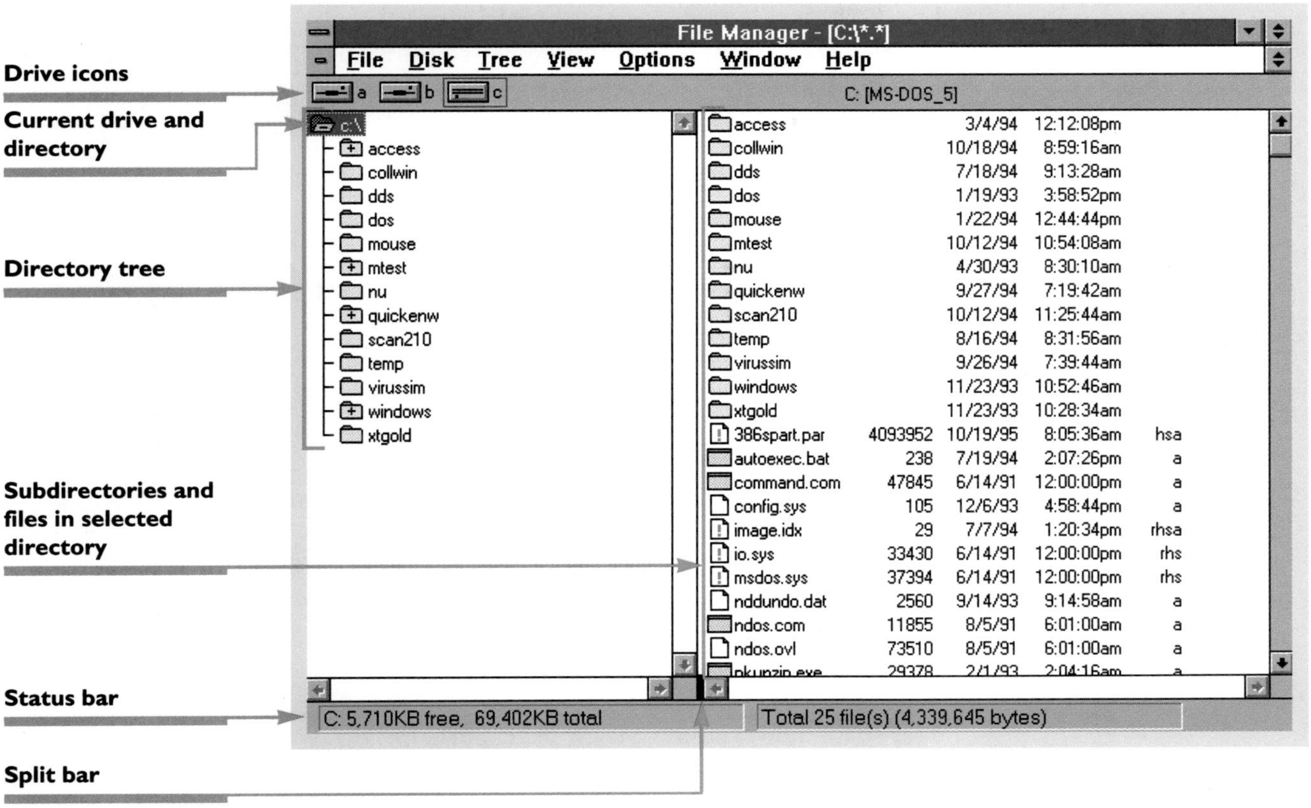

TABLE 2-3: Drive Icons

DRIVE ICON	TYPE OF DRIVE
	Floppy drive
	Hard drive
	Network drive
	CD ROM drive

TROUBLE?

Click the maximize button in the File Manager window to maximize this window.■

Creating a directory

A **directory** is similar to a file folder in a filing cabinet. It is a part of a disk where you can store a group of related files. For example, you might create a directory called PROJECT1 and store all of the files relating to a particular project in that directory. Directories can contain both files and other directories, called **subdirectories**. The directory at the top of the directory tree is called the **root directory** and is usually the drive itself. ▶ Explore the directory structure of the hard disk in your computer. Then use File Manager to create a directory called MY_FILES on your Student Disk.

STEPS

1. **Click the drive C icon to display the contents of this drive**
   The directories appear in the left side of the directory window and a list of the files and directories in the selected directory appear in the right side of the window. You can use the Tree menu to see all of the branches of the directory tree.

2. **Click Tree on the menu bar, then click Expand All**
   You can now view the entire tree structure of drive C, or the root directory, as shown in Figure 2-5. You might have to scroll up and down to view all the subdirectories. Now that you can navigate through a directory tree you are ready to create a directory on your Student Disk.

3. **Make sure your Student Disk is in the disk drive, then click the drive A icon (or the drive B icon if your Student Disk is in drive B)**
   File Manager pauses while your computer reads the contents of your Student Disk. You want to create the directory below the root directory.

4. **Click File on the menu bar, then click Create Directory**
   The Create Directory dialog box opens. The Current Directory line should read A:\. You will name the new directory MY_FILES. Directory names can have up to 11 characters but cannot include spaces, commas, or backslashes.

5. **Type my_files in the Name text box, then click OK**
   Be sure to type the underscore. This new directory appears on your Student Disk, as shown in Figure 2-6. You can use this directory to store all of the files you create and save. In the next lesson, you will move the SMILE.BMP file into this directory.

FIGURE 2-5: Directory tree

Indicates an open directory

Indicates subdirectories displayed

Your list of directories will be different

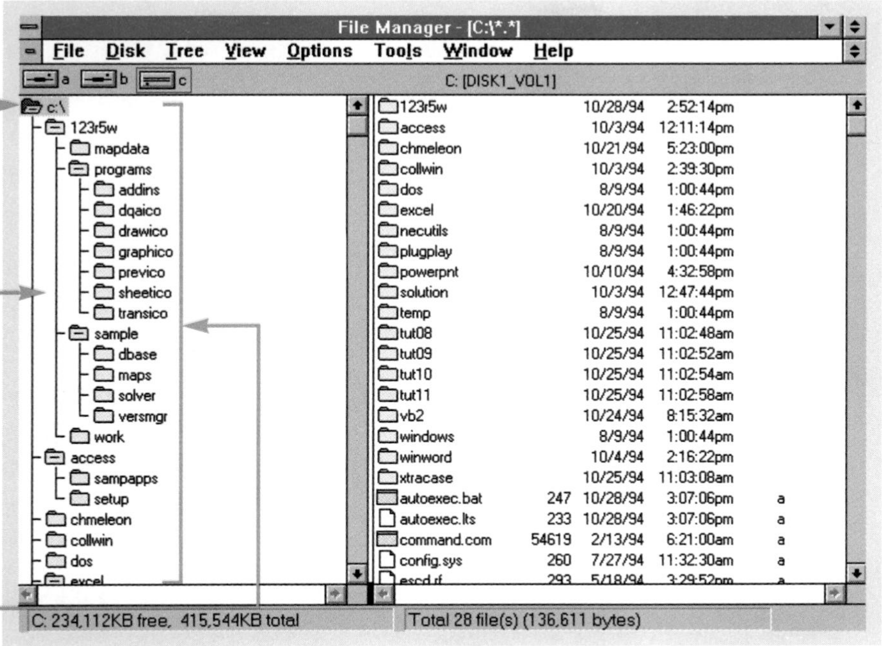

FIGURE 2-6: MY_FILES directory on your Student Disk

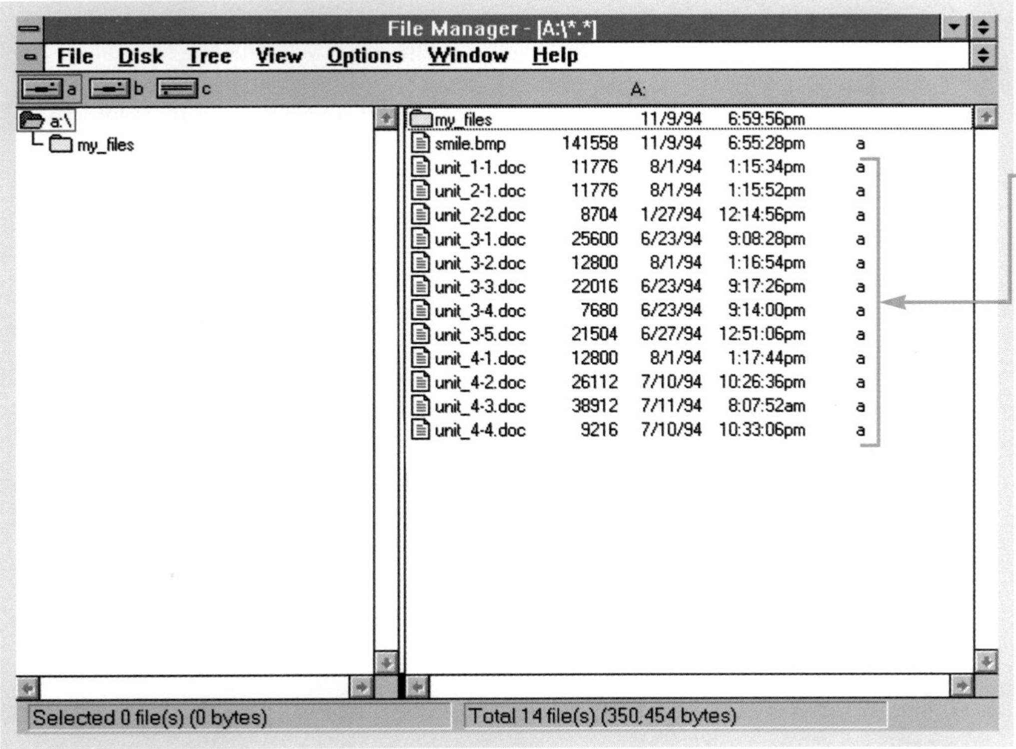

Your files might be different depending on what you are using for a Student Disk

TROUBLE?

If you create the directory in the wrong place, select it then press [Delete]. Two confirmation dialog boxes will appear. They will ask you if you are sure you want to delete the directory. Make *absolutely sure* that you selected the MY_FILES directory. Click YES in both dialog boxes, then create the directory again.

Moving, copying, and renaming files

File Manager allows you to move, copy, and rename files and directories. These commands appear on the File menu. Often you will need to move files from one drive or directory to another. At other times you might want to copy a file to create an identical file in a new location. ▶ Use File Manager to move the SMILE.BMP file to the MY_FILES directory on your Student Disk. Then, make a copy of this file and rename it.

STEPS

1. Make sure that File Manager displays the root directory on your Student Disk

2. Click the **SMILE.BMP file icon**, then drag it slowly to the left
   The mouse pointer changes to ⬚, as shown in Figure 2-7. The new pointer shape indicates that you are performing a drag-and-drop operation. **Drag-and-drop** is one method for moving and copying files. You can also move files by clicking Move on the File menu, then typing the filenames of the files you wish to move.

3. Drag the SMILE.BMP file icon over the MY_FILES directory on your Student Disk until the MY_FILES directory is selected, then release the mouse button and click Yes to confirm
   The file does not appear in the root directory anymore—it appears in the MY_FILES directory. Don't worry if you move a file to the wrong place; simply drag it again to the correct location. Now, make a backup copy of SMILE.BMP in the root directory of your Student Disk.

4. Click the **SMILE.BMP file icon** in the MY_FILES directory to select it, click **File** on the menu bar, then click **Copy**
   The Copy Dialog box opens, as shown in Figure 2-8. It shows the current directory and the currently selected files. You need to type the new location in the To text box.

5. Type **a:** in the To text box, then click **OK**
   File Manager creates a copy of SMILE.BMP on the root directory of your Student Disk. Note that you can also copy files using the Drag-and-Drop method. Simply press [Ctrl] as you drag the file. The mouse pointer changes to ⬚.

   Now you can rename the file using a backup extension, .BAK. See Table 2-4 for a description of some other file extensions.

6. Click the **SMILE.BMP file icon** on the root directory, click **File** on the menu bar, then click **Rename**
   The Rename dialog box opens with SMILE.BMP in the From text box. You will type the new name in the To text box.

7. Click in the To text box to place the insertion point if necessary, type **smile.bak**, then click **OK**
   You should now have two copies of the Paintbrush file on your Student Disk: one in the MY_FILES directory, and a backup in the root directory.

FIGURE 2-7: Moving a file

Drag-and-drop pointer

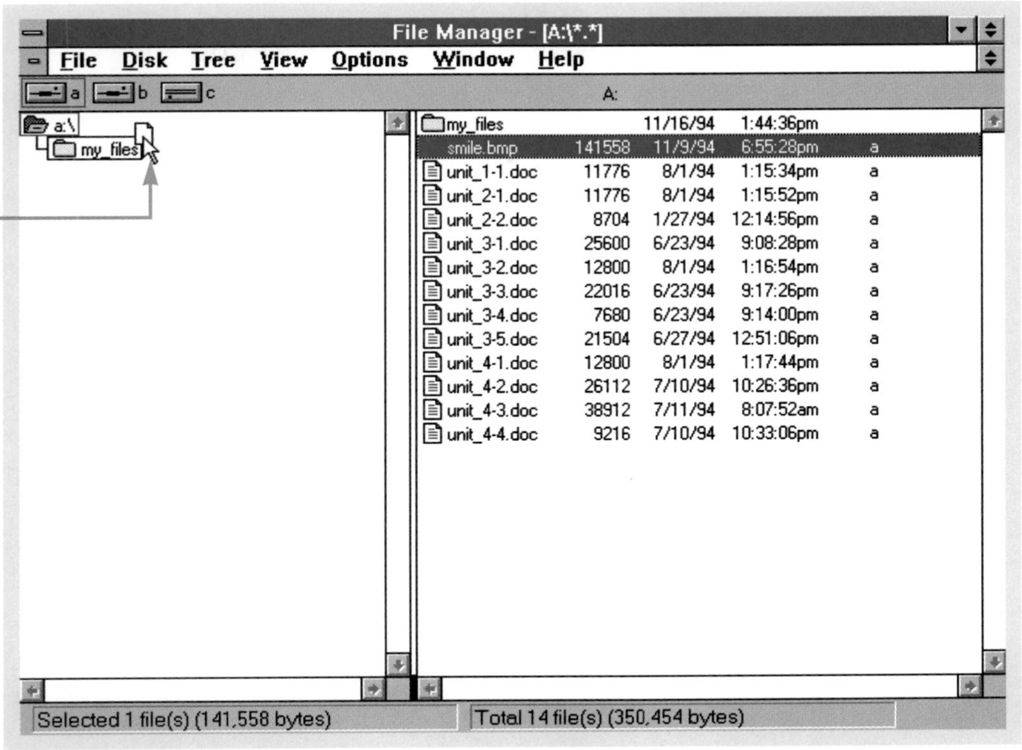

FIGURE 2-8: Copy dialog box

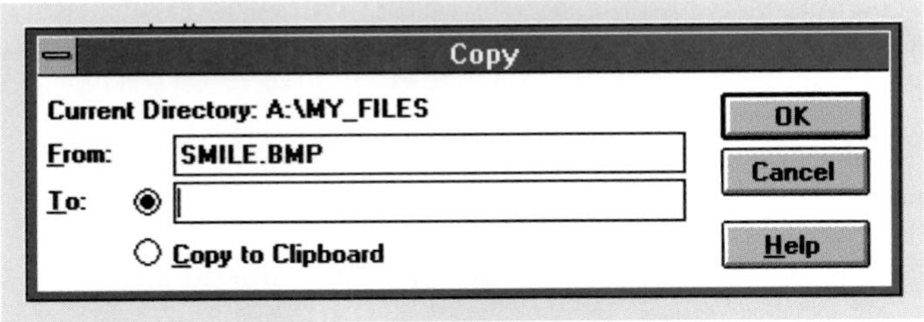

QUICK TIP

To select several files for moving or copying, press and hold [Ctrl] while clicking each file icon. Your mouse pointer will change to when you drag them to another location.

TABLE 2-4: Common file extensions

EXTENSION	FILE TYPE	EXTENSION	FILE TYPE
.txt	Text file	.exe	Executable files
.doc	MS Word document file	.com	Executable files
.bmp	Windows bitmap file	.bat	Batch files
.xls	MS Excel spreadsheet file	.wri	Windows Write file
.tmp	Temporary file	.drv	Windows driver file
.wmf	Windows metafile	.hlp	Help file
.wk4	Lotus 1-2-3 worksheet file	.bak	Backup file

Formatting and copying disks

You must format disks before using them. **Formatting** a disk erases any data on it and allows a computer to read it. You use File Manager to format disks and to copy the entire contents of one disk to another disk. You should make backup copies of your most important disks (for example, program disks). ▶ ***Do not complete these steps until your instructor tells you to.*** Read these steps now to become familiar with the process of formatting and copying disks.

STEPS

1. Place an unformatted, 3.5-inch disk in drive A or drive B
2. Click **Disk** on the File Manager menu bar, then click **Format Disk**
   The Format Disk dialog box opens. This dialog box contains a list box to select both the drive and the capacity of the disk you want to format. **Capacity** indicates whether the disk is double density or high density. See Table 2-5 for a description of each command on the Disk menu.
3. Select the appropriate drive and capacity, then click **OK**
   Figure 2-9 shows an example of how your dialog box might look if you want to format a 1.44 MB high density disk in drive A. Another dialog box opens, warning you that all data will be erased from your disk.
4. Click **Yes**
   A dialog box opens, indicating that the disk is being initialized. When the operation is complete, File Manager displays a dialog box, showing the amount of space on your newly formatted disk. The dialog box also asks if you want to format another disk.
5. Click **No**
   Remove the formatted disk from the drive and attach a disk label that identifies the contents of the disk. Now you are ready to copy information to this disk.
6. Click **Disk** on the menu bar, click **Copy**, then specify the source and destination drives
   The Copy dialog box opens with two list boxes. Use these boxes to specify the source and destination drives. When copying a disk, File Manager takes all the information from one disk, called the **source**, and copies it onto a new disk, called the **destination**. Be careful what you use for a destination disk because all of its original information will be lost. Also, the Copy command will only work if both disks are of the same type, for example, both 3.5-inch high-density disks. Figure 2-10 shows an example of this completed dialog box.
7. Place your source disk in the appropriate drive, then click **OK**
   A dialog box appears to warn you that all data will be lost on the destination disk.
8. Click **Yes** then press **[Enter]** when you are prompted to insert the source disk
   Copy shows its progress as a percentage as it copies the source disk into memory. At some point, Copy will stop reading from the source disk and ask you to insert the destination disk.
9. Remove your source disk and insert your destination disk, then click **OK**
   File Manager now places all the information from the source disk onto the destination disk.
10. Double-click the **control menu box** in the File Manager window to exit File Manager

FIGURE 2-9: Format dialog box

Check the drive and capacity before clicking OK

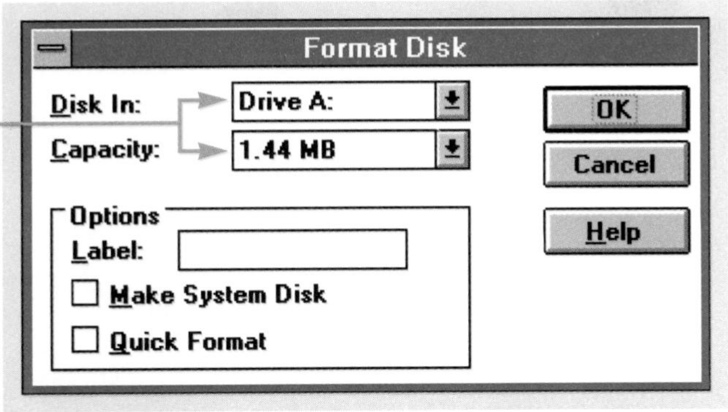

FIGURE 2-10: Completed Copy Disk dialog box

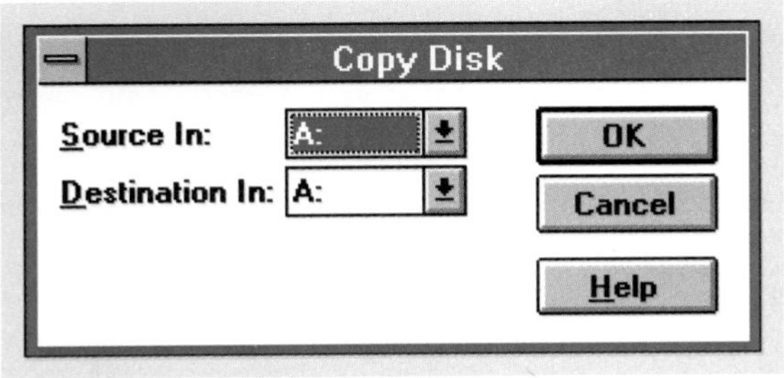

TABLE 2-5: Disk menu commands

COMMAND	DESCRIPTION
Copy Disk	Copies a floppy disk
Label Disk	Assigns an electronic label to a disk
Format Disk	Makes a floppy disk usable to your computer
Make System Disk	Copies special system files to a disk
Select Drive	Chooses a drive to view

TROUBLE?

If you're not sure if your disk is formatted, place it in the drive and click the corresponding drive icon. If File Manager can read the disk, it is already formatted.

CONCEPTS REVIEW

Label each of the elements of the File Manager window shown in Figure 2-11.

1 ____

5 ____

2 ____

3 ____

4 ____

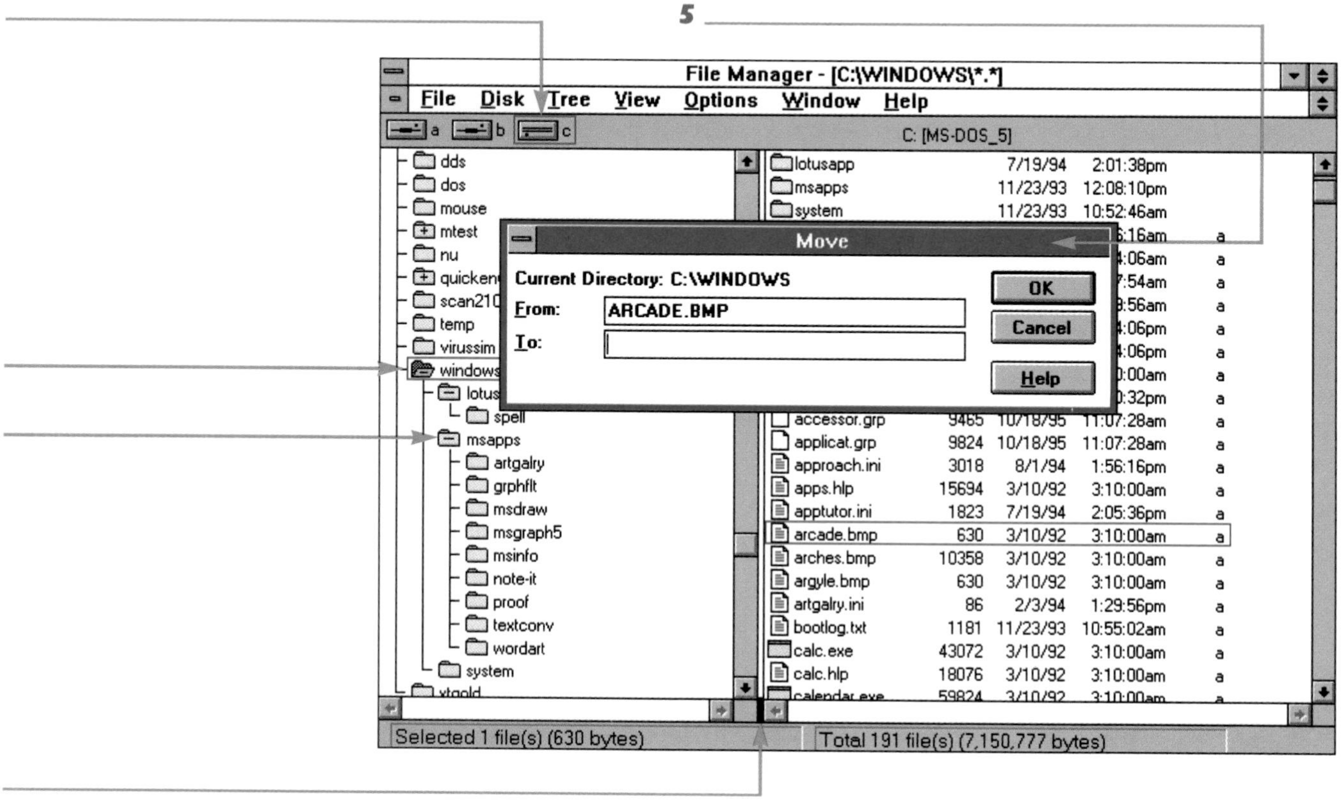

FIGURE 2-11

Match each of the descriptions with the appropriate icon.

6 

7 

8 

9 

10 

a. Directory that contains other undisplayed directories

b. Document or File associated with an application

c. Application File

d. Up one directory

e. Directory

11 Which extension is associated with Paintbrush files?

a. .txt

b. .bmp

c. .tmp

d. .wk4

Select the best answer from the list of choices.

12 Which tool would you use to add text to your Paintbrush drawing?

a. 

b. 

c. abc

d. 

13 File Manager is a Windows application that lets you

a. Select different desktop wallpaper

b. Move a file from one location to another

c. Type entries into a text file

d. Determine what programs begin automatically when you start Windows

14 In which program group can you usually find the File Manager application icon?

a. Accessories

b. File Manager

c. Startup

d. Main

15 The temporary storage space used by your computer when you work is called

a. A hard disk

b. RAM

c. A monitor

d. A file

16 For most Windows applications, the Save command is usually located on which menu?

a. File

b. Edit

c. Help

d. Save

17 The icon that File Manager uses to represent a floppy drive is

a. 

b. 

c. 

d. 

18 C:\ means

a. The root directory on drive C

b. It is a subdirectory

c. Not on drive C

d. All of the above

19 A directory tree is

a. A listing of file contents

b. A list of drives

c. The way File Manager organizes your directories

d. None of the above

20 If you want to backup a file on your disk

a. Copy the file and rename the original file using the .BAK extension

b. Click Backup on the File menu

c. Rename the file using the .BAK extension

d. Move the file to a backup directory

21 When you copy a disk, the source disk

a. Is the location where files will be placed

b. Contains the information that will be placed on the second disk

c. Is the same as the destination disk

d. Will be erased

22 Before a computer can read or write to a disk, you must __________ it.

a. Copy

b. Format

c. Erase

d. Open

APPLICATIONS REVIEW

1 Create and save a Paintbrush file.

a. Start Windows, then start Paintbrush.

b. Create your own unique, colorful design using several colors with several of Paintbrush's tools.

c. Insert your Student Disk in the appropriate disk drive, then save the picture as ART.BMP to the MY_FILES directory.

d. Exit Paintbrush.

2 Start and view File Manager.

a. Open File Manager.

b. Be sure your Student Disk is in either drive A or drive B, then double-click the drive icon containing your Student Disk.

c. Double-click the drive C icon.

d. Double-click the c:\ directory icon on the left side of the drive C window, then scroll down the left side of the drive window to see the available directories. When you see the Windows directory icon, double-click it to see the directories and files available in the Windows directory.

3 Create a Directory.

a. Create a subdirectory under the MY_FILES directory on your Student Disk.

b. Click the drive A icon to display the contents of your Student Disk. The new subdirectory will go below the MY_FILES directory.

c. Click the MY_FILES directory icon on the left side of the window. This tells File manager that the new subdirectory will go below the MY_FILES directory.

d. Click File on the menu bar, then click Create Directory. The Create Directory dialog box opens and prompts you to name the new directory. Type "unit2" in the Name text box, then click OK.

e. If you don't want to keep this directory on your disk, click the UNIT2 directory, then press [del] to delete this directory.

4 Move, copy, and rename files.

a. Copy the ART.BMP file into the root directory on your Student Disk.

b. Rename the ART.BMP file in the root directory ART.BAK.

c. Move the ART.BAK file into the MY_FILES directory on your Student Disk.

5 Format and copy a disk.

a. Format a new blank disk using the Format Disk command on the Disk menu. Check that the drive and capacity is correct.

b. Make a copy of your Student Disk using the Copy Disk command on the Disk menu. In the Copy dialog box, make sure that drive A (or drive B) is both the source and the destination drive, then click OK. Your Student Disk is the source disk.

c. When File Manager prompts you, remove your Student Disk and insert the newly formatted disk. This is the destination disk.

d. Close File Manager, then exit Windows.

INDEPENDENT CHALLENGE

It is important to develop a sound, organized plan when you manage files and directories. Practice your skills by organizing the following list of names into a coherent and logical directory tree. Rewrite the following list of directories as it might appear in File Manager. Pay special attention to the contents of each directory and use as many or few subdirectories as you feel are necessary. Feel free to use the directory tree on your computer as a model for your work. Also, you might want to create a directory to hold related subdirectories.

C:\	
\wrdprcsr	(Word Processor)
\sprdshet	(Spreadsheet)
\graphs	
\sheets	
\resumes	
\report92	
\report93	
\docs	
\pong	(Game)
\blaster	(Game)
\report94	
\windows	
\system	
\games	

Glossary

Active application The software program you are currently working in, indicated by a highlighted title bar.

Active window The window you are currently working in, indicated by a highlighted title bar.

Applications Useful, task-oriented software programs.

Check box The box you click that turns a dialog box option on or off.

Click To press and release the mouse button one time. You click to select items, choose commands, and work in applications.

Command button The button you click that executes the dialog box command.

Command prompt Usually represented as C:\>, it gives you access to MS-DOS commands and applications.

Copy To create a duplicate item. You can choose to place this duplicate item in a new location.

Cursor The blinking vertical line that indicates where you are on the screen. Also known as the insertion point.

Dialog box A box that opens giving you more options for executing a command.

Dimmed command A menu command that is not currently available.

Directory tree A graphical structure of a directory that shows the root directory, files, and subdirectories.

Double-click To press the mouse button twice quickly. You double-click to start and exit applications.

Drag To point at an item, press and hold the mouse button, move the mouse to a new location, then release the mouse button.

Drag-and-drop A method used to move items with the mouse instead of the keyboard.

Ellipsis Portion of a menu command that indicates that choosing this command will open a dialog box that asks for further information.

File Manager An application that comes with Windows that helps you to organize your files and work with disks.

List box A box containing a list of items. To choose an item, click the list arrow, then click the desired item.

Maximize button Enlarges an application window to its largest possible size.

Menu A list of commands that you can use to accomplish certain tasks.

Menu bar A set of menus that appear at the top of an application window.

Minimize button Reduces an application window to an icon at the bottom of the screen.

Mouse A handheld input device.

Mouse pointer A graphical representation showing where the mouse is positioned on the desktop. The shape changes, depending on where it is positioned.

Move To place an item in a new location.

Multitasking The ability for more than one application to run at the same time.

Point To position the mouse pointer on an item on the desktop.

Radio button The small circle you click to select or deselect a single dialog box option.

Random Access Memory (RAM) Temporary storage space that is erased when the computer is turned off.

Restore button Restores an application to its previous size.

Root directory The directory at the top of the directory tree, usually the drive itself.

Run Operate.

Scroll arrows (left and right) The arrows in scroll bars that you click to move along the scroll bar in small increments.

Scroll bars (horizontal and vertical) Appear when a window contains more information than can be displayed at one time and allow you to navigate the window. Scroll bars contain scroll boxes and scroll arrows.

Screen saver A moving pattern that fills your screen after your computer has not been used for a specified amount of time.

Scroll boxes (horizontal and vertical) Located in scroll bars and used to move along the scroll bar in larger increments.

Select Click an item to select it. When you select an item, it becomes highlighted, or active.

Source disk The original disk when copying disks.

Split bar The bar that divides the directory window in the File Manager.

Subdirectory A directory within another directory.

Target disk The disk that the source disk copies to when you are copying disks.

Task List A window that displays a list of applications you are currently running and allows you to switch between applications. Double-click anywhere on the desktop or press [Ctrl] [Esc] to display.

Text box A box in which you type text.

Index

PageMaker® 5 for Windows™

Read This Before You Begin PageMaker® 5 for Windows

To the Student

To use this book you must have eight Student Disks. Your instructor will either provide you with them or ask you to create your own by completing the lesson entitled "Creating your Student Disks" in Unit 1. Use the following to determine which Student Disk to use with each unit:

Student Disk	Unit(s)
1	1,2
2	3,4
3	5,6
4	7,8
5	9
6	10 (Lessons 1–4)
7	10 (Lessons 5–6)
8	10 (Lesson 7)

Using Your Own Computer

If you are going to work through this book using your own computer, you need a computer system running Microsoft Windows 3.1, PageMaker 5 for Windows, and eight Student Disks. *You will not be able to complete the step-by-step exercises in this book using your own computer until you have your own Student Disks.* This book assumes the default settings under a complete installation of PageMaker 5 for Windows. Be sure to install all of the additions. The student exercises in this book use mainly the Arial and Times New Roman fonts that are standard in a Windows installation. If you should receive a missing font message, PageMaker will substitute the font with another font that is available on your system. You can simply accept this font substitution and continue with the exercises.

To the Instructor

Bundled with the instructor's copy of this book is the CTI WinApps Setup Disk, which contains an automatic Student Disk generating program. Once you install the Setup Disk on a network or standalone workstation, students can easily make their own Student Disks by double-clicking the "Make PageMaker 5 Student Disks" icon in the CTI WinApps icon group. Double-clicking this icon transfers all the files your students need to complete the step-by-step lessons in the units, Application Reviews, and Independent Challenges to eight high-density disks in drive A or B. If some of your students will use their own computers to work through this book, they must first get eight Student Disks. The lesson entitled "Creating your Student Disks" in Unit 1 provides complete instructions on how to make the Student Disks. The instructions in this book assume that the students know which drive and directory contain the Student Disks, so it's important that you provide disk location information before the students start working through the units.

As an adopter of this text, you are granted a license to install this software on any computer or network used by you or your students. For instructions on how to install the CTI WinApps icon group from the Setup Disk, see the README.TXT file included on the Setup Disk. A printout of this file is included in the Instructor's Manual.

Using the Student Disk Files

In this book, you will be asked to save your files with the same filename, thus replacing the original student file. We encourage you to make a backup copy of the original files before you begin. This procedure will ensure that the student files will remain unmodified in case you wish to redo the exercise.

UNIT 1

OBJECTIVES

- ▶ Create your Student Disks
- ▶ Define desktop publishing software
- ▶ Start PageMaker 5.0 for Windows
- ▶ Open a publication
- ▶ View the PageMaker publication window
- ▶ Set the zero point and use ruler guides
- ▶ Work with tools in the toolbox
- ▶ View the publication
- ▶ Get Help
- ▶ Close a publication and exit PageMaker

Getting Started

Now that you've learned the basics of Microsoft Windows 3.1, you are ready to use Aldus PageMaker 5.0 for Windows, a popular desktop publishing application. In this unit, you will learn how to start PageMaker and how to use the elements of the PageMaker window. You will also view a publication, use on-line Help, close a publication, and exit the application. ▶ Joe Martin works in the Marketing Department at New World Airlines. Before installing PageMaker, the Marketing Department used third parties to produce all company publications, which was both time-consuming and expensive. Patricia Fernandez, the communications manager, wants Joe to use PageMaker to create many of the publications in-house. ▶

Creating your Student Disks

To complete the lessons and exercises in this book, you must have eight (8) Student Disks. These Student Disks contain all the files you need for the Units, Applications Reviews, and Independent Challenges. If your instructor or technical support person provides you with your Student Disks, you may skip this lesson. If your instructor asks you to make your own Student Disks, you need eight blank, formatted high-density disks and a computer with Microsoft Windows 3.1, PageMaker 5 for Windows, and the CTI WinApps icon group installed on it. Once you have these items, complete the following steps.

STEPS

1. Label eight blank, formatted high-density disks as follows: PageMaker Student Disk 1, PageMaker Student Disk 2, PageMaker Student Disk 3, PageMaker Student Disk 4, PageMaker Student Disk 5, PageMaker Student Disk 6, PageMaker Student Disk 7, PageMaker Student Disk 8
2. Start Windows and make sure the Program Manager window is maximized
   If you need help starting Windows, refer to the lesson called "Starting Windows" at the beginning of this book.
3. Insert the first formatted disk labeled "PageMaker Student Disk 1" in drive A or B
   In this book, we assume that you will copy and retrieve files from drive A.
4. In the Program Manager window, look for an icon labeled "CTI WinApps" like the one in Figure A or a window labeled "CTI WinApps" like the one in Figure B
   If you cannot find anything labeled "CTI WinApps," the CTI software might not be installed on your computer. If you are in the computer lab, ask your technical support person for help. If you are using your own machine, you will not be able to create your Student Disks. Ask your instructor or technical support person for further information on where to locate the CTI WinApps icon group.
5. Double-click the **CTI WinApps icon**
   The CTI WinApps group window opens. If the CTI WinApps group window is already open, as shown in Figure B, skip to Step 6.
6. In the CTI WinApps group window, double-click the **Make PageMaker5 Illust Student Disks icon**
   The Make PageMaker 5 Illust Student Disks dialog box opens, as shown in Figure C.
7. Make sure the formatted disk that you labeled "PageMaker Student Disk 1" is in the disk drive and the drive that contains your disk corresponds to the radio button that is selected, then click **OK**
   For example, if you want to copy the Student Disk files to drive A, make sure that the Drive A radio button is selected.
8. Click **Make Disk**
   When copying is complete, a message appears indicating the number of files copied to your disk.
9. Clik **OK**, insert the blank, formatted disk that you labeled "PageMaker Student Disk 2" into your disk drive, then click **Make Disk**
   Follow the instructions on the screen to copy all the necessary files onto all eight Student Disks.
10. Click **Exit** when you are finished copying all of your Student Disks
    Now the files you need to work through this book are on your Student Disks. Refer to the "Read This Before You Begin PageMaker 5" page for instructions on which Student Disk to use with each unit.

FIGURE A:
CTI WinApps icon

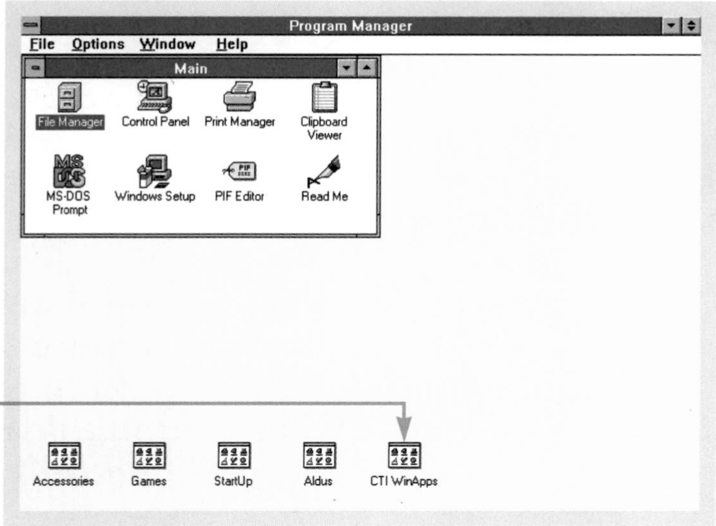

CTI WinApps icon

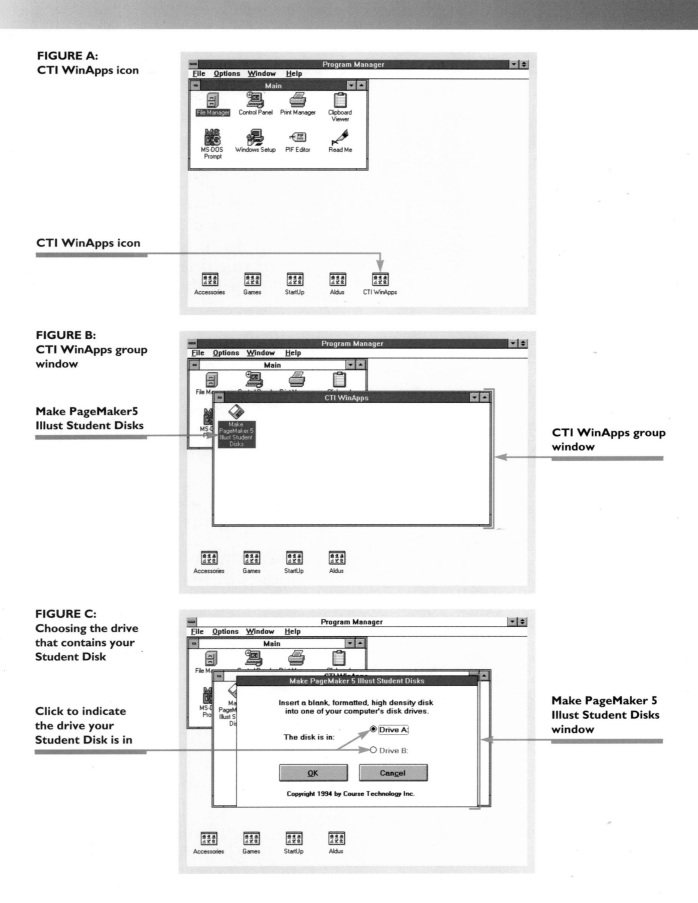

FIGURE B:
CTI WinApps group window

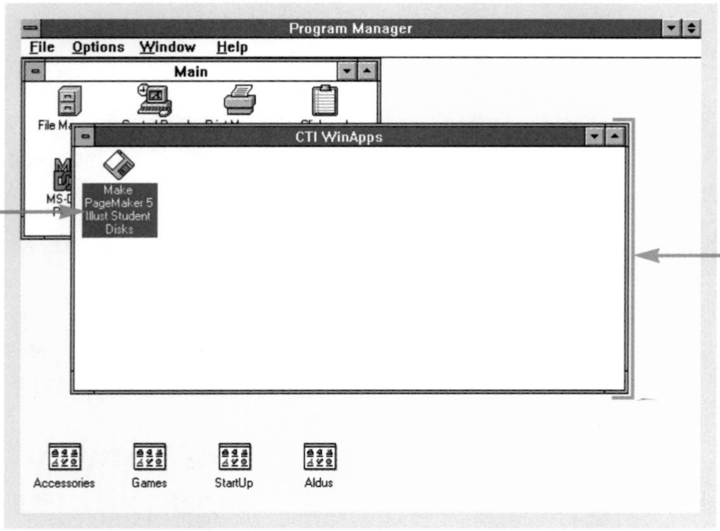

Make PageMaker5 Illust Student Disks

CTI WinApps group window

FIGURE C:
Choosing the drive that contains your Student Disk

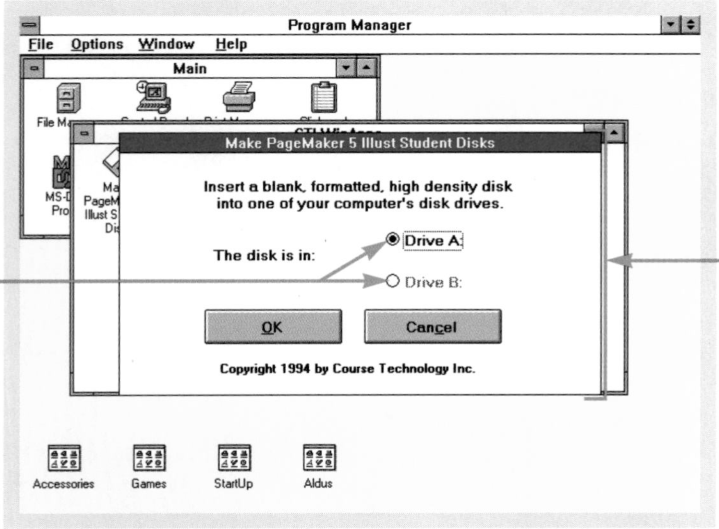

Click to indicate the drive your Student Disk is in

Make PageMaker 5 Illust Student Disks window

Defining desktop publishing software

PageMaker is a desktop publishing application. A **desktop publishing** application lets you integrate text, graphics, spreadsheets, and charts created in different applications into one document on a personal computer, condensing into hours what used to take days in traditional publishing. With PageMaker, you can create many types of publications, including brochures, newsletters, and even books. A **publication** is any document produced in PageMaker. Figure 1-1 is one example of a publication. Some types of publications you can create with PageMaker are listed in Table 1-1. ▶ Joe is excited about using PageMaker. He knows that some of the benefits of using PageMaker include:

- **Saving money**
  By creating publications in-house at New World Airlines, Joe saves the cost of hiring graphic designers to create the company's publications.
- **Saving time**
  In the past, Joe had to consider the time third parties spent completing the publication. Depending on a designer's workload, it took a few days to a week to finish publications. Now Joe can control when publications will be completed and work them into his agenda—not someone else's.
- **Controlling the production process**
  By creating the company's publications at his personal computer, Joe has control of all the steps in the production process—from design to final layouts.
- **Providing security**
  Some publications that Joe needs to create contain special airline fares or confidential company financial data. In the past, New World Airlines managers were apprehensive about sending this information outside the company.
- **Offering color**
  Joe creates many color publications. Some use just one color in a particular area, called a **spot color**. Other publications, such as a color advertisement, use four basic colors (known as the **process colors**) printed over each other to create other colors. The result is a **full-color** publication. PageMaker lets you create spot and full-color publications.

TABLE 1-1: Examples of PageMaker publications

PUBLICATION	EXAMPLES
Periodical	Magazines, newsletters, newspapers
Promotional	Advertisements, flyers, press releases, prospectuses
Informational	Brochures, bulletins, catalogs, data and fact sheets, schedules, programs
Stationery	Business cards, envelopes, fax cover sheets, interoffice memos, letterheads
Instructional	Training manuals, employee handbooks
Presentation	Overheads, posters

FIGURE 1-1: A PageMaker publication

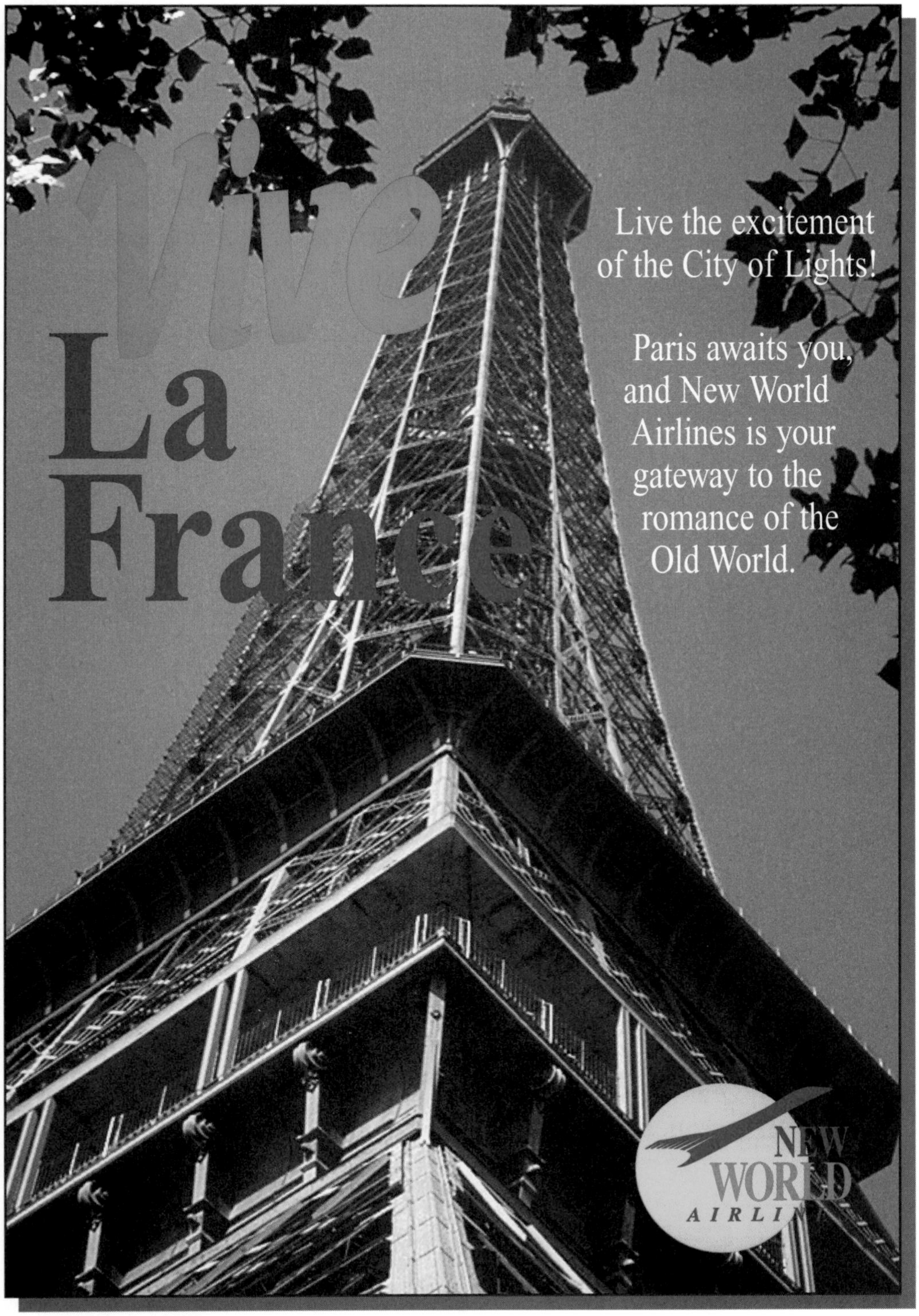

Starting PageMaker 5.0 for Windows

To start PageMaker, you first start Windows, as described in "Microsoft Windows 3.1." Then, you open the program group window that contains the PageMaker application icon, usually the Aldus program group. A slightly different procedure might be required for computers on a network and for those that use utility programs to enhance Microsoft Windows. If you need assistance, ask your instructor or technical support person for help. ► Try starting PageMaker now.

STEPS

1 Make sure the Program Manager window is open
The Program Manager icon might appear at the bottom of your screen. Double-click to open it, if necessary.

2 Double-click the **Aldus program group icon**
The Aldus program group window opens, and the Aldus PageMaker icon appears, as shown in Figure 1-2. Your screen might look different depending on the applications installed on your computer. The Aldus program group might already be maximized. If you cannot locate the Aldus program group icon, click Window on the Program Manager menu bar, then click Aldus.

3 Double-click the **Aldus PageMaker 5.0a application icon**
Your PageMaker icon might say "Aldus PageMaker 5.0." If it does, double-click this instead. PageMaker opens and displays a blank screen with the PageMaker menu bar across the top, as shown in Figure 1-3. In the next lesson, you learn how to open a publication.

FIGURE 1-2: Aldus program group

PageMaker application icon

Your desktop might look different depending on the applications installed on your computer

Aldus program group window

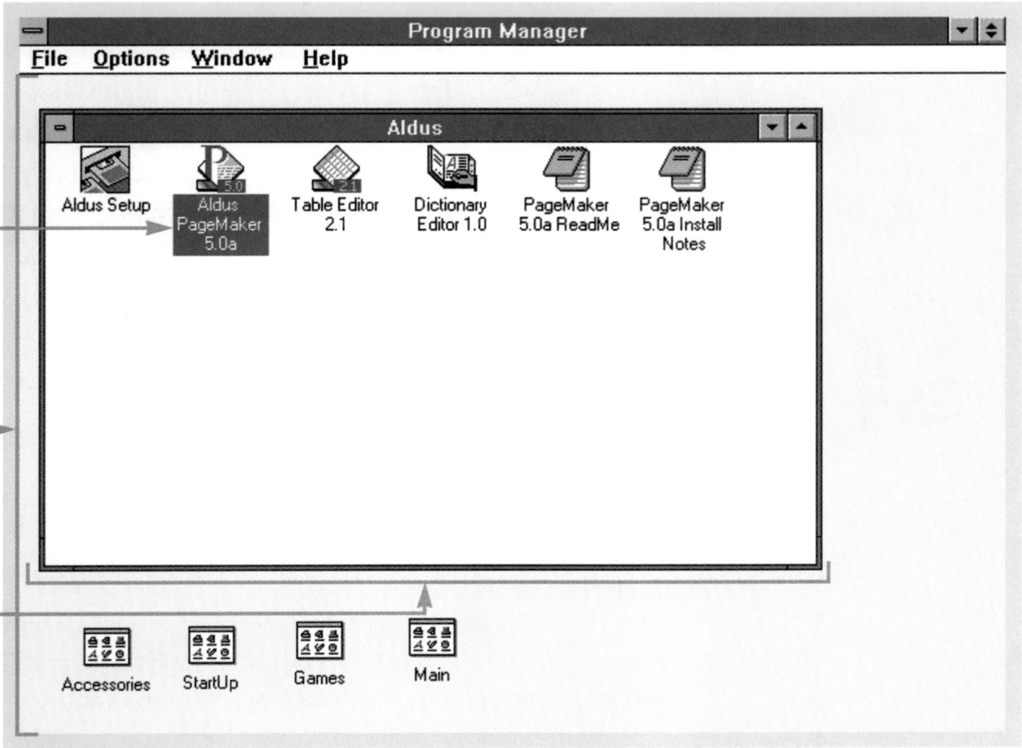

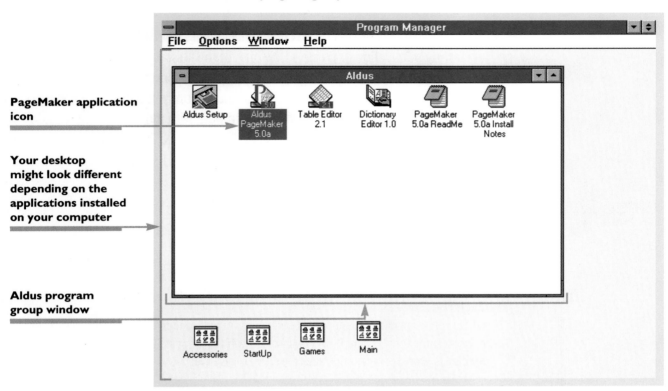

FIGURE 1-3: Blank screen after PageMaker is opened

Application title bar

PageMaker menu bar

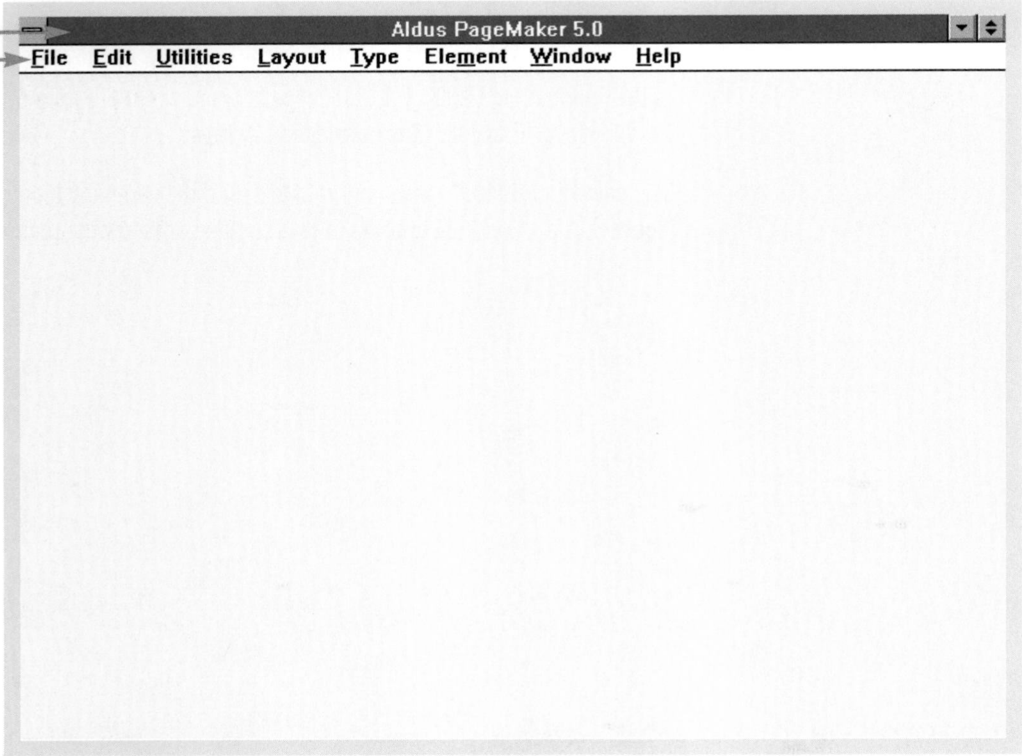

Opening a publication

To view the window in which you create PageMaker publications, you need to open an existing publication or create a new one. In this lesson you will open a file from your Student Disk. See your instructor or technical support person for a copy of the Student Disk if you do not already have one. Make sure you have made a working copy of your Student Disk before you begin to work with it. For more information about your Student Disk, refer to the page entitled "Read This Before You Begin Aldus PageMaker 5" at the beginning of this section. ▶ Joe wants to open a newsletter he created earlier to review it.

STEPS

1 Insert your Student Disk in the appropriate drive

2 Click **File** on the menu bar, then click **Open**
The Open publication dialog box opens, as shown in Figure 1-4. The files, directories, and drive names on your computer might be different from those shown in the figure.

3 Click the **Drives list arrow**
A list of your available drives appears. Locate the drive that contains your Student Disk. These lessons assume your Student Disk is in drive A. If you are using a different drive, or if your practice files are stored on a network, click the appropriate drive.

4 Click **a:**
A list of files on your Student Disk appears in the File name list box.

5 In the File name list box, click **unit_1-1.pm5**, then click **OK**
You could also double-click the filename in the File name list box to open the file. Pages 2 and 3 of the publication, UNIT_1-1.PM5, appear, as shown in Figure 1-5. UNIT_1-1.PM5 contains the New World Airlines company newsletter—Wings.

The newsletter includes a photograph, text, and the company logo at the bottom of the page. Notice that the filename appears in its own title bar below the menu bar.

FIGURE 1-4: Open publication dialog box

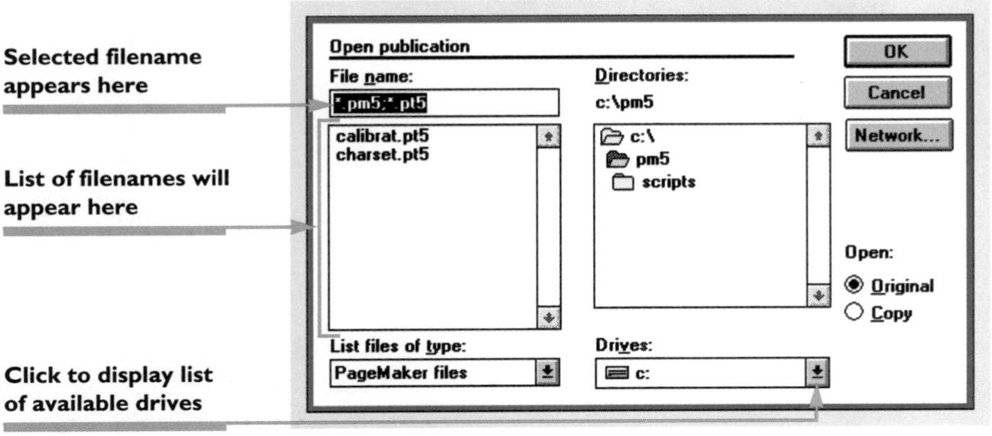

FIGURE 1-5: Pages 2 and 3 of UNIT 1-1.PM5

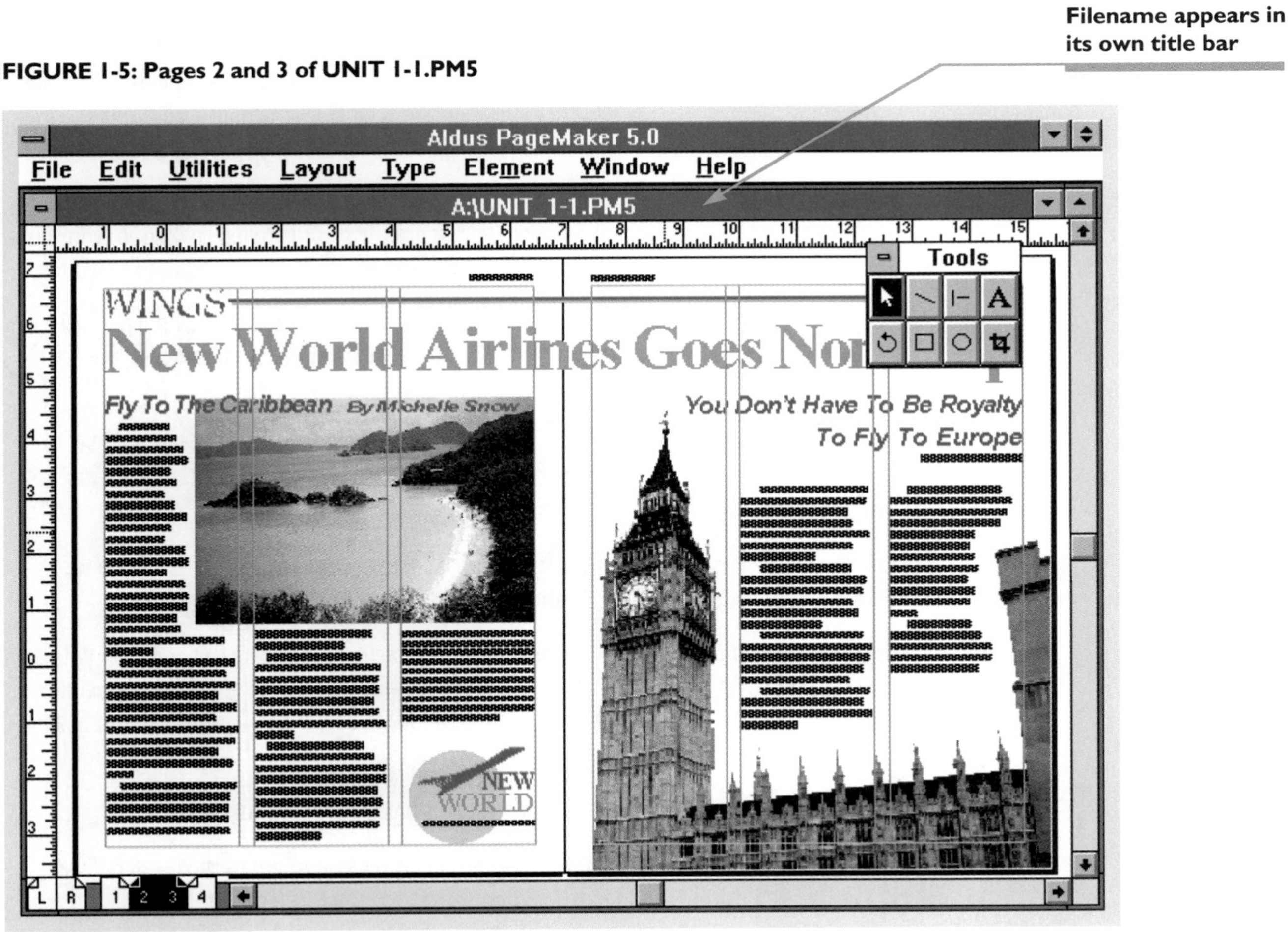

Viewing the PageMaker publication window

When you open a publication in PageMaker, it appears in the publication window. The **publication window** is the area that includes the page where you modify an existing publication or create a new one. ▶ Joe's newsletter appears in the publication window. Familiarize yourself with the elements of the publication window by comparing the descriptions below to Figure 1-6.

- The **publication page** is the solid-lined, boxed area in which you create and modify text and graphics to build a publication. The maximum page size allowed in PageMaker is 42 inches by 42 inches. The publication page can be displayed as a single page or with two facing pages. The publication page is shadowed on the bottom and outer page borders so that you can see if you are working on a right or a left page.
- The **margin guides** are magenta-colored boxes inside the page borders. The margin guides show you where the margins are relative to the page borders. The vertical margin guides in this publication are obscured by blue **column guides**, vertical lines that indicate columns.
- The **pasteboard** is the white area surrounding and including the publication page. You can use the pasteboard as a work area to hold text or graphics until you place them in your publication. Any area beyond the pasteboard is represented by yellow or a color other than white.
- **Page icons** are numbered rectangles that appear in the lower-left corner of the publication window. They represent the pages in a publication. To move to a different page, click the desired page icon.
- **Master page icons** appear to the left of the page icons and access the right and left master pages. **Master pages** are nonprinting pages used for placing text and/or graphics that will appear on all pages of the publication.
- **Scroll bars** are located on the right and bottom edges of the window. You use them to display portions of the pasteboard that are not visible in the current view.
- The **toolbox** contains eight tool icons that you use to create and modify text and graphics. The toolbox is a **floating palette**, which is a movable window within the publication window. You can work with it just like any other window—it has a title bar and a control menu box.
- **Rulers** are located on the top (horizontal ruler) and left (vertical ruler) of the window. You use the rulers to size and align your text and graphics precisely and accurately.
- The **zero point marker** is the intersection of the horizontal and vertical rulers. The **zero point** is the point at which the zero marks on the rulers intersect.
- The **menu bar** contains menus where you choose PageMaker commands.

FIGURE 1-6: PageMaker publication window

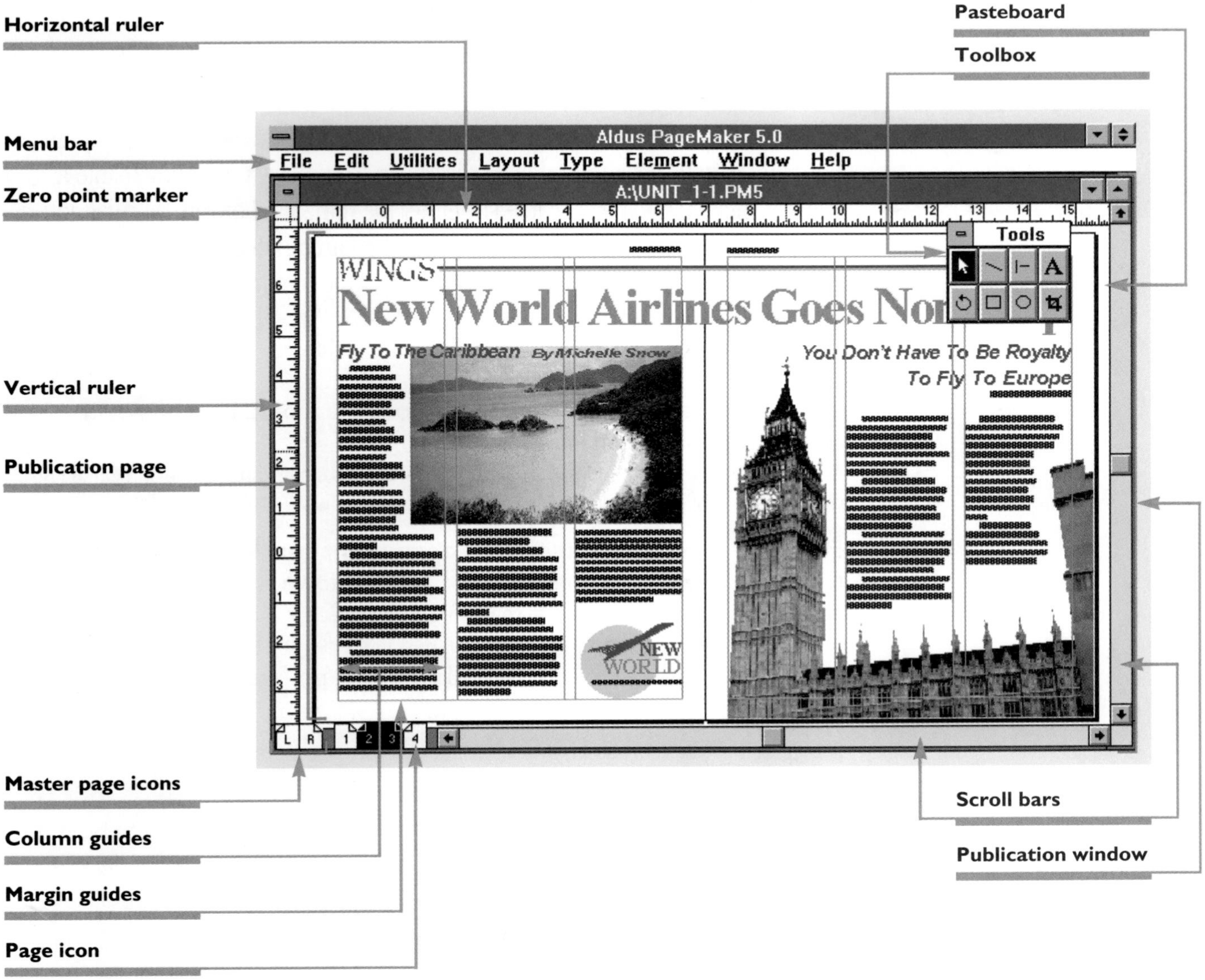

Setting the zero point and using ruler guides

You can easily place and precisely align text and graphics on a page in PageMaker by using its ruler guide system. **Ruler guides** are nonprinting lines that usually appear in blue on the screen. You move a ruler guide onto a page by clicking the area occupied by either the horizontal or vertical ruler and dragging the guide into place. Publication pages accommodate up to 40 ruler guides. The **zero point** is the point at which the zero mark on the rulers meets. The default zero point is the top left page border. ▶ Try setting the zero point and using the ruler guides now.

STEPS

1. **Without pressing the mouse button, move the mouse pointer slowly around the publication window**
   As you move the pointer, watch as the **pointer guides**, dotted lines in the horizontal and vertical rulers, follow the pointer. Try changing the zero point.
2. **Position the mouse pointer on the zero point marker, press and hold the left mouse button, then drag the pointer down and to the right to the point where the top and left margin guides meet**
   Notice that as you drag, the zero point icon appears in reverse, and the intersection of two dotted lines that go the length and width of the window follow the movement of the pointer.
3. **Release the mouse button**
   See Figure 1-7. The zero point is now at the intersection of the top and left margin guides. Now try creating a horizontal ruler guide.
4. **Place the mouse pointer over the horizontal ruler, then press and hold the left mouse button**
   The pointer changes to ↕.
5. **Drag ↕ down until the pointer guide on the vertical ruler is at the 5" mark, then release the mouse button**
   A dotted line moves with ↕. See Figure 1-8. After you release the mouse button, the ruler guide changes to blue and stays on the page. Don't worry if it is not exactly at the 5" mark. You can reposition the ruler guides anywhere on the publication page.
6. **Place the mouse pointer over the horizontal ruler, then drag a second ruler guide to the 1" mark on the vertical ruler**
   If you didn't move the ruler guide exactly to the 1" mark, position the mouse pointer over the ruler guide, then drag it again. You can remove a ruler guide any time you want to by moving it off the publication page.
7. **Drag the ruler guide at the 1" mark up or down until it is off the publication page and on the pasteboard or the horizontal ruler, then release the mouse button**
   The ruler guide disappears. You create vertical ruler guides in the same manner.

FIGURE 1-7: The repositioned zero point

FIGURE 1-8: Placing the ruler guides

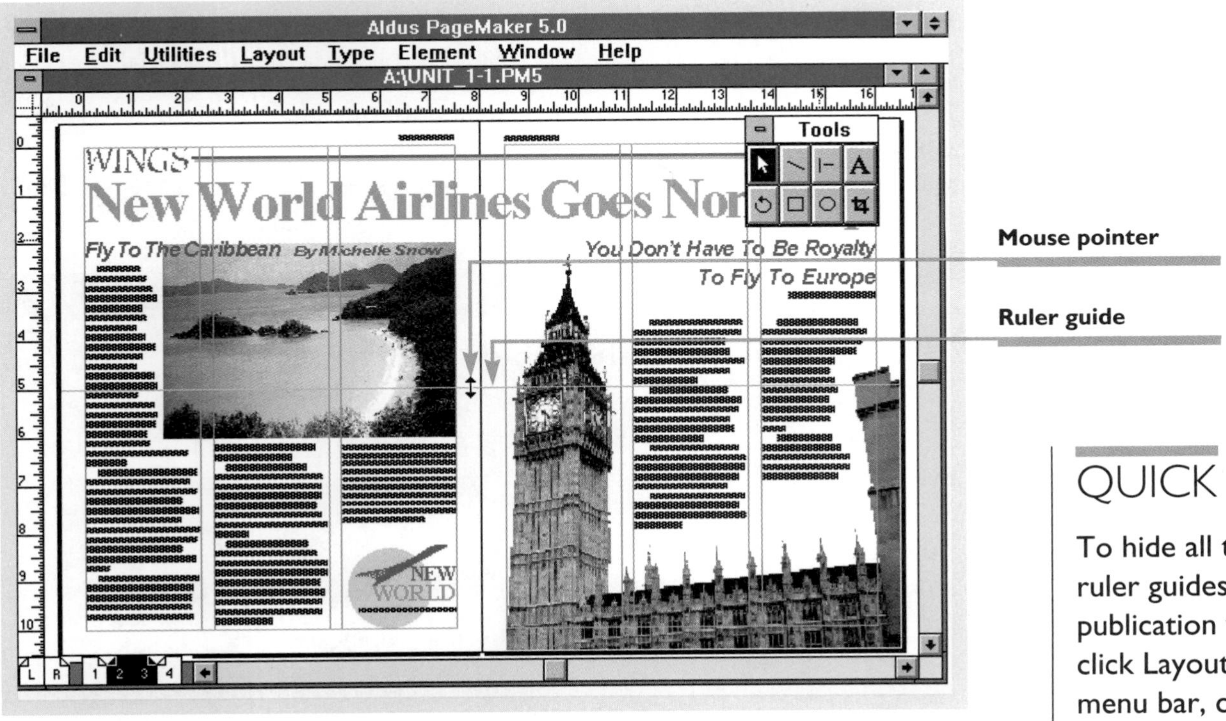

QUICK TIP

To hide all the ruler guides in the publication window, click Layout on the menu bar, click Guides & rulers, then click Guides. To show them again use the same command.

Working with tools in the toolbox

Just as conventional designers used their tools (rulers, pens, and knives) to create publications, users of desktop publishing software use electronic tools to perform the same tasks. PageMaker's **toolbox** usually appears in the upper-right corner of the publication window. The toolbox gives today's designers the same range of tools that conventional designers use, but these electronic tools have even more capabilities. Each of the eight tools is represented by an icon in the toolbox, and each tool has a different mouse pointer shape when it is selected. See Table 1-2 for a list of the tools, their pointer shapes, and brief descriptions of their functions. ▶ Joe needs to use one of the tools to add a line to his newsletter.

STEPS

1. **Click the Constrained-line tool  in the toolbox**
   The pointer changes to +. You position the pointer where you want to begin drawing the line.
2. **Position + above the logo on page 2 directly on top of the third column's left column guide**
   See Figure 1-9. If it is positioned correctly, you will not be able to see the blue column guide under the vertical line of +.
3. **Press and hold the left mouse button, drag + across the column until + is directly on top of the right margin guide, *but do not release the mouse button***
   A line appears as you drag the pointer.
4. **Move + down the page until the line jumps down by 45 degrees**
   See Figure 1-10. The line drawn by the Constrained-line tool is always straight at a 45-degree angle.
5. **Move + back up the right margin guide until the line is straight across the page, then release the mouse button**
   When you release the mouse button, the line stays on the screen as shown in Figure 1-11. Don't worry if your line isn't in exactly the same location as the one in the figure.

TABLE 1-2: Toolbox tools

TOOL	ICON	POINTER SHAPE	DESCRIPTION
Pointer			Selects, moves, and resizes objects
Line		+	Draws a straight line at any angle
Constrained-line		+	Draws a straight line at 45-degree angles
Text			Allows you to enter and modify text
Rotating			Rotates any object around an axis to any angle
Rectangle		+	Draws a rectangle or a square
Ellipse		+	Draws an ellipse or a circle
Cropping			Adjusts the borders of a graphic by eliminating unwanted portions

FIGURE 1-9: Positioning the Constrained-line tool

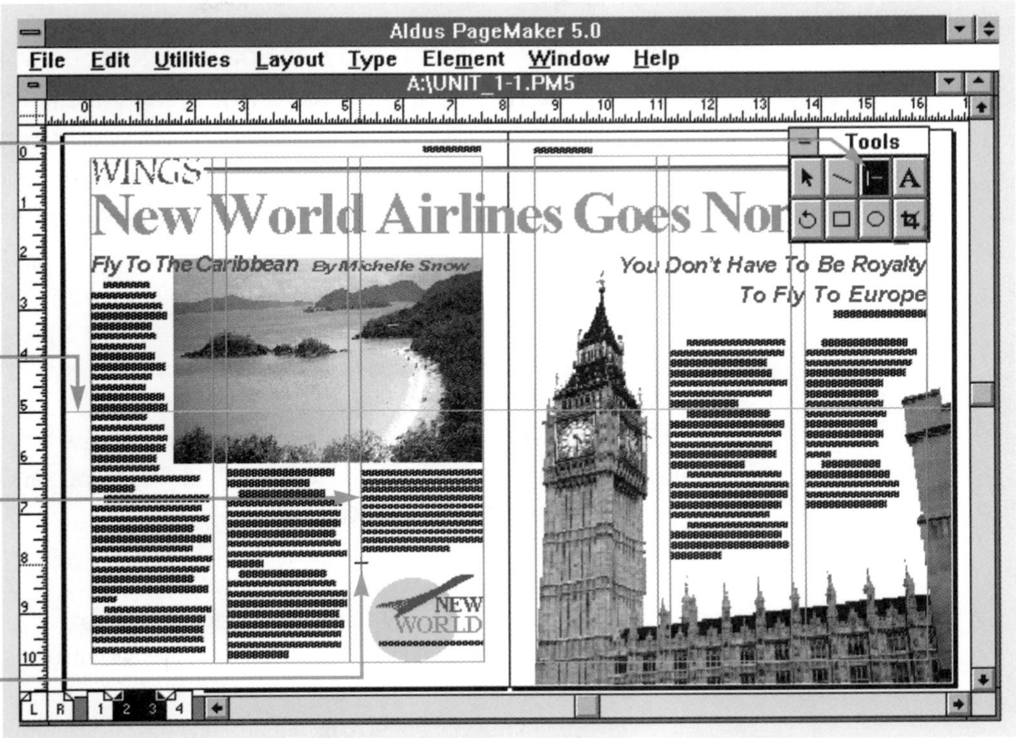

FIGURE 1-10: Changing the angle of a constrained-line

FIGURE 1-11: The final line

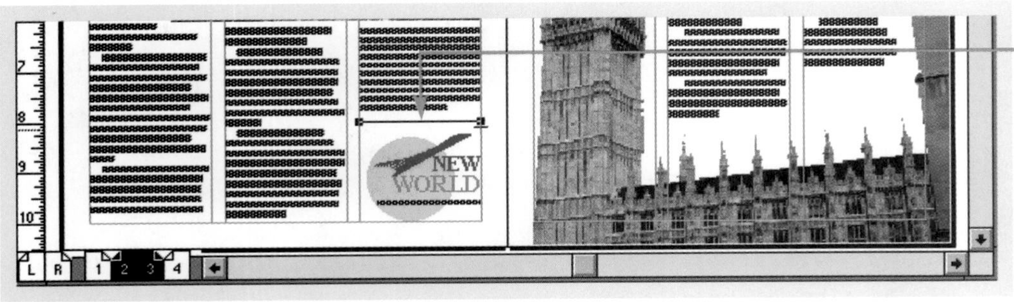

QUICK TIP

The toolbox is a window. If it blocks your view of part of the page, click the toolbox's title bar, then drag it to a new position anywhere on the pasteboard.

Viewing the publication

In PageMaker, you can change the **page view**, or the magnification of the page. Table 1-3 describes the views. Higher magnifications allow you to fine-tune documents. Lower magnifications allow you to view an entire page at once. You can also use the scroll bars to see portions of the publication that are not displayed in the window. For information on another method of scrolling, see the related topic "Using the grabber hand." ▶ Try changing the page view and using the scroll bars now.

STEPS

1. **Click the Pointer tool in the toolbox**
   The pointer changes to ↖.
2. **Click Layout on the menu bar, then click View**
   The View menu appears, as shown in Figure 1-12. The check mark next to the Fit in window option indicates that this is the current view.
3. **Click 200% size**
   The publication appears at four times its actual size.
4. **Click the down arrow on the vertical scroll bar**
   The page scrolls up about one inch, revealing a lower section of the page.
5. **Click in the vertical scroll bar anywhere above the scroll box**
   The page moves in a larger increment than when you clicked the down arrow. You use the horizontal scroll bar in the same manner.
6. **Click Layout on the menu bar, click View, then click Show pasteboard**
   A full view of the white pasteboard appears with the pages centered. Yellow shading marks the area beyond the largest possible page size.
7. **Click the Photo of the beach in the upper-right corner on page 2, click Layout, click View, then click 75% size**
   The view changes to ¾ of the actual size of the page with the photo centered in the view. Compare your screen with Figure 1-13.

TABLE 1-3: Publication page views

VIEW	DESCRIPTION
Show pasteboard	Displays the entire pasteboard with the page(s) centered on it
Fit in window	Adjusts page(s) to fill publication window so you see all of the page(s) and some of the surrounding pasteboard
25% size	Displays the page at ¼ the actual size
50% size	Displays the page at ½ the actual size
75% size	Displays the page at ¾ the actual size
Actual size	Displays the publication at the size specified when the publication was created
200% size	Displays the page at twice the actual size
400% size	Displays the page at four times the actual size

FIGURE 1-12: Layout and View menus

Checkmark indicates this option is selected

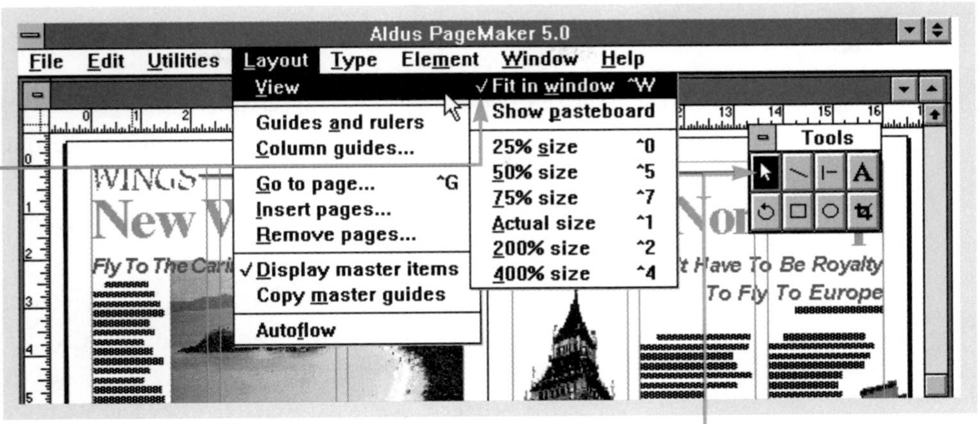

Pointer tool

FIGURE 1-13: Publication page at 75% size

Using the grabber hand

Instead of using the scroll bars to move around the pasteboard, you can use the grabber hand. The **grabber hand** acts like a hand on a piece of paper and lets you move the page in any direction in the publication window. To use the grabber hand, press and hold [Alt], then press and hold the left mouse button. The pointer changes to ☟, and the page moves in the direction you move the mouse. The grabber hand is active only while you continue to hold [Alt] and the left mouse button.

QUICK TIP

To change the view quickly to Actual size from any other view, press the right mouse button. This is called **right-clicking**. Press the right mouse button again to change the view to Fit in window.

Getting Help

PageMaker provides an extensive on-line Help system that gives you immediate access to definitions, explanations, and useful tips. Help information appears in its own window that you can resize and refer to as you work. ▶ Use PageMaker's on-line Help to learn how to close a publication and exit PageMaker.

STEPS

1. **Click Help on the menu bar, then click Contents**
   The Help Contents window opens listing available Help topics, as shown in Figure 1-14. This window has its own menu bar and five buttons. See Table 1-4 for a description of each button.

2. **Click the green, underlined topic Commands in the Reference Information section**
   A list of PageMaker's menus appears.

3. **Under the Commands topic, click File Menu, then click Close**
   A Help window opens, displaying a definition of the Close command on the File menu and a basic explanation of how to close a publication. Read the information on the File Close command.

4. **Click Search**
   The Search dialog box opens, as shown in Figure 1-15. You use this dialog box to locate a specific topic or feature. The insertion point appears in the Search text box.

5. **In the Search text box, type Exit**
   As you type each character, the list of available topics scrolls to display topics beginning with those letters. The topic "Exit" appears in the list box.

6. **Click Show Topics**
   Help displays all the topics relating to the Exit command in the lower list box.

7. **Click Exit (File Menu) in the lower list box, then click Go To**
   A Help window appears, displaying a definition of the Exit command on the File menu and a basic explanation of how to exit PageMaker and return to Windows. Read the information on the Exit command, then close the Help window.

8. **Click File on the Help window menu bar, then click Exit**
   The Help window closes and returns you to the publication. You can also double-click the control menu box on the Help window to close it.

FIGURE 1-14: Help Contents window

Help window buttons

Click to see PageMaker menu commands

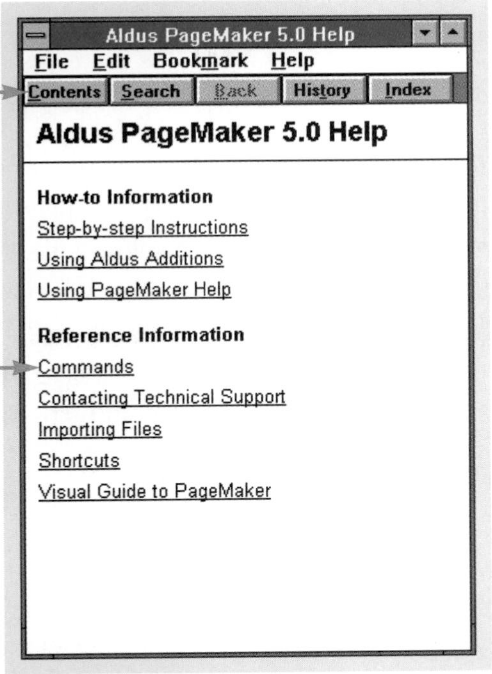

FIGURE 1-15: Search dialog box

Insertion point

List of available topics

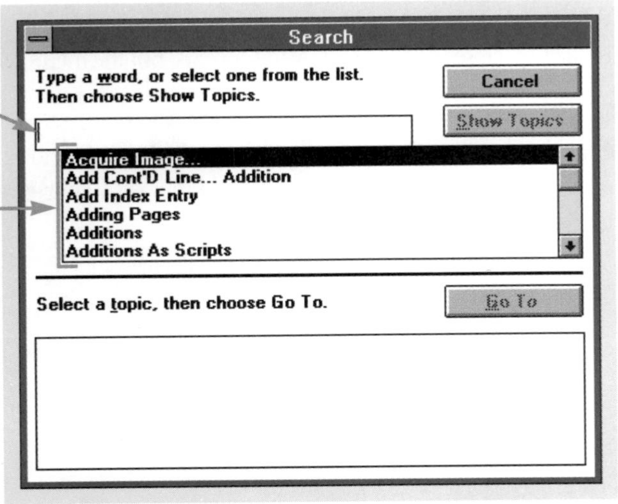

TABLE 1-4: Help window buttons

BUTTON	DESCRIPTION
Contents	Displays the contents of the Help file by topic categories
Search	Opens a dialog box in which you specify the topic you want help with
Back	Returns you to the previous topic
History	Displays a list of Help topics to which you have referred
Index	Displays an alphabetical listing of all Help topics

QUICK TIP

To access Help quickly, press [F1].■

Closing a publication and exiting PageMaker

When you are finished working on a publication, you generally save your work, then close the file. You won't save the changes you made to this publication because you were only practicing. When you close a file, the publication window no longer appears, but PageMaker remains open. When you have completed all your work in PageMaker, you can exit the application. Table 1-5 explains the difference between closing a file and exiting PageMaker. ▶ Joe is finished reviewing his newsletter, so he closes the publication and exits PageMaker.

STEPS

1. Click **File** on the menu bar
   See Figure 1-16.
2. Click **Close**
   You could also double-click the publication control menu box instead of choosing File Close. A warning box opens, as shown in Figure 1-17, asking if you want to save changes to the file before closing. Because this was a practice session, you do not need to save the file.
3. Click **No**
   The publication closes and the toolbox disappears, but the menu bar is still visible.
4. Click **File** on the menu bar, then click **Exit**
   You could also double-click the application control menu box to exit the application. PageMaker closes, and you are returned to the Program Manager window.

TABLE 1-5: PageMaker's Close and Exit commands

CLOSING A FILE	EXITING PAGEMAKER
Puts a file away, closing the active publication window	Puts all files away, closing all open publication windows
Leaves PageMaker loaded in computer memory	Frees computer memory for other uses

FIGURE 1-16: Closing a publication using the File menu

Close command

Exit command

FIGURE 1-17: Save changes warning

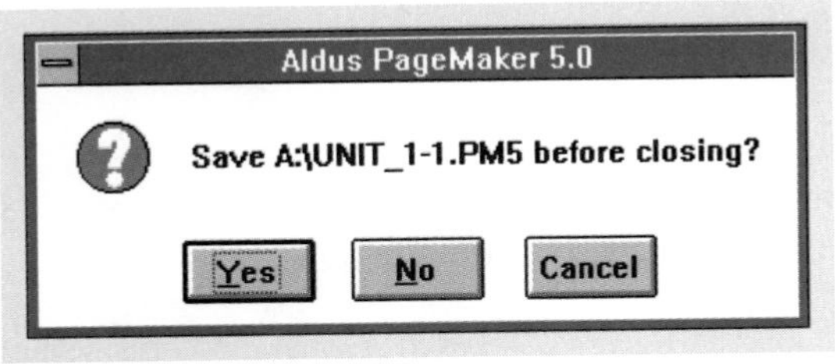

QUICK TIP

To exit PageMaker and close several files at once, click File on the menu bar, then click Exit. PageMaker will prompt you to save changes to each publication before exiting.

CONCEPTS REVIEW

Label each of the publication window elements shown in Figure 1-18.

1 Constrained-line tool

2 Zero Point marker

3 Pointer tool

4 Rule guide

5 Vertical Rule

6 Publication page / Margin Guides

7 Tool Box

8 Master Page Icon

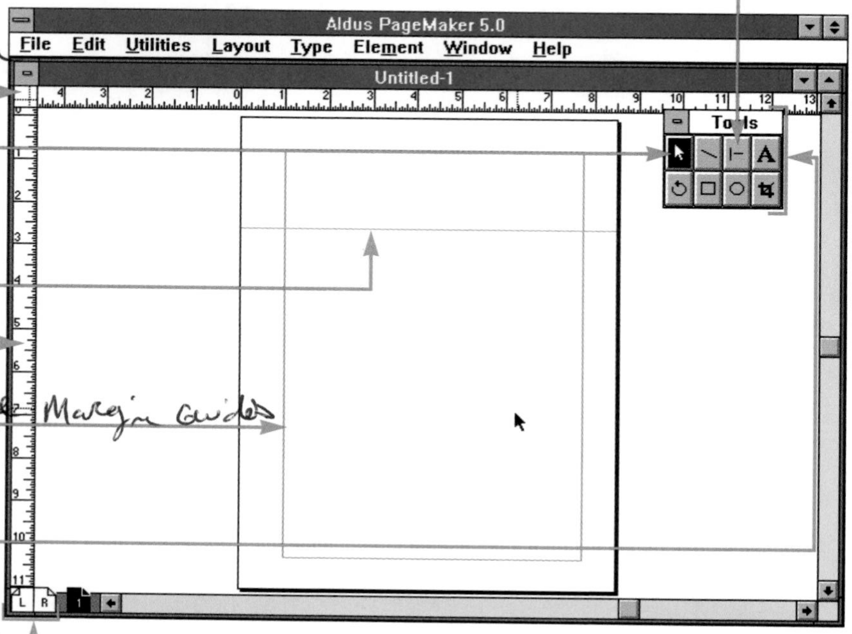

FIGURE 1-18

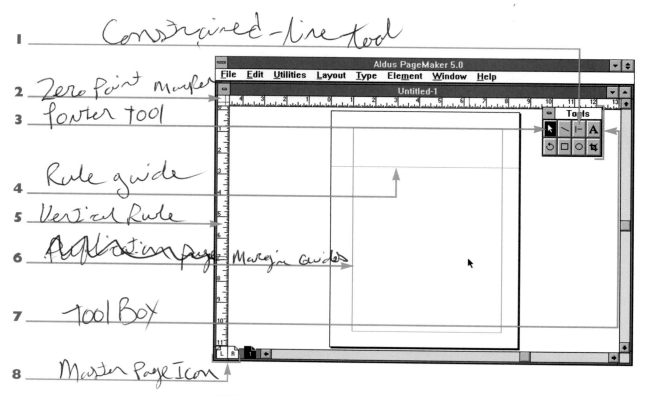

Match each of the terms with the statement that describes its function.

9 Magenta-colored lines that identify the page margins

10 The intersection of the horizontal and vertical rulers

11 Area in which you create and modify text and graphics

12 Work table area that can hold text and graphics

13 Contains tools for creating and modifying text and graphics

a. Zero point marker
b. Pasteboard
c. Margin guides
d. Toolbox
e. Publication page

Select the best answer from the list of choices.

14 To precisely make small adjustments to a publication, which of the following would you choose from the Layout View menu?

a. Show pasteboard
b. 25% size
c. Actual size
d. 400%

15 Which tool do you use to modify text?

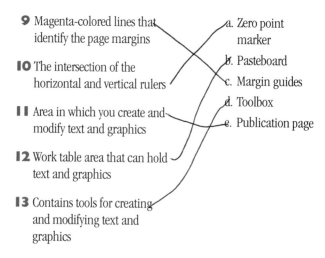

a. 
b. 
c. 
d. 

16 Desktop publishing software can create all of the following publications, except

a. Newsletter

b. Brochure

c. Advertisement

d. All of the above can be created in PageMaker

17 To repeat text and graphics on all pages of a publication, place the text and graphics on the

a. Default pages

b. Page icons

c. Master pages

d. Publication pages

18 You can get Help in any of the following ways, except

a. Clicking Help on the menu bar

b. Pressing [F1]

c. Selecting a topic in the Help window

d. Minimizing the application window

APPLICATIONS REVIEW

1 Start PageMaker.

a. Double-click the Aldus program group icon in the Program Manager window.

b. Double-click the PageMaker application icon.

2 Open a publication and identify elements in the publication window.

a. Click File on the menu bar, then click Open.

b. Select the drive containing your Student Disk from the Drives list box.

c. Open the file UNIT_1-2.PM5.

d. Identify as many elements of the publication window as you can without referring to the unit.

3 View the publication window.

a. Click the right arrow on the horizontal scroll bar.

b. Click the down arrow on the vertical scroll bar.

c. Click Layout on the menu bar, click View, then click 25%.

d. Click Layout on the menu bar, click View, then click 200%.

e. Click Layout on the menu bar, click View, then click Fit in window.

4 Change the zero point and use ruler guides.

a. Drag the zero point marker to the corner where the top and left corners of publication page meet.

b. Drag a horizontal ruler guide to the .5" mark on the vertical ruler.

c. Drag another horizontal ruler guide to the 5" mark on the vertical ruler.

d. Drag a vertical ruler guide to the 1" mark on the horizontal ruler.

e. Remove the horizontal ruler guide at the 5" mark.

5 Explore the toolbox.

a. Click the Constrained-line tool.

b. Move the pointer below the word "France."

c. Draw a line to underline the word.

6 Explore Help.

a. Click Help on the menu bar, then click Search.

b. Scroll through the Search Topic list box to view the available topics.

c. Select a topic from the list box which you want to know more about, then click Show Topics.

d. Select a topic to read, then click Go To. Read the topic.

e. Click File on the menu bar, then click Exit.

7 Close the publication and exit PageMaker.

a. Click File on the menu bar, then click Close.

b. Click No when you are asked if you want to save changes.

c. If needed, close any other documents you might have opened using the same technique.

d. Click File on the menu bar, then click Exit.

INDEPENDENT CHALLENGE 1

PageMaker provides three on-line Guided Tours: Quick Tour, Tutorial, and New Features. Quick Tour is a brief introduction and demonstration of PageMaker features. Tutorial is a self-paced demonstration and interactive practice session. New Features is an overview of the new and enhanced features in the current version of PageMaker. Use the Quick Tour to find out more about PageMaker.

To complete this independent challenge:

1 Click Help on the menu bar, click Learning PageMaker 5.0, then click Quick Tour.

2 Follow the on-line tutorial directions.

3 At the end of the tutorial, click Close to return to the publication window.

INDEPENDENT CHALLENGE 2

Some examples of how PageMaker can be used are mentioned at the beginning of this unit. Search for examples of publications that could be produced using PageMaker and compile them into a sample design packet.

To complete this independent challenge:

1 Gather at least five different publications. Make sure at least one of your samples is in full color and another includes only spot color.

2 Keep this design packet. Refer to it as necessary as you learn about design features in later units.

UNIT 2

OBJECTIVES

- Plan a publication
- Create a new publication
- Place a graphic
- Resize a graphic
- Move objects
- Add text and lines to a publication
- Format text
- Save a publication
- Print a publication
- Design Workshop: Letterhead

Creating A PUBLICATION

Now that you know how to start PageMaker, use the on-line Help system, and move around a PageMaker publication window, you are ready to plan and create your own publication. When working with a publication, you can include text and graphics created in other application programs. You can also use PageMaker's tools to create and modify text and graphics directly in your publication. After you create a publication, you can save and print it. ▶ Joe Martin needs to create a new company letterhead for New World Airlines. Creating simple publications is one of the many ways that PageMaker is useful for businesses. ▶

Planning a publication

Before you create a publication in PageMaker, you need to plan and design it. Planning and designing a publication organizes your thoughts and ideas about what to include and how it should look. At the beginning of each unit, you will learn design tips for creating different types of publications. ▶ One of Joe's first assignments is to create a new letterhead for New World Airlines. Letterhead should be eye-catching and memorable. It should contain the company logo and the company name, and can also contain the company address, telephone and fax numbers, and electronic mail address. Joe keeps the following guidelines in mind as he plans and designs the letterhead:

STEPS

1. **Place the company logo in a logical position on the page**
   A company's logo is used in almost all forms of visual communication to reinforce the connection between the graphic logo and the company name. Logos on letterhead are often at the top of the page, but they can run down a side or be at the bottom. The logo should be large enough the catch the reader's attention, but not so large that it is overwhelming. Joe decides to place the New World Airlines logo at the top of the page in the center.

2. **Include the company address and any relevant telephone numbers**
   The placement of the address and telephone numbers is usually based on the placement of the logo. Joe decides to put the address and the company's toll free telephone number below the logo.

3. **Consider adding the company motto or slogan**
   Adding the motto or slogan is not required, but it can help reinforce the company's image. Joe decides to put the New World Airlines slogan, "The Wings of America," above the address line.

4. **Evaluate the final design, and add lines, boxes, or shading, if necessary**
   Joe wants the logo and the address line to be visually distinct from the rest of the page, so he adds a thin horizontal line below the logo. Figure 2-1 shows Joe's sketch of the letterhead.

FIGURE 2-1: Joe's sketch of the new letterhead

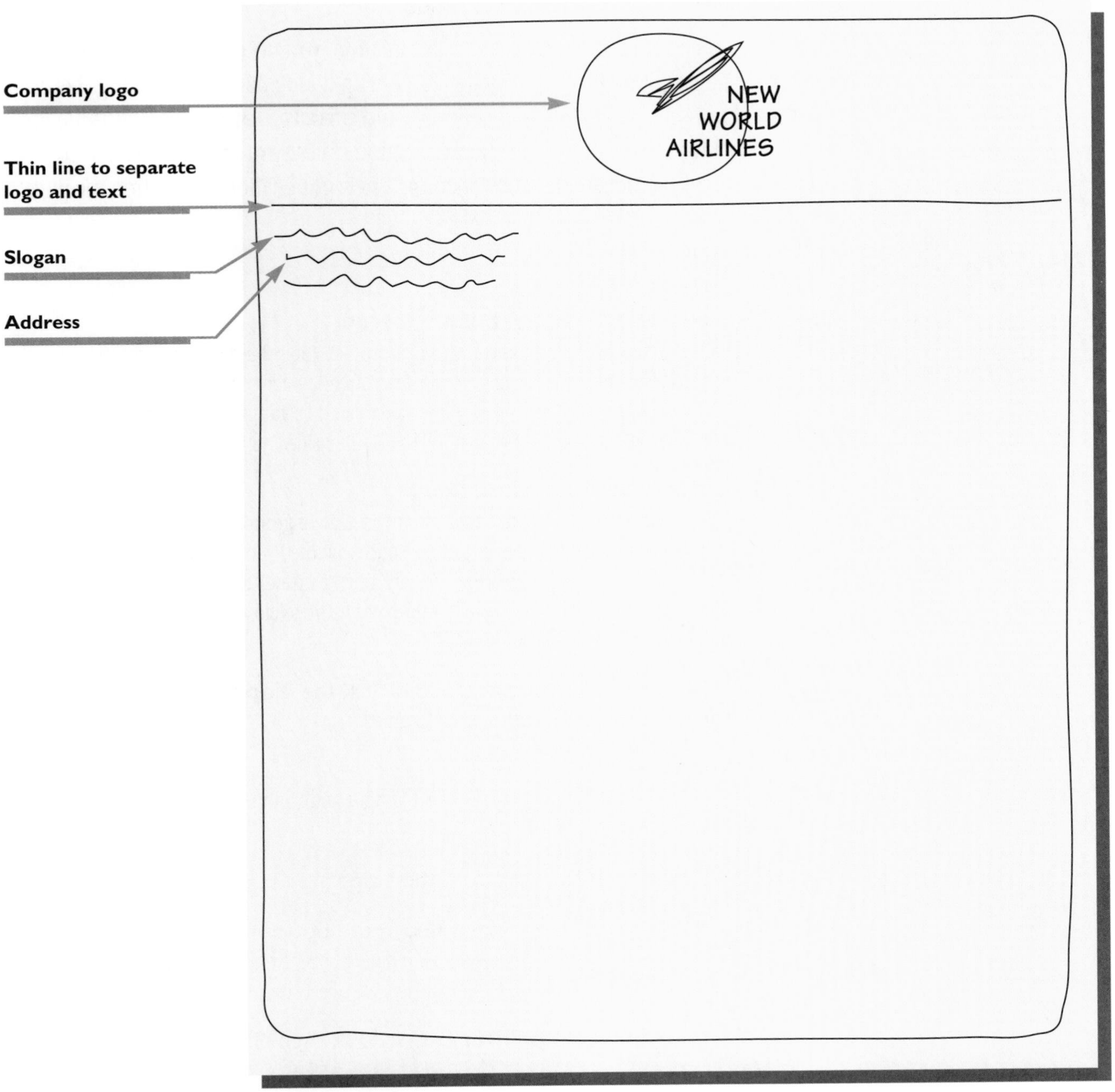

Creating a new publication

Before you can begin creating a new publication, you need to select the settings for the pages. To do this, you use the Page setup dialog box. These settings become the default settings for the publication. The **default settings** determine the general layout of each page in the publication unless you specify otherwise. ▶ Joe begins creating the letterhead by opening a new publication and setting the page defaults.

STEPS

1 **Start PageMaker**

2 **Click File on the menu bar, then click New**
The Page setup dialog box opens, as shown in Figure 2-2. Table 2-1 describes the options in the Page setup dialog box. The company letterhead is a one-page publication that will be on standard 8½" x 11" paper, so most of the PageMaker default settings are fine. Because this is only a single-page publication, Joe turns off the Double-sided option.

3 **Click the Double-sided check box**
Turning this feature off sets each page individually instead of grouping even and odd pages together as you saw in the newsletter in Unit 1. Notice that the Facing Pages option is dimmed and that the margin options change from "Inside" and "Outside" to "Left" and "Right." Joe looks at his sketch again and sees that he wants to put the logo closer to the top edge of the page, so he decides to change the top margin to .5".

4 **In the Margin in inches section, double-click the Top text box**
The current value, .75, is **selected**, or highlighted.

5 **Type .5**
The top margin is now set at .5". Next, Joe sets the right and bottom margins to be the same as the left margin, 1".

6 **Double-click the Right text box, then type 1**

7 **Press [Tab] twice to select the value in the Bottom text box, then type 1**
You can place the insertion point in a text box in dialog boxes by clicking in the text box or by pressing [Tab] to move from option to option. Now Joe selects his printer.

8 **Click the Compose to printer list arrow, then click the name of your printer**
If you are unsure of the name of your printer, ask your instructor or technical support person.

9 **Click OK**
The Page setup dialog box closes, and a new Untitled publication window with a blank publication page opens, displaying a letter-size page with the top margin guide set at .5" from the edge and the right and bottom margin guides set at 1" from the edge. Notice that there is only one master page icon because this is a single-sided publication.

FIGURE 2-2: Page setup dialog box

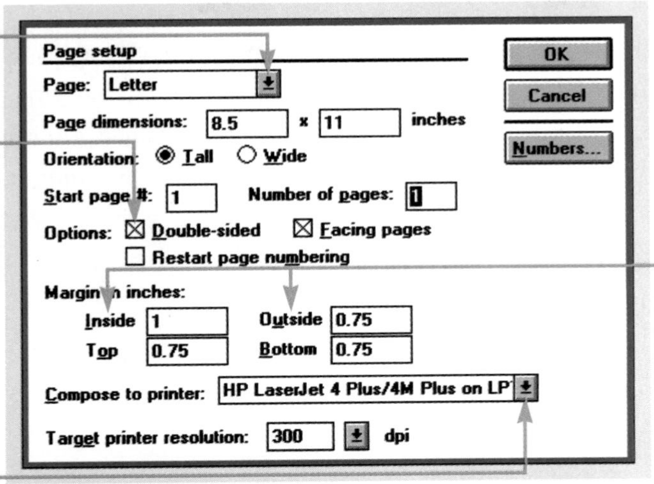

TROUBLE?

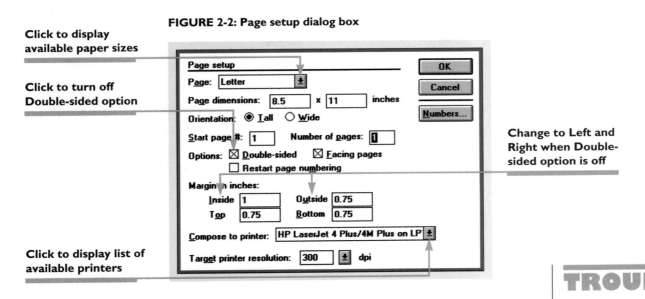

If you need help starting PageMaker, refer to the lesson "Starting PageMaker 5.0 for Windows" in Unit 1.

TABLE 2-1: Page setup dialog box options

OPTION	DESCRIPTION
Page	Select a standard paper size or choose Custom to specify your own dimensions
Page dimensions	Enter custom page dimensions; if you change the page dimensions to non-standard measurements, Custom is automatically displayed in the Page list box
Orientation	Choose Tall (vertical) or Wide (horizontal)
Start page #	Specify the first page number of the publication
Number of pages	Specify the total number of pages in the publication
Double-sided	Indicate that a publication has left and right pages
Facing pages	Only available when Double-sided is checked; when selected, displays left and right pages side by side
Restart page numbering	For publication files that are linked, or connected, to another publication file, starts the page numbering at the specified start page number instead of continuing from the end of the publication it is linked to
Margin in inches	Specify the margins for the publication
Compose to printer	Select the name of the printer to be used for printing the publication
Target printer resolution	Choose the **resolution**, or print quality, measured in dots per inch (the higher the number of dots, the better the image quality), you can choose a higher resolution only if you have a higher resolution printer

Placing a graphic

With PageMaker, you can easily **import**, or include, graphics in your publication. **Graphics** are images created in a drawing or painting program or photographs or art scanned into the computer using a scanner. You import graphic files using the Place command on the File menu. Placing graphics allows you to enhance your page layouts with images that cannot be created with PageMaker's basic design tools. ▶ Joe has already scanned the New World Airlines logo. He now wants to place it at the top of the letterhead.

STEPS

1. **Click File on the menu bar, then click Place**
   The Place document dialog box opens. Notice that it is similar to the Open publication dialog box you saw in Unit 1.
2. **Make sure your Student Disk is in the disk drive, then click the Drives list arrow**
3. **Click a:**
   If you are using a different drive, click the appropriate letter. A list of files on your Student Disk appears in the File name list box. Only the files that can be imported into a PageMaker publication are listed.
4. **In the File name list box, click logo.tif then click OK**
   The Place document dialog box closes and the mouse pointer changes to . This pointer identifies the format of the graphic file as **Tagged Image File Format (TIF)**. There are other graphic file formats and each format has a place pointer. Each type of graphic file gives a different resolution and takes up a different amount of disk space. See Table 2-2 for a description of graphic file types.
5. **Position the top border of along the top margin guide with the pointer guide on the horizontal ruler at 3.25", as shown in Figure 2-3. Notice the top border of the pointer is on top of the top margin border.**
6. **Click the left mouse button**
   The graphic appears on the page and the mouse pointer changes back to , as shown in Figure 2-4. The **selection handles**, the small black squares at the corners and sides of the graphic, indicate that the graphic is selected.

TABLE 2-2: Graphic file types

PLACE POINTER	FILE EXTENSION	DESCRIPTION
	.BMP	Bitmap file. Image created by dot resolution; used in Windows Paintbrush application
	.EPS	Encapsulated PostScript file. File created using PostScript code to create an image. EPS files are usually large.
	.PIC	Picture/Draw file. Generally geometric drawings or charts and graphs.
	.TIF	Tagged Image File Format. A standardized file format used by most major software developers for standard drawing, paint, and scanned images.

FIGURE 2-3: TIF pointer on the publication page

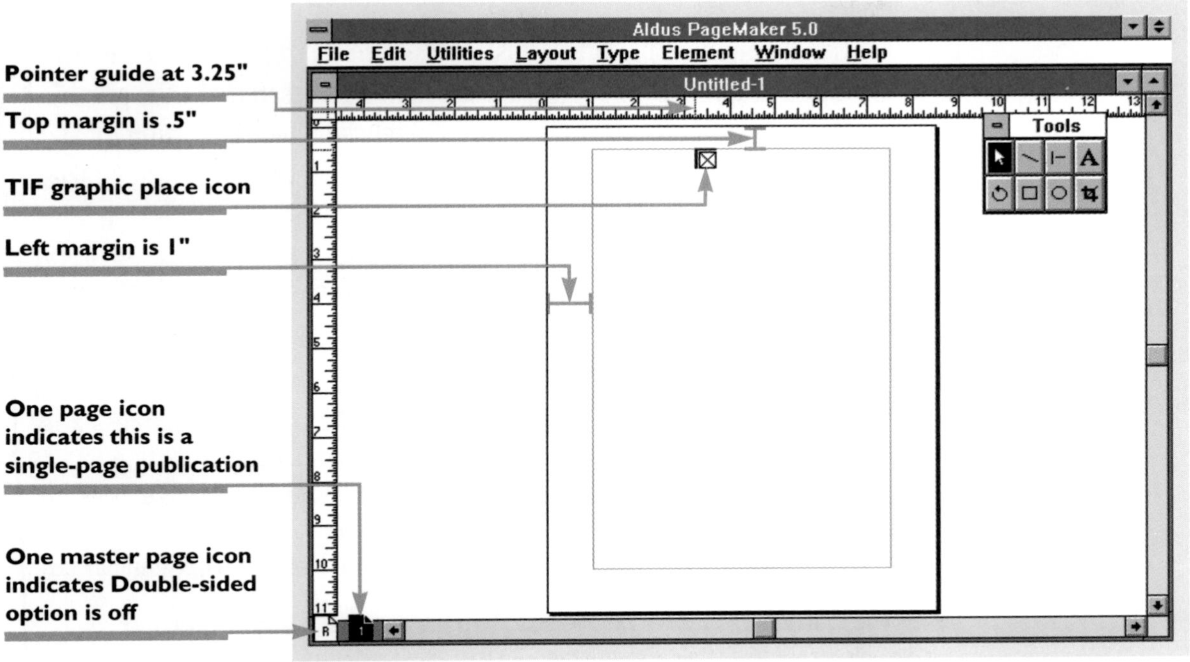

FIGURE 2-4: Placed graphic

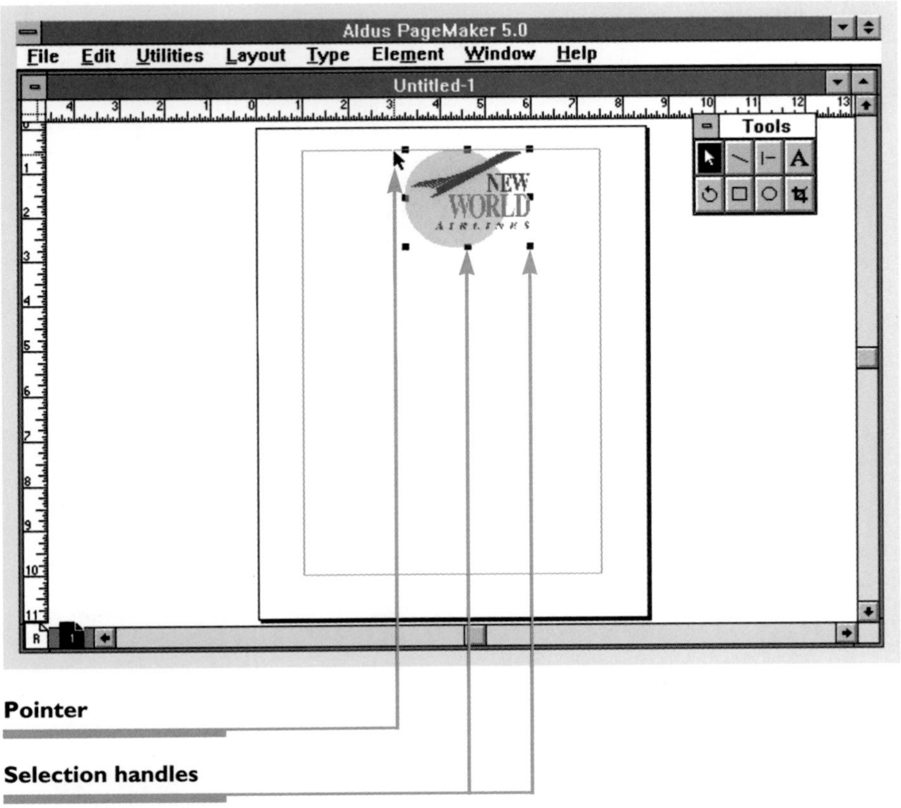

DESIGN TIP

Try to position the upper-left corner of the place pointer where you want the upper-left corner of the graphic to be. This saves time moving the graphic to the correct position after it is placed.

TROUBLE?

Unless otherwise indicated, always click the left mouse button. If you click the right mouse button, also known as right-clicking, you get a different view of the document. Use the View command on the Layout menu to return to your original view.

Resizing a graphic

Usually when a graphic is imported, it is not the correct size, so you need to resize it. You **resize** graphics by dragging the selection handles to make the graphic larger or smaller. For more information, see the related topic "Distorting the image design." ▶ Joe needs to resize the New World Airlines logo so that it takes up less space at the top of the page.

STEPS

1. **If the graphic is not selected, move the pointer to the middle of the logo, then click to select it**
   Clicking once on a graphic selects it.
2. **Move the pointer to the lower-right corner handle of the logo, press and hold [Shift], then press and hold the mouse button**
   The pointer changes to ⤡, and a box appears around the graphic to show you its dimensions. Pressing [Shift] while you resize a graphic maintains the proportions of the graphic as you resize it. By dragging a corner handle, you change the length and width of the image simultaneously.
3. **Drag the handle until it is at the 5.25" mark on the horizontal ruler**
   Use the pointer guides to help you size the logo correctly. See Figure 2-5.
4. **Release the mouse button and the [Shift] key**
   The logo is resized as shown in Figure 2-6.

FIGURE 2-5: Preparing to resize the logo

Pointer guide in horizontal ruler

Pointer guide in vertical ruler

Outline shows the dimension of the graphic

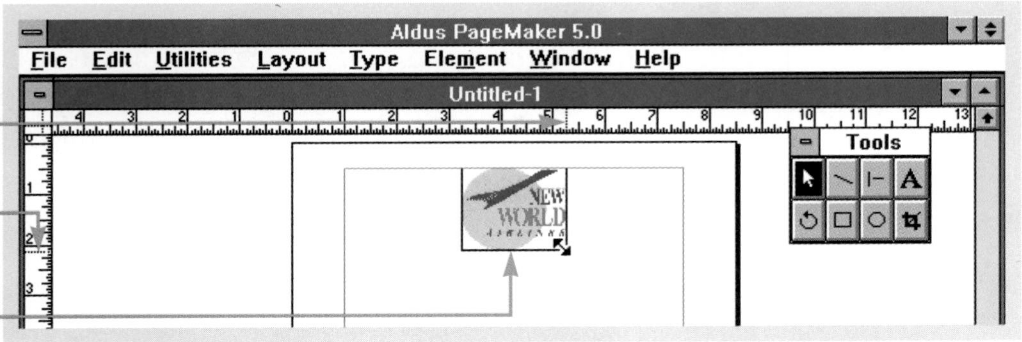

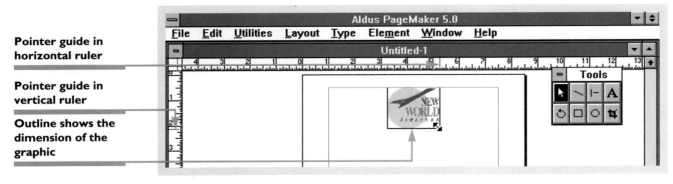

FIGURE 2-6: Resized logo

Pointer guide

Selection handles indicate the graphic is still selected

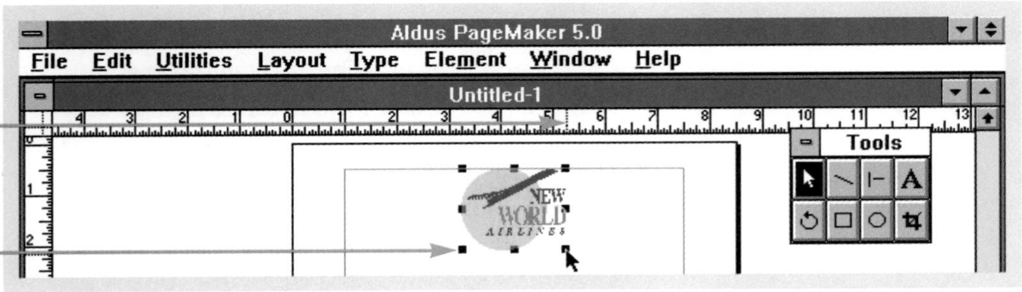

Distorting the image design

Sometimes you will want to resize a graphic without maintaining its proportions. To do this, you drag a selection handle without pressing [Shift]. This distorts the image. When you need to fit an image within a certain area, it can be helpful to distort it. Distortion can also be used as a method of creative design in your publication. It is important to make sure that the distortion does not affect the integrity of the image. If you decide to resize an image to its original proportions after it was distorted, press [Shift], then drag the handle to the desired size, and the graphic will again be proportionally sized.

DESIGN TIP

The easiest way to determine the measurement of a graphic you are resizing is to move the zero point to the upper-left corner of the image.

TROUBLE?

If you forget to press [Shift] when you resize a graphic and the proportions are no longer true, resize it again, this time pressing [Shift]. The proportions return to their original dimensions when you resize the image with the Shift key.

Moving objects

An **object** is an item, such as a graphic logo or a line that you can select and then size or move. You can move objects between pages or onto the pasteboard for temporary storage outside the page. For more information on selecting objects, see the related topic "Selecting a group of objects." ▶ Joe decides he wants to reposition the logo on the page.

STEPS

1 Click the **Pointer tool** in the toolbox, if necessary
The mouse pointer changes to ↖. If your toolbox is not visible, click Window on the menu bar, then click Toolbox.

2 Click anywhere on the New World Airlines logo to select it, if necessary

3 Position the pointer anywhere over the logo, but *not* over any of the handles, then press and hold the **mouse button**
The pointer changes to ✥, the graphic seems to disappear, and an outline showing the borders of the graphic appears. Note that if you hold down the mouse button too long no outline appears. If you clicked one of the handles, you would resize the object instead of moving it.

4 Drag the logo to the upper-left corner of the page so that the top and left borders of the outline are on top of the top and left page margins, then release the mouse button
When you release the mouse button, the logo appears in its new location. Compare your screen with Figure 2-7.

5 Click anywhere on the page, except on the logo, to deselect the graphic

FIGURE 2-7: Repositioned logo

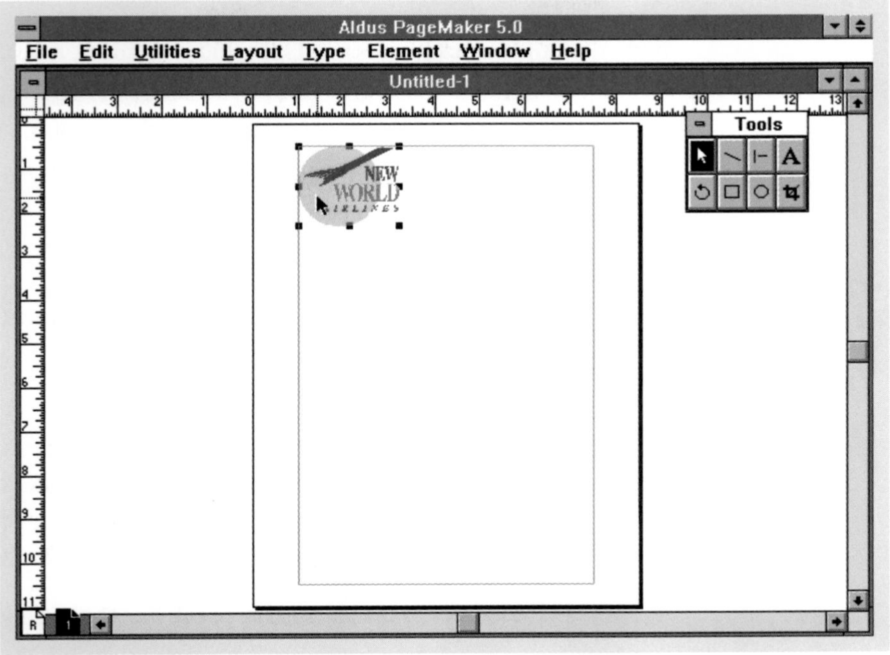

Selecting a group of objects

You can select several objects at once in PageMaker by dragging a **selection marquee** around the group of objects you want to move or edit. As you drag the pointer, you see a rectangle consisting of moving dashed lines that resemble a theater marquee, as shown in Figure 2-8. When you think all the objects are enclosed by the selection marquee, release the mouse button. The marquee disappears and selection handles appear on all of the objects. If handles do not appear around an object you wanted to select, the marquee was probably not large enough to select all the objects. Redraw the marquee so it is large enough to select all the objects.

TROUBLE?

If you accidentally resize a graphic instead of move it, click Edit, then click Undo stretch to return the graphic to its original size.

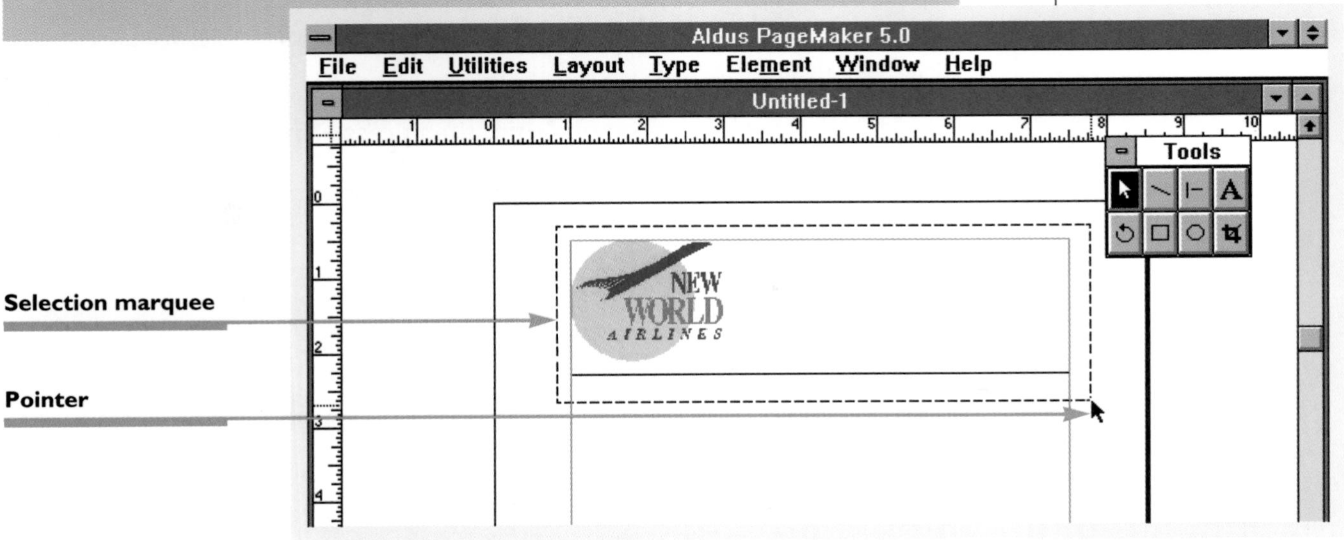

FIGURE 2-8: A selection marquee

Adding text and lines to a publication

PageMaker provides tools so you can add text and lines to a publication easily and quickly. To add text to a publication, you select the Text tool from the toolbox, click the page, then type. To add a straight line to a publication, you use the Constrained-line tool, which you used earlier. ► Joe needs to add the company's address and telephone number to the letterhead. He also wants to draw a line to separate the logo from the rest of the page.

STEPS

1 Click the **Constrained-line tool** in the toolbox
The pointer changes to +.

2 Position + just below the graphic on the left margin guide, then drag to the right until the + is directly on top of the right margin guide
See Figure 2-9. A horizontal line appears just below the logo. Next Joe wants to add the company address. First, he changes the view so that he can see the letters he types. Joe selects the logo before changing views so that, when the page is magnified, the logo will be centered on the screen.

3 Click the **Pointer tool** in the toolbox, then click the **logo** to select it

4 Click **Layout** on the menu bar, click **View**, then click **Actual size**
The screen appears at 100% with the selected logo in the center of the screen. Now Joe is ready to enter the airline's address and telephone number with the Text tool.

5 Click the **Text tool** A, then position the pointer over the page
The pointer changes to I.

6 Click I below the line and next to the left margin guide
A blinking cursor appears, also called the insertion point. The **cursor** shows where the next character you type will appear. If you click in the wrong place, reposition the cursor by clicking the Text tool pointer again in the correct place. (See Figure 2-10 for correct placement.)

7 Type **"The Wings of America"** then press **[Enter]**
Notice that characters appear as you type and the cursor moves down one line when you press [Enter]. See Figure 2-10.

8 Type **1845 North Lindbergh Blvd.** then press **[Spacebar]** three times

9 Type **Charlotte, NC 28204**, press **[Spacebar]** three times, then type **800-HORIZON**

FIGURE 2-9: Horizontal line added

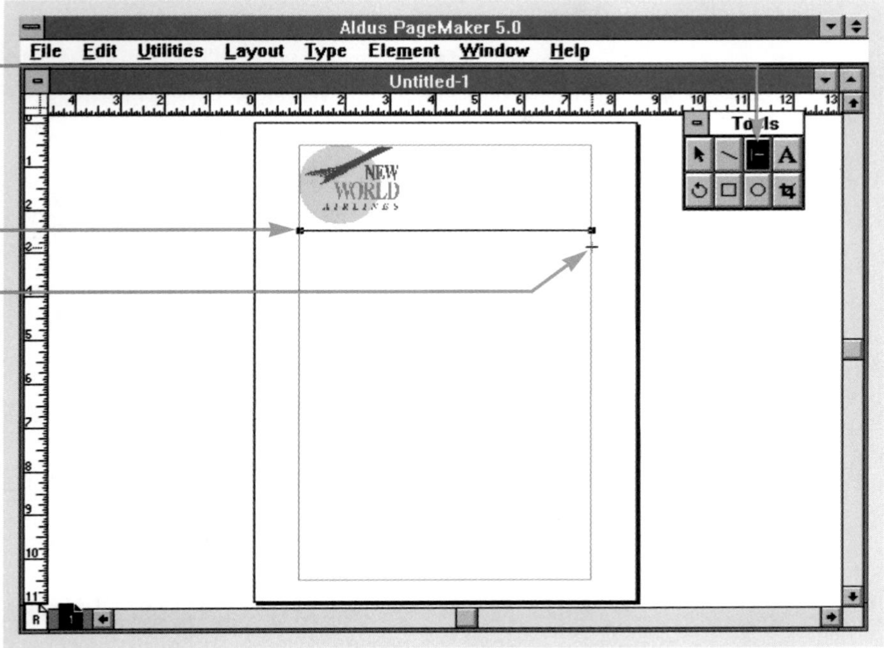

FIGURE 2-10: Text entered on page

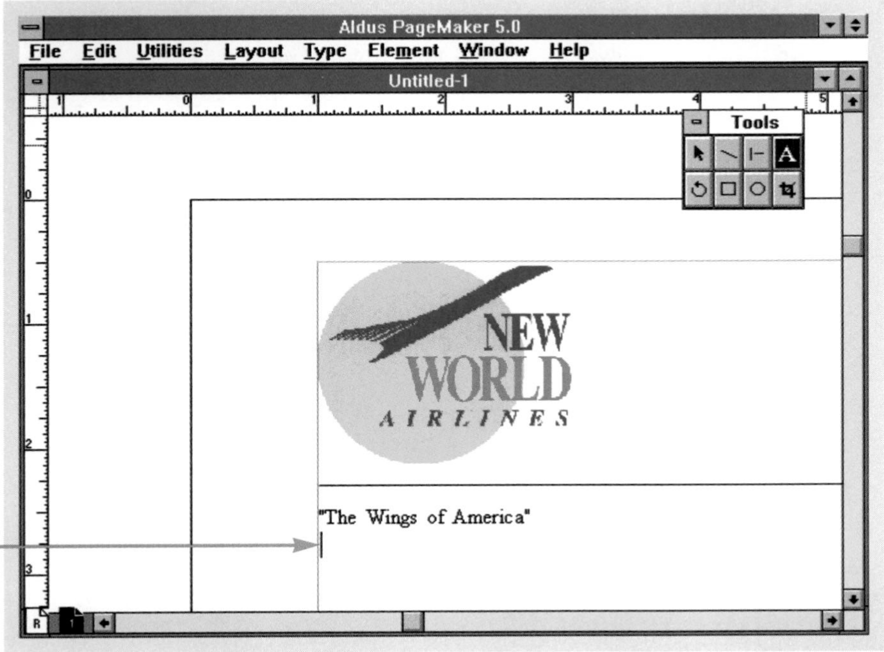

TROUBLE?

If you make a typing error, press [Backspace] to erase the error, then type the correct text.

Formatting text

When you **format** text, you change its appearance. You can change the font, size, and style of the text. The **font** is a set of characters using a specific design. The **size** of the characters is usually measured in points. A **point** is 1/72 of an inch. The **style** of the text is how the design is displayed, for example, in italics or bold. Table 2-3 shows examples of fonts, sizes, and styles. The easiest way to format text is to select the text you want to format, then choose the appropriate command from the Type menu. ▶ Joe wants to format the company's address and telephone number.

STEPS

1. **Position I at the end of the address line, then drag the pointer to the left until you reach the beginning of the address line**
   The address line is selected, as shown in Figure 2-11. If you accidentally select the line above, click outside the highlighted area to deselect the text and try again.
2. **Click Type on the menu bar, then click Font**
   The Font menu appears, as shown in Figure 2-12, with a list of all the fonts available on your computer. Joe wants to change from the default font of Times New Roman to Arial.
3. **Click Arial**
   Notice that the font changes. Next, Joe thinks that the address line will look better if the text is smaller.
4. **Click Type on the menu bar, click Size, then click 9**
   Joe also wants to italicize the address line.
5. **Click Type on the menu bar, click Type style, then click Italic**
   The selected text now reflects all the changes you made.
6. **Click anywhere on the page to deselect the text**
   Joe is pleased with the letterhead. Compare your screen with Figure 2-13.

TABLE 2-3: Types of fonts and formatting

FONT	12 POINT	24 POINT	12 PT BOLD	12 PT ITALIC
Arial	PageMaker	PageMaker	**PageMaker**	*PageMaker*
Brush Script	PageMaker	PageMaker	**PageMaker**	*PageMaker*
Times New Roman	PageMaker	PageMaker	**PageMaker**	*PageMaker*

FIGURE 2-11: Selected text

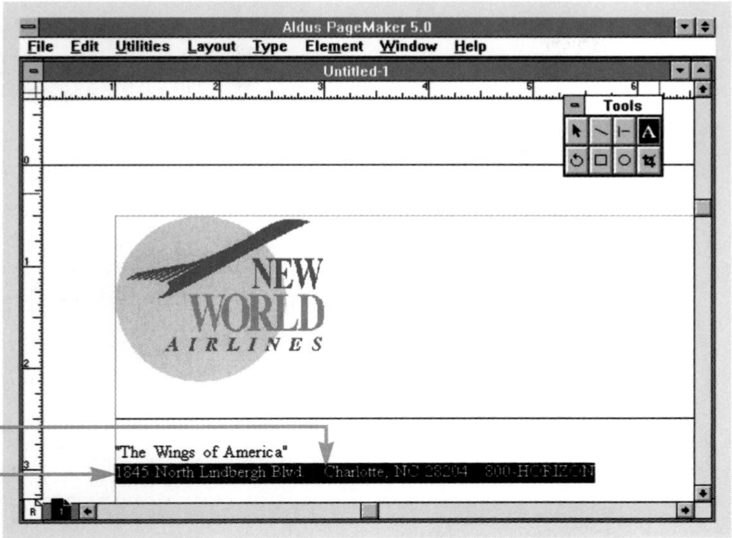

Selected text

Pointer

FIGURE 2-12: Font menu

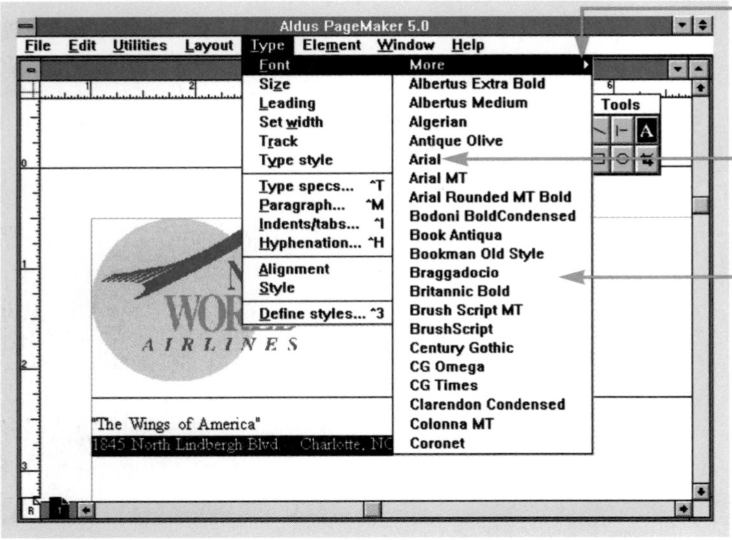

Click to display more font names

Click to choose Arial

Your list of fonts might be different

FIGURE 2-13: Joe's completed letterhead

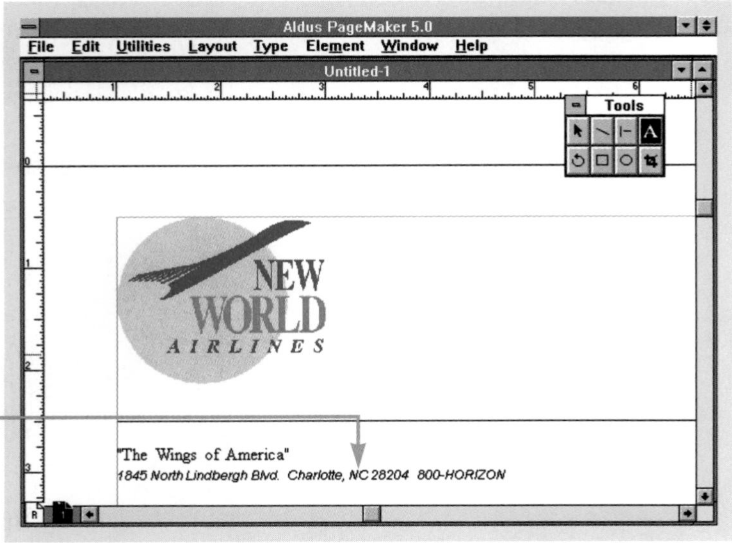

9-point italicized type

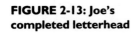

DESIGN TIP

The size of the text should be proportional to the importance of the message.

QUICK TIP

To select a word quickly, double-click it with I. To select an entire line quickly, triple-click anywhere in it with I.

Saving a publication

As you learned in "Microsoft Windows 3.1," you must save a file to disk to save it permanently. As you work on your publication, it's a good idea to save it every 10 or 15 minutes. Frequent saving prevents losing your work unexpectedly in case of a power or equipment failure. It's also a good practice to save your work before you print it. You will save all the files on your Student Disk. For more information on protecting files, see the related topic "Creating backup files." ▶ Joe wants to save his publication with the name LTRHEAD.

STEPS

1. **Click File on the menu bar, then click Save As**
   The Save publication dialog box opens.
2. **Make sure your Student Disk is in the appropriate drive**
3. **Click the Drives list arrow, then click a:**
   If you are using a different drive for your Student Disk or you are storing your practice files on a network, click the appropriate drive.
4. **Double-click the File name text box to select the filename if necessary, then type ltrhead**
   See Figure 2-14. Filenames can contain up to eight characters. These characters can be lower- or uppercase letters, numbers, or any symbols except for spaces, commas, periods, and the following symbols: \ / [ ] " ^ : * ?.
5. **Click OK**
   The Save publication dialog box closes, and the publication is saved as a file named LTRHEAD.PM5 on your Student Disk. PageMaker automatically adds the file extension .PM5 to your filename so that it can later recognize it as a PageMaker file. The filename appears in the title bar at the top of the page window. After looking over the letterhead one more time, Joe decides that he wants to change "Blvd." to "Boulevard."
6. **Double-click the word Blvd., type Boulevard, then press [Delete] to delete the period**
   Now that Joe has changed his publication, he needs to save it again.
7. **Click File on the menu bar, then click Save**
   The Save command saves the changes to a file that has already been named. Table 2-4 shows the difference between the Save and Save As commands.

TABLE 2-4: The difference between the Save and Save As commands

COMMAND	DESCRIPTION	PURPOSE
Save As	Saves file, requires input name	To save a file the first time, to change the filename, or to save the file for use in a different application. Useful for backups.
Save	Saves named file	To save any changes to the original file. Fast and easy—do this often to protect your work.

FIGURE 2-14: Completed Save publication dialog box

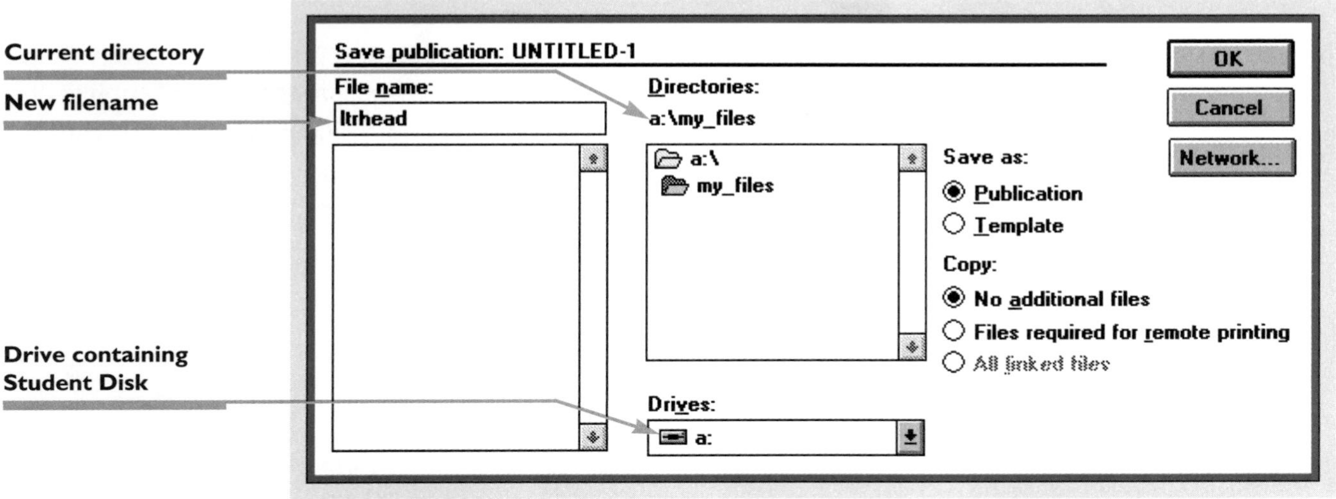

Creating backup files

It's good practice to back up your files in case something happens to your disk. To create a backup copy of a file, save the file again to a second disk with another file extension such as .BAK.

QUICK TIP

You can use the shortcut key combination [Ctrl][S] to save a file.

Printing a publication

Printing publications allows you to edit, or proof, your work. Sometimes it's easier to see how the elements work together on a page in a printed publication than on the screen. You also print your publication when it is completed. When you print your publications on a laser printer, you capitalize on one of desktop publishing's strengths—creating camera-ready copy at your desk. **Camera-ready copy** is paper copy that is ready to be photographed for reproduction without further alteration. ▶ With the New World Airlines letterhead saved to disk, Joe prints it to show it to Patricia Fernandez, his manager.

STEPS

1 **Check the printer**
Make sure that the printer is on, has paper, and that it is on-line or ready to print. If you send a file to a printer that is not ready, an error message appears.

2 **Click File on the menu bar, then click Print**
The Print document dialog box opens, as shown in Figure 2-15. The name of the printer in the Print to list box matches the name of the printer you chose in the Page setup dialog box when you created the new publication. The default settings are correct for this publication. Table 2-5 explains the five middle command buttons, each of which opens a different dialog box.

3 **Click Setup**
The Setup dialog box opens as shown in Figure 2-16. If you have a PostScript printer attached to your computer, you will have a Paper button instead of a Setup button. Click Paper. The Paper dialog box opens as shown in Figure 2-17. You can choose the paper size on which to print and whether the source of paper will be the trays or a manual feed bypass tray.

4 **Make sure the Size list box near the top of the Setup dialog box displays the paper size as Letter 8.5 × 11 in**
If you are using a PostScript printer, make sure the Size list box displays US Letter.

5 **Click OK to close the Setup dialog box, then click Print in the Print document dialog box**
If you are using a PostScript printer, you can simply click Print. A status window appears while the printer receives the publication's information. Note that a Cancel button in the status window allows you to cancel the printing if you want to. Don't worry if you don't have a color printer. Your printer will convert the colors you see on the screen to black, white, and shades of gray. Joe can now exit PageMaker, close the publication and save his work.

6 **Click File on the menu bar, click Exit, then click Yes when you are asked if you want to save the changes**
After Patricia approves the letterhead, Joe will send the file to a professional print shop where the letterhead will be printed in a large quantity with the colors that should appear in the logo.

FIGURE 2-15: Print document dialog box

Selected printer

Pages to be printed

Number of copies

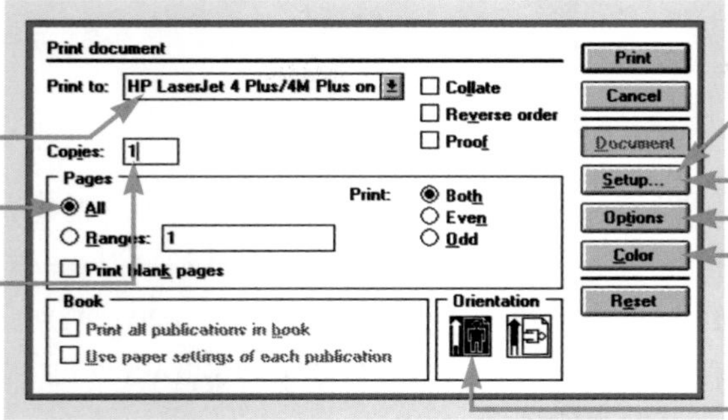

This button changes to "Paper" for Postscript printers

Click to display additional printing options

Tall orientation selected

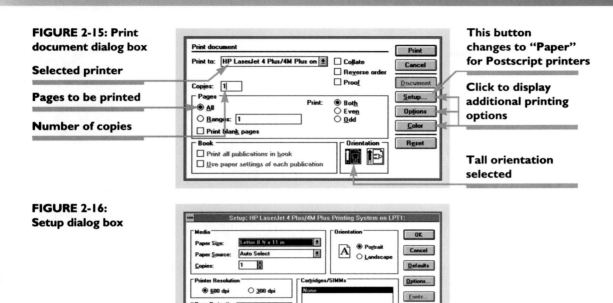

FIGURE 2-16: Setup dialog box

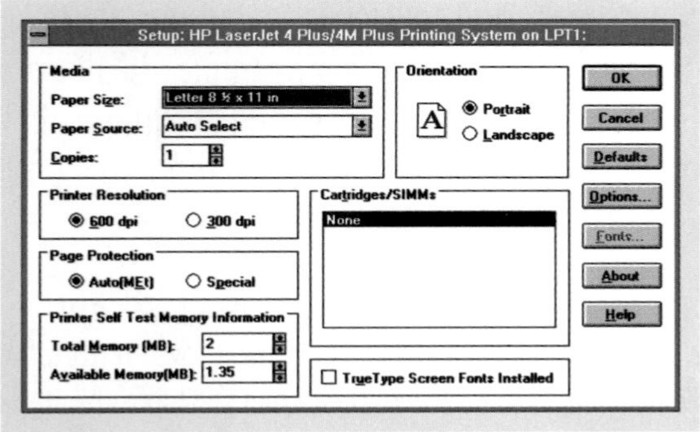

FIGURE 2-17: Paper dialog box

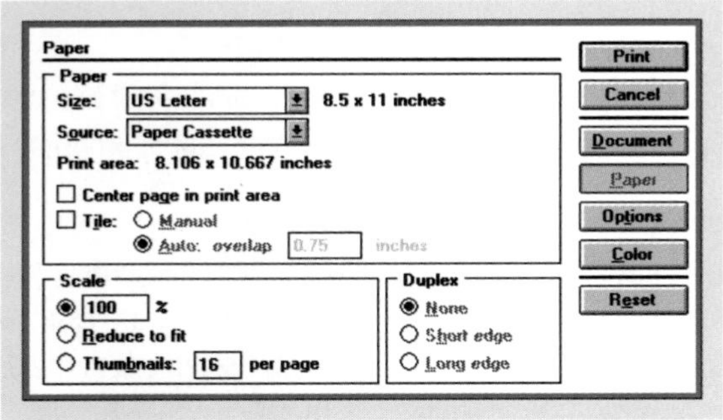

TABLE 2-5: Print dialog box buttons

BUTTON	DESCRIPTION
Document	General settings and options to print the document, including the choice of printer, number of copies, range of pages and orientation.
Paper	Settings to change the printing resolution, paper size, and the paper source for PostScript printers.
Setup...	Settings to change the printing resolution, paper size, and the paper source for non-PostScript printers.
Options	Options to choose the scale of the printed publication, from 5% to 1600%, duplex printing (double-sided printing), and options for applying printer marks on the page. Printer marks are used in final output by commercial printers.
Color	Settings to determine how color objects in the document will be printed.

TROUBLE?

If you are having trouble printing or unsure whether your printer is PostScript, see your instructor or technical support person for assistance.

QUICK TIP

You should save your publication prior to printing, so if anything happens to the file as it is being sent to the printer, you will have a copy of the final version saved to your disk.

Design Workshop: Letterhead and other office stationery

At the end of each unit, you will see the final output of the publication you created. After you create a publication, it is important to critique your final output to see if it meets your original goals. Designing letterhead can seem simple, but there are certain techniques that can make your company's letterhead and stationery stand out. When creating office stationery including letterhead, memoranda, business cards, fax cover sheets, and envelopes, it is important to keep a consistent design among all the types of stationery. For example, the placement of the logo and fonts, sizes, and style used should be similar. ▶ Joe would like to critique his design of the New World Airlines letterhead shown in Figure 2-18 before he gives it to his boss for approval.

STEPS

1. **Did the logo placement add to the overall design?**
   Joe added his company logo to the letterhead and moved it from the center to the top-left corner of the page. He could have positioned the logo at the top right, in the center, or on the bottom of the page. It seems to be an appropriate size and does not overwhelm the information on the page.

2. **Was all the relevant information included?**
   Joe did include all the relevant information. He decided not to include the fax number and electronic mail address because these numbers are not appropriate for the general public.

3. **Was the use of the slogan appropriate?**
   Joe added the New World Airlines slogan to reinforce his company's message. Depending on the audience, slogans or mottos might not be appropriate or necessary. As with the company information, he could have placed the slogan across the bottom of the page to serve as an **anchor**, or border, for the overall design of the letterhead.

4. **Did the placement of lines enhance the layout?**
   Joe separated the logo from the rest of the layout by adding a line below the logo across the page. He could have placed the logo and address vertically down the left side of the page and then added a vertical line from the top to bottom margin to separate this information from the body of the letter.

5. **Are you pleased with the overall appearance of the letterhead?**
   Joe is pleased because the smaller size and different font of the address distinguish this information from the slogan and from the text of the letters that will be printed on the letterhead. But he could have created a more balanced layout by placing the text above the line in the upper-right corner or across the bottom of the page.

FIGURE 2-18: Joe's final letterhead

NEW WORLD AIRLINES

"The Wings of America"

1845 North Lindbergh Boulevard, Charlotte, NC 28204   800-HORIZON

CONCEPTS REVIEW

Label each of the publication window elements shown in Figure 2-19.

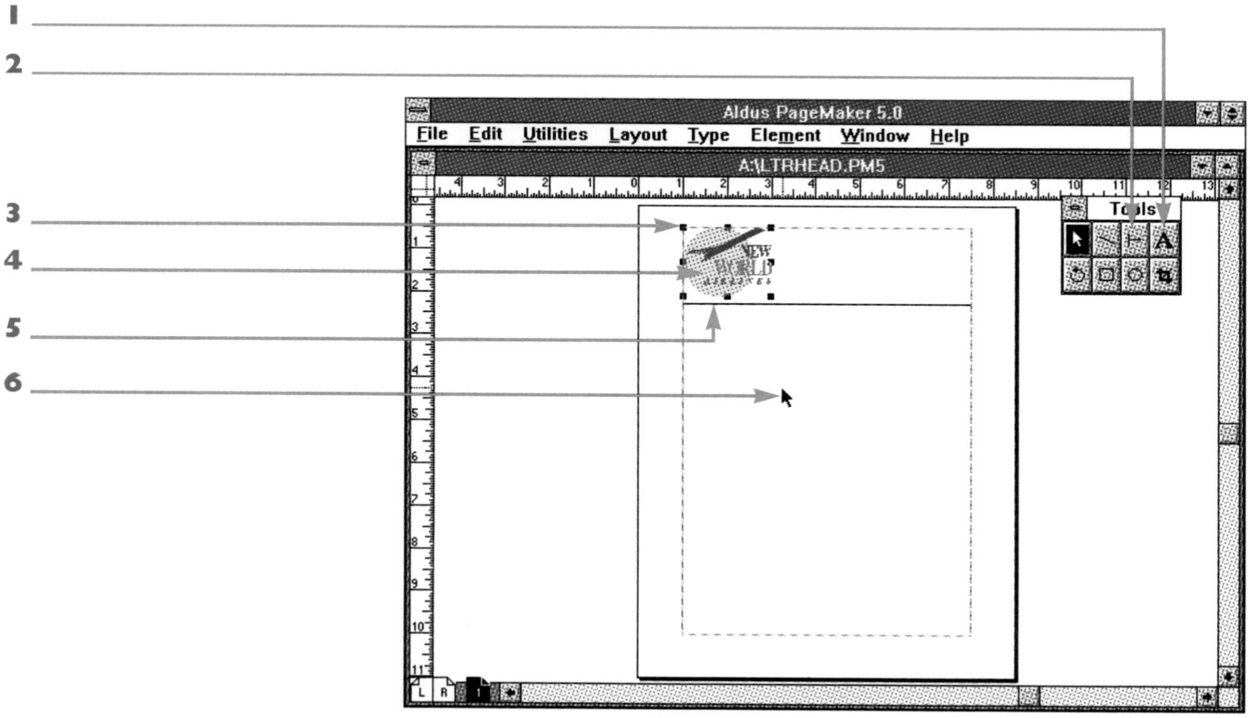

FIGURE 2-19

Match each of the terms with the statement that describes its function.

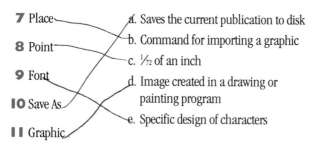

7 Place

8 Point

9 Font

10 Save As

11 Graphic

a. Saves the current publication to disk

b. Command for importing a graphic

c. $1/72$ of an inch

d. Image created in a drawing or painting program

e. Specific design of characters

Select the best answer from the list of choices.

12 The term used to describe image quality and clarity of a publication's output is

a. Image view

b. Resolution

c. Laser print

d. None of the above

13 In the Page setup dialog box, you can make the following settings, except

a. Number of columns

b. Size of the page

c. Number of pages

d. Both a and c

14 In the Page setup dialog box, you can set "Compose to printer" which means

a. Choose the print quality in dots per inch

b. Choose the printer to be used for printing

c. Choose the document format for exporting to another program

d. None of the above

15 All of the following are true statements concerning filenames, except

a. Filenames are less than eight characters

b. Numbers can be used as the first character

c. Punctuation can be used as the first character

d. All of the above are true statements

16 PageMaker allows you to place all of the following, except

a. Text files

b. Graphic images

c. Images created with a paint program

d. All of the above can be placed in a PageMaker publication.

17 While dragging a graphic's corner handle, which key do you press to resize a graphic image proportionally?

a. [Alt]

b. [Shift]

c. [Ctrl]

d. The image automatically resizes proportionally

18 Selecting text allows you to

a. Change the format

b. Enlarge the size of text

c. Add bolding or italics

d. All of the above

19 A printed publication that can be sent directly to a commercial printing company is called

a. Selection marquee

b. Camera-ready

c. Image-ready

d. Both a and c

APPLICATIONS REVIEW

1 Create a new publication.

a. Start PageMaker and open the Page setup dialog box.

b. Make sure Letter appears in the Page list box.

c. Make sure the orientation is Tall.

d. Set all margins to 1".

2 Place a graphic on a page.

a. Use the Place document dialog box to select the file LOGO.TIF from your Student Disk.

b. Using the rulers as guides, position the place pointer at the .5" mark on the vertical ruler and 6" mark on the horizontal ruler.

3 Resize and move the graphic.

a. Proportionally resize the graphic to 6" on the horizontal ruler and 2" on the vertical ruler.

b. Drag the logo until it is centered between the two margins.

4 Add text to the publication.

a. Select the Text tool in the toolbox

b. Position the cursor at the top left margin.

c. Change the view to Actual size.

d. Type the following memo:

MEMO
TO: Patricia Fernandez
FROM: Joe Martin
DATE: January 12, 1995
RE: Letterhead & Envelope design

Enclosed you will find the final draft for the company letterhead. I believe these designs meet your specifications. If you have any questions, please call me.

Pending your approval, the printer informed me that the final production of the letterhead could be completed in one week.

5 Format text.

a. Select the word "Memo."

b. Change the size to 14 points.

c. Bold and underline the selected word.

6 Add lines to the publication.

a. Select the Constrained-line tool in the toolbox.

b. Place the pointer on the left margin guide just below the word "Memo."

c. Draw a line from the left margin to the right margin. The screen will scroll automatically.

d. Deselect the line by selecting the Pointer tool in the toolbox.

e. Draw a second line from below the words "RE: Letterhead."

7 Save the publication.

a. Open the Save publication dialog box.

b. Name the publication MEMO1.PM5.

8 Print the publication, and exit PageMaker.

a. Check the printer to make sure that it is on-line.

b. Using the Print document dialog box, make sure that the paper size is Letter.

c. Make any other adjustments necessary.

d. Exit the application, saving your changes when prompted.

INDEPENDENT CHALLENGE 1

You are the graphic designer for Johnson Printing Company. Your manager has asked you to create letterhead, memo letterhead, and a business card design. The logo is shown in Figure 2-20 and is supplied on your Student Disk as JLOGO.TIF.

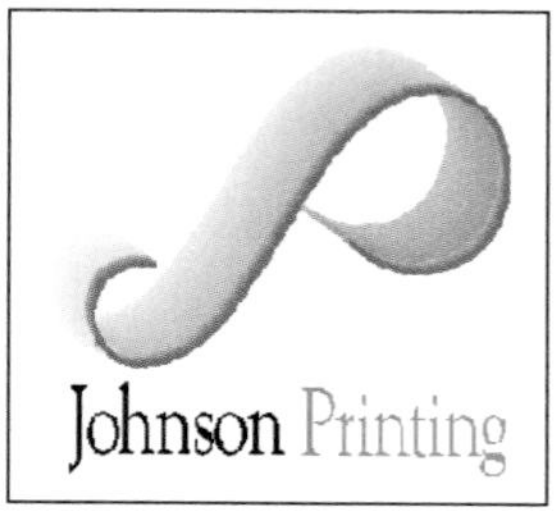

FIGURE 2-20

To complete this Independent Challenge:

1 Plan the letterhead, the memo letterhead, and the business card by sketching them on paper. Where will the logo go? Should it be centered or off to one side? Do you need any lines?

2 Open a new one-page publication and save it as JLETTER.PM5 to your Student Disk.

3 Place the image JLOGO.TIF on the page. Resize the logo to a more appropriate size. Move the logo to an appropriate position.

4 Draw a line on the page, if necessary.

5 Use the Text tool to add text for the company address and telephone number.

6 Save your work, then print the publication and close the file.

7 Open a new one-page publication and save it as JMEMO.PM5 to your Student Disk.

8 Place the logo JLOGO.TIF on the page. Resize the logo to a more appropriate size. Move the logo to an appropriate position.

9 Add a single line in a location that you feel enhances the design of the memo.

10 Use the Text tool to add the words "TO:," "FROM:," "DATE:," "RE:" in the appropriate places.

11 Save your work, then print the publication and close the file.

12 Open a new single-sided publication. In the Page setup dialog box, choose Custom in the Page list box and make the dimensions 2" × 3.5", make all four margins equal to .25", and choose Wide as the orientation.

13 Save the publication as JBUSCARD.PM5 to your Student Disk.

14 Place the logo JLOGO.TIF on the page. Resize it so it fits within the page margins, then move it to the position on your business card indicated by your design sketch.

15 Type your name, title, the company's address, and telephone number.

16 Select your name, change the type style to bold, and change the type size until it is the size you want. Change the size and style of the company address and telephone number.

17 Save your work, then print the publication and close the file.

18 Submit all printouts.

INDEPENDENT CHALLENGE 2

You are a freelance graphic artist hired by your school or company to redesign their stationery. Obtain a sample of the letterhead, or memo letterhead currently in use. Compare this example to what you learned in this unit and think about the following:

- Is a logo used in the publication? Is the logo large enough to be seen but not overwhelming?
- Is all the relevant information included? Should you include a fax number or the electronic mail address?
- Is the company's or school's slogan included in the letterhead? Is it appropriate to include it for this company or school?
- Do you need a graphic element to separate the logo and company information from the body text of the letterhead?

To complete this independent challenge:

1 Sketch a new design for the letterhead.

2 What information did you include? Why?

3 Did you include the company's or school's slogan? Why or why not?

4 Did you include any graphics? Explain.

5 Evaluate the overall appearance of the letterhead. Are you pleased with it? Sometimes it helps to not look at a design for a day and then reevaluate it. Now, what do you think?

UNIT 3

OBJECTIVES

- Plan a fact sheet
- Create columns
- Import and place text
- Control the text flow
- Manipulate text blocks
- Move and resize text blocks
- Drag-place text
- Use reverse text
- Design Workshop: Fact sheets

Working WITH TEXT

Now that you know how to create a publication in PageMaker, you are ready to learn more about working with text. In this unit, you will learn how to create columns, how to import, place, and manipulate text, and how to format headlines. ▶ Joe needs to create a fact sheet describing package tours that New World Airlines has arranged with Sunset Tours, a travel agency. ▶

Planning a fact sheet

A **fact sheet** is an informational publication. It can contain one page or a set of pages that describes in detail the company's products or services. Fact sheets usually contain heavy amounts of text, so it is important to plan the layout carefully and use graphical elements to support the text. ▶ As part of the publicity campaign on the New World Airlines package deals with Sunset Tours, Joe Martin wants to create fact sheets that describe available tours to Europe and Asia. Travel agents at Sunset will send the fact sheets to potential customers who request more information about specific vacation packages. He plans to describe charters to three different cities. He keeps the following guidelines in mind as he plans his first fact sheet:

STEPS

1 **Keep the layout simple**
While it is important to catch the reader's attention, fact sheets should provide detailed information about a product or service in a succinct and organized way. If your fact sheet relies too heavily on creative design, some of your message might get lost. Joe has decided to have three columns. Each column will provide information about a specific tour.

2 **Keep the format consistent among fact sheets in a series**
Fact sheets in a series should present repetitive types of information consistently. Joe's fact sheets will provide the same information: name of tour, description, and point of response. **Point of response** is the phone number or the address where the reader can respond to information in the fact sheet. Formatting this text in the same manner creates a consistent look.

3 **Use graphical elements strategically to enhance the overall layout**
Graphical elements is an umbrella term that describes anything on a page other than the text. Graphical elements, such as lines or photos, can make your fact sheets more interesting. Because fact sheets should provide information, graphical elements should support the text without overshadowing the message you are trying to convey. Joe decides to include a photograph of a famous site in each city.

4 **Include a headline that instantly conveys the purpose of the fact sheet**
Publications with a lot of text can be so intimidating that the reader might simply ignore the fact sheet; therefore, the headline should convey the purpose of the publication immediately and clearly. Joe wants a headline identifying the purpose of his fact sheet across the top of the page. He also decides to set the headline for his fact sheet in **reverse text**, white text on a black background, so the reader will know at the first glance what information the fact sheet contains.

5 **Use high-quality paper stock**
People keep fact sheets as reference material, so it's important to print a fact sheet on paper able to withstand repeated handling.

Figure 3-1 shows Joe's final sketch of his fact sheet.

FIGURE 3-1: Joe's sketch of his fact sheet

DESIGN TIP

Use lines to provide structure in your publication. A line can separate headlines from descriptive text or separate columns of text. Lines give the layout some creativity without burdening the reader with too many graphical elements.

Creating columns

One way of presenting text is to organize the information into columns. To create a column in PageMaker, you use column guides. **Column guides** define columns on a publication page to control the flow of text or to help you align text and graphics. In the Column guides dialog box, you specify how many columns you want on the page and the space between columns, called the **gutter**. PageMaker allows up to 20 columns on one page. For more information on columns, see the related topic "Changing column widths." ▶ Joe Martin begins setting up the fact sheet by creating three columns.

STEPS

1. **Open PageMaker, click File on the menu bar, then click New**
   The Page setup dialog box opens.
2. **Click the Double-sided check box to turn this option off**
3. **Change all margin settings to .5", then click OK**
   The Page setup dialog box closes, and a new blank publication opens in the publication window.
4. **Click Layout on the menu bar, then click Column guides**
   The Column guides dialog box opens, as shown in Figure 3-2.
5. **In the Number of columns text box, type 3**
   This tells PageMaker to create three columns on the publication page. The gutter adjusts automatically to .167", which is about ⅙". Although he can change the gutter, Joe accepts the amount of space specified by PageMaker.
6. **Click OK**
   The dialog box closes and blue column guides (if you're using a color monitor) appear on the page dividing the page into three equal columns, as shown in Figure 3-3.

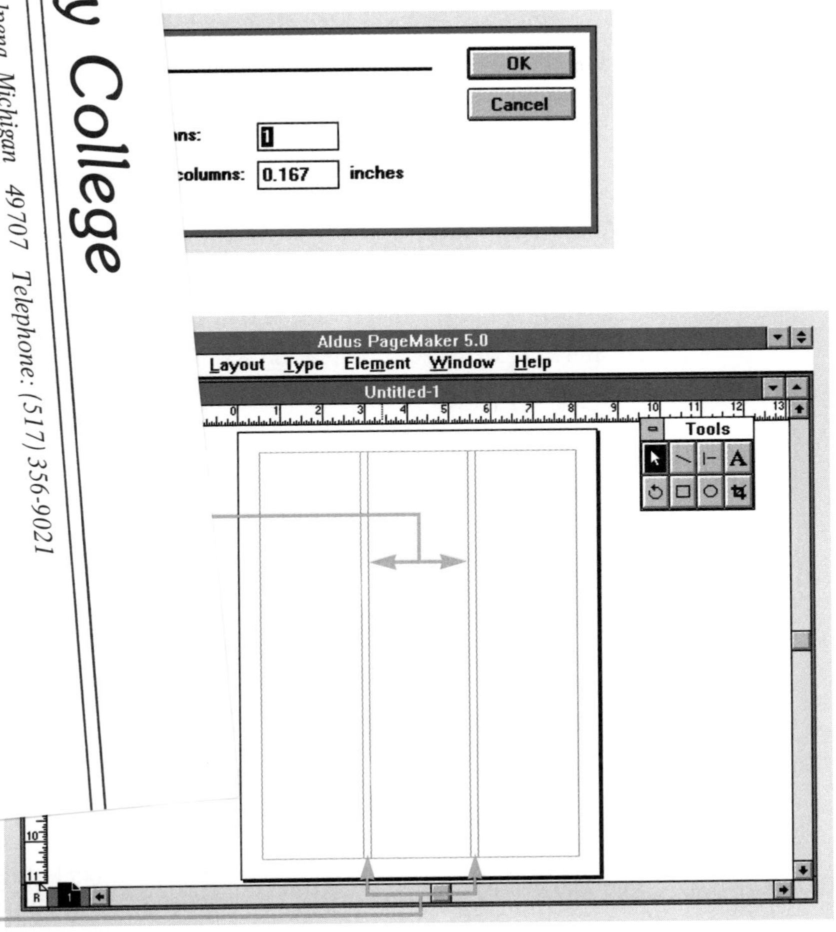

Gutter

Changing column widths

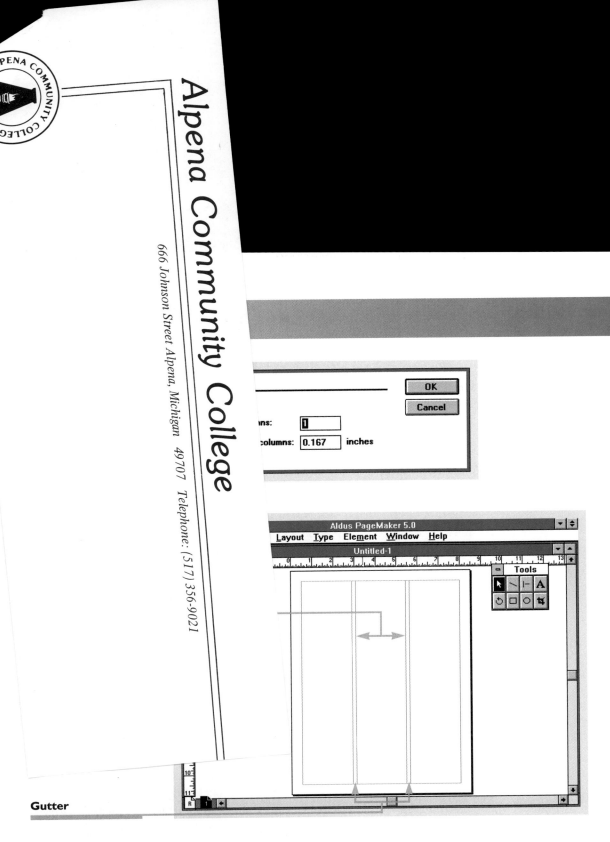

PageMaker automatically creates columns of equal width. You can change these widths by simply moving the column guides. After you create the number of columns you want, position the pointer over one of the two lines that make up the column guide, then press and hold the mouse button. The pointer changes to ↔. Drag the column guide to widen or narrow the column width. As you move the column guide, the width of the gutter does not change. In Figure 3-4, the first column is wider.

Gutter stays the same

Column guide moves to right as you drag

Mouse pointer moving column guide to the right

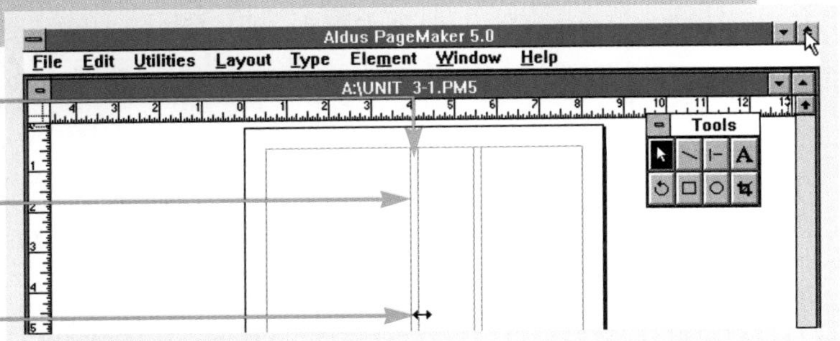

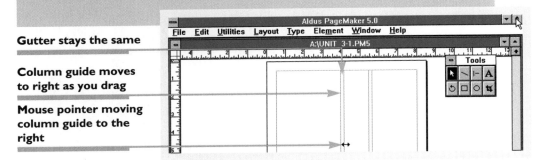

FIGURE 3-4: Adjusting column widths manually

DESIGN TIP

Most publications should have no more than four to five columns per page, depending on the page size. This is because the narrower the column, the harder it is to read the text.

QUICK TIP

Create columns on the master pages to set columns for an entire publication.

Importing and placing text

Just as you imported graphics into your publication, you can import text files from word processing applications, using the Place command on the File menu. Importing text and graphics will save you time; you won't have to recreate anything you've created in another application. See Table 3-1 for a partial list of word processing file types that you can place in a PageMaker publication. ▶ Joe has a fact sheet that already contains the photographs he needs. He needs to open that file. Then he wants to place in his publication a point of response that he wrote using his word processing application.

STEPS

1 **Click File on the menu bar, click Close, then click No when asked if you want to save "Untitled-1"**
The untitled publication with the three columns is now closed. Next you will open the file UNIT_3-1.PM5 which contains columns and the photos that Joe has already placed.

2 **Open the file UNIT_3-1.PM5 on your Student Disk**
If you need help opening a file, refer to "Opening a PageMaker publication" in Unit 1.

Now you can place the point of response text.

3 **Click File on the menu bar, then click Place**

4 **Select the drive containing your Student Disk, if necessary, click unit_3-2.doc in the File name list box, then click OK**
The pointer changes to ▤. Unlike the pointers for placing graphic files, the pointer shape does not change depending on the type of file being placed. When this text flow pointer appears, it is said to contain, or be **loaded**, with text.

5 **Position ▤ in the third column at the top margin, as shown in Figure 3-5, then click the mouse button**
The text appears on the page bordered on the top and bottom by empty windowshade handles, as shown in Figure 3-6. The **windowshade handles** define the **text block**, which is an object that consists of horizontal lines above and below the text. The width of the text block is determined by the width of the page or column.

6 **Right-click to change the view to Actual size so you can read the text and scroll the window to see the point of response**

FIGURE 3-5: Manual text flow icon

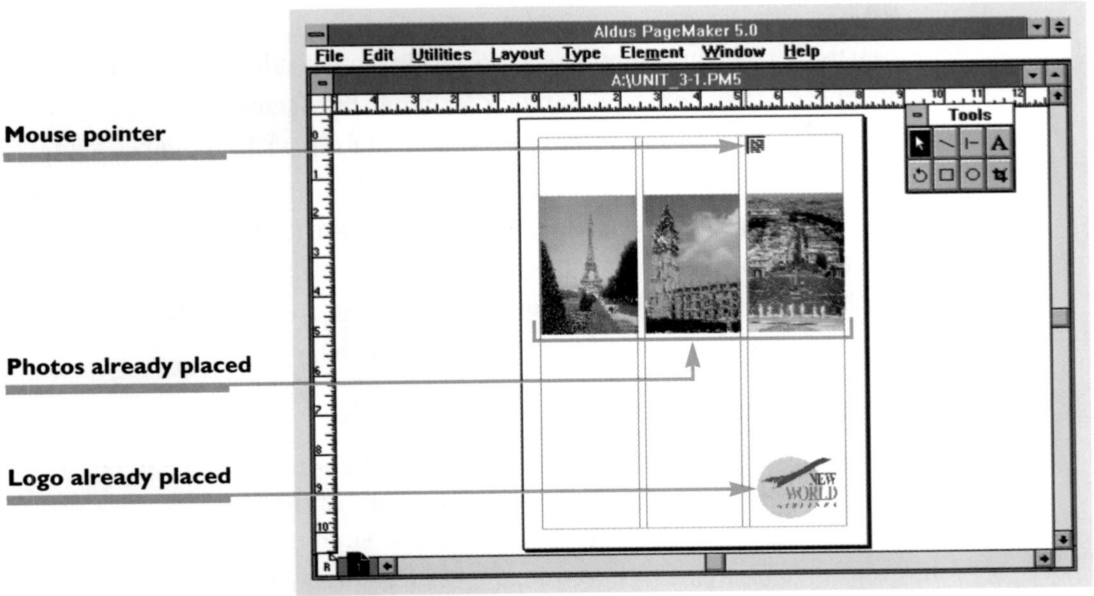

FIGURE 3-6: Text block on page

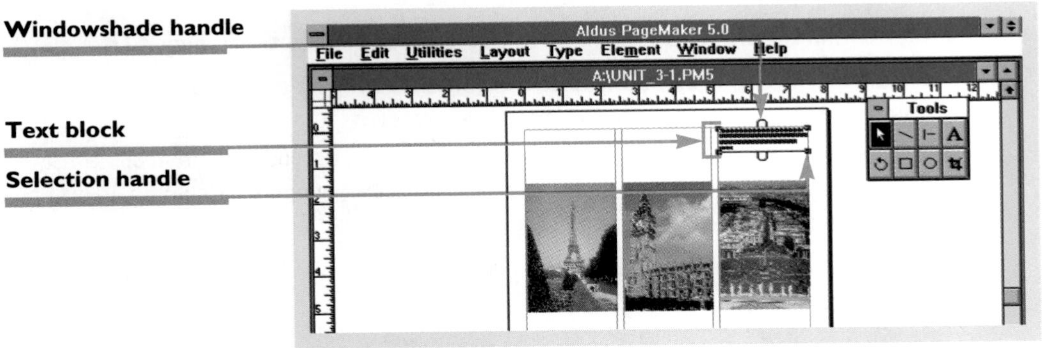

QUICK TIP

If you open File Manager and a publication window next to each other, you can drag a text file icon from the File Manager window to an open PageMaker publication window. PageMaker then places the document in your publication.■

TABLE 3-1: Types of word processing files that PageMaker accepts

FILE EXTENSION	WORD PROCESSING APPLICATION
.SAM	Ami Pro
.DOC	Microsoft Word Macintosh and Microsoft Word for Windows
.DOC	MultiMate
.WPD	WordPerfect 5.x DOS and WordPerfect for Windows 5.x
.RTF	Rich Text Format
.TXT	Text or ASCII file

TROUBLE?

If you need to find out which versions of word processing files PageMaker can import, click Help on the menu bar, click Contents, click Importing Files then click Text filters.■

Controlling the text flow

There are three ways you control the flow of text in a publication: automatic (Autoflow), semi-Autoflow, and manual flow. When the **Autoflow** feature is turned on, text you place flows from one column to the next, filling up as many columns and pages as necessary. Table 3-2 reviews the three methods of text flow. ▶ The Sunset Tours representative, Sheree Jackson, gave Joe a text file containing a description of her company's tours to Europe. Joe is ready to place the text describing the tours in his fact sheet. Because he wants to control where he places text in the columns, he will turn the Autoflow option off.

STEPS

1. **Right-click** to change the view to Fit in Window
2. Click **Layout** on the menu bar, then make sure there is no check mark before the Autoflow option listed at the bottom of the menu
   The default for PageMaker is for the Autoflow feature to be turned off. See Figure 3-7.
3. If there is a check mark beside the Autoflow option, click **Autoflow** to turn it off
4. Click **File** on the menu bar, then click **Place**
5. Select the file **unit_3-3.doc** from your Student Disk, then click **OK**
6. Position in the first column at the left margin guide at the 5.25" mark on the vertical ruler, then click the **mouse button**
   The text is placed and flows from the pointer down the page to the bottom margin of the first column. A triangle appears in the windowshade handle at the bottom of the column, indicating more text needs to be placed, as shown in Figure 3-8.
7. Click at the bottom of the first column
   The pointer changes to .
8. Position in the second column at the 5.25" mark on the vertical ruler, then click the **mouse button**
   Once again, text flows within the column to the bottom of the page. This time an empty windowshade handle appears at the bottom of the second column, indicating there is no more text to be placed. See Figure 3-9. Notice that the windowshade handle at the top of the second column contains a plus sign. This indicates that the text is **threaded**, or connected, to another text block, in this case, the text block in the first column.
9. Click **File** on the menu bar, then click **Save** to save the changes to the publication

TABLE 3-2: Text flow methods

METHOD	ICON	DESCRIPTION
Manual		Text flows from the insertion point to the bottom of a column or page. You have to specify where to place additional text, if necessary.
Autoflow		Text flows from one column to the next, filling up as many columns and pages necessary to place the text.
Semi-Autoflow		With Autoflow turned off, press and hold [Shift] while placing text. Text flows to the bottom of the page or column, then the semi-Autoflow text icon automatically appears ready to place more text.

FIGURE 3-7: Autoflow option turned off

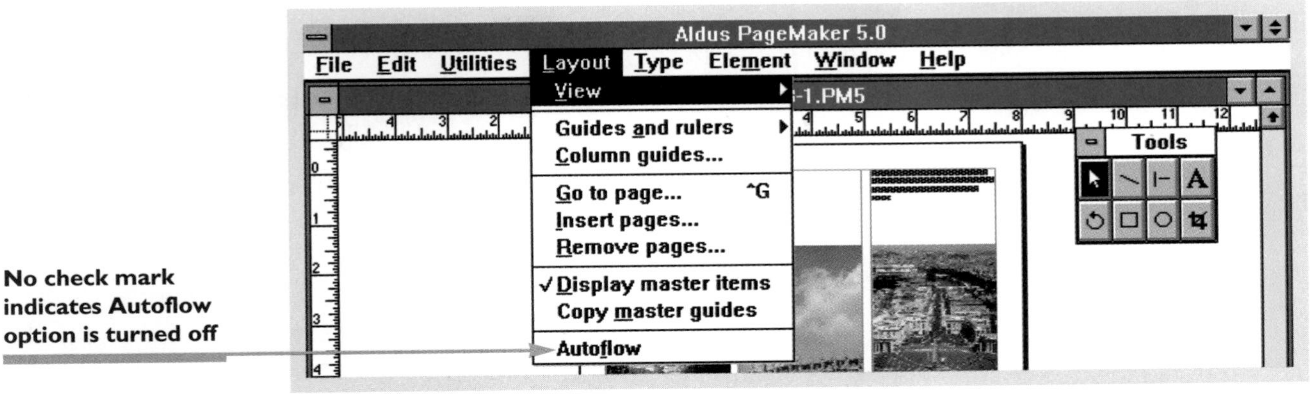

FIGURE 3-8: Placed text flowing to the bottom of the first column

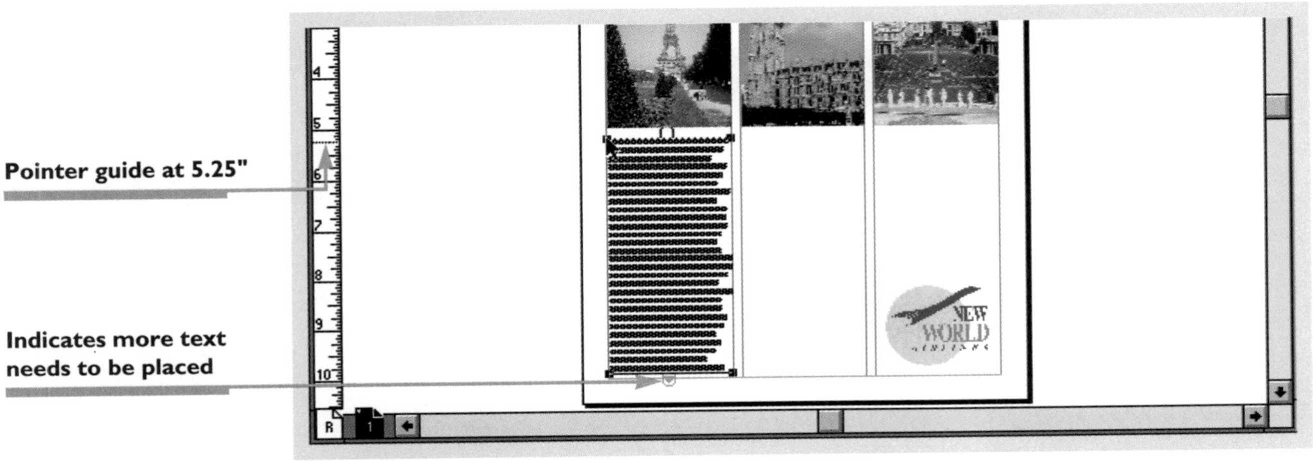

FIGURE 3-9: Threaded text block

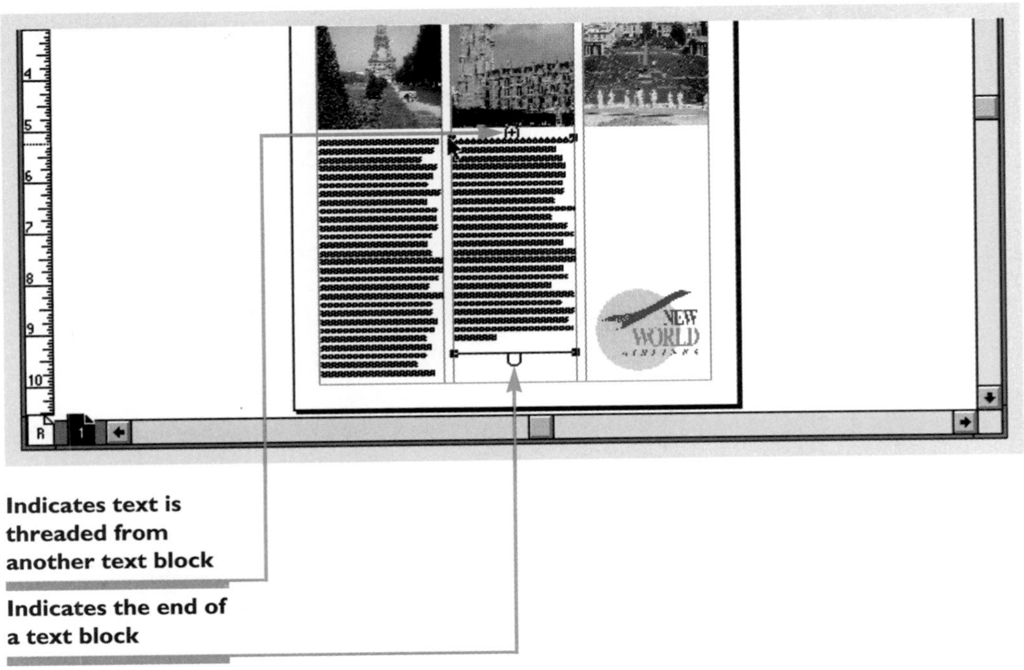

QUICK TIP

When the text flow pointer is loaded, you can switch between manual flow and semi-Autoflow by pressing and holding [Shift], and you can switch between manual flow and Autoflow by pressing and holding [Ctrl].

Manipulating text blocks

You can change the size and shape of any text block on a page. When you select a text block, the windowshade handles appear across the top and bottom border of the text block. You change the length of a text block by dragging the windowshade handle up or down. ▶ Joe wants to change the length of the text blocks so that the text under each photo corresponds to that photo.

STEPS

1. **Click Layout on the menu bar, click View, then click 75% size**
   The text in the first column describes Paris and London. Joe needs to manipulate the text blocks so that the text under each photo corresponds to the photo in the column.
2. **Click the text block in the first column**
   This selects the text block in the first column.
3. **Position the pointer on the bottom windowshade handle, then press and hold the mouse button**
   ↕ appears, as shown in Figure 3-10.
4. **Drag the windowshade handle up to the end of the paragraph describing Paris, France, as shown in Figure 3-11**
   After you release the mouse button, the text from the end of the first column now appears at the beginning of the second column. If you didn't drag the windowshade handle up far enough in the first column, click it again, then drag it to the correct position.
5. **Click the text block in the second column**
   The text has flowed past the bottom of the column.
6. **Scroll down to see the bottom of the text block in column two**
7. **Drag the bottom windowshade handle up so that only the paragraph describing London, England, appears in the text block**
   Don't worry if it takes a couple of tries to position the paragraph.
8. **Click at the bottom of the second column**
   The pointer changes to .
9. **Position in the third column at the 5.25" mark on the vertical ruler, then click the mouse button**
   The text "Rome, Italy" should be at the top of the third column, as shown in Figure 3-12. The empty windowshade handle appears at the bottom of the third column.

FIGURE 3-10: Changing the length of the text block

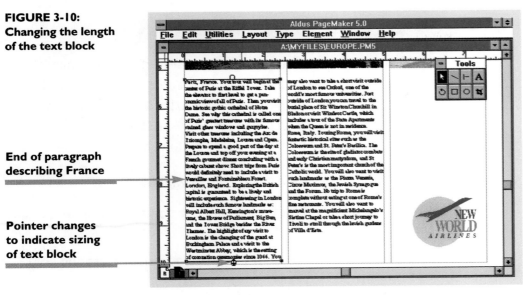

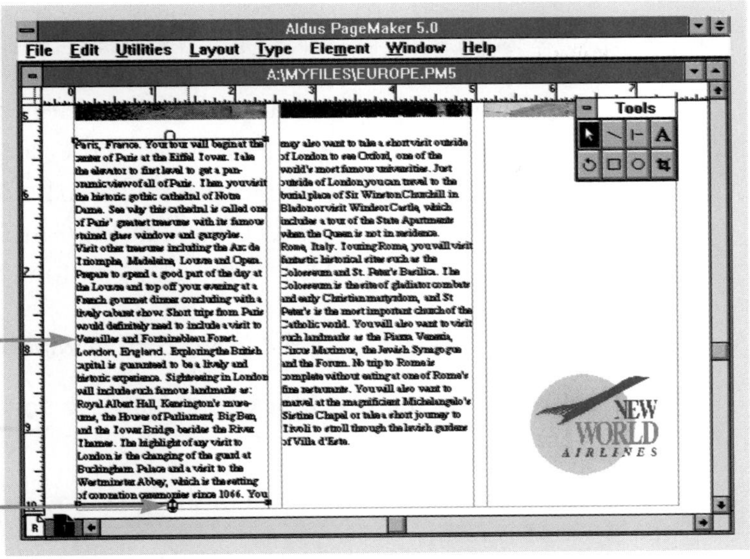

End of paragraph describing France

Pointer changes to indicate sizing of text block

FIGURE 3-11: First column after text block is resized

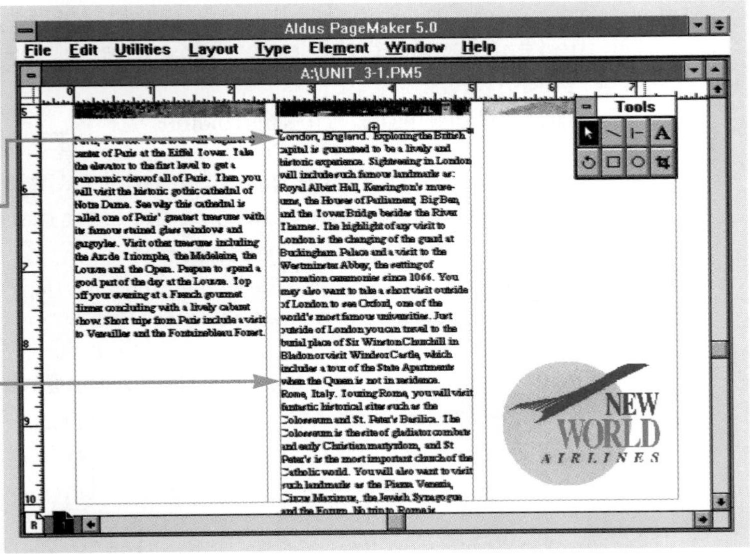

Paragraph describing London moved to top of second column

End of paragraph describing London

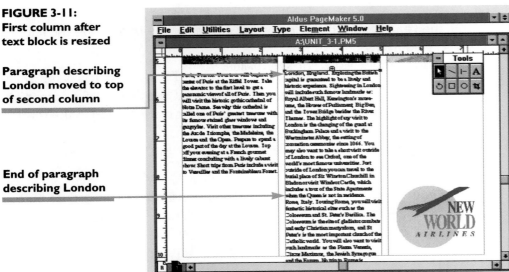

FIGURE 3-12: Second column after resizing text block

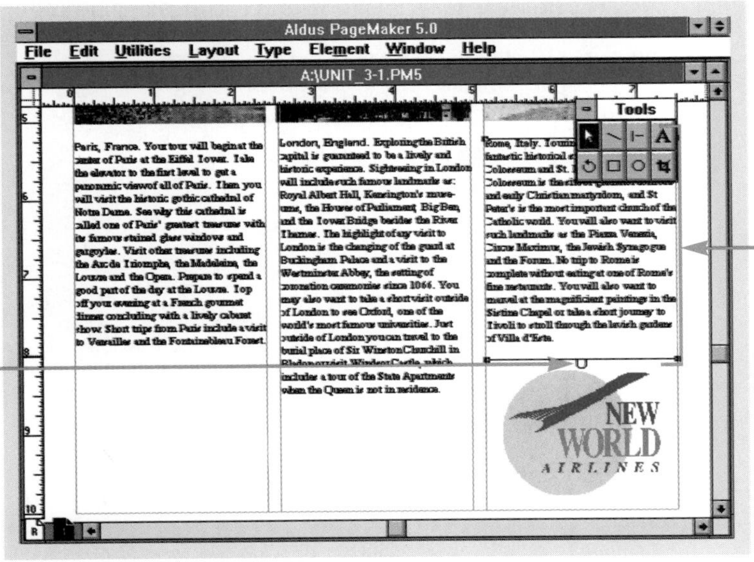

Indicates end of text block

Text describing Rome

QUICK TIP

Use ruler guides to make sure text blocks are aligned across all columns.

Moving and resizing text blocks

One of PageMaker's most powerful options is its extensive ability to manipulate text blocks. You can adjust the dimensions and the location of text blocks. The process for sizing and moving text blocks is similar to the method used for graphics. ▶ Joe decides to move the text block containing the point of response to the bottom of the page. He will resize it so it stretches across the three columns.

STEPS

1. **Right-click** twice to change the view to Fit in window
2. Click anywhere on the text block containing the point of response located in the upper-right corner of the page
3. Position the pointer in the middle of the text block, then press and hold the **mouse button**
   The pointer changes to ✥.
4. Drag the **text block** to the lower-left corner of the page inside the left margin guide
   Now Joe wants to stretch the text across the columns.
5. Position the pointer over the selection handle at the lower-right corner of the text block, then drag the handle to the right margin guide in the third column, but *do not release the mouse button*
   The pointer changes to ⤡ as you drag the handle, and a box appears around the text block to show its dimensions, as shown in Figure 3-13.
6. When you are satisfied with the new dimensions, release the mouse button
   The text is now resized from margin to margin, as shown in Figure 3-14. The text block on your screen might be in a different spot depending on how far you dragged the text block. The text block in Joe's fact sheet needs to be moved again because it overlaps the logo.
7. Position the pointer in the middle of the text block, then drag the **text block** until it is just above the bottom margin guide
8. Click **File** on the menu bar, then click **Save** to save the changes to the publication

FIGURE 3-13: Resizing a text block

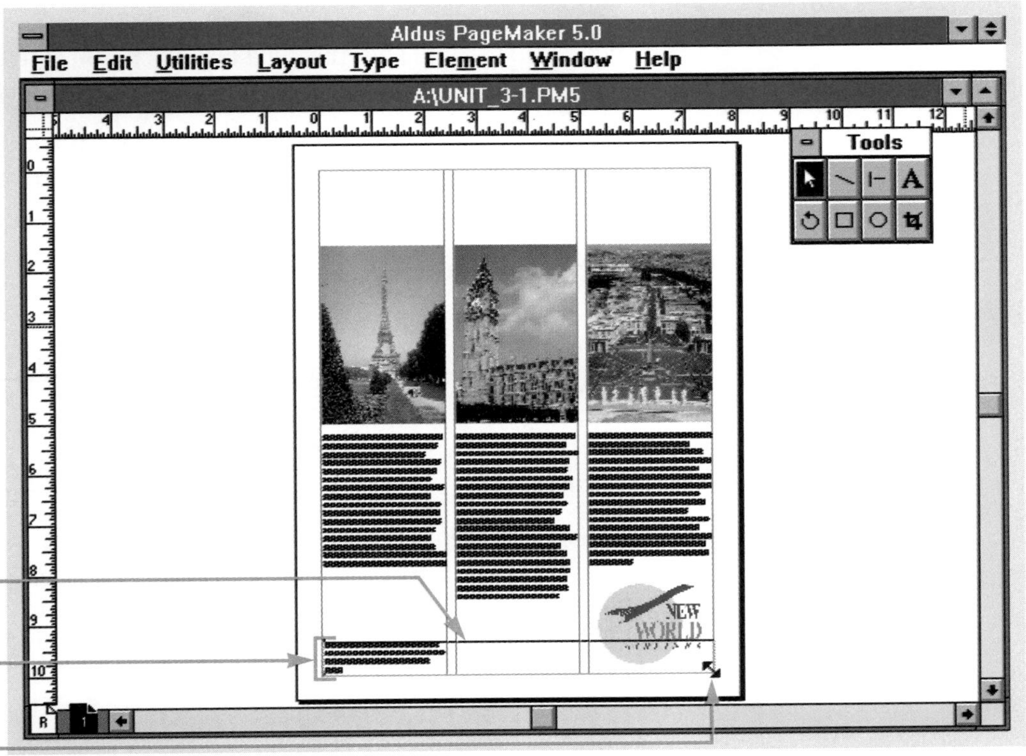

Box shows dimensions of text block

Point of response text block in new location

Mouse pointer

FIGURE 3-14: The resized text block

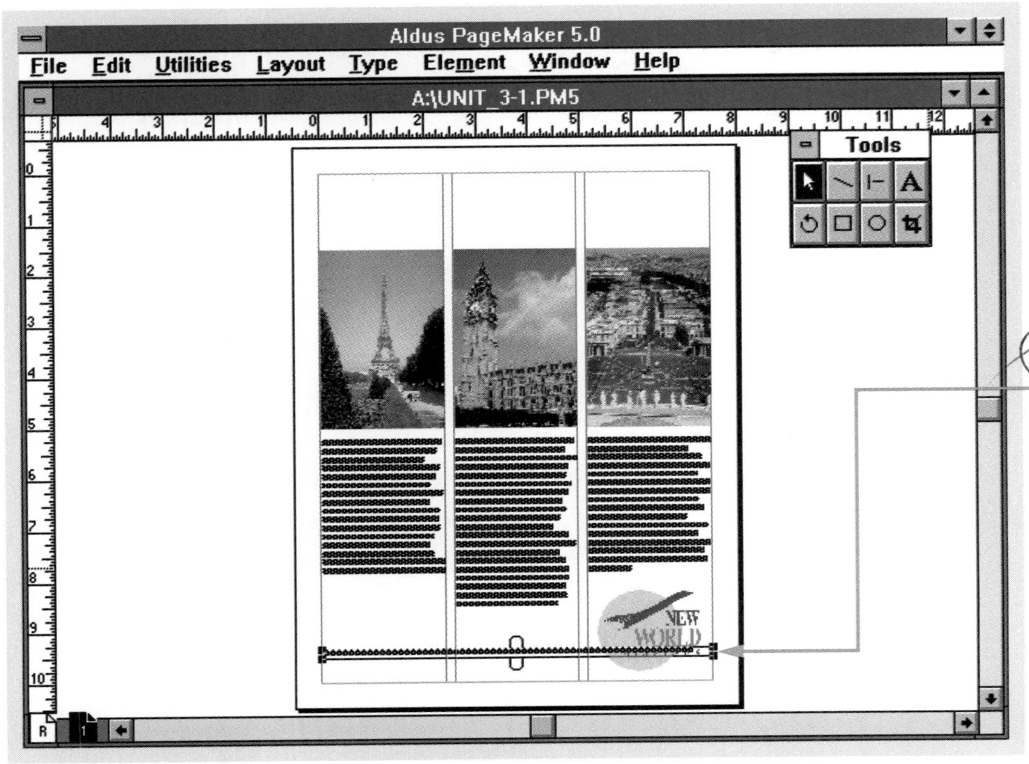

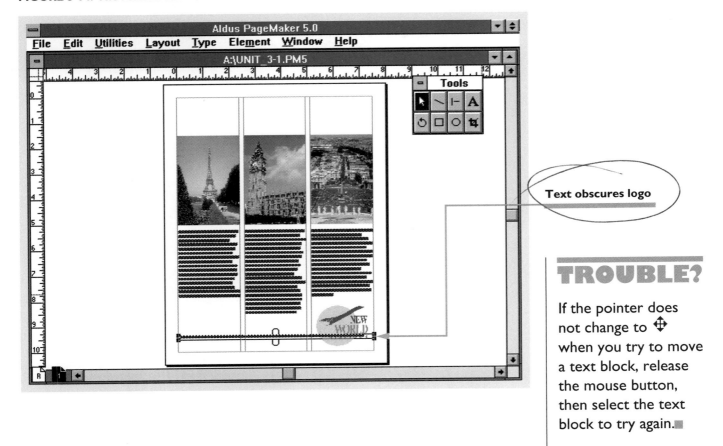

Text obscures logo

TROUBLE?

If the pointer does not change to ✥ when you try to move a text block, release the mouse button, then select the text block to try again.

Drag-placing text

In addition to resizing and moving a text block, you can automatically position text across columns or a page using the drag-place method. The drag-place method allows you to define the size of a text block at the same time you import text from another location. You can use this method with both manual and automatic text flows. You can also drag-place graphics. ▶ Joe wants to place a headline that his co-worker Sheree created across the top of all three columns in his fact sheet.

STEPS

1. Click **File** on the menu bar, then click **Place**
2. Select the file **unit_3-4.doc** from your Student Disk, then click **OK**
3. Position at the top-left margin guide
4. Drag down to the 1.25" mark on the vertical ruler and all the way to the right margin guide, but *do not release the mouse button*
   A box appears to show you the text block dimensions, as shown in Figure 3-15.
5. When you are satisfied with the text block dimensions, release the mouse button
   The headline appears in a text block that stretches from margin to margin, as shown in Figure 3-16. The text does not span from margin to margin because the point size isn't big enough. The headline was formatted as a large point size and bold in the word processed file. Text retains its format when it is placed in a PageMaker publication.
6. Click **File** on the menu bar, then click **Save** to save the changes to the publication

FIGURE 3-15: Drag-placing a text block

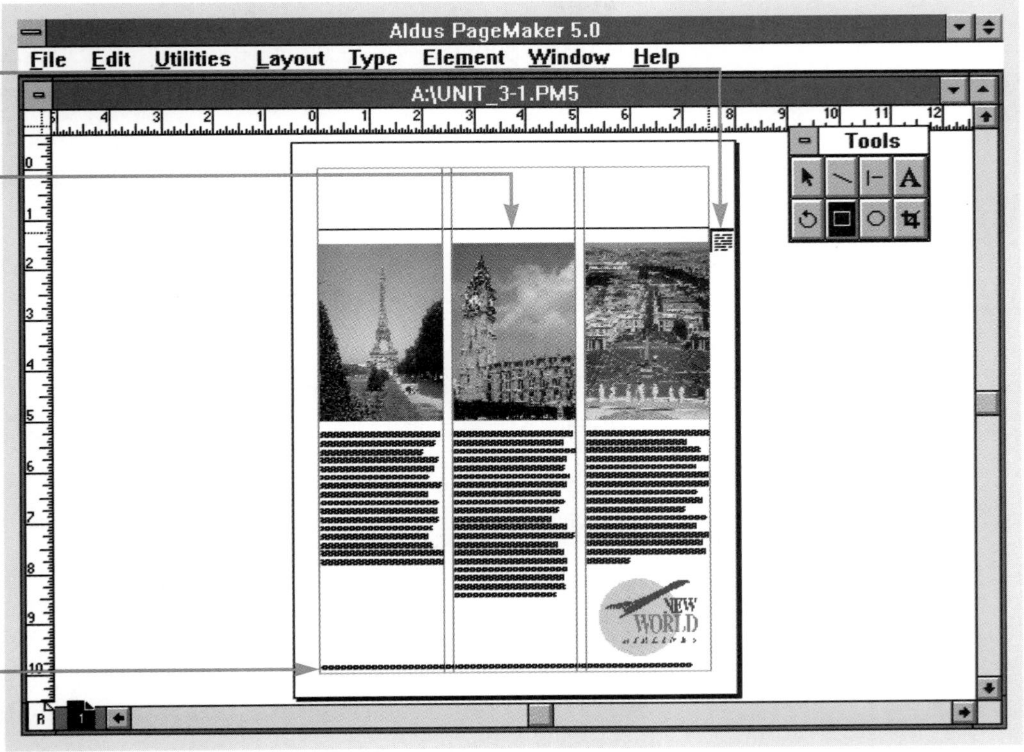

FIGURE 3-16: Headline placed across three columns

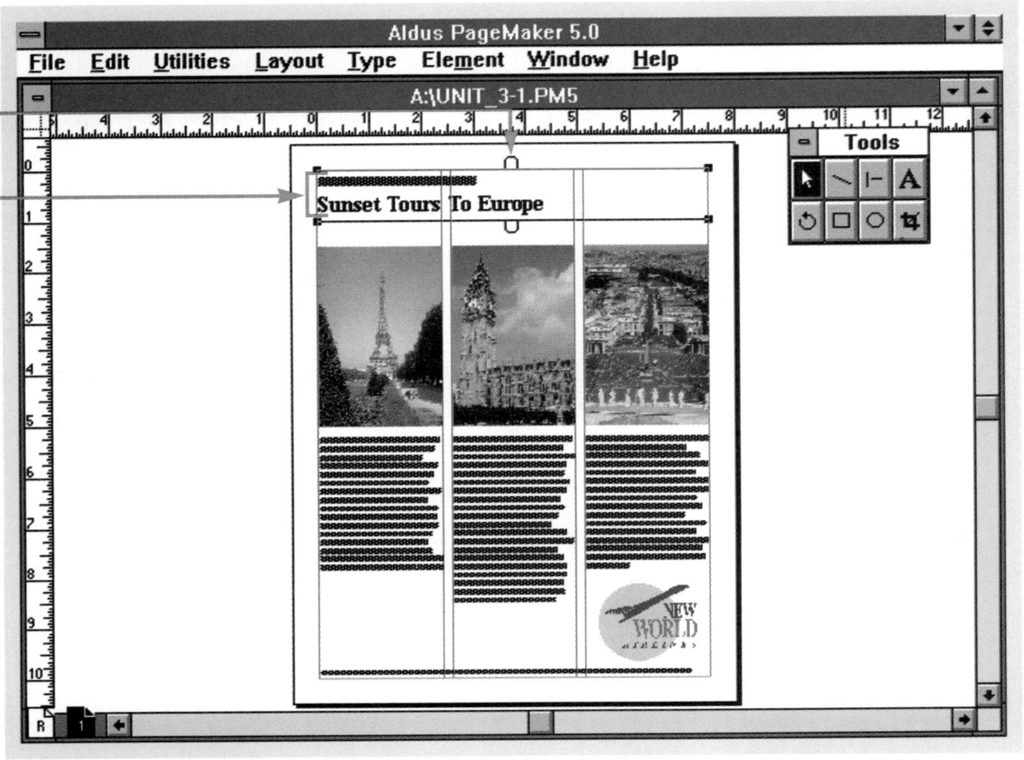

Using reverse text

Headlines in publications need to be eye-catching. One way to do this is to draw a box around the headline, then use reverse text. **Reverse text** is white or lightly-shaded letters and lines against a dark background. The contrast makes the text more noticeable. ▶ Joe formats the headline on the fact sheet with reverse text. He also wants to draw a box around the headline.

STEPS

1. **Click the Text tool in the toolbox, then drag over the two lines of text containing the headline to select them**
2. Click **Type** on the menu bar, click **Alignment** then click **Align center**
   The headline is centered in the text block.
3. Click **Type** on the menu bar, click **Type style**, then click **Reverse**
   The text changes to white, and because it's on a white background, it seems to disappear.
4. Click the **Rectangle tool** in the toolbox
   The pointer changes to +.
5. Position + at the top left intersection of the margin guides, then drag the pointer to the 1" mark on the vertical ruler and the right edge of the third column
   A box appears with selection handles around it, as shown in Figure 3-17. Next, Joe needs to make this box black.
6. Click **Element** on the menu bar, click **Fill**, then click **Solid**
   The box fills with black. The box is an object that is on top of the text block. To see the text in the text block, Joe needs to move the box behind, or in back of the text block.
7. Click **Element** on the menu bar, then click **Send to back**
   The selected object, in this case the box, is sent behind the white text, so you can read the white text on the black box. See Figure 3-18. You will learn more about this in Unit 6.

   Satisfied with his fact sheet, Joe saves and prints it.
8. Click **File** on the menu bar, then click **Save**
9. Click **File** on the menu bar, click **Print**, then click **Print** in the Print dialog box
   Note that depending on your printer, this might take moments or minutes. Also, if you do not have a color printer, your printout will look different.
10. Click **File** on the menu bar, then click **Close** to close the file

FIGURE 3-17: A box drawn with three columns

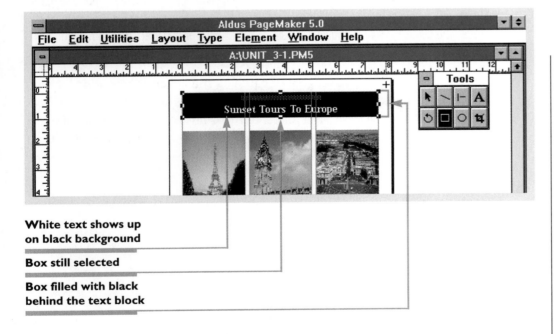

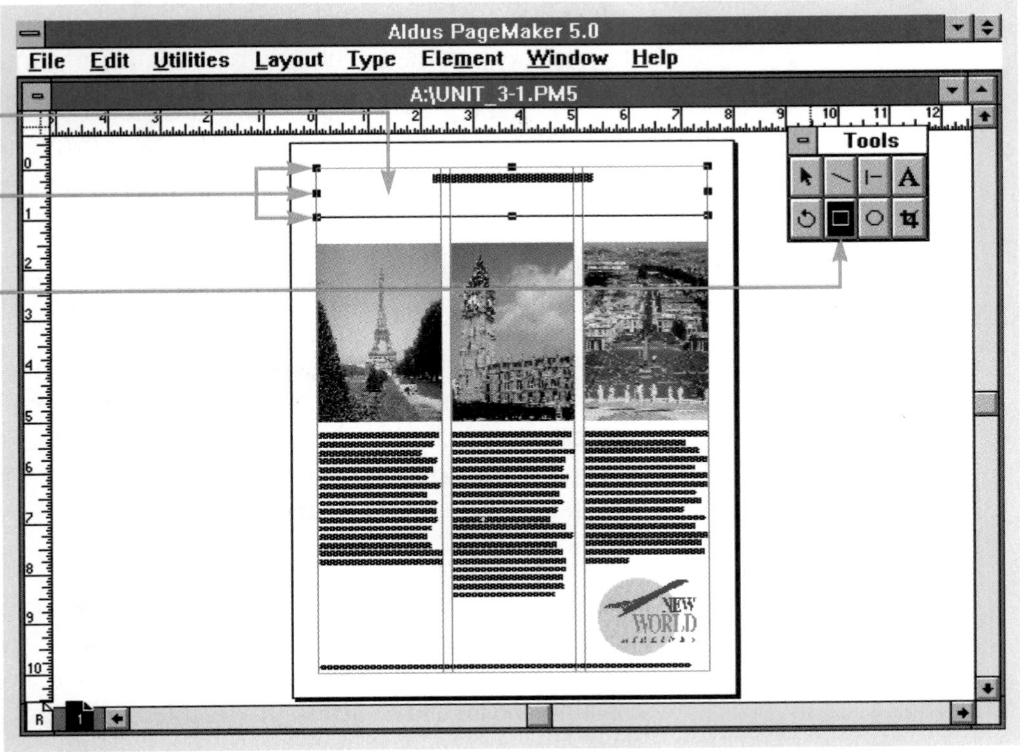

FIGURE 3-18: White text on black background

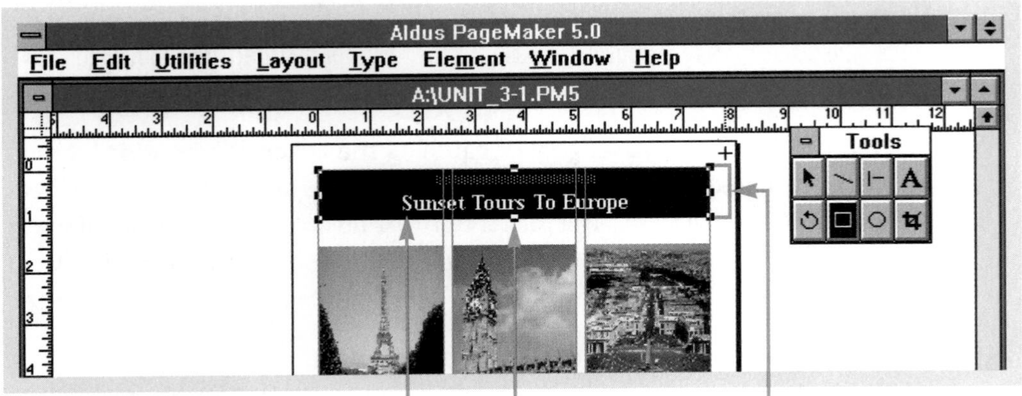

DESIGN TIP

Reverse text is an effective method to draw the reader's attention to headlines or subheadlines if the type is large enough.■

TROUBLE?

If you have trouble finding text that is reverse, click Edit on the menu bar, then click Select all to display the windowshade handles of all the text blocks.■

Design Workshop: Fact sheets

Fact sheets are important publications for many companies. These documents are the first contact with potential customers often describing products and services available. It is therefore important that fact sheets convey all the information in an organized fashion. Consistency is essential in fact sheets that describe multiple products or services. ▶ Joe critiques his design for the European tours fact sheet shown in Figure 3-19.

STEPS

1 **Is the layout simple?**
You should try to balance large amounts of text with graphical elements. Graphical elements help to break up the text. When you add graphical elements, be careful not to add too many, or the publication will look cluttered. Joe's layout is simple and well balanced. Each of the three columns contains a photo and an equal amount of text. The headline at the top and the point of response at the bottom pull the fact sheet together.

2 **Is the format consistent with other fact sheets?**
It is important to portray your company's products and services in an organized fashion to the reader. Joe will create additional fact sheets for the other Sunset Tours in Europe and Asia. He will use the same layout that includes a headline, small photos, an equal amount of text describing the specific tour destination, and the point of response.

3 **Do the graphical elements on the page enhance the overall layout?**
Graphical elements can help the reader gain an immediate understanding of the purpose of the publication. Joe has included photos of some of the most famous landmarks of Europe to help stimulate the reader's desire for travel. He also used the New World Airlines logo to help identify which airline flies to Europe. Both of these graphical elements enhance the fact sheet message.

4 **Does the headline achieve its goal of catching the reader's attention?**
Using reverse text immediately draws the attention of the reader to the fact sheet. Joe could have used a bolder font like Arial and a larger point size to make his headline more striking. Before he completes the other fact sheets in the series, he will make these changes to the headlines.

FIGURE 3-19: Completed European Vacation fact sheet

New World Airlines Presents:

Sunset Tours To Europe

Paris, France. Your tour will begin at the center of Paris at the Eiffel Tower. Take the elevator to the first level to get a panoramic view of all of Paris. Then you will visit the historic gothic cathedral of Notre Dame. See why this cathedral is called one of Paris' greatest treasures with its famous stained glass windows and gargoyles. Visit other treasures including the Arc de Triomphe, the Madeleine, the Louvre and the Opera. Prepare to spend a good part of the day at the Louvre. Top off your evening at a French gourmet dinner concluding with a lively cabaret show. Short trips from Paris include a visit to Versailles and the Fontainebleau Forest.

London, England. Exploring the British capital is guaranteed to be a lively and historic experience. Sightseeing in London will include such famous landmarks as: Royal Albert Hall, Kensington's museums, the Houses of Parliament, Big Ben, and the Tower Bridge besides the River Thames. The highlight of any visit to London is the changing of the guard at Buckingham Palace and a visit to the Westminster Abbey, the setting of coronation ceremonies since 1066. You may also want to take a short visit outside of London to see Oxford, one of the world's most famous universities. Just outside of London you can travel to the burial place of Sir Winston Churchill in Bladon or visit Windsor Castle, which includes a tour of the State Apartments when the Queen is not in residence.

Rome, Italy. Touring Rome, you will visit fantastic historical sites such as the Colosseum and St. Peter's Basilica. The Colosseum is the site of gladiator combats and early Christian martyrdom, and St Peter's is the most important church of the Catholic world. You will also want to visit such landmarks as the Piazza Venezia, Circus Maximus, the Jewish Synagogue and the Forum. No trip to Rome is complete without eating at one of Rome's fine restaurants. You will also want to marvel at the magnificient paintings in the Sistine Chapel or take a short journey to Tivoli to stroll through the lavish gardens of Villa d'Este.

NEW WORLD AIRLINES

For more information about New World Airlines/Sunset Tours to Europe, call your travel agent or call us at 1-800-HORIZON.

CONCEPTSREVIEW

Label each of the numbered publication window elements shown in Figure 3-20.

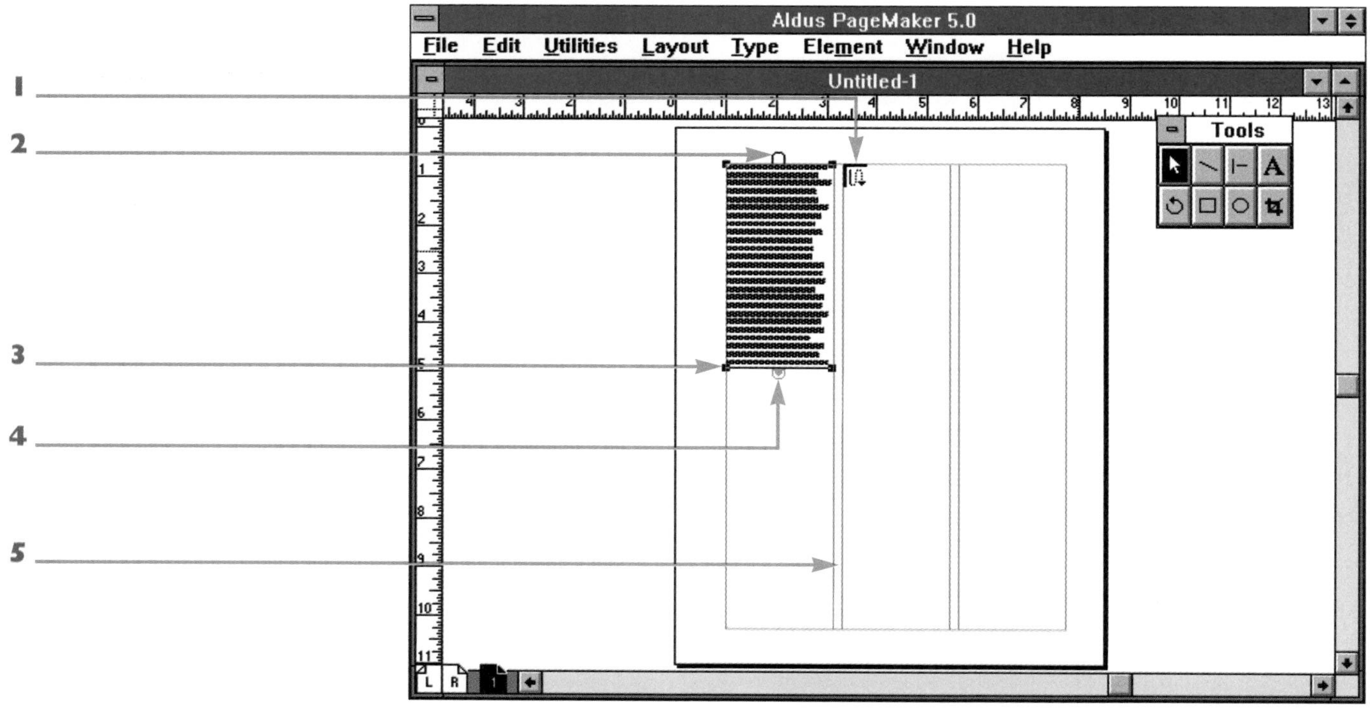

FIGURE 3-20

Match each term with the statement that describes its function.

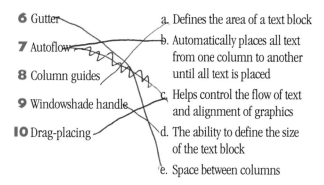

6 Gutter
7 Autoflow
8 Column guides
9 Windowshade handle
10 Drag-placing

a. Defines the area of a text block
b. Automatically places all text from one column to another until all text is placed
c. Helps control the flow of text and alignment of graphics
d. The ability to define the size of the text block
e. Space between columns

Select the best answer from the list of choices.

11 Informational fact sheets are similar to flyers, except
  a. Information sheets have larger headlines to compensate for heavy text descriptions.
  b. Information sheets give more comprehensive explanations.
  c. Flyers have a simpler layout.
  d. Flyers use a higher quality paper stock.

12 Fact sheets are used for
  a. Conveying a message instantly
  b. Product descriptions
  c. A call for action
  d. Both a and b
  e. All of the above

13 A gutter is

a. The space between margins and the end of the page

b. The space between columns

c. The margin of a column

d. None of the above

14 You can automatically place all text from one column to the next, filling up as many pages as necessary, using

a. Drag-placing

b. Autoflow

c. Semi-Autoflow

d. Balance columns

15 You can change column widths by

a. Drag-placing text

b. Clicking and dragging column guides

c. Clicking and dragging ruler guides

d. Entering custom settings in the Column guides dialog box

16 When using semi-Autoflow, you press

a. [Ctrl]

b. [Shift]

c. [Alt]

d. [Shift] [Alt]

APPLICATIONS REVIEW

1 Create a publication with three columns.

a. Start PageMaker and make sure your Student Disk is in the disk drive.

b. Open the publication Unit_3-5.PM5 from your Student Disk.

c. Use the Column guides dialog box to create three columns.

2 Place text on the page using Autoflow.

a. Use the Place document dialog box to select the file Unit_3-3.DOC from your Student Disk.

b. Make sure the Autoflow option is on.

c. Use the Autoflow pointer to make sure the text flows on the page inside the first two columns.

3 Manipulate text blocks.

a. Use the Pointer tool to select the first text block.

b. Use the windowshade handle to move the bottom of the text block up to the 5.5" mark on the vertical ruler.

4 Move and resize the text block.

a. Move the text block so the bottom of the text block touches the bottom margin guide on the page.

b. Drag a horizontal ruler guide above the first line of text in the first column.

5 Move the text block in the second column so the top of text is aligned with the top line of text in the second column. Use the ruler guide to assist you in aligning the text.

a. Use the Page setup dialog box to change the left and right margins to .5".

b. Move the text blocks in the first and second column so the left windowshades touch the left column guides respectively.

c. Use the text block selection handles to resize both text blocks to fit within their respective column guides.

d. Make sure the top lines of text are still aligned.

6 Drag-place text.

a. Use the Place document dialog box to select the file Unit_3-2.DOC from your Student Disk.

b. Drag-place the text so that you place it across two columns above the body text.

7 Create a headline in reverse text

a. Change the view to 75%.

b. Use the Text tool to type the following two lines:

Paris, London and Rome
Escorted Tour from $2500

c. Select the first line, then using the Type menu, change the font to Arial and the size to 32 points.

d. Select the second line, then change the font to Arial and the size to 24 points.

e. Select both lines of text and apply Reverse type.

f. Use the Rectangle tool to draw a box from the top left intersection of the margin guides to the 2" mark on the vertical ruler.

g. Fill the box with a solid color.

h. Send the box behind the headline.

i. Save and print your publication, then exit PageMaker.

INDEPENDENT CHALLENGE 1

You work in the Admissions Office at Medfield College. One of your tasks is to standardize the descriptions for all degree programs in the various schools. You decide to keep a consistent format and give each major its own fact sheet. Your next fact sheet is for the bachelor of science degree in management information systems. The staff of that department provides you with the program description. You need to conform it to your standards.

To complete this independent challenge:

1. Open a new one-page, letter-sized publication with three columns.
2. Drag-place the file UNIT_3-6.DOC from your Student Disk across the top of the page. This file contains the headline, "Medfield College, Management Information Systems."
3. Change the font, size, and style of the headline so it is eye-catching and appealing. Use reverse text for the headline.
4. Place the file UNIT_3-7.TIF on the publication page. This file contains a photo of the building that houses the MIS offices. Resize and move the graphic as necessary.
5. Place the file UNIT_3-8.DOC from your Student Disk on the publication page. The text in this file should flow from one column to another.
6. Manipulate the text blocks and the graphic to make the layout appealing.
7. Use your own judgment to add lines or boxes to enhance the layout of the fact sheet.
8. Save your work as MIS.PM5.
9. Print the fact sheet and close the publication.

INDEPENDENT CHALLENGE 2

Visit a computer store or an automotive dealer and get the informational fact sheets used to describe the products offered. Review the examples, then redesign one of them to improve its performance. Answer the following questions as you plan your design:

1. Is the layout simple? Or are there too many graphics?
2. Is there a way to cut some of the text and add graphical elements without sacrificing the overall purpose of the publication?
3. Does the headline stand out and immediately catch your attention?
4. Can your overall design be consistently applied to other product description/fact sheets?

To complete this independent challenge:

1. Sketch your version of the fact sheet.
2. Open a new single-sided, one-page publication and save it as NEWFACT.PM5 on your Student Disk.
3. Create columns in your publication if necessary.
4. The file PLACEHLD.TIF on your Student Disk is a dummy graphic file. A **dummy** file is a temporary file that you use as a placeholder. Place this file in your fact sheet for each graphic you want to include. Use the drag-place method to place the graphics, and resize and move them as necessary.
5. The file TEXTHLD.DOC on your Student Disk is a dummy text file that was typed in a word processor. Place this file in the publication.
6. Adjust the text flow of the story in the fact sheet as necessary so that the fact sheet is visually balanced. Hint: If there is too much text in the file for your fact sheet, use the Text tool in the Toolbox to select some of the text, then press [Delete] to delete it.
7. Add a headline by typing directly on the page. Format the headline to be eye-catching. Resize and move the text block and change the alignment of the headline so that it appears where you want it to. Hint: If you are having trouble finding the text block, click the Pointer tool in the Toolbox, then click anywhere on the text.
8. Add a point of response if necessary by typing directly on the page.
9. Add lines as necessary.
10. Save the publication and print it.

UNIT 4

OBJECTIVES

- Plan a business report
- Add and place text using story editor
- Edit text in story editor
- Use the spell checker in story editor
- Find and change text in story editor
- Format text using Type specifications
- Format paragraphs
- Adjust leading
- Insert and remove pages in a publication
- Design Workshop: Business reports

Modifying TEXT

PageMaker has many features to help you create professional-looking publications. A built-in word processor called story editor allows you to edit, format, and then check the spelling of text. You can also format paragraphs, change the space between lines of text, and add or delete pages. ▶ Joe Martin will use these features as he completes his first big project, a five-page business report that proposes expanding New World Airlines' flights into the Caribbean. ▶

Planning a business report

When developing a business report, consider that most business people have limited time to read your document. Your goal should be to create high-impact reports and proposals that take advantage of innovative design and concise writing. It's important that the report be organized in a logical, consistent, and sequential fashion. A report that quickly and clearly conveys a message using a creative design captures the attention of busy people. ▶ New World Airlines' marketing director, Sarah Pohl, wants to add flights to the Caribbean. Working with Sarah, Joe plans a concise report proposing these additional flights. This proposal will be read by the president and vice presidents of the company. Joe created the thumbnail sketches shown in Figure 4-1 as he planned the proposal. A **thumbnail** is a small sketch that shows only the large elements of the page. He uses the following guidelines to create a high-impact proposal:

STEPS

1 **Use a coherent writing style**
Keep report language simple, clear, and concise. Use headlines and subheads to organize the report in a logical, consistent, and sequential fashion. Joe makes sure that his proposal has logical headlines, and he writes concisely and clearly.

2 **Include an abstract**
An **abstract** is a summary at the beginning of the report. The abstract highlights the main points of the report. Joe's proposal will include a short, one-paragraph abstract. Joe decides to place the abstract on the proposal's cover.

3 **Add a business-like cover**
The cover sets the tone for the report. It should not entertain the reader, rather it should emphasize the importance of the report and introduce the visual style used in the report. The cover for Joe's proposal will include a title, the logo for New World Airlines, and the names of the people who prepared the proposal.

4 **Include graphics to enhance text pages**
By using graphics, you can balance the excessive text used in reports. Graphics include charts, tables, photographs, or illustrations. The graphics should reinforce the information in the report. Joe plans to include photos of the Caribbean and charts to show how New World Airlines' revenue will increase with the new flights.

5 **Maintain a consistent design**
Using a consistent design provides continuity through all sections of the report.

6 **Consider using a three-column page layout**
A columnar layout allows you to include more text on a page. A page with three columns gives you more flexibility in placing graphics. Layouts with only one or two columns limit the size of graphics, and letter-size pages look cramped with more than three columns. Joe decides to use three columns for the body of the proposal so he needs to use graphics that are one, two, or three columns wide.

FIGURE 4-1: Joe's sketch of his business proposal

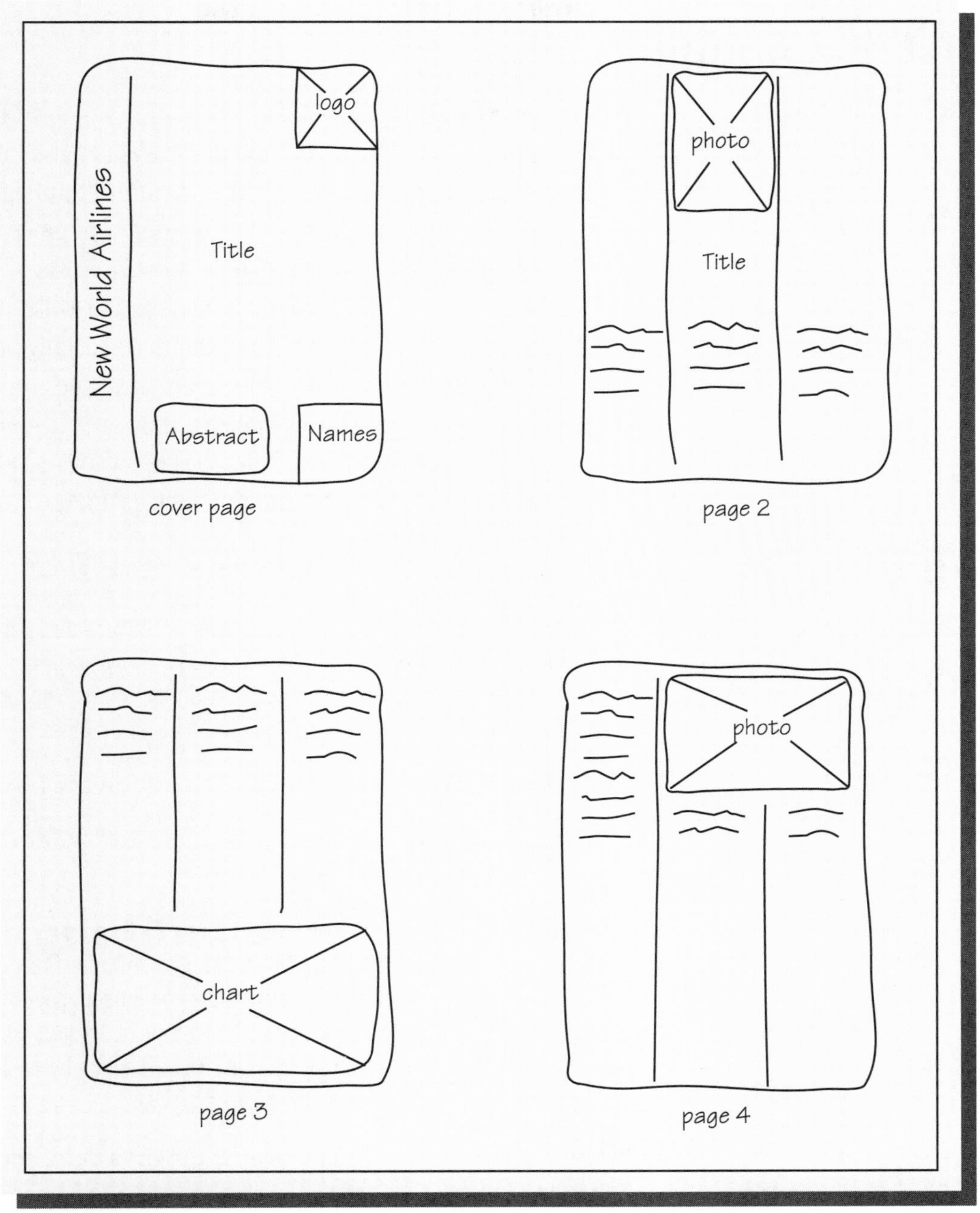

Adding and placing text using story editor

You can edit text in the PageMaker publication window, but this can be slow. If you have to insert a large amount of text in PageMaker, use PageMaker's story editor. **Story editor** is a word processing program within PageMaker. For information about exporting text from story editor to other word processing applications, see the related topic "Exporting text to other word processors." In addition to inserting text, you can edit text, check the spelling of all the words in a publication, and find text and change it to other text. Story editor is especially helpful when you make multiple changes to a story that spans several text blocks on multiple pages, because the entire story displays in the story editor window. ▶ Joe already wrote the proposal and placed it in his publication. Now he is ready to create the abstract for the business proposal using story editor and place it on the cover.

STEPS

1. **Start PageMaker, then open the document UNIT_4-1.PM5 from your Student Disk**
   This file contains Joe's proposal. The cover page of the proposal, page 1 of the publication, appears in the publication window. Joe wants to place the abstract in the middle of the page, but he wants it to be wider than the middle column. He decides to add ruler guides one-half inch from either side of the middle column guides to help him place the abstract text block.

2. **Drag a vertical ruler guide to the 6" mark on the horizontal ruler**

3. **Drag a second vertical ruler guide to the 2½" mark on the horizontal ruler**
   See Figure 4-2. Joe is ready to type the abstract.

4. **Click Edit on the menu bar, then click Edit story**
   The story editor window appears as shown in Figure 4-3. The Story menu replaces the Layout menu in the menu bar and the Element window no longer appears. The publication window is visible behind the story editor window. The left side of the story editor window is where Style names appear. You will learn about styles in Unit 5. The filename of the current publication and the story name appear in the title bar.

5. **Move the pointer anywhere over the right side of the story editor window**
   Notice that the pointer changes to I.

6. **Move the pointer anywhere over the left side of the story editor window**
   Notice that the pointer changes to ↖.

See the continuation of this lesson to type the abstract and place it in the publication.

FIGURE 4-2: Page 1 of the proposal with ruler guides

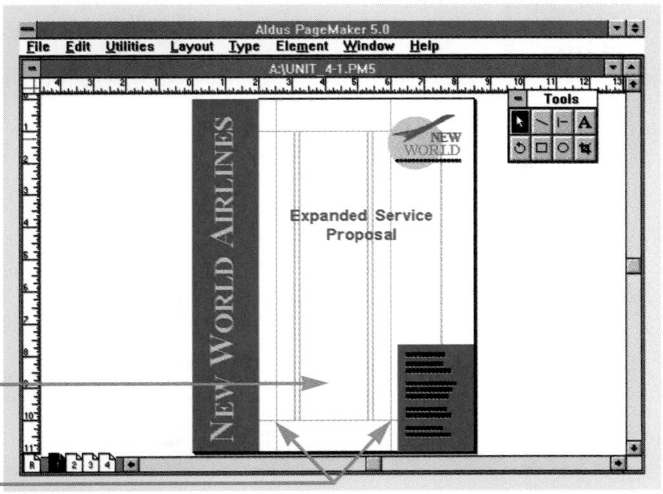

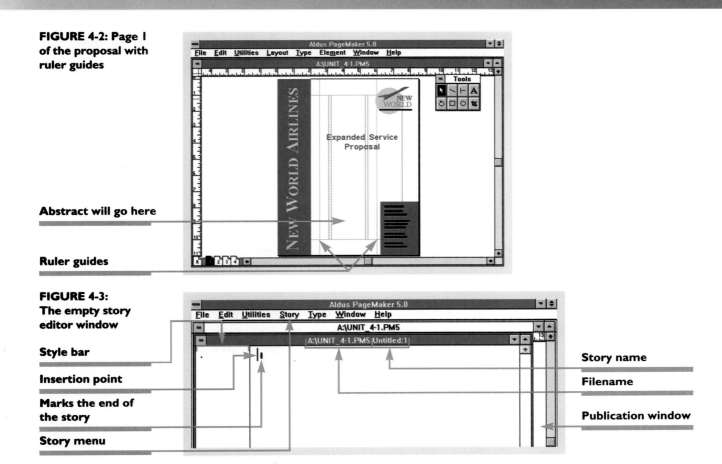

Abstract will go here

Ruler guides

FIGURE 4-3: The empty story editor window

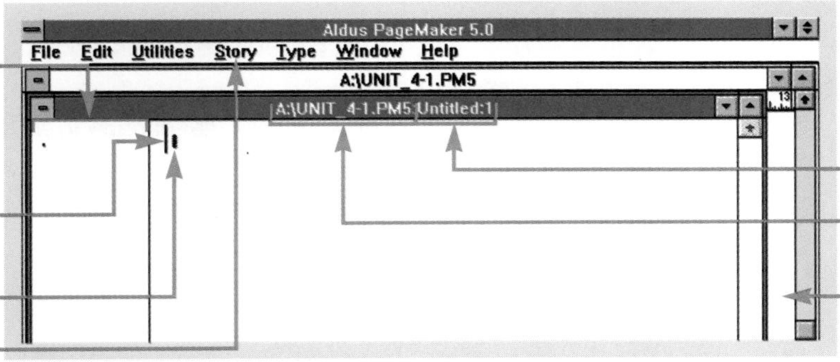

Style bar

Insertion point

Marks the end of the story

Story menu

Story name

Filename

Publication window

Exporting text to other word processors

You might need to export text created in PageMaker to a word processing program such as WordPerfect or Microsoft Word. You do this by selecting the Export command on the File menu. If you do this in layout view, you first need to use the Text tool to select the text you want to export. The Export document dialog box opens as shown in Figure 4-4. You can choose to save text in a specific word processing program's format or as text-only, which saves the text without the formatting originally applied in PageMaker. Text-only can be imported into most word processors. After you click OK, a new text file, separate from the original PageMaker file, is created and saved to the drive you specified. You can export only text, not graphics or page layouts.

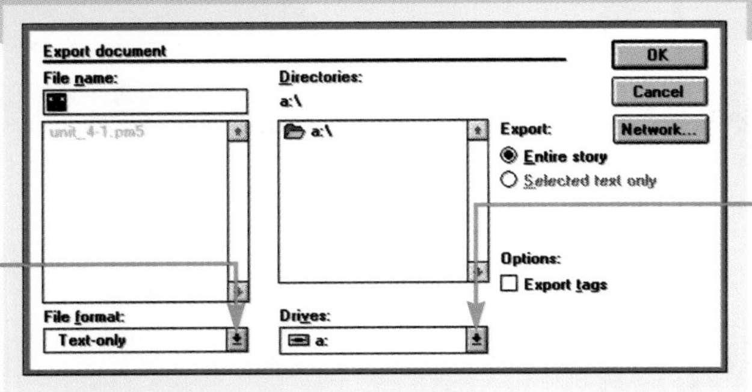

Click to select format of exported text

Click to specify drive to save the new file to

FIGURE 4-4: Export document dialog box

Adding and placing text using story editor, continued

With story editor open, Joe is ready to type the text of the abstract and place it in the publication.

STEPS

7 **Type ABSTRACT then press [Enter]**

8 **Click Story on the menu bar, then click Display ¶**

If the command Display ¶ already has a checkmark next to it, then this option is already turned on, so skip this step. The Display ¶ command displays nonprinting characters such as paragraph markers, spaces, and tab markers. ¶ is the symbol for a new paragraph. Displaying the non-printing symbols makes it easier to place precisely the cursor within the story.

9 **Type New World Airlines has mapped success in the past 10 years by,** *but do not press [Enter]*

Don't worry if you make typing errors. You will find out how to correct them in a later lesson. Notice that as you typed the word "by," the word moved down to the next line. This feature is called **word wrap**. The only time you press [Enter] is to start a new paragraph.

10 **Type the rest of the abstract shown in Figure 4-5**

Now Joe needs to place the abstract in the publication.

11 **Click Story on the menu bar, then click Close story**

You could also double-click the control menu box on the story editor window. A small dialog box opens giving you three options, Place, Discard, or Cancel. See Table 4-1 for a description of each of these commands. Joe wants to place the story.

12 **Click Place**

Story editor closes, and page 1 appears in layout view. The pointer changes to [pointer icon].

13 **Position [pointer icon] on the lefthand ruler guide at 8.5" on the vertical ruler, then drag-place the pointer to the intersection of right ruler guide and the bottom margin guide**

See Figure 4-6. The abstract is placed on page 1, as shown in Figure 4-6. If you see [windowshade handle icon] at the bottom of the text block, drag it down below the bottom margin guide.

14 **Click File on the menu bar, then click Save to save your changes**

TABLE 4-1: Dialog box commands to place story editor text

COMMAND	DESCRIPTION
Place	Closes story editor and opens the layout view
Discard	Deletes the text you just typed and returns to the layout view
Cancel	Stops the action and keeps story editor open

FIGURE 4-5: The abstract in the story editor window

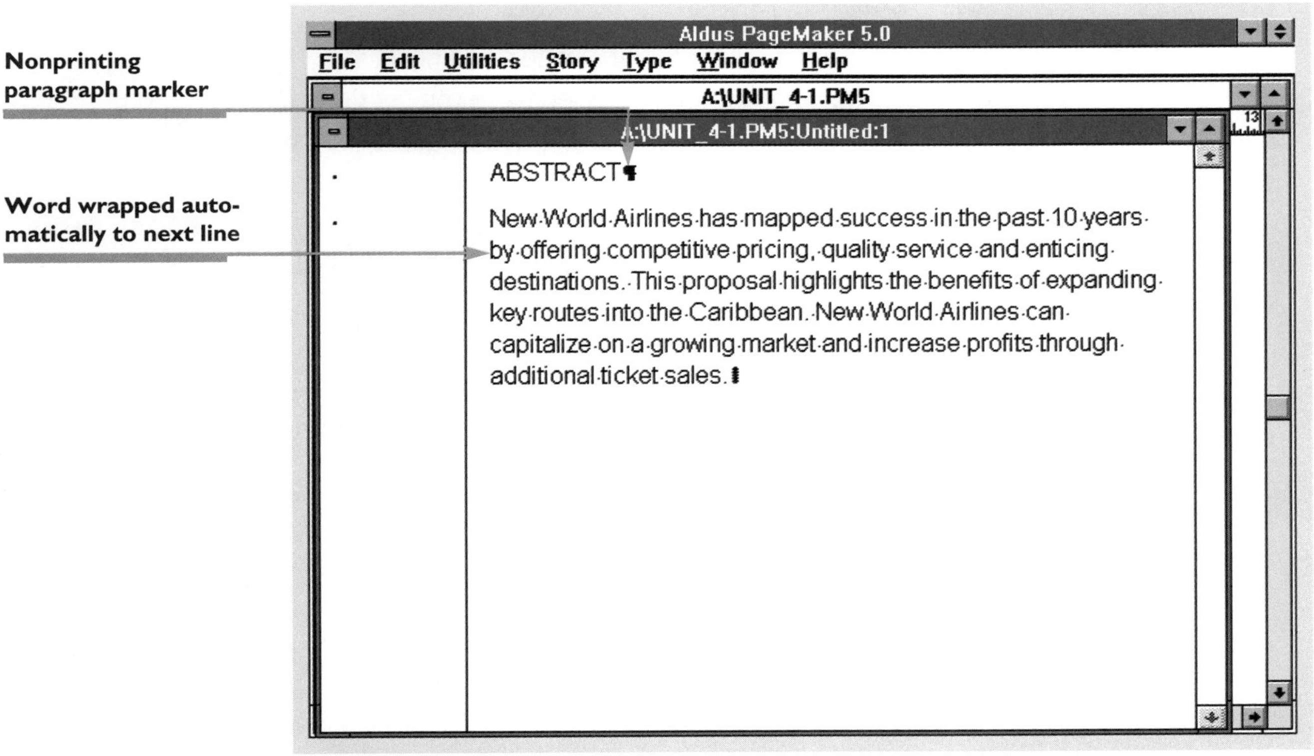

FIGURE 4-6: Abstract on page 1

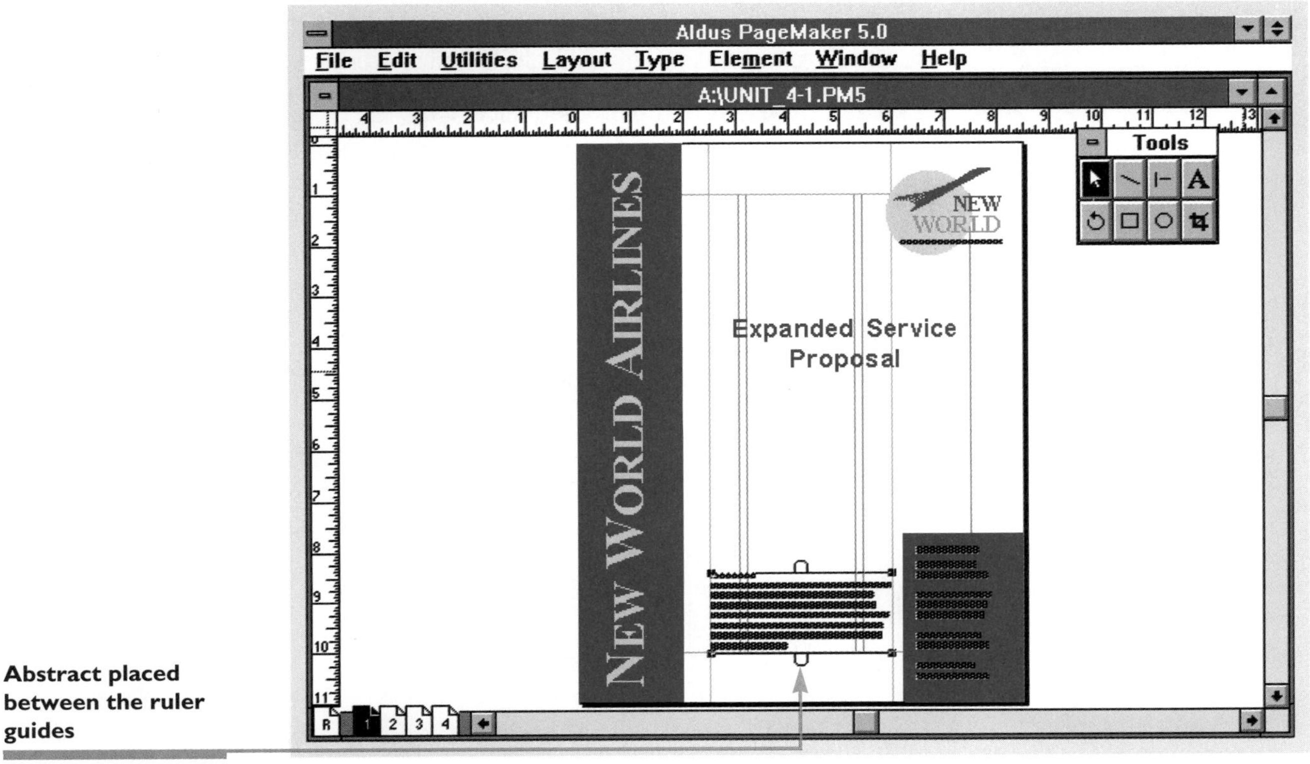

Editing text in story editor

You can use story editor to edit any story in a publication, even if the story was placed from another word processor. When you use story editor to edit your stories rather than making changes directly in the publication, you can see all parts of a story at one time, even if the story is threaded over multiple pages. You edit text by deleting and retyping characters or by using the Cut, Copy, and Paste commands on the Edit menu. When you cut or copy selected text, you place the selected text on the Clipboard. The **Clipboard** is a temporary storage area for cut or copied text or graphics. See Table 4-2 for a brief description of the Cut, Copy, and Paste commands and their corresponding keyboard shortcuts. ▶ After looking over the proposal, Joe wants to move one of the paragraphs in the publication.

STEPS

1. **Click the page 2 icon in the lower-left corner of the publication window**
   Page 2 of the publication appears in the publication window. Joe wants to edit the proposal. To open a story in story editor, select it in the publication window before you open story editor.
2. **Click the text block in the first column, click Edit on the menu bar, click Edit story, click Story on the menu bar, then click Display ¶**
   Story editor opens with the text of the proposal in the story editor window. Normal is the name of the style that was imported with the text. You will learn more about styles in Unit 5. Notice that the filename of the story is the first few words of the story. Don't worry about any errors you notice; you will correct them later.
3. **Click I at the beginning of the second paragraph, then triple-click the mouse pointer to highlight the entire paragraph**
   Make sure the entire paragraph including the ¶ symbol is selected, as shown in Figure 4-7.
4. **Click Edit on the menu bar, then click Cut**
   PageMaker removes the selection from the story editor and places it on the Clipboard.
5. **Click in the vertical scroll bar anywhere below the scroll box**
   The text scrolls up one window.
6. **Click I at the beginning of the paragraph that begins "Existing aircraft"**
   The insertion point appears at this point.
7. **Click Edit on the menu bar, then click Paste**
   PageMaker pastes the contents of the Clipboard at the insertion point, as shown in Figure 4-8. The paragraphs will run together if you didn't highlight the paragraph marker at the end of the paragraph you moved. If the paragraphs run together here, press [Enter] to insert a new paragraph marker. Joe notices that the second sentence in the paragraph he just moved begins with "Bye," and it should begin with "By."
8. **Drag I over the "e" in "Bye" to select it**
9. **Press [Delete] or [Backspace]**
   The "e" is deleted from the story. When you use this method of deleting text, the deleted text is not placed on the Clipboard, and you cannot use the Paste command to paste it back in to the publication.

FIGURE 4-7: Highlighted selection in story editor

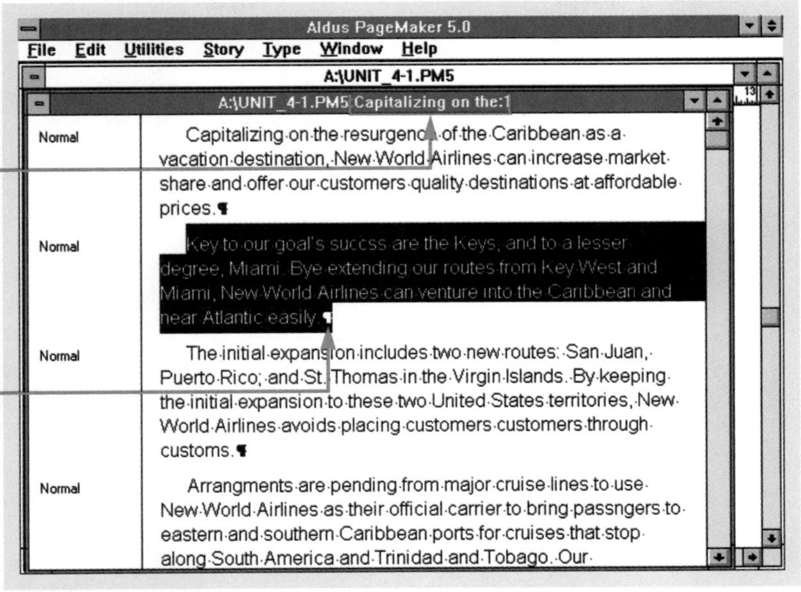

FIGURE 4-8: Paragraph pasted in new location

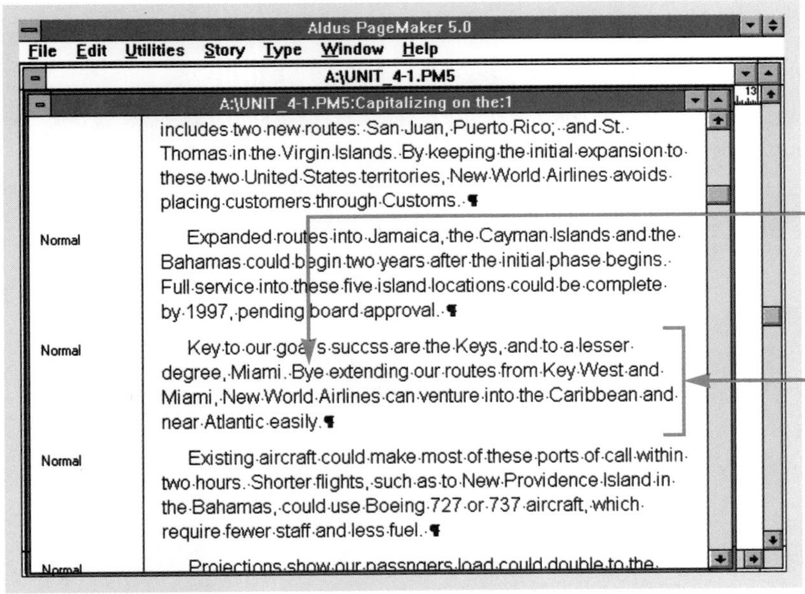

TABLE 4-2: Editing commands

COMMAND	KEYBOARD SHORTCUT	DESCRIPTION
Cut	[Ctrl][X]	Removes the selection to the Clipboard
Copy	[Ctrl][C]	Copies the selection to the Clipboard but leaves the selection in place
Paste	[Ctrl][V]	Moves the Clipboard contents to a new location

QUICK TIP

You can access story editor quickly by triple-clicking a text block with the Pointer tool.

TROUBLE?

If you use [Delete] by mistake instead of the Cut command to delete something, click Edit on the menu bar, then click Undo edit.

Using the spell checker in story editor

It's a good idea to check the spelling in a story before you print the publication. You can do this using the spell checker in story editor. You can check the spelling in the current story, a highlighted portion of the story, all stories in the current publication, or all stories in open PageMaker publications. Spell checking is available only when you are in story editor. ▶ Joe wants to check the spelling in the current story.

STEPS

1 **Scroll to the top of the story editor window so that the beginning of the story is visible, then click I before the "C" in "Capitalizing"**
PageMaker starts checking spelling from the insertion point, so now it will check the whole story.

2 **Click Utilities on the menu bar, then click Spelling**
The Spelling dialog box opens. See Table 4-3 for descriptions of the options in the Spelling dialog box. Notice the Current story radio button is selected. This means that PageMaker will check the spelling in only the current story that appears in the story editor window.

3 **Click Start**
PageMaker begins searching the story for unknown words. "Juan" is flagged by the spell checker as a possible misspelled word, as shown in Figure 4-9. Juan is not misspelled, but PageMaker does not have Juan in its dictionary. Joe decides to add it to the dictionary because he knows he will use this word in the future.

NOTE: If you are working in a lab, you might not be allowed to add words to the dictionary; check with your instructor or technical support person before completing the next step. If the first word flagged is "Puerto," then someone else might have already added "Juan" to the dictionary. Read Steps 4, 5, and 6, but do not perform any mouse actions, then continue with Step 7.

4 **Click Add**
The Add word to user dictionary dialog box opens, as shown in Figure 4-10. If the word were more than one syllable, PageMaker inserts a tilde (~) to indicate the word would hyphenate if it appeared at the end of a line. Three tildes after a syllable indicate the least desirable place to hyphenate the word.

5 **Click OK to accept PageMaker's hyphenation and capitalization of the word and to close the dialog box**
See the continuation of this lesson to finish spell checking the story.

FIGURE 4-9: Spelling dialog box with unknown word

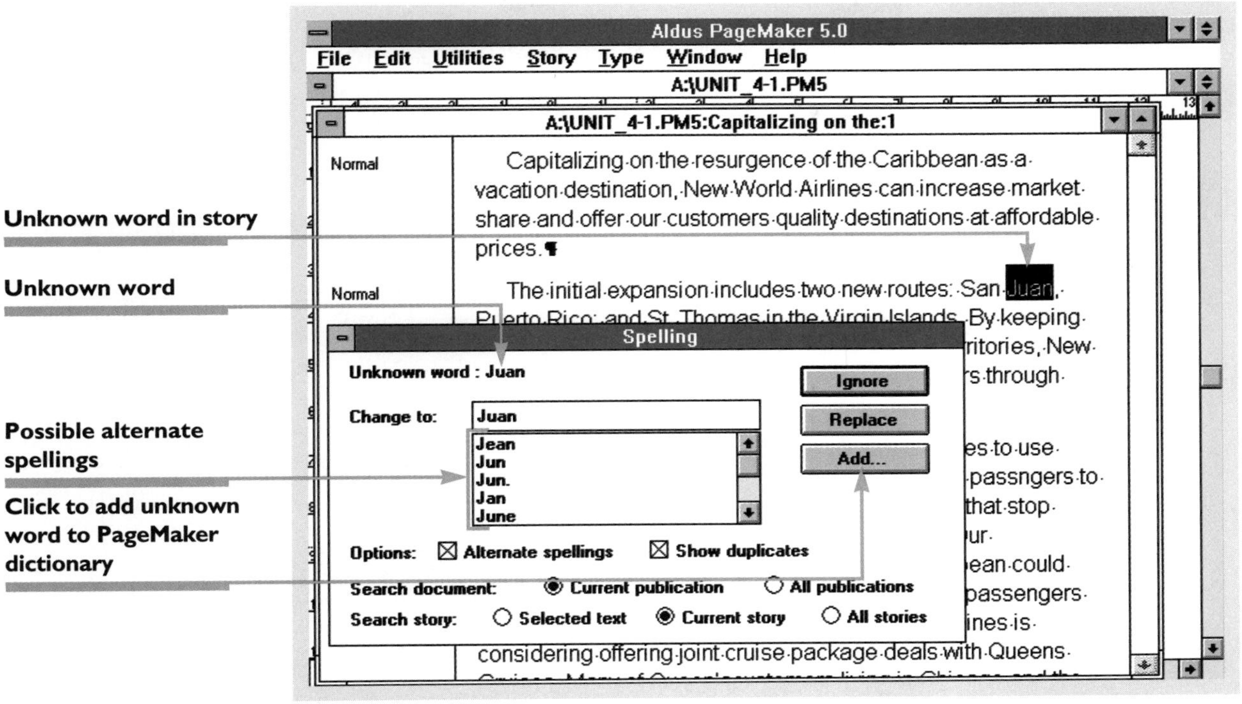

FIGURE 4-10: Add word to user dictionary dialog box

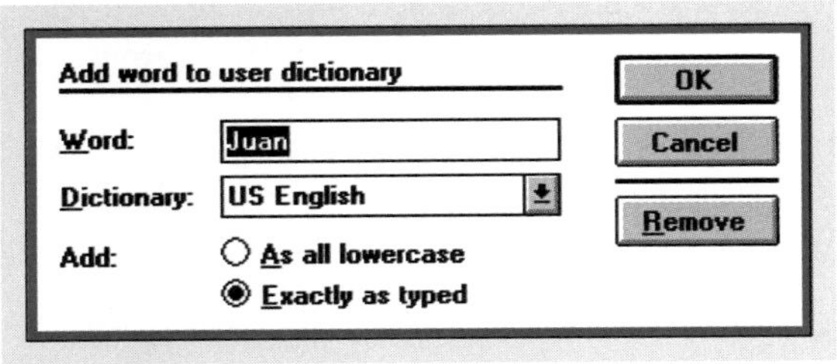

TABLE 4-3: Spelling dialog box options

OPTION	DESCRIPTION
Alternate spellings	When turned on, lists alternate spellings for each word the PageMaker dictionary does not recognize; turn this feature off to speed up the spell check
Show duplicates	When turned on, flags duplicate words such as "the the;" turn this feature off to speed up the spell check
Current publication	Checks spelling in the current publication only
All publications	Checks spelling in all open publications
Selected text	Checks spelling in the selected text only
Current story	Checks spelling in the current story only
All stories	Checks spelling in all stories in the current publication

Using the spell checker in story editor, continued

Joe continues checking the spelling in the story.

STEPS

6 **Click Continue in the Spelling dialog box**
The next word flagged is "Puerto" in the city name "Puerto Rico." This is not misspelled, so Joe decides to tell PageMaker to ignore this error.

7 Click **Ignore**
Next PageMaker flags "Rico."

8 Click **Ignore**
The next word flagged is "customers." This word is flagged as a duplicate word, as shown in Figure 4-11.

9 Click **Replace** to delete the second "customers" from the story
The next word flagged, "Arrangments," as shown in Figure 4-12, is spelled incorrectly.

10 Click **Arrangements** in the list of alternate spellings
"Arrangements" appears in the Change to text box.

11 Click **Replace** to accept the spelling in the Change to text box
The misspelled word in the story is replaced with the correct spelling. PageMaker corrects the misspelled word and moves on to the next unknown word.

12 Continue making spelling changes to the story, choosing the appropriate action for each potential error
When PageMaker is finished checking the story, the message "Spelling check complete" appears at the top of the Spelling dialog box.

13 Double-click the **control menu box** on the Spelling dialog box to close it
The Spelling dialog box closes.

14 Click **File** on the menu bar, then click **Save** to save your publication

FIGURE 4-11: Spell checker flagging a duplicate word

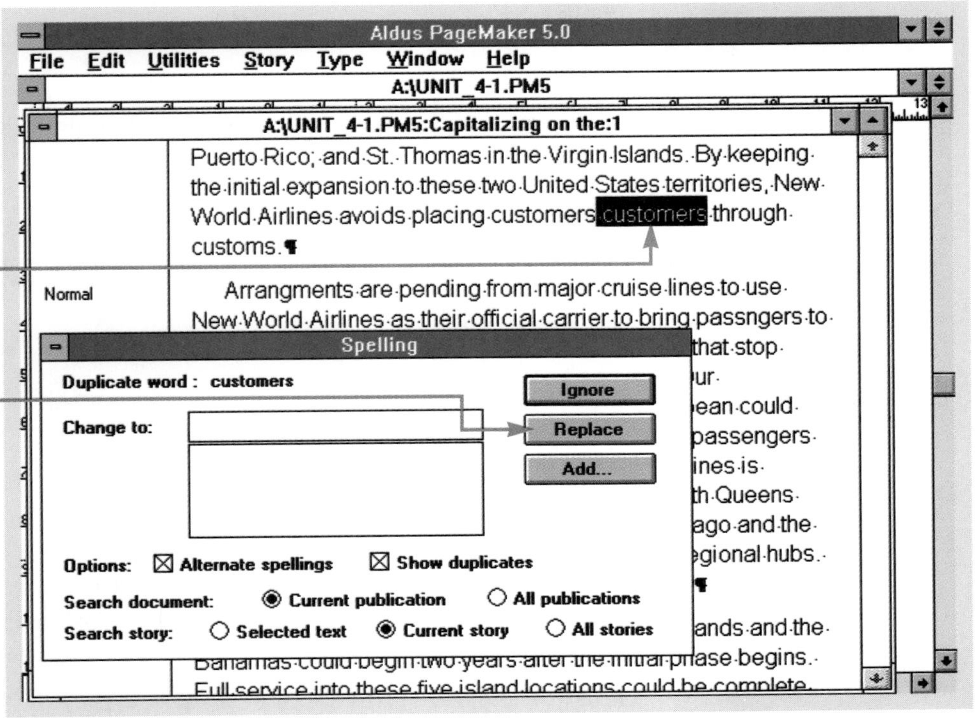

Duplicate word flagged

Click to delete duplicate word

FIGURE 4-12: Replacing a misspelled word

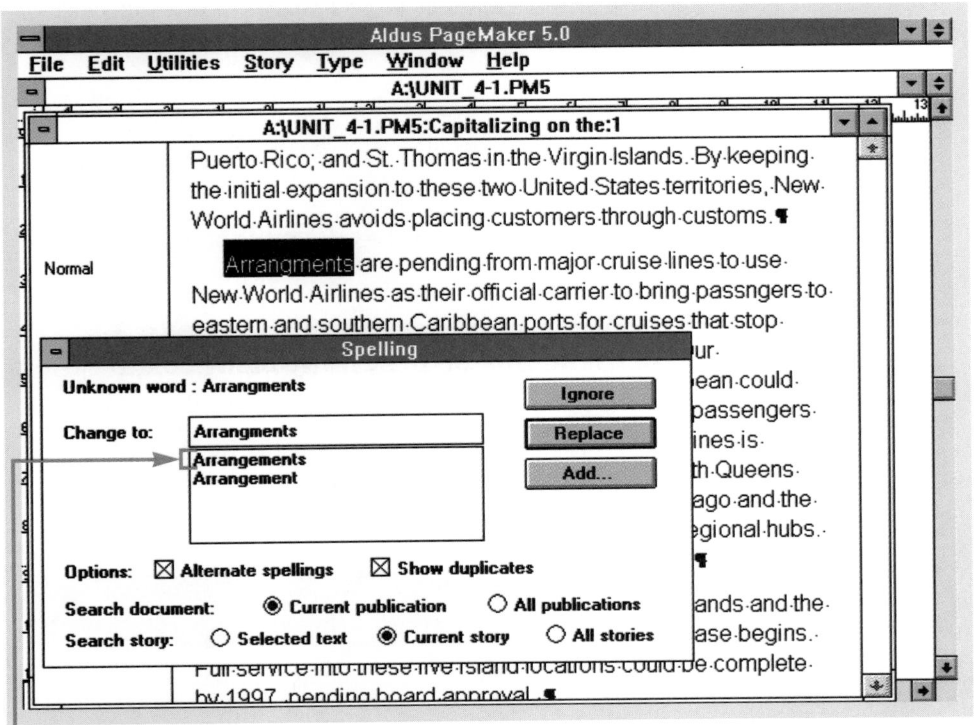

Click to put this spelling in the Change to text box

TROUBLE?

If you accidentally choose Ignore for a word that is spelled incorrectly, you must save the file and exit PageMaker, then reopen the file before the spell check will recognize the mis-spelled word again.

Finding and changing text in story editor

When you are in story editor, you can use the Change command to search for specific text in a story and change it to different text. You can also search for and change format attributes such as fonts, type styles, or font size. For more information on changing format attributes, see the related topic "Expanding the Find and Change attributes." ▶ Joe used the phrase "ports of call" in the proposal. He wants to change it to "destinations."

STEPS

1 Scroll to the top of the story editor window so that the beginning of the story is visible, then click I before the "C" in "Capitalizing"
PageMaker searches for the text from the insertion point.

2 Click **Utilities** on the menu bar, then click **Change**
The Change dialog box opens, as shown in Figure 4-13. If you had selected the Find command on the Utilities menu instead, a similar dialog box would have opened, but the three command buttons for Changing text would not appear. You use the Find command to search for specific text only. Joe wants to find the phrase "ports of call" and change it to "destinations."

3 Click I in the **Find what text box**, then type **ports of call**

4 Click I in the **Change to text box**, then type **destinations**

5 Click **Find**
PageMaker searches the story. When it finds the text in the Find what text box, it stops, and the Change and Change & find command buttons are now available to you. See Figure 4-14. Table 4-4 describes the Change options.

6 Click **Change**
The text is replaced with the new text. Joe checks the rest of the story for the phrase.

7 Click **Find next**
The Search complete dialog box opens. This means that PageMaker did not find any more occurrences of the phrase.

8 Click **OK** to close the dialog box

9 Double-click the **control menu box** on the Change dialog box to close it
The Change dialog box closes. Joe is finished editing the proposal. He wants to return to layout view now.

10 Click **Story** on the menu bar, then click **Close story**
Story editor closes and the layout view appears.

TABLE 4-4: Change options

CHANGE OPTION	DESCRIPTION
Change	Replaces the selected text with the text in the Change to text box
Change & find	Finds the next occurrence of the text in the Find what text box and changes it to the text in the Change to text box
Change all	Finds all occurrences of the text in the Find what text box and changes each of them to the text in the Change to text box

FIGURE 4-13: Change dialog box

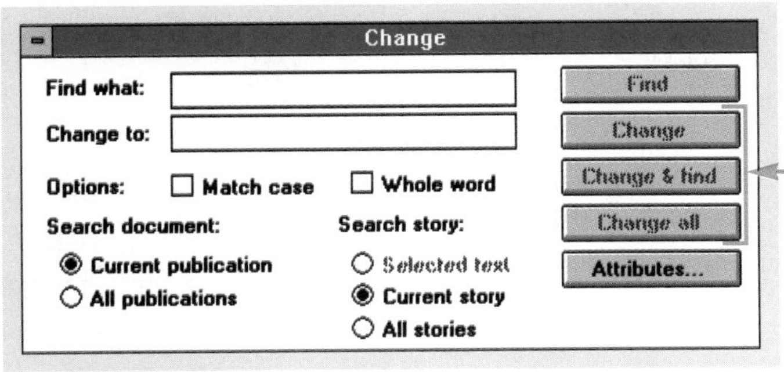

Change options do not appear in Find dialog box

FIGURE 4-14: Change dialog box and found text

Found text

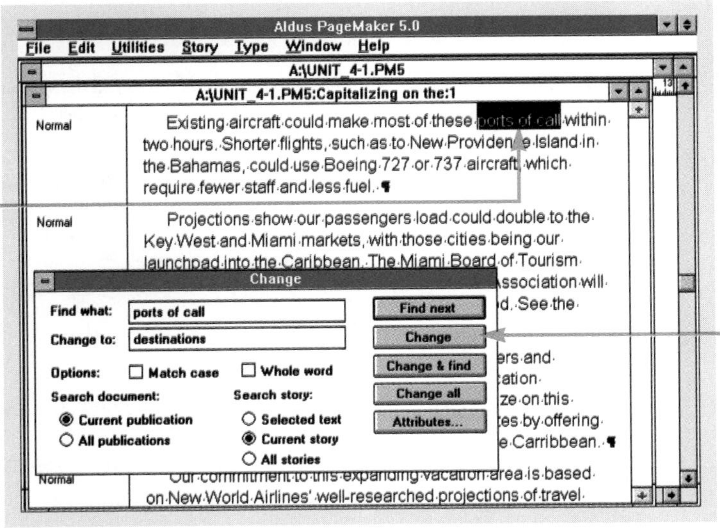

Click to change found text

Expanding the Find and Change attributes

You might need to find or change text that is formatted in a particular way. If you click Attributes in the Find dialog box or the Change dialog box, the Find attributes or Change attributes dialog box appears. The Change attributes dialog box is shown in Figure 4-15. Using this dialog box, you can find and change specific format attributes for paragraph styles, font, size, and type styles. The Change attributes dialog box is divided into two sides. On the left side, you set the attributes you want to find. On the right side, you set the new format attributes. Only the left side appears in the Find attributes dialog box.

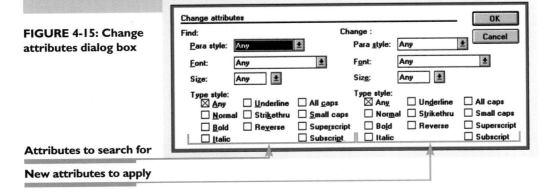

FIGURE 4-15: Change attributes dialog box

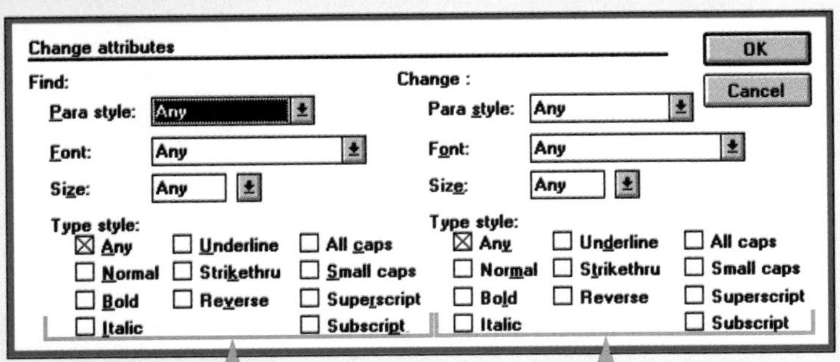

Attributes to search for

New attributes to apply

QUICK TIP

You cannot find or change text that is part of a graphical element.

Formatting text using Type specifications

You already know how to change text formats using the submenus on the Type menu. If you choose the Type specs command on the Type menu, you open the Type specifications dialog box in which you can set multiple formats at once. You can use the Type specifications dialog box in either layout view or story editor. ▶ The current font in the proposal is Arial, a sans serif font that can be difficult to read when it's small. Joe decides to change the font for the entire proposal to a serif font.

STEPS

1. **Click Layout on the menu bar, click View, then click 75%**
   This will allow you to see the changes you'll make to the text.
2. **Click the Text tool [A] in the Toolbox, then click I anywhere in the text**
3. **Click Edit on the menu bar, then click Select all**
   The Select all command selects all the text in a story.
4. **Click the page 4 icon [4], click Layout on the menu bar, click View, then click 75% size**
   Notice the text is selected because it is one story threaded throughout the publication.
5. **Click Type on the menu bar, then click Type specs**
   The Type specifications dialog box opens, as shown in Figure 4-16. Joe wants to change the font.
6. **Click the Font list arrow, then click Times New Roman**
   If you don't have Times New Roman, choose another serif font such as a variation of Times New Roman, Palatino, or Garamond. The current font size is 11.5 points. Joe chose this point size when the font was Arial because he didn't think 12 point would fit. Now that he's changed the font, he can change the point size to the more common 12 point.
7. **Click the Size list arrow, then click 12**
8. **Click OK**
9. **Click anywhere outside of the selected text block**
   This deselects the text. See Figure 4-17. Notice that the type in the third column does not flow down as far as it did before because you changed the font and the point size. Satisfied with his changes, Joe saves the publication.
10. **Click File on the menu bar, then click Save**

FIGURE 4-16: Type specifications dialog box

Click to display list of fonts

Click to display list of sizes

Click to display additional formatting options

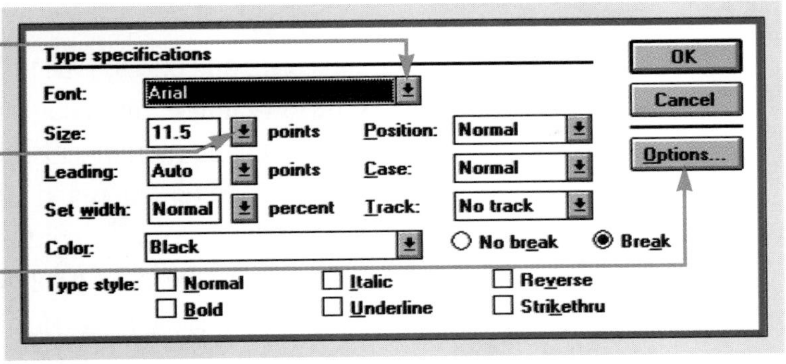

FIGURE 4-17: Type changes applied

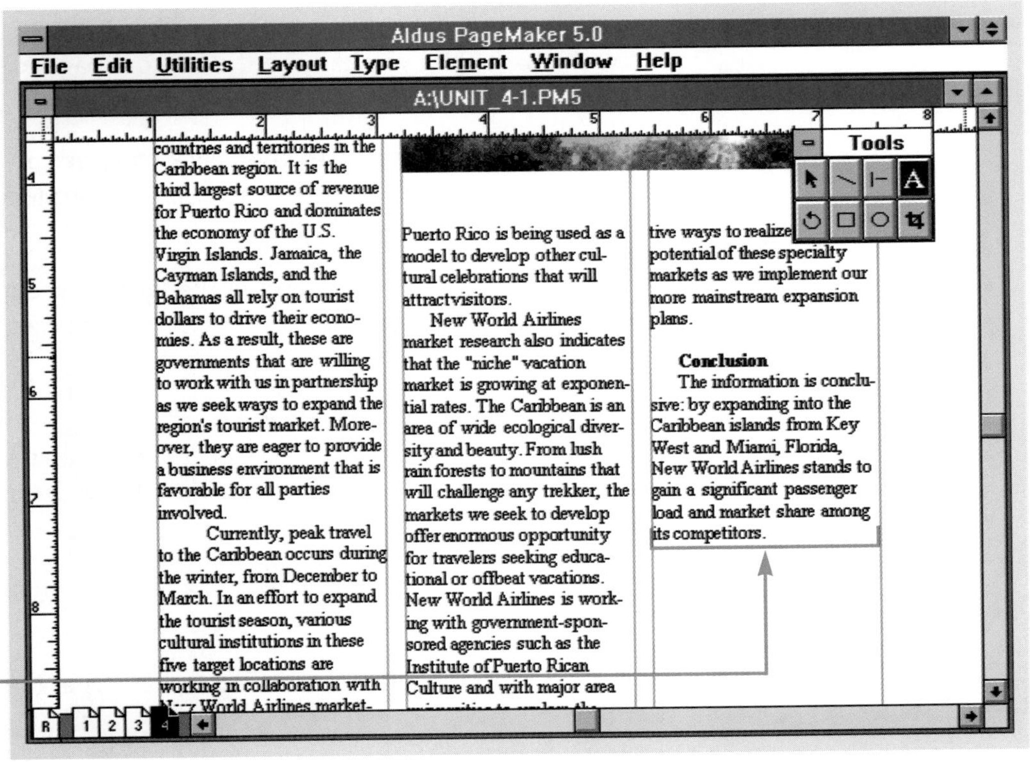

Text reflowed after font and font size changed

DESIGN TIP

Depending on the font, a range of 10 to 12 points is a good size for a large body of text.

Formatting paragraphs

When you select the Paragraph command on the Type menu, the Paragraph specifications dialog box opens. You can use this dialog box for a variety of formatting needs. For example, you can set paragraph indents, change the space between paragraphs, adjust the alignment, or turn on widow and orphan control. A **widow** is a line that begins a paragraph at the bottom of a column or page. An **orphan** is a line that ends a paragraph but falls at the top of a column or page. ▶ Joe thinks the paragraph indent on the paragraphs is too large. He also wants to eliminate widows and orphans.

STEPS

1. **Click I anywhere in the last paragraph, click Edit on the menu bar, then click Select all**

2. **Scroll the page until you can see the bottom page margin**
   See Figure 4-18. Notice any widows and orphans.

3. **Click Type on the menu bar, then click Paragraph**
   The Paragraph specifications dialog box opens. First, Joe wants to decrease the paragraph indents on all the paragraphs in the proposal.

4. **Double-click the First text box in the Indents section, then type 0.15**
   This sets an indent of .15" on the first line of every paragraph. Next, Joe turns the widow and orphan control on.

5. **Click the Widow control check box**
   An "X" appears in the check box, and widow control is turned on. Now Joe needs to tell PageMaker how many lines of text make up a widow. Joe decides that two lines constitutes a widow.

6. **Double-click the Widow control text box, then type 2**
   See Figure 4-19.

7. **Click the Orphan control text box, then type 2 in the Orphan control text box**

8. **Click OK**
   PageMaker moves lines of text up to the next column or page or down to the previous column or page to eliminate widows and orphans.

FIGURE 4-18: Widowed text at the bottom of column two

Orphan

Widow

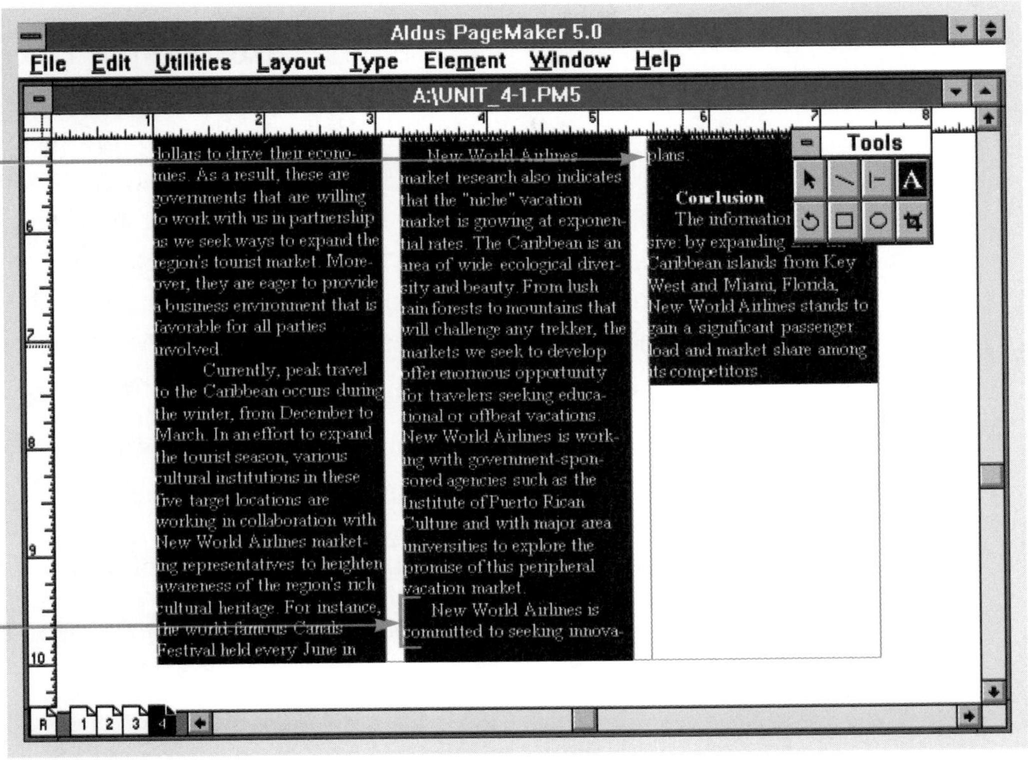

FIGURE 4-19: Widow control turned on

Widow control turned on

Click to turn on orphan control

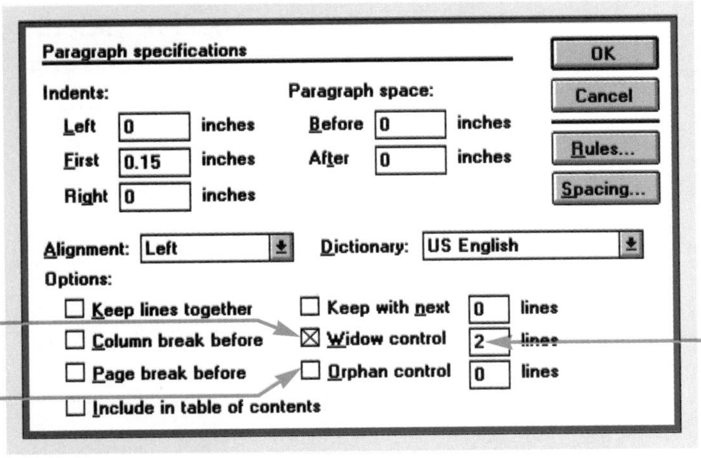

Widow defined as 2 lines or less

DESIGN TIP

The absence of widows and orphans in a layout shows quality design.■

Adjusting leading

Leading is the vertical space between lines of text. Specifically, leading is the total height of a line from the top of the tallest characters in the line to the top of the tallest characters in the line below. Leading is measured in points, the same as font size. PageMaker's default for leading is 20% greater than the font size. This means that if the text is 10 points, the leading would be 12 points. This is referred to as 10 (font size) over 12 (leading), or $^{10}/_{12}$. For more information on leading, see the related topic "Positioning text within its leading." ▶ Joe wants to make the lines of text a space and a half apart; in other words, he wants to increase the leading by 50%.

STEPS

1. Click **Layout** on the menu bar, click **View**, then click **Fit in window**
2. Click I anywhere in the text
3. Click **Edit** on the menu bar, then click **Select all**, if necessary
4. Click **Type** on the menu bar, then click **Type specs**
   The Type specifications dialog box opens. Joe wants to increase the space between each line of text.
5. Click the **Leading text box** to select it, type **18**, then click **OK**
   You could also click Leading on the Type menu, then select a leading from the submenu. The story flows below the bottom margin of the third column, as shown in Figure 4-20.
6. Click the **Pointer tool** in the Toolbox, click the **text block** in the third column, then drag up to the bottom margin even with the second column
   The windowshade handle appears at the bottom of the third column, indicating that there is still text to be placed, as shown in Figure 4-21. Joe will need to add additional pages to the proposal.

Continue with the next lesson to insert a page into the proposal.

FIGURE 4-20: Text after leading is increased

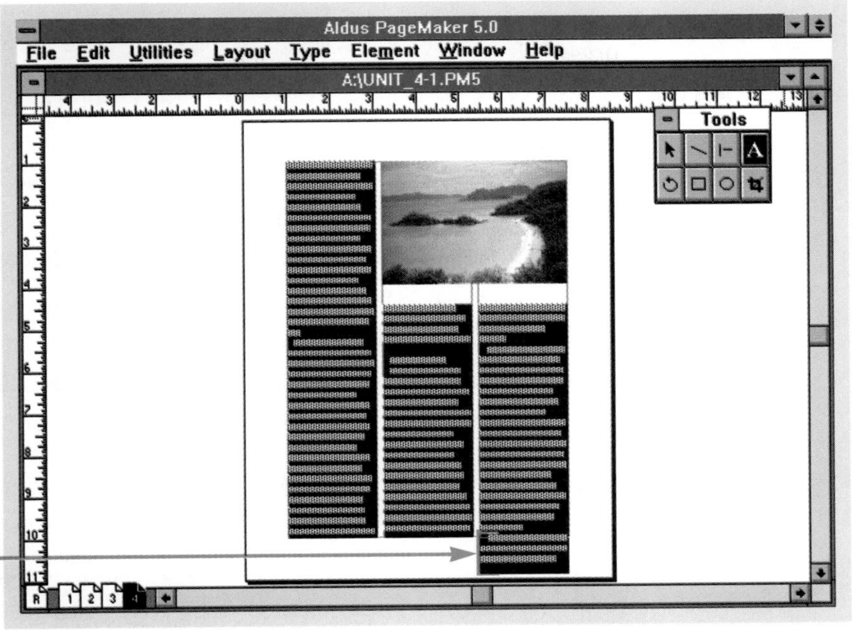

Story flows below margin

FIGURE 4-21: Text block shortened in the third column

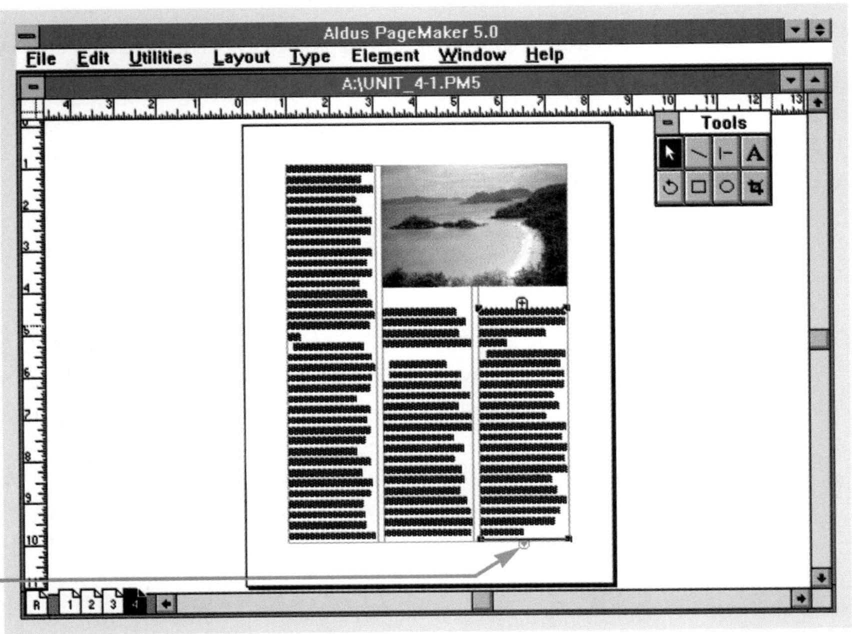

Indicates more text needs to be placed

Positioning text within its leading

PageMaker gives you three choices for adjusting the text once the leading is chosen. **Proportional leading** is the default setting that allows for proportional amounts of space above the tallest character and the lowest character in a line. **Top of caps leading** measures the leading from the highest point on any character in a line. **Baseline leading** measures the leading from the baseline of the line of text. To change the way leading is measured, click Type on the menu bar, click Paragraph, then click Spacing.

TROUBLE?

If you try to set different leading in the same line, PageMaker uses the largest leading for the entire line.■

Inserting and removing pages in a publication

You can insert pages before, after, or between the current pages in the publication window. PageMaker allows a maximum of 999 pages in a publication. You can also remove pages from a publication. PageMaker automatically rethreads text blocks and updates page icons when you add or delete pages. For more information on moving between pages, see the related topic "Using the Go to page command."

▶ Because Joe increased the leading, the text no longer fits on four pages, so he needs to add pages to the publication.

STEPS

1 **If the text block in the third column is not selected, click it, then click**
This loads the place pointer with the text that doesn't fit on page 4.

2 **Click Layout on the menu bar, then click Insert pages**
The Insert pages dialog box opens, in which you specify how many pages you want to insert and where you want to insert them, as shown in Figure 4-22.

3 **Type 2 in the Insert pages text box, make sure the After current page radio button is selected, then click OK**
The dialog box closes, and a new page 5 appears in the window. Notice two additional page icons for pages 5 and 6 appear in the lower-left corner of the window. Joe uses the semi-Autoflow method to place the rest of the text.

4 **Press [Shift], then click at the top of the first column, *but do not release [Shift]***

5 **Click at the top of the second column, then release [Shift]**
The windowshade handle appears at the end of the text in the second column, as shown in Figure 4-23. Joe realizes he added an extra page so he needs to remove page 6.

6 **Click Layout on the menu bar, click Remove pages, type 6 in the Remove page(s) text box, type 6 in the through text box, then click OK**
An alert message appears, asking if you want to delete the specified pages.

7 **Click OK**
PageMaker removes page 6. Notice that the icon no longer appears in the lower-left corner of the window. Satisfied with the proposal, Joe decides to save and print it.

8 **Click File on the menu bar, click Save, click File on the menu bar, click Print, then click Print in the Print document dialog box**
The publication prints.

9 **Click File on the menu bar, then click Exit to exit PageMaker**

FIGURE 4-22: Insert pages dialog box

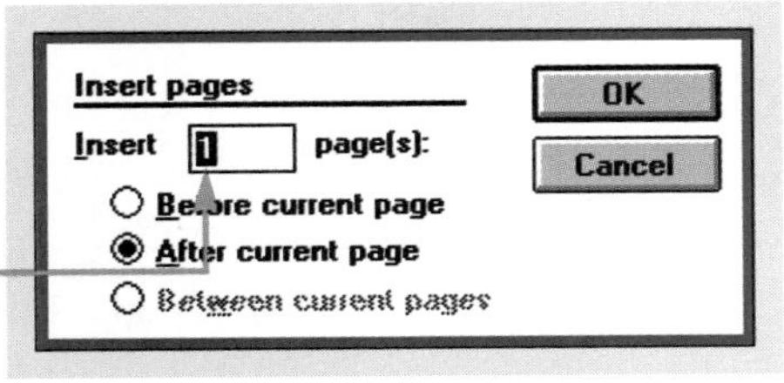

Type number of pages you want to insert

FIGURE 4-23: Text placed on the new page

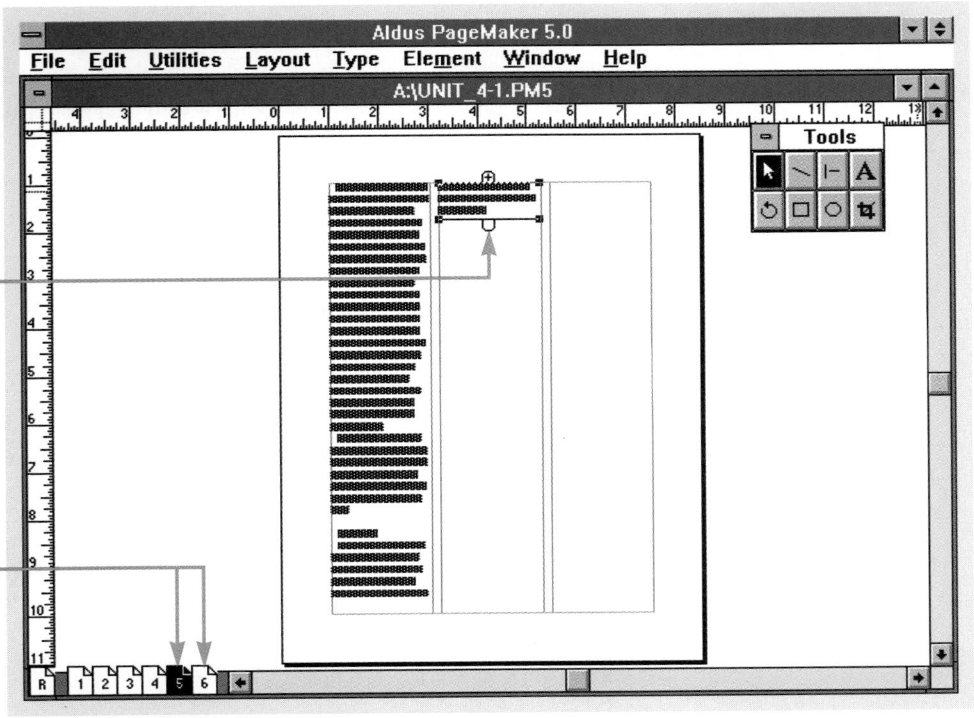

No more text to place

Two more pages

Using the Go to page command

In addition to clicking page icons to move to a specific page in a publication, you can use the Go to page command on the Layout menu. This command is helpful if you are working on a large multiple-page document (usually more than 20 pages) and all the page icons do not appear at the bottom of the publication window. Click Layout on menu bar, then click Go to page to open the Go to page dialog box. Click the Page number radio button, type the page number you want to go to in the text box, then click OK. See Figure 4-24.

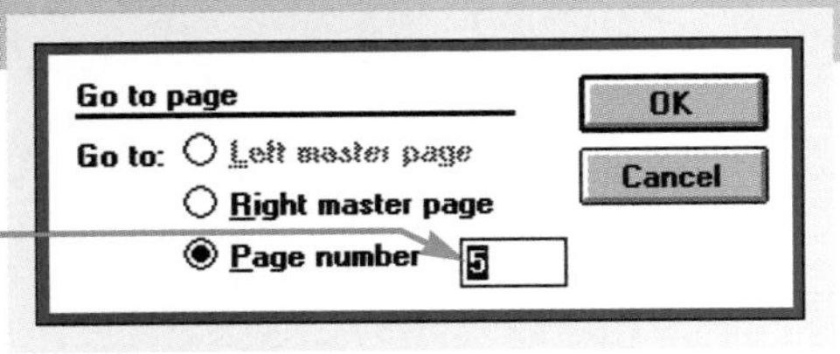

Type the page number you want to go to

FIGURE 4-24: Go to page dialog box

QUICK TIP

To quickly move forward one page, press [F12]; to quickly move back one page, press [F11].

Design Workshop: Business reports

Using innovative design and concise writing when creating business reports will capture your reader's attention. It's important that the report be organized in a logical, consistent and sequential fashion. ▶ Figure 4-25 shows the cover page and page 2 of the final proposal. Let's critique the final publication.

STEPS

1 **Does the cover invite the reader to read the report?**
The cover sets the tone for the report. It should emphasize the importance of the report and introduce the visual style used in the report. You should not spend so much time creating the cover page that you sacrifice the quality of the text in the report; however, there are several small additions that can enhance your cover and invite the reader continue to read the report. The large headline and the abstract on the cover of Joe's proposal immediately let the reader know what the report contains. The New World Airlines logo on the cover adds a nice touch without crowding any important information.

2 **Is the text organized in a logical fashion?**
It is critical that the text in a business report be coherent. PageMaker's story editor gives you some of the tools commonly available in word processing applications to edit your stories, including a spell checker and commands for finding and changing text. Joe checked the spelling in his report before he printed it. He also replaced an overused phrase with a better word. Note also that Joe included headlines and subheads within the body of the report to organize the information.

FIGURE 4-25: Pages 1 and 2 of the proposal

NEW WORLD AIRLINES

NEW WORLD AIRLINES

Expanded Service Proposal

Prepared By:

Michelle Snow
New World Airlines

Mary V. Kountzman
Greater Caribbean
Board Of Tourism

Francis Bellach
New World Airlines

Joseph Martin
New World Airlines

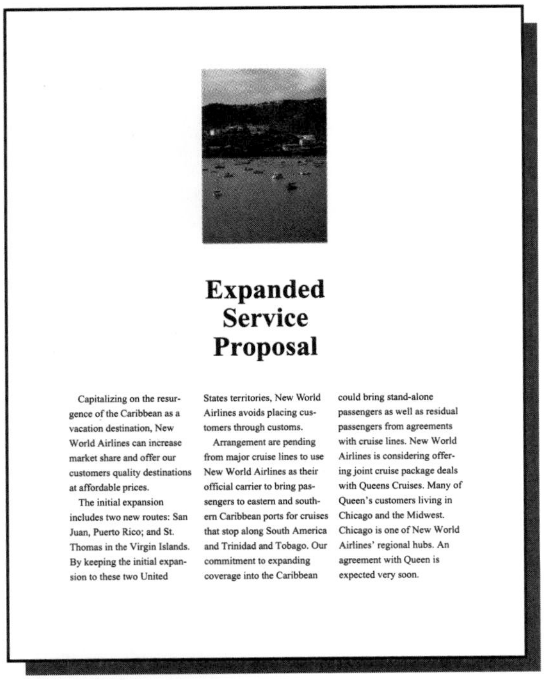

Expanded Service Proposal

Capitalizing on the resurgence of the Caribbean as a vacation destination, New World Airlines can increase market share and offer our customers quality destinations at affordable prices.

The initial expansion includes two new routes: San Juan, Puerto Rico; and St. Thomas in the Virgin Islands. By keeping the initial expansion to these two United States territories, New World Airlines avoids placing customers through customs.

Arrangement are pending from major cruise lines to use New World Airlines as their official carrier to bring passengers to eastern and southern Caribbean ports for cruises that stop along South America and Trinidad and Tobago. Our commitment to expanding coverage into the Caribbean could bring stand-alone passengers as well as residual passengers from agreements with cruise lines. New World Airlines is considering offering joint cruise package deals with Queens Cruises. Many of Queen's customers living in Chicago and the Midwest. Chicago is one of New World Airlines' regional hubs. An agreement with Queen is expected very soon.

Design Workshop: Business reports, continued

Let's continue critiquing Joe's design. Figure 4-26 shows pages 3 and 4 of the proposal. Refer to this and to Figure 4-25 as necessary.

STEPS

3 **Are the pages too heavy with text?**
If possible, you should balance the excessive text used in reports with graphics. As with a fact sheet, you should add graphics to reinforce the information in the report, not just decorate it. Joe included a chart on page 3 to reinforce text explanations, and photos of the Caribbean on pages 2 and 4 to add interest to the text. Joe also adjusted the leading to space out the text in the proposal, giving the pages more white space. This forced him to add a new page, page 5, to his proposal.

4 **Does each page of the report have a consistent design?**
Using a consistent design provides continuity through all sections of the report and makes it easier for the reader to find information. Joe set up the proposal with three columns which gave him more flexibility for placing the text and graphics. His placement of graphics helps the pages look consistent. Looking back, Joe should have included a graphic on page 5 to tie the entire publication together.

FIGURE 4-26: Pages 3 and 4 of the proposal

Expanded routes into Jamaica, the Cayman Islands and the Bahamas could begin two years after the initial phase begins. Full service into these five island locations could be complete by 1997, pending board approval.

Key to our goal's success are the Keys, and to a lesser degree, Miami. Bye extending our routes from Key West and Miami, New World Airlines can venture into the Caribbean and near Atlantic easily.

Existing aircraft could make most of these destinations within two hours. Shorter flights, such as to New Providence Island in the Bahamas, could use Boeing 727 or 737 aircraft, which require fewer staff and less fuel.

Projections show our passengers load could double to the Key West and Miami markets, with those cities being our launchpad into the Caribbean. The Miami Board of Tourism and the Keys Regional Commerce and Growth Association will waive certain fees and taxes for a two-year period. See the accompanying graph on Page 3 of this report.

Surveying the Caribbean, its cobalt-blue waters and breathtaking scenery encapsulate a fantastic vacation destination. New World Airlines hopes to capitalize on this ever-growing hot spot so close to the United States by offering flights directly to some of the best areas within the Caribbean.

Our commitment to this expanding vacation area is based on New World Airlines' well-researched projections of travel trends and airline capacity in the near Atlantic, and our close collaboration with the various governments and tourism officials in each of the five island locations.

New Horizons

Hurricane Hugo did more than damage property when it blew through the Caribbean

Projected Increases In Passengers And Revenue

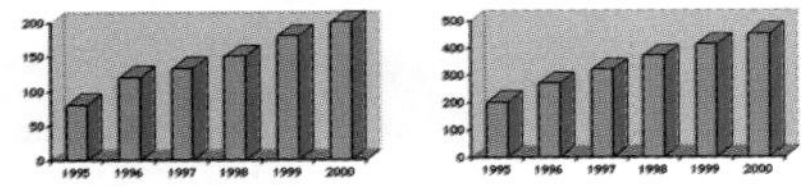

Passengers In Thousands

Revenues In Thousands

and up the coast of the United States in 1989; it virtually devastated Caribbean tourism. Although more than 490 million tourists visited the region during the past several years, it has only been during the past year that regional services and accommodations have been restored to levels that will entice large numbers of tourists to return to the Caribbean. New World Airlines believes our company is uniquely positioned to capitalize on this expanding service area.

Our market research has shown that vacationers prefer to visit places they perceive as exotic while at the same time they choose destinations that ensure a certain cultural "comfort zone." What makes these five locations particularly attractive for our potential customers, who will be predominantly from the United States, is that English is the official language of most and is widely spoken in all. In addition, the historical European influence on the cultures of these particular Caribbean locations makes them a comfortable choice for travelers, while the island location satisfies their desire for a "foreign" experience, romance, excitement, and sun.

Strategic Alliances

Tourism is the largest source of revenue for most countries and territories in the Caribbean region. It is the third largest source of revenue for Puerto Rico and dominates the economy of the U.S. Virgin Islands. Jamaica, the Cayman Islands, and the Bahamas all rely on tourist dollars to drive their economies. As a result, these are governments that are willing to work with us in partnership as we seek ways to expand the region's tourist market. Moreover, they are eager to provide a business environment that is favorable for all parties involved.

Currently, peak travel to the Caribbean occurs during the winter, from December to March. In an effort to expand the tourist season, various cultural institutions in these five target locations are working in collaboration with New World Airlines marketing representatives to heighten awareness of the region's rich cultural heritage. For instance, the world-famous Canals Festival held every June in Puerto Rico is being used as a model to develop other cultural celebrations that will attract visitors.

CONCEPTSREVIEW

Label each of the publication window elements as shown in Figure 4-27.

1 ____

2 ____

3 ____

4 ____

5 ____

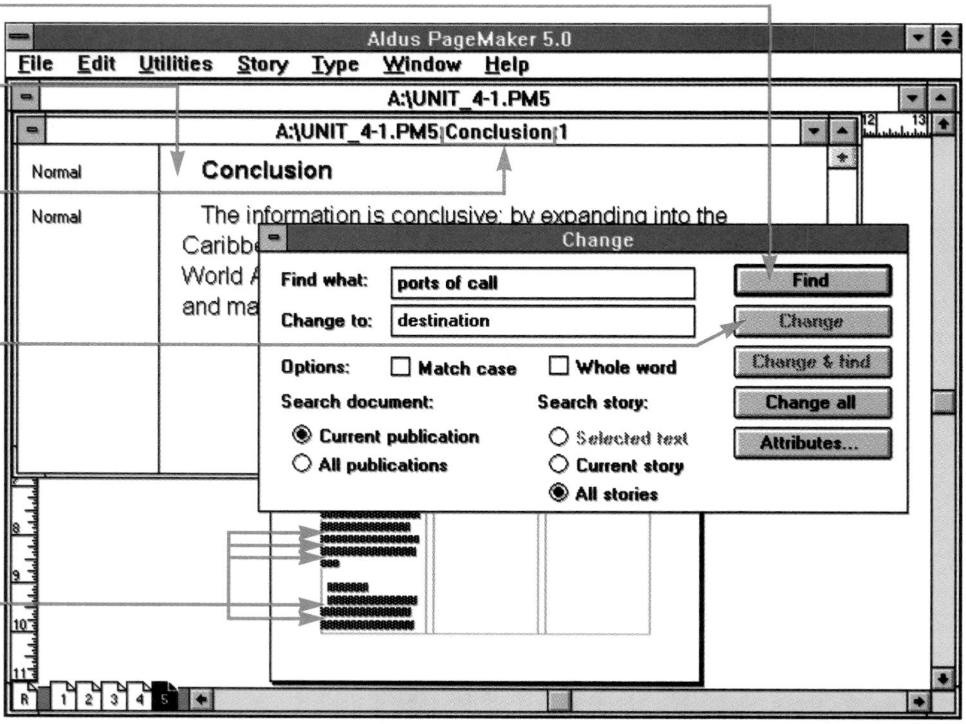

FIGURE 4-27

Match each of the terms with the statement that describes its function.

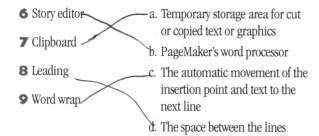

6 Story editor
7 Clipboard
8 Leading
9 Word wrap

a. Temporary storage area for cut or copied text or graphics
b. PageMaker's word processor
c. The automatic movement of the insertion point and text to the next line
d. The space between the lines

Select the best answer from the list of choices.

10 All of the following are advantages of using story editor, except
- a. You can insert large amounts of text easily
- b. You can make multiple changes to a story that spans several text blocks
- c. You can use powerful utilities such as the spell checker and the Find and Change utility
- d. You can see how the story fits on the page

11 When you use the spell checker, you can check only
- a. The current story
- b. All stories in the publication
- c. All stories in the publications currently opened
- d. All of the above

12 An advantage of using the Type specifications dialog box is
- a. You can spell-check your entire document
- b. Multiple formats can be set at one time
- c. You can set paragraph specifications also
- d. Both b and c

13 All of the following are true statements about leading, except
- a. You change the height of the characters when you set leading
- b. Leading is measured in points, the same as text
- c. PageMaker's default for leading is 20% greater than font size
- d. Leading is automatically set when you choose a different font size

14 PageMaker's spell checker allows you to

a. Add new words to the dictionary

b. Check for spelling in all stories in the publication

c. Find a word accidentally typed consecutively

d. All of the above

15 Typing "2" in the Widow control text box means

a. PageMaker will allow two lines together at the end of a page or column

b. PageMaker will allow three lines together at the end of a page or column

c. PageMaker will allow two lines together at the top of a page or column

d. PageMaker will not allow three lines together at the bottom of a page or column

APPLICATIONS REVIEW

1 Place text using story editor.

a. Open the file on your Student Disk called UNIT_4-2.PM5.

b. Open story editor.

c. Type the following text:

Story by Janice Owens

Janice is a business editor for the New Orleans Star. She has closely monitored the large food warehouse chains nationwide because many of these companies are headquartered in New Orleans and the surrounding areas in Louisiana. She can be reached at her office at (504) 564-5433 or through email at Owens@NOSTAR.VCA.

d. Close story editor, then drag-place the story below the headline across the first two columns only.

2 Insert pages.

a. Insert four pages after the current page.

b. Move to page 1, then reflow the text from the first page to the new pages.

3 Edit text in story editor.

a. Return to page 1, then open story editor with the main story open at the beginning.

b. Display the nonprinting symbols.

c. Use the Cut command to remove the entire second paragraph including the paragraph symbol.

d. Position the insertion point at the beginning of the paragraph that begins "Kemper cited ...," then paste the paragraph you just cut.

4 Use the spell checker in story editor.

a. Move the insertion point to the beginning of the story.

b. Open the Spelling dialog box.

c. Check the spelling in the current story.

d. When you are finished, close the Spelling dialog box.

5 Find and change text in a story.

a. Return to the beginning of the story, then open the Change dialog box.

b. Type the text "Kemper Foods" in the Find what text box.

c. Type "Kemper Distributors Inc." in the Change to text box.

d. Find the first occurrence of the text you are searching for.

e. Change the text to the replacement text.

f. Find all occurrences of the text you are searching for and change them to the new text.

g. When you are finished, close the Change dialog box, then close story editor.

6 Format text using type specifications.

a. Select all the text in the main story in the publication.

b. Open the Type specifications dialog box.

c. Change the font to Palatino or Garamond.

d. Change the size to 10 points.

e. Close the Type specifications dialog box.

7 Adjust the leading.

a. Make sure all the text in the main story is still selected.

b. Change the leading to 20.

c. Click at the end of the last text block and continue to flow the text to the next page.

8 Format paragraphs.

a. Make sure all the text in the main story is still selected.

b. Open the Paragraph specifications dialog box.

c. Change all of the paragraph indents to .15".

d. Turn widow control on and define a widow as one line.

9 Remove pages.

a. Open the Remove dialog box.

b. Remove pages 4 and 5.

c. Save your work and print the publication. Close the publication, then exit PageMaker.

INDEPENDENT CHALLENGE 1

As the on-site desktop publisher for Johnson Printing, you need to petition your manager for an upgrade of your computer equipment. You must justify the expense in a report that proves the upgrade will ensure an increase in productivity. The increase in productivity will translate into more time to do more projects, which equals more revenues. You decide to make the report simple and straightforward.

To complete this independent challenge:

1 Create a new four-page publication with three columns. Save the publication as JOHNPROP.

2 Place the file JLOGO.TIF, the Johnson Printing logo, on page 1, which is the cover page. Open a new story in story editor, then type a headline and your name to go on the cover page. Place these elements anywhere on the page. Format this text. Add other design elements to the cover page to make it more eye-catching.

3 The file CHART.TIF on your Student Disk contains a chart showing how much your productivity will be increased if you get the upgraded equipment. Place this chart on page 3. Drag-place it across the two left columns starting in the upper-left corner of the publication. The bottom of the graphic should be at the 4" mark on the vertical ruler.

4 Type a headline on page 2 that corresponds to the computer request for Johnson Printing. Stretch the headline's text block across all three columns. Format the headline.

5 Place the file PROPOSAL.DOC on pages 2 through 4. This text is the same as the text you placed earlier in the unit for New World Airlines. Here, you're using it as dummy text, which is sample text placed in a document strictly for the purposes of design approval. Ignore any leftover text on page 4.

6 Open the dummy text in story editor and write a custom introduction for Johnson Printing. Make the introduction two paragraphs long with at least three sentences per paragraph describing your goals for upgrading the computers at Johnson Printing.

7 Select the introduction you just typed, then open the spell checker and check the spelling in your introduction.

8 Deselect the introduction, move the insertion point to the beginning of the story, then use the Change command to find the phrase "New World Airlines" and change it to "Johnson Printing Company."

9 Exit story editor and evaluate the final design. Is the proposal to text heavy? Do you need to increase the leading? Would a different font be easier to read? Do you need to add more graphics? Make any changes necessary.

10 Save and print your work.

INDEPENDENT CHALLENGE 2

Choose an issue or problem at your school or place of employment that you would like to address. Use PageMaker to create either a proposal for the school's board of trustees, your department, your boss, or the president of your company. Define the issue, then discuss your proposed solution.

To complete this independent challenge:

1 Open a new single-sided publication with at least four pages. Save it as MYPROP.PM5.

2 Create a cover page that includes a short two- to three- paragraph abstract describing the contents of your report. Make sure the cover page is eye-catching.

3 Place the file JLOGO.TIF as a dummy graphic file, or if you have another graphic file you would like to use, use that instead. Consider placing a second graphic in the publication. On your final printout, label these graphics to identify what they would be if you were not using dummy files.

4 Type the text of your proposal in story editor. Use the spell checker to check the spelling. Place the text in the publication. Add the necessary pages to place the entire text or remove empty pages.

5 Format the text of the proposal. Change the font, size, and leading as necessary. Consider double-spacing the text.

6 Add headlines and subheadlines to enhance the overall appearance of your report.

7 Evaluate the final design. Do you need to add any lines to visually separate graphics and text? Do the pages have a consistent design? Is your cover page eye-catching without looking cluttered? Make any necessary changes.

8 Save and print the publication.

UNIT 5

OBJECTIVES

- Plan a newsletter
- Use master pages
- Define styles
- Apply styles
- Create a table of contents
- Edit styles
- Balance columns
- Create drop caps
- Design Workshop: Newsletters

Working WITH MULTIPLE PAGES

Making multiple-page publications cohesive and consistent is one of PageMaker's strengths. In this unit, you will learn about master pages and styles and how they help control repetitive elements and type usage in multiple-page publications. Text and graphics placed on the master pages appear on all pages of your publication. Styles enhance productivity by quickly applying set attributes to paragraphs and by modifying a style to change its appearance throughout the publication. Also, you will learn about features designed to improve the layout of your publication. ▶ In this unit, Joe Martin uses PageMaker to enhance the final appearance of the New World Airlines quarterly frequent flyer newsletter. ▶

Planning a newsletter

Newsletters are one of the most common types of publications produced using PageMaker. The challenge is to create a newsletter so it will capture the reader's attention. Before creating your newsletter in PageMaker, take time to determine the overall layout of your newsletter. ▶ Joe needs to design *Wings*, the New World Airlines frequent flyer newsletter. The newsletter is on letter-size paper and is four pages long. Joe takes the following points into consideration as he plans the layout:

STEPS

1. **Include a flag at the top of the newsletter**
   The **masthead**, **nameplate**, or **flag**, is the graphical element that serves as your identification and gives a purpose to your newsletter. The flag includes the name of the newsletter and the date of the publication. It might also include the volume number, the company name or the source of the newsletter, and other identifications. Be careful not to crowd the area with too much information. Joe creates a flag using a drawing application, and he places it at the top of page 1.
2. **Focus the attention of the reader to the main story on each page**
   The reader should immediately know which story is the most important story on each page. Creating a main focus gives readers a place to begin reading the pages of the newsletter. The headline for the main story can be larger than other headlines on the page. Generally, the importance of stories ranks from the top left to the bottom right because of the natural way we read.The story about bonuses on special trips is the most important story on page 4, so Joe places it on the page's upper left corner.
3. **Use graphics to show the information's importance**
   Graphics capture the reader's attention and motivate him or her to read the story. Generally, graphics associated with the main story are larger. Smaller stories might not even contain graphics. Joe designs the first three pages of the newsletter to contain many graphics, especially pages 2 and 3, which represent a **spread**, or two facing pages that can work together in one design package.
4. **Use shading, lines, or white space to break up text**
   You don't want to congest your newsletter by having stories run into each other. Try to include only one or two stories on a page for a newsletter of this size. However, there might be times when you have many short stories on a page; in these cases, use shading or lines to separate the stories. Joe uses page 4 of the newsletter as a "catch-all" for the shorter stories and plans to use shading on one of the stories to help it stand out from the other three stories on the page.
5. **Select appropriate fonts for headlines and body text**
   Like photos and graphics, the headline must invite your audience to read the story. In general, you should design headlines in a bold font no smaller than 18 points. Headlines compete for attention on the page, so you need to visually separate them from the page's other design elements. Body text is usually a serif font 10 to 12 points in size. Joe plans to use a mix of styles for headlines and use 12-point Times New Roman for body text.
6. **Include a preview section on the first page of the newsletter**
   A preview section lets the reader know what to expect inside. This serves as a teaser to get your readers to open the newsletter and read the stories. Joe plans a preview section at the bottom of the first page.

FIGURE 5-1: Joe's sketch of his newsletter

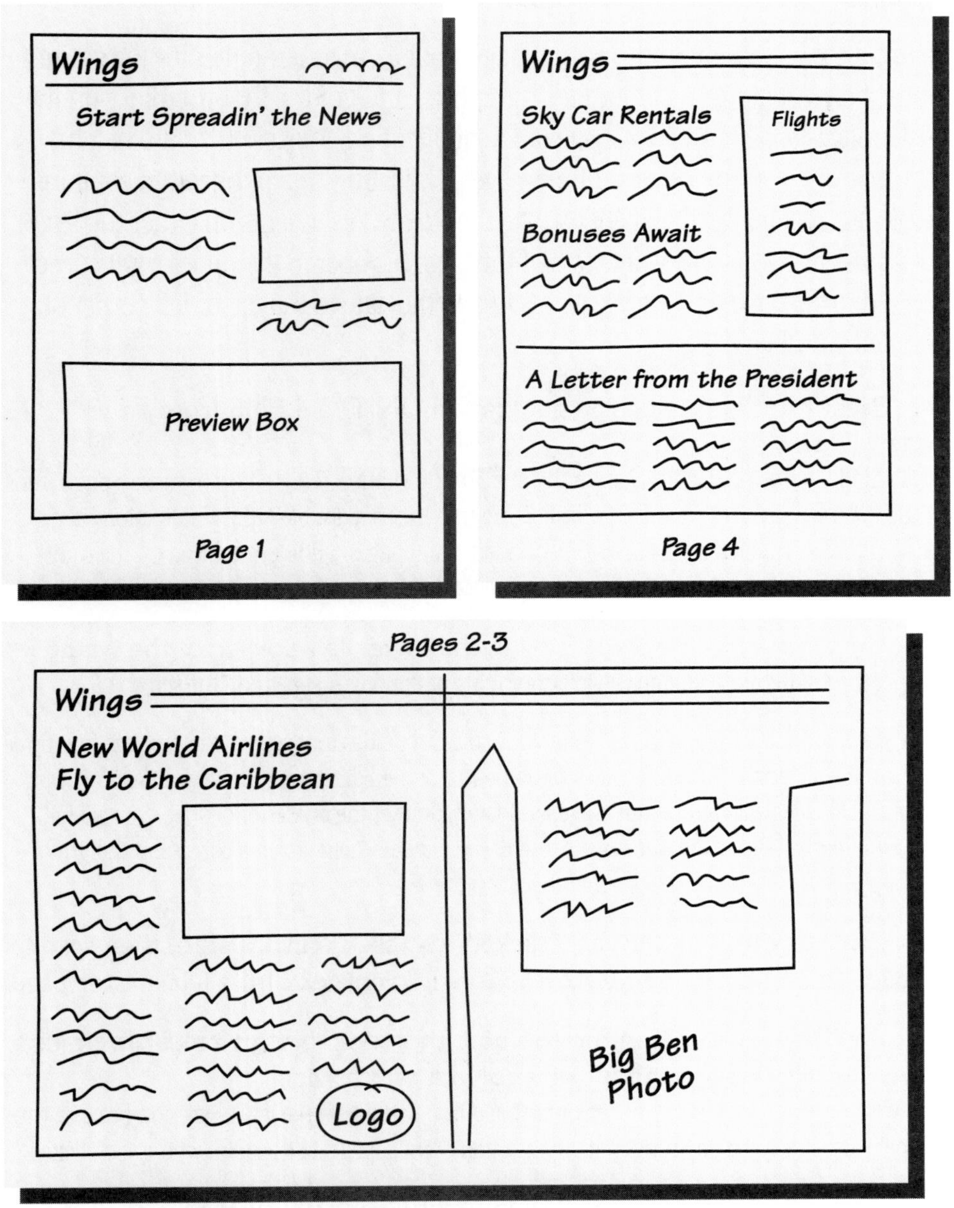

DESIGN TIP

Too many fonts distract the reader. A small newsletter should contain only two fonts, one for headlines and one for body text. Use type styles (bold, italic, etc.) to create contrast without changing the font.

Using master pages

Master pages are non-printing pages that serve as templates for the entire publication. All items, including text, graphics, and guides, that you place on the master pages appear on every page of the publication. Master pages are helpful when you are working on a multiple-page publication. If a publication contains double-sided pages, you can choose whether to place elements on either the left or right master page. ▶ Joe wants to add the page number to the upper-right corner of all even-numbered pages. He wants to add the date to the upper-left corner of each odd-numbered page.

STEPS

1 **Start PageMaker and open the publication UNIT_5-1.PM5 from your Student Disk**
Pages 2 and 3 of the newsletter open in the publication window. There are two master page icons in the lower-left corner of the window indicating that this is a double-sided publication. Items placed on the left master page appear only on left-hand pages, and items placed on the right master page appear on right-hand pages.

2 **Click the master page icon [L|R] in the lower-left corner of the window [L|R] becomes highlighted, and the left and right master pages appear on the screen**

See Figure 5-2. The pages are blank, except for column guides that separate each page into three columns. Joe added the column guides when he first started designing the newsletter. This way, the column guides appear on every page, and Joe had to set the guides only once. He also had placed the *Wings* logo and a line for the tops of the pages to help create a consistent design for each page.

3 **Click Layout on the menu bar, click View, click Actual size, then scroll the page to move the view to the upper-right corner of the left master page**

4 **Click the Text tool [A] in the toolbox, then drag-place a text block just above the third column about one column-width wide**
You have created a text block at the top of the page. You cannot see the text block now because you have not placed or typed anything in it. An insertion point appears at the point where you clicked.

5 **Type Page, press [Spacebar], then press [Shift][Ctrl][3]**
See Figure 5-3. "Page LM" appears at the insertion point. LM is the page number symbol for the left master page.

6 **Click Type on the menu bar, click Alignment, then click Align right**
The text becomes right-aligned in the text block.

7 **If your text block extends beyond the right margin, drag the text block to the left until the right edges of the text block are just touching the right margin guide**
See the continuation of this lesson to add the publication date to the right master page.

FIGURE 5-2: Elements placed on the master pages

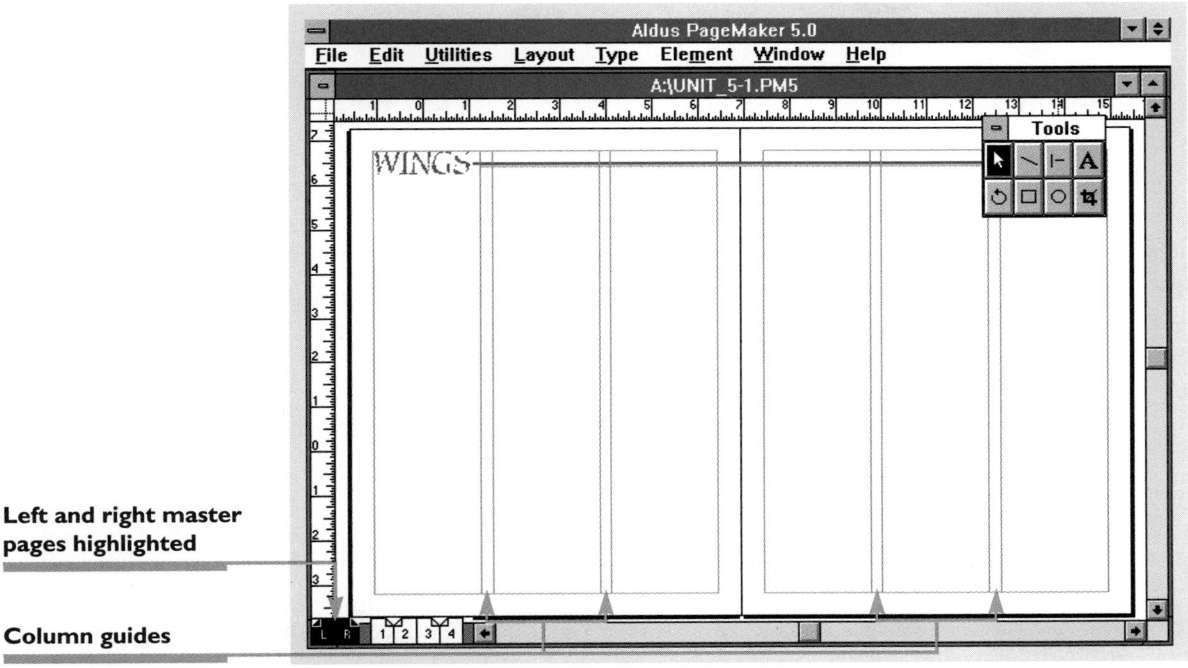

FIGURE 5-3: Page number symbol on left master page

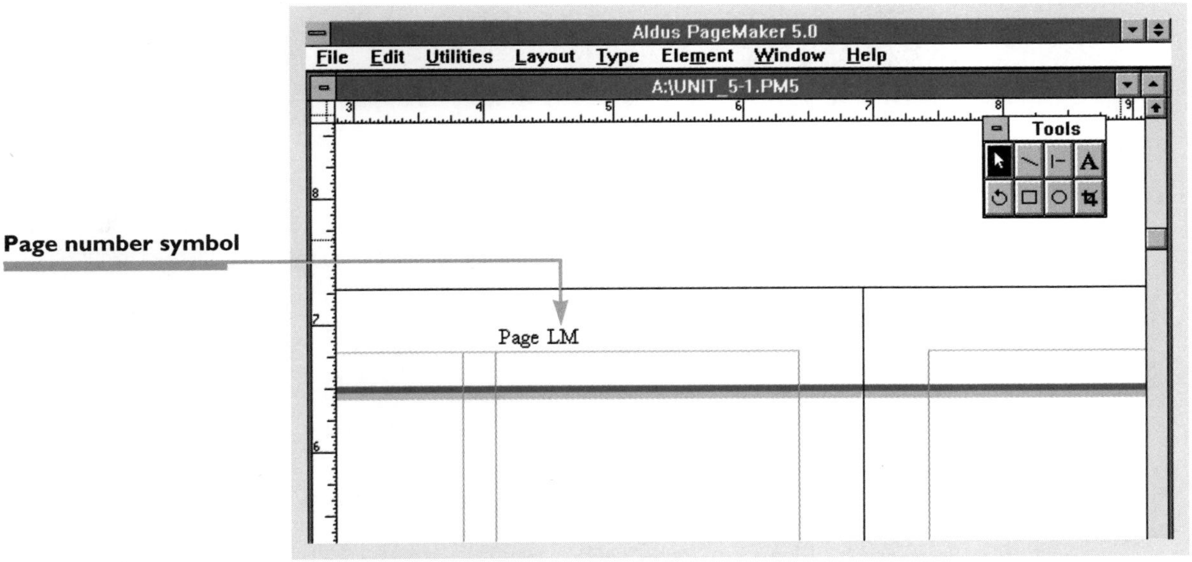

TROUBLE?

Master pages cannot be deleted, but you can delete any element placed on the master pages as you would on a normal page.

Using master pages, continued

For more information on master pages, see the related topic "Partially displaying master page items." ▶ Joe needs to add the publication date to the right master page.

STEPS

8 **Click the right arrow in the horizontal scroll bar until the upper-left corner of the right master page appears in the publication window**
You should see the top left corner of the right master page.

9 **Drag-place a text block about one column-width wide above the first column on the right master page**

10 **Type September 25, 1996**
Make sure the text block doesn't start in the left margin. If necessary, drag the text block to the right until the left edge of the text block aligns with the left margin guide. Also make sure that the two text blocks on the two master pages are aligned. See Figure 5-4 for reference.

11 **Click the page 2 and 3 page icon**

12 **Position the mouse pointer near the top of the page where pages 2 and 3 intersect, then right-click**
See Figure 5-5. The information you typed on the master pages appears on these pages. The number 2 replaces the LM page number symbol.

13 **Click the page 1 page icon**
Page 1 appears in the publication window. The text Joe typed on the master pages appears on all pages of the publication, but Joe doesn't want the date and Wings logo and line to appear above the flag on page 1, so he hides it using the Display master items command on the Layout menu.

14 **Click Layout on the menu bar, then click Display master items**
This feature hides the elements you add to the master pages. When Display master items is checked (the default), all items on the master page appear on the page in the publication window. When Display master items is unchecked, the master page items disappear from view. Because you used this command with page 1 selected, only page 1 does not display the master page items. The information you saw on pages 2 and 3 remains on those pages.

15 **Save the publication**

FIGURE 5-4: Aligned items on master pages

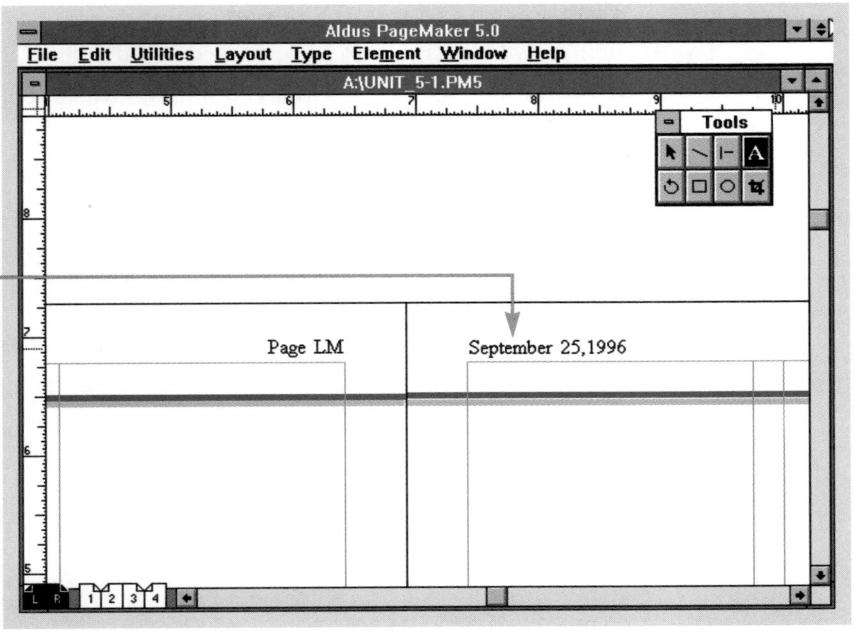

Date appears on right master page

FIGURE 5-5: Page 2 page number and date

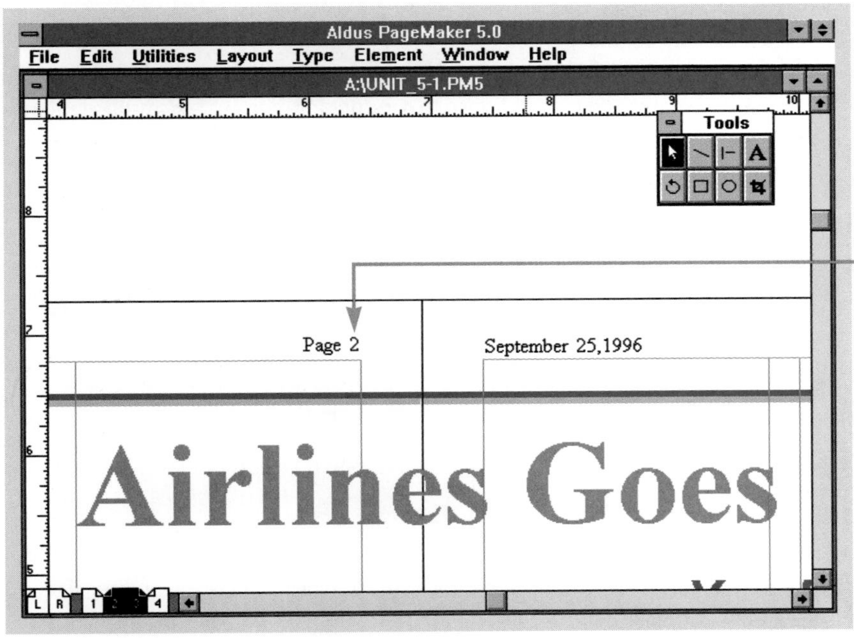

Page number replaces symbol

Partially displaying master page items

Sometimes you might want to hide certain elements from a master page. For example, you might want to display a graphic but not a page number. To hide the unwanted elements, draw a box around the element, click Element on the menu bar, click Fill, then click Paper. You might have to remove the line as well, depending on your default line weight.

QUICK TIP

The Display master items command affects both facing pages in a two-page spread.

TROUBLE?

Elements placed on master pages always lie behind all other layers in the publication window.

Defining styles

You define styles using the Define styles command on the Type menu. **Styles** are sets of formatting instructions that you name, save, and apply to paragraphs. Styles let you quickly apply formatting instructions to text with a simple click on the Styles palette. Using styles saves time and consistently formats text throughout a multiple-page publication. After you define styles, the style names appear in the Styles palette. You can also edit styles at any time. Once you edit a style, all occurrences of the style in the open publication are automatically updated with the new formatting instructions. For more information on PageMaker styles, see the related topic "PageMaker's default styles." ▶ Joe has already created styles for the headlines and the body text of the newsletter. Now he needs to create a style for the cutlines. **Cutlines** are text describing photos or graphics in a newsletter.

STEPS

1. **Click the page 4 page icon**

2. **Click Window on the menu bar, then click Style palette**
   The Styles palette appears with the styles that Joe already created listed. Like the toolbox, the Styles palette is a floating palette. You can move it anywhere around the screen and resize it.

3. **Click anywhere within the headline about SkyCar rentals on page 4**
   The style Reg. Headline is highlighted in the Styles palette. This style defines the text as Arial, 24 points, bold, left justified, with auto leading. **Justified** means that the space between characters will be adjusted so that the text is aligned to a particular margin. Left-justified aligns the text along the left margin. **Leading** is the space between characters. Autoleading means that PageMaker adjusts the spacing automatically.

4. **Click anywhere in the story below the headline**
   The style Body text is highlighted in the Styles palette. This style is defined as Times New Roman, 11 points, 12-point leading, justified, first indent at 1 pica, and auto hyphenation. Picas are a unit of measurement that you will learn more about in Unit 6. Autohyphenation means that PageMaker will hyphenate words automatically.

5. **Click in the toolbox**
   The [No style] option is highlighted in the Styles palette because no text is presently selected.

6. **Click Type on the menu bar, then click Define styles**
   The Define styles dialog box opens. See Figure 5-6. Because the insertion point was in the body text when you opened the Define styles dialog box, [Selection] appears at the top of the style list. Joe continues defining the Cutline style by selecting character and paragraph formats.

7. **Click New**
   The Edit style dialog box opens with the insertion point in the Name text box. Each of the four buttons on the right side of the dialog box opens the corresponding dialog box. You set specifications in each of these dialog boxes for the style you are creating. Joe decides to name the new style Cutline.

8. **Type Cutline in the Name text box**
   See Figure 5-7. This gives a name to your new style. See the continuation of this lesson to finish defining the cutline style.

FIGURE 5-6: Define styles dialog box

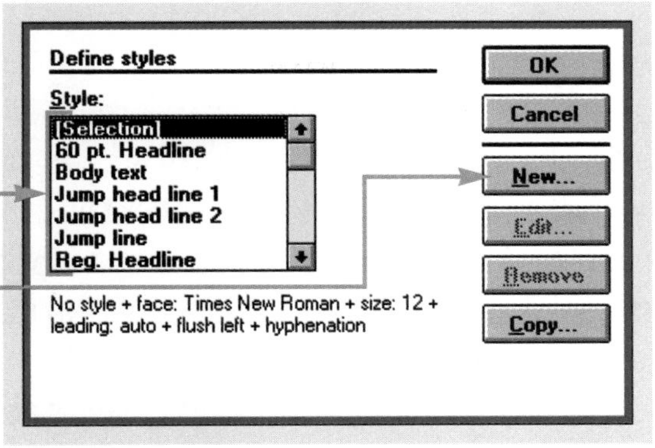

List of styles

Click to create a new style

FIGURE 5-7: Edit style dialog box

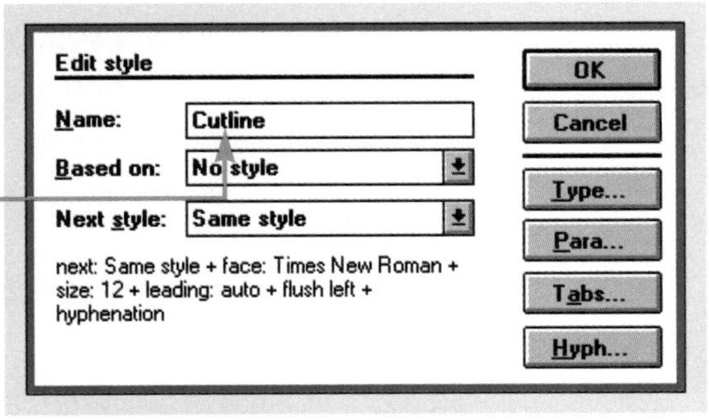

New style name

PageMaker's default styles

When you open a new publication, a set of default styles already exists. See Table 5-1 for a description of the default styles. The style description includes the style that it is based on, which style will be applied to the next paragraph, and all of the formatting instructions to be applied by the style. The "+" (plus sign) signifies each formatting instruction that you add to the style. You can modify these styles and their names to suit your publication or remove them from the styles list and start a new list.

TABLE 5-1: PageMaker's default styles

STYLE NAME	DESCRIPTION
[Selection]	No style + face: Times New Roman + size: 12 + leading: auto + flush left + hyphenation
Body text	next: Same style + face: Times New Roman + size: 12 + leading: auto + flush left + first indent: 0.333 + hyphenation
Caption	next: Same style + face: Times New Roman + italic + size: 10 + leading: auto + flush left
Hanging indent	next: Same style + face: Times New Roman + size: 12 + leading: auto + flush left + left indent: 0.167 + first indent: -0.167 + hyphenation
Headline	next: Same style + face: Times New Roman + bold + size: 30 + leading: auto + flush left + incl TOC
Subhead 1	Headline + next: Same style + size: 18
Subhead 2	Subhead 1 + next: Same style + size: 12

Defining styles, continued

The Based on list box lets you select a style to base your new style upon. For example, the Reg. Headline used for headlines on page 4 is based on the 60-point Headline style. When you select a style from the Based on list box, PageMaker copies the formatting attributes for the new style. You then can modify these attributes. The Next style list box lets you select the style that applies to the next paragraph in a story if that paragraph does not already have a style. The Cutline style is based on the "No style" selection from the Style palette. PageMaker assigns the formatting characteristics from the Selection default. PageMaker also provides predesigned templates which already have the style defined for you. See the related topic "Using PageMaker's predesigned templates" for more information. ▶ Joe continues defining the Cutline style by selecting character and paragraph formats.

STEPS

9 Click **Type**
The Type specifications dialog box opens.

10 Click the **Font list arrow**, then click **Arial**

11 Type **10** in the Size text box

12 Click the **Italic check box** in the Type style section, then click **OK**

13 Click **Para**
The Paragraph specifications dialog box opens. Because some of the cutlines are more than one line long, Joe wants the Cutline style to be justified.

14 Click the **Alignment list arrow**, click **Justify**, then click **OK**
The Paragraph specifications dialog box closes. The description of the style at the bottom of the dialog box reflects the changes you made. The Justify command forces text to align between both the right and left margins. See Figure 5-8.

15 Click **OK** in the Edit style dialog box
The Edit style dialog box closes. The new Cutline style name is highlighted in the Style list box in the Define styles dialog box.

16 Click **OK** to close the Define styles dialog box
You return to the publication window. Cutline has been added to the Styles palette.

FIGURE 5-8: Edit style dialog box after Cutline style is defined

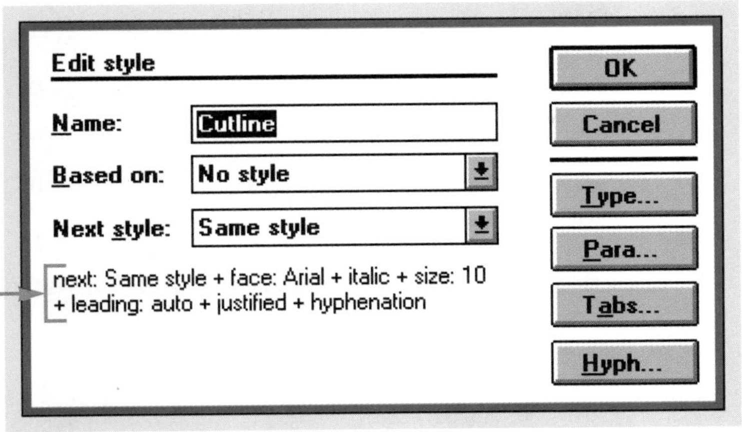

Description of Cutline style

Using PageMaker's predesigned templates

To save you time and energy, you can chose one of PageMaker's predesigned templates as a starting point for creating your own publications. You can choose from two different newsletter templates. These newsletter templates have dummy text and graphics laid out on the page which you replace with your own text and graphic objects. The templates also include styles for headlines, body text, titles and cutline captions. Other publications that you can create from predesigned templates include: mailing labels, brochures, calendars, labels or linings for cassettes, compact disks, or video tapes, envelopes, fax cover sheets, invoices, manuals or purchase orders. To open a predesigned template, click Utilities on the menu bar, click Aldus Additions, then click Open template. After you choose your desired template rename the new untitled file to leave the original template unchanged. You could also create your own template by clicking the Template radio in Save as dialog box.

QUICK TIP

To access the Define styles dialog box quickly, press [Ctrl][3].

Applying styles

Once you've defined a style, you need to apply it to the text. To apply a style, you select the characters or paragraph you want to format, then click the style name in the Styles palette. For more information on styles, see the related topic "Formatting text after applying a style." ▶ Joe applies his new Cutline style to the cutlines in the newsletter.

STEPS

1. **Click the page 2 and 3 page icon, then scroll to fit the cutline below the photo on page 2**
   See Figure 5-9.

2. **Click the Text tool in the toolbox, then click anywhere within the cutline text block**
   The style won't be applied if you use the Pointer tool to select the text block; the text must be selected or the insertion point must be in the paragraph you are applying the style to. Notice "[No style]" is selected in the Styles palette.

3. **Click Cutline in the Styles palette,**
   The cutline text changes to match all the specifications you defined earlier. See Figure 5-10.

4. **Click the page 1 page icon**
   Page 1 appears in the publication window.

5. **Click anywhere within the cutline under the photo, right-click to change the view to Actual size, then click Cutline in the Styles palette**
   The text changes to conform to the Cutline style.

FIGURE 5-9: Text before Cutline style is applied

New style in Style palette

Cutline text block

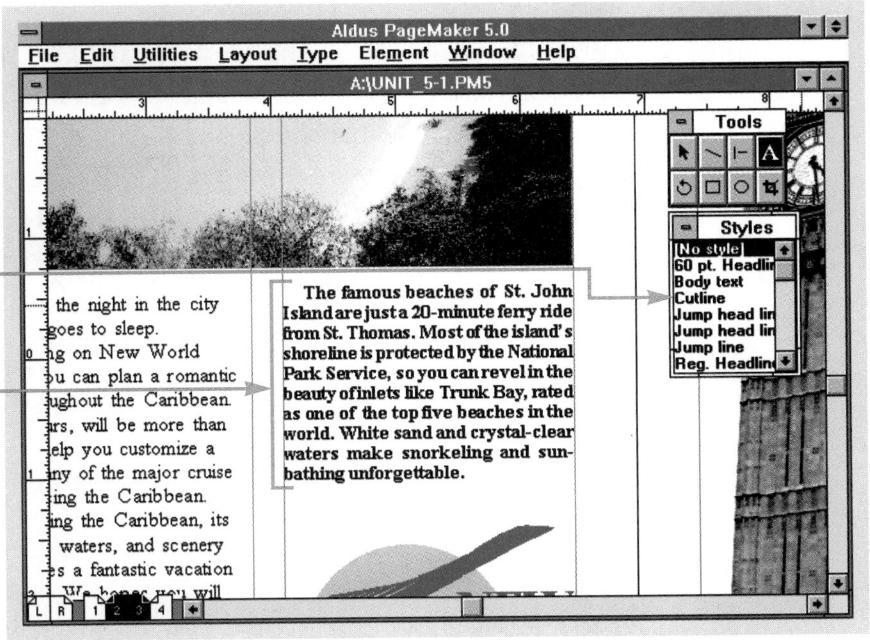

FIGURE 5-10: Text after Cutline style is applied

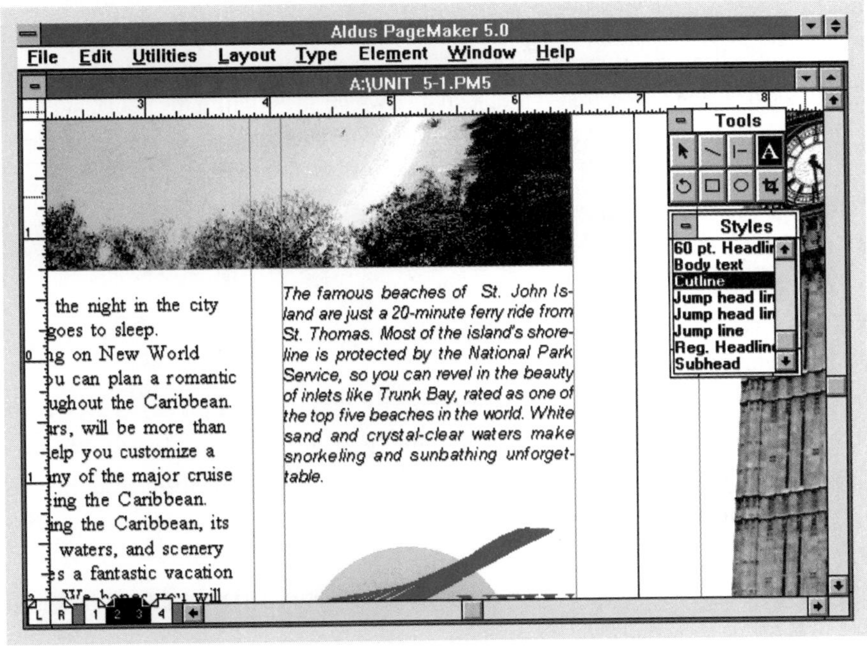

Formatting text after applying a style

You can edit text after applying a style using commands available on the Type menu. Any changes you make to a selected range of text affect only that text. When you further format text with an applied style, a plus sign (+) appears behind the name of the style in the Styles palette. This tells you that additional formatting changes have been made to the style after it was originally applied to that text.

TROUBLE?

If you try to apply a style and the text you want to format does not change, make sure you have selected all the characters for a character style or that the insertion point is in the paragraph for a paragraph style before you apply the style.

Creating a table of contents

PageMaker can automatically generate a table of contents (TOC) for your publication. You select styles or individual paragraphs for the TOC and use the Create TOC command on the Utilities menu. PageMaker then searches for the paragraphs you selected for the TOC and creates a new story, the TOC, to be placed in your publication. When you place this new story, PageMaker creates new TOC styles and adds them to the Styles palette. For more information on creating a TOC, see the related topic "Marking individual paragraphs to be included in a TOC." ▶ Joe uses the Create TOC command for the preview section on the first page of the newsletter.

STEPS

1. **Click Layout on the menu bar, click View, click 50% size, then scroll down to the bottom half of the page**
2. **Click Type on the menu bar, then click Define styles**
   The Define styles dialog box opens.
3. **Click Reg. Headline in the Style list box, then click Edit**
   The Edit style dialog box opens. Joe needs to select the styles to be included in the table of contents. He decides to include the Reg. Headline style; that way every story with a headline will appear in the TOC.
4. **Click Para..., click the Include in table of contents check box, then click OK three times**
   Choosing Paragraph tells PageMaker what page the story appears on in the publication. The Define styles dialog box closes. Now that you've identified which styles within the publication will appear in the TOC, Joe is ready to use the Create TOC command to generate the TOC and then place it on page 1.
5. **Click Utilities on the menu bar, then click Create TOC**
   See Figure 5-11. The Create table of contents dialog box opens. Note that the default title for a TOC is "Contents," which is selected automatically when you open the dialog box.
6. **Type In This Issue... in the Title text box**
   Don't forget to type the ellipsis (...).
7. **In the Format section, click the Page number after entry radio button**
   Joe wants the page number to appear after every headline.
8. **Make sure "^T" appears in the Between entry and page number text box**
   This code (^T) tells PageMaker to insert a tab between the text and page number.
9. **Click OK**
   The dialog box closes and PageMaker generates the table of contents. The manual text-flow icon appears. Now Joe needs to place the text in the preview section.
10. **Drag-place the manual text-flow icon from the upper-left corner of the blue box to the lower-right corner of the blue box**
    See Figure 5-12. If the page numbers wrap to the next line, widen the text box as necessary. Drag down the page if you want to see the entire TOC. The new text is a table of contents with "In This Issue" as the title. If you scroll through the Styles palette, you'll notice PageMaker created two new styles based on the Reg. Headline style called TOC Reg. Headline and TOC title. Next, Joe edits the styles.

FIGURE 5-11: Create table of contents dialog box

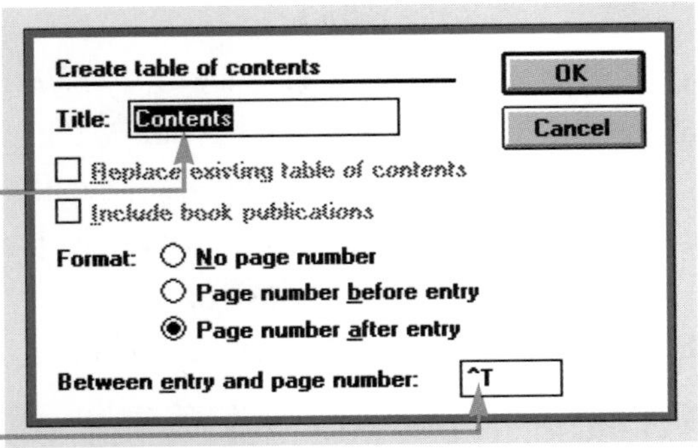

Title will appear in publication

Code indicates tab

FIGURE 5-12: Table of contents placed on page 1

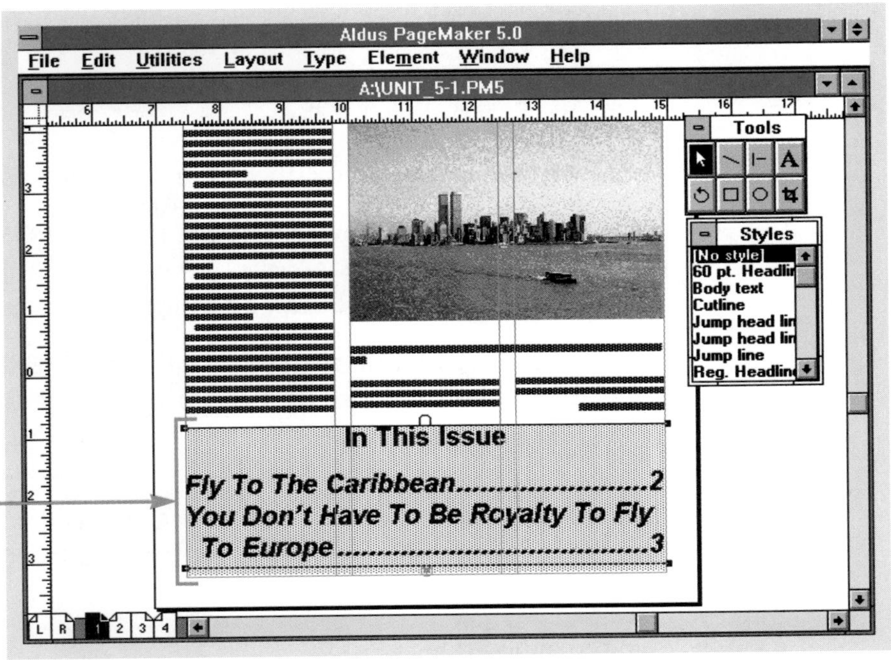

Not all of the text will fit in the preview section

Marking individual paragraphs to be included in a TOC

You can add more styles or select individual paragraphs to include more items within the table of contents. To add an individual paragraph to the table of contents, click the Text tool [A] within the paragraph you want included, click Type on the menu bar, then click Paragraph. The Paragraph specifications dialog box opens. Click the Include in table of contents check box, then click OK. Click the Create TOC command on the Utilities menu, then click OK in the Create table of contents dialog box to regenerate the TOC with the new paragraph.

TROUBLE?

Don't worry if the font displayed on your computer is different than the one in Figure 5-12. ■

Editing styles

After you define a style, you can change it at any time. When you edit a style definition in the Define and Edit styles dialog boxes, PageMaker automatically updates all occurrences of the style in the open publication. You don't have to select every paragraph that is formatted with that style. For more information on styles, see the related topic "Copying styles from another PageMaker publication."

▶ Joe wants to edit the styles PageMaker created when it generated the TOC.

STEPS

1. **Click Type on the menu bar, then click Define styles**
   The Define styles dialog box opens.
2. **Click TOC title in the Style list box, then click Edit**
   The Edit style dialog box opens. Joe wants the title to be larger and to stand out more.
3. **Click Type**
   The Type specifications dialog box opens.
4. **Type 40 in the Size text box, then type 36 in the Leading text box**
5. **Click the Color list arrow, click Red, then click OK twice**
   The Type specifications and Edit style dialog boxes close, and TOC title is highlighted in the Styles list box. The description of the style has changed to reflect the changes you made.
6. **Click TOC Reg. Headline in the list, then click Edit**
   Joe wants to decrease the size of the TOC entries to make them fit within the preview section.
7. **Click Type**
8. **Type 20 in the Size text box, then click OK three times**
   The dialog boxes close. Notice that the table of contents headline and references reflect the changes you made. See Figure 5-13.
9. **Save the publication**

FIGURE 5-13: Edited styles

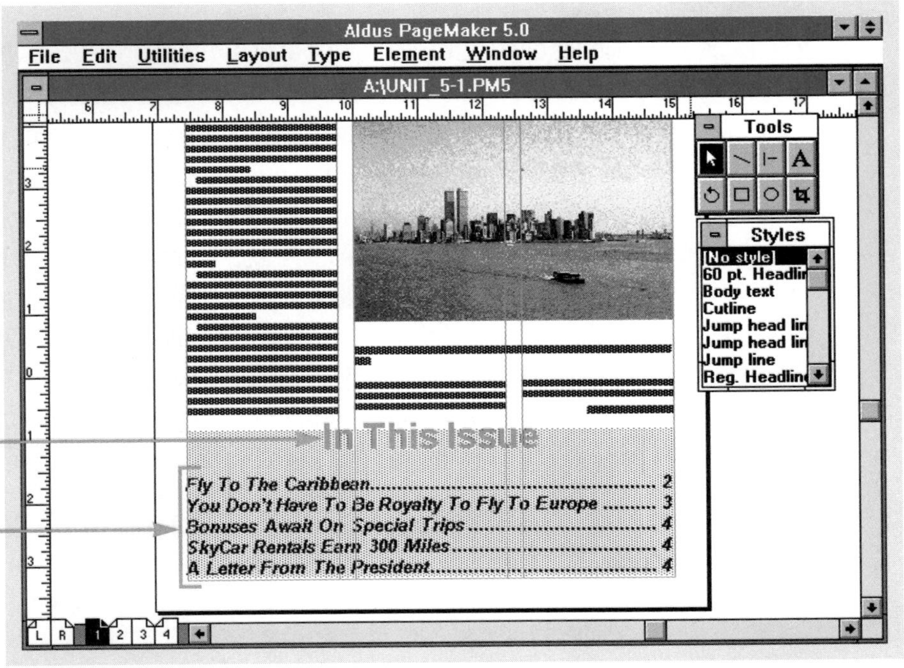

Title is larger and more eye-catching

All the text fits within the preview section

Copying styles from another PageMaker publication

Each publication has its own set of styles. You can add styles from another PageMaker publication to the publication you are working on. Open the Define styles dialog box, then click Copy. The Copy styles dialog box opens as shown in Figure 5-14. Select the filename of the publication you want to copy the style from, then click OK to close the Define Styles dialog box. PageMaker imports the styles. If the message "Copy over existing files?" appears, note that PageMaker will write over styles with the same name when you copy styles from another publication.

Type filename of publication you want to copy styles from

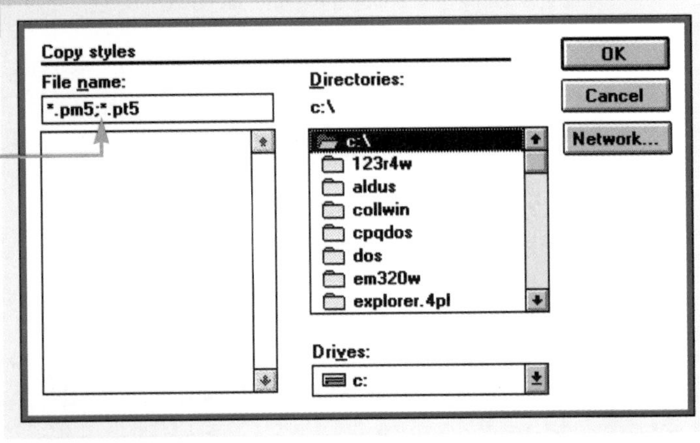

FIGURE 5-14: Copy styles dialog box

QUICK TIP

To open the Edit style dialog box quickly, press and hold [Ctrl] then click the name of the style you want to edit on the Styles palette.

Balancing columns

Newsletter or magazine designs appear more organized when all columns are **balanced**, or the same length. PageMaker contains a feature called **Balance columns** that lets you easily align the tops or bottoms of text blocks threaded in a story on a single page or facing pages. Balance columns is an Aldus Addition. For more information on Aldus Additions, see the related topic "Aldus Additions." When you use Balance columns, PageMaker calculates the average length of each text block and resizes them to equal lengths across the number of columns they span. Balancing columns manually usually requires a few minutes worth of moving windowshade handles and text blocks. Using the Balance columns feature, PageMaker performs the calculations within seconds. ▶ Joe improves the layout of his newsletter by balancing the text blocks of a story he places on page 4.

STEPS

1. **Click the page 4 page icon, click Layout on the menu bar, click View, click 75% size, then use the scroll bars and arrows to center the lower third of the page in the publication window**
   Page 4 appears in the publication window.
2. **Click File on the menu bar, click Place, select the file UNIT_5-2.DOC from your Student Disk, then click OK**
3. **Click in the first column under the headline "Letter From The President"**
   The company president's letter flows into the first column. The triangle windowshade indicates more text needs to be placed.
4. **Click, press and hold [Shift], click in the second column under the headline, click in the third column to place the rest of the story, then release [Shift]**
   See Figure 5-15. The story contains three text blocks of uneven lengths across three columns. Joe wants to balance these columns to make the president's letter appear as one "unit" on the page.
5. **Click the Pointer tool, then drag the pointer to form a selection marquee around the three text blocks you just placed to select all three text blocks**
   If you have trouble dragging the selection marquee, see the related topic "Selecting a group of objects" in Unit 2.
6. **Click Utilities on the menu bar, click Aldus Additions, then click Balance columns**
   The Balance columns dialog box opens, as shown in Figure 5-16. Joe wants to align the columns at the bottom rather than the top. This means PageMaker realigns the text blocks so their bottom lines are even across all three columns.
7. **Click the Balance Column Top icon in the Alignment section of the dialog box**
   Now Joe needs to decide where to place the lines of text that cannot be divided equally among the selected text blocks. He decides to have the extra lines, if any, added to the left column.
8. **Click the Balance Column Left icon in the Add leftover lines section of the dialog box**
9. **Click OK to close the Balance columns dialog box, then click anywhere outside the page to deselect the text blocks**
   See Figure 5-17. The columns are now balanced.

FIGURE 5-15: Columns before balancing

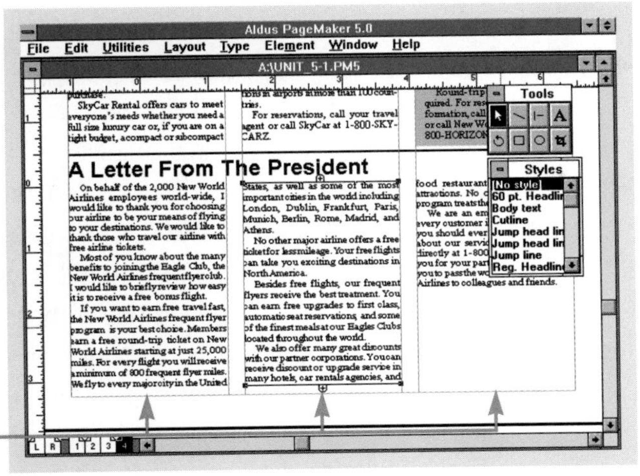

Three uneven text blocks

FIGURE 5-16: Balance columns dialog box

Balance Column Top icon

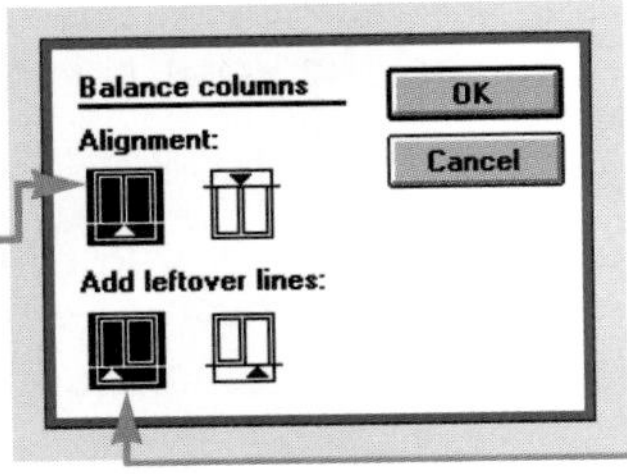

Balance Column Left icon

FIGURE 5-17: Columns after balancing

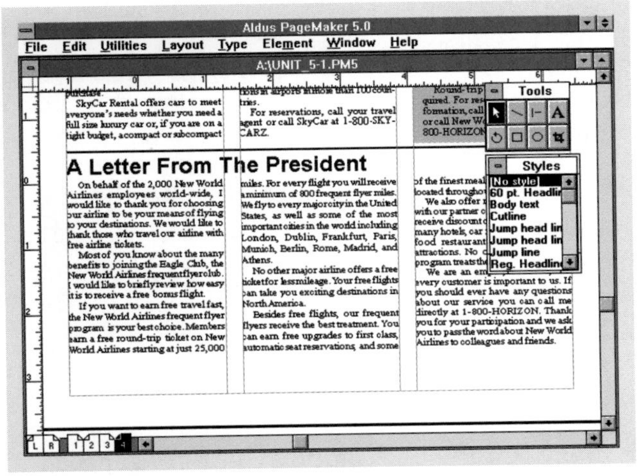

Aldus Additions

Aldus Additions provide customized features to automate repetitive or complex publishing tasks. PageMaker 5.0 is shipped with 24 Additions. Third-party vendors also supply Additions to enhance PageMaker. All of the Additions are listed in the Aldus Additions submenu on the Utilities menu. PageMaker separates Additions into three categories: text Additions, page layout Additions, and color and printing Additions. The text Additions can create drop caps and add bullets and numbering for lists. The Additions for page layout can balance columns and sort pages. The Additions for color and printing allow you to define printer styles, build booklets, and create keylines. You will learn about most of the Aldus Additions provided by PageMaker in this book.

TROUBLE?

The Aldus Additions must be installed in order to use them. They install automatically with a standard installation of PageMaker.

Creating drop caps

Many newsletters use a design feature called a drop cap. A **drop cap** is the first letter in a story that is enlarged and lowered so the top of the letter is even with the first line of text, and the base of the letter drops next to the rest of the paragraph. You determine the size of the drop cap based on how many lines you want it to descend into the paragraph. The Drop Cap command is an Aldus Addition. For more information on improving the appearance of the stories in your newsletter, see the related topic "Creating pull quotes." Joe wants to add a drop cap to the first paragraph of the page 1 story to help the story stand out on the page.

STEPS

1 Click the **page 1 page icon**, click **Layout** on the menu bar, click **View**, then click **Actual size**

2 Scroll to center the first paragraph of the story in the publication window

3 Click the **Text tool** in the toolbox, then click anywhere within the first paragraph

4 Click **Utilities** on the menu bar, click **Aldus Additions**, then click **Drop cap**
See Figure 5-18. The Drop cap dialog box opens. Joe wants the drop cap to descend four lines into the paragraph.

5 Type **4** in the Size text box, then click **Apply**
The Apply button previews the drop cap action before you close the dialog box. A drop cap four lines appears next to the first paragraph. Joe decides to accept this addition by closing the dialog box.

6 Click **Close**
The dialog box closes. See Figure 5-19.

7 Save then print the publication and exit PageMaker

FIGURE 5-18: Drop cap dialog box

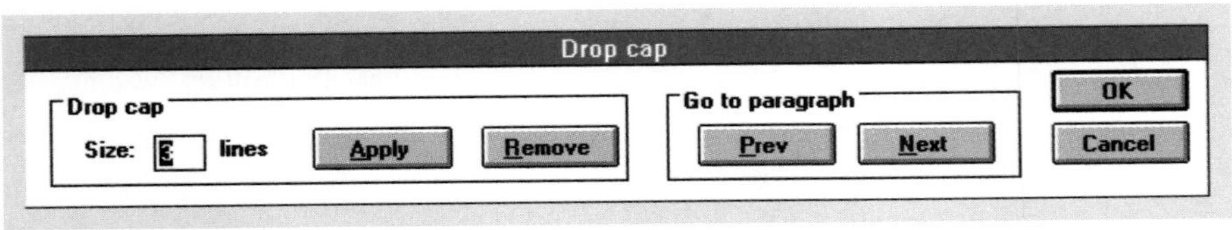

FIGURE 5-19: Drop cap placed in first paragraph

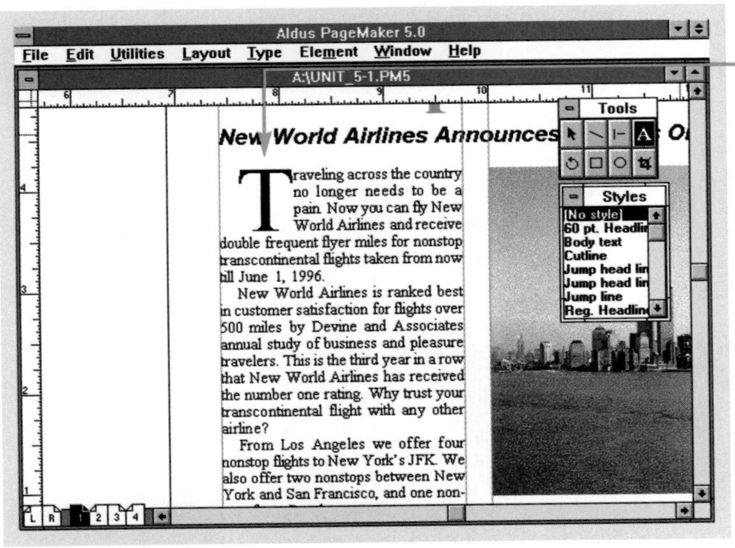

Drop cap is 4 lines tall

Creating pull quotes

A pull quote is a small amount of text enlarged within a story to catch the reader's attention. To create pull quotes, click the text tool in the text that you want to use for the pull quote, click Type on the menu bar, click Paragraph, then click Rules. The Rules dialog box opens allowing you to add a line above and below a specified paragraph of text. The rule lines will set off the text from the rest of the story. All you need to do then is increase the size of text in the paragraph. See Figure 5-20. Using lines attached to a paragraph of text is beneficial because the lines stay attatched to the paragraph and flow with that paragraph when the text is modified.

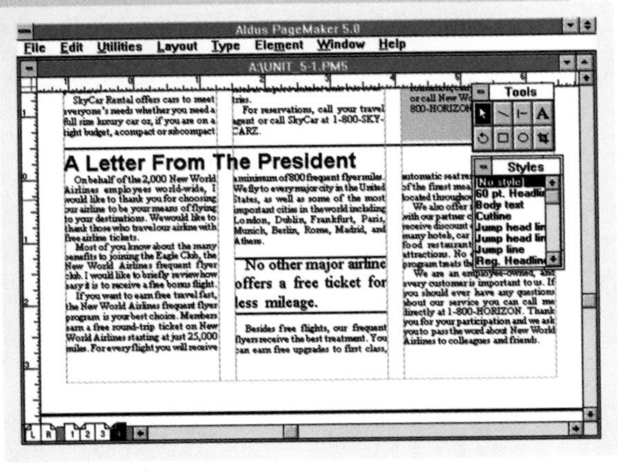

FIGURE 5-20

TROUBLE?

If you have a blank line between paragraphs or a drop cap that runs into the paragraph that follows, the paragraphs containing the drop cap has fewer lines than you specified in the Drop cap dialog box.■

Design Workshop: Newsletters

Although most of this newsletter was completed when you opened the document, you learned what is required to create a newsletter. This unit provided the lessons you needed to learn how to work with master pages and defining styles. ▶ Before creating your newsletter, you must carefully plan your overall layout to capture your reader's attention and draw the reader's eye to the main story. ▶ Pages 1 and 4 of the redesigned *Wings* newsletter for New World Airlines' frequent flyers are shown in Figure 5-21. Let's review Joe's design.

STEPS

1 **Does the newsletter's flag stand out?**
The newsletter's flag serves as a graphic that quickly identifies the newsletter for readers. The *Wings* logo in Joe's flag is easily identifiable. Joe also includes the date of the publication and the company name. Because the newsletter is published only quarterly, Joe decides not to clutter the flag with a volume number.

2 **Does the newsletter's first page invite the reader to continue to read the newsletter?**
The first page is design-intensive. A large photo and creative headline make the first glance at the newsletter a noticeable one. The reader is instantly drawn to the story after seeing the photo and reading the headline. They want to discover why they should "Start spreadin' the news." Joe included a preview section that contains a table of contents for the newsletter. He hopes the TOC will motivate his audience to continue reading the newsletter.

3 **Are the pages too congested or too crowded?**
Joe wanted to make page 1 visually appealing. To accomplish this, he sacrificed the space needed to place other stories or photos on this page. The result is a strong first page. Page 4 acts as a "catch-all" page for Joe, where he placed the continuation of the page 1 story, which is called a **jump**, and other smaller, less important stories. He separates the information presented on page 4 with lines and a box shaded gray.

4 **Is the reader's attention drawn to the main story on each page?**
Only page 4 contains more than one story, so the stories on the first three pages compete only with graphics for attention. On page 4, the story about special trips is understood to be the most important because it is at the top of the page. Joe placed the jump from page 1 next to the top story and shaded it gray to separate it.

FIGURE 5-21: Pages 1 and 4 of the newsletter

WINGS

THE NEW WORLD AIRLINES CUSTOMER QUARTERLY
SEPTEMBER 1996

Start Spreadin' The News

New World Airlines Announces Specials On Transcontinental Flights

Traveling across the country no longer needs to be a pain. Now you can fly New World Airlines and receive double frequent flyer miles for nonstop transcontinental flights taken from now till June 1, 1996.

New World Airlines is ranked best in customer satisfaction for flights over 500 miles by Devine and Associates annual study of business and pleasure travelers. This is the third year in a row that New World Airlines has received the number one rating. Why trust your transcontinental flight with any other airline?

From Los Angeles we offer four nonstop flights to New York's JFK. We also offer two nonstops between New York and San Francisco, and one non-stop from Seattle.

New York City is the financial capital of the country, the city of the Broadway lights and the home of Statue of Liberty. And you can earn an additional 25% mileage bonus in addition to the double mileage by staying at the Madison Majestic Hotel. The Madison is in the center of Manhattan and is only a few short blocks from either Wall Street and the lights of Broadway and Times Square. This hotel, one of New York's finest with its 700 beautifully appointed, oversized rooms and suites,

Your little town blues will melt away with double mileage on fares to New York City.

See Flights, Page 4

In This Issue

WINGS

Bonuses Await On Special Trips

Are you planning a pleasure trip to the Caribbean, Europe, Russia, South Korea, Japan, Australia, or the United States? If you are, why not fly New World Airlines and take a tour with our travel planning partner, Sunset Tours? Sunset Tours offers vacation packages spanning four continents. And once again, New World Airlines frequent flyers can receive a bonus of 1500 frequent flyer miles when they make their flight reservations and book a Sunset tour.

Sunset Tours travel agents are experienced travel guides who pride themselves on providing the most comfortable and comprehensive tours.

Sunset Tours offers you a choice of more than 400 hotel packages and more than 100 motor coach tours, for every budget.

Sunset Tours travel agents pride themselves on the variety of European tours they offer starting at any of your favorite New World Airlines destinations whether it be London, Dublin, Frankfurt, Paris, Munich, Berlin, Rome, Madrid, or Athens.

For reservations or for more information call your travel agent, or call New World Airlines at 1-800-FLY-AWAY.

SkyCar Rentals Earn 300 Miles

New World Airlines frequent flyers who fly to any location in the continental United States and rent a car from SkyCar Rental will receive a bonus of 300 miles at the time of your ticket purchase.

SkyCar Rental offers cars to meet everyone's needs whether you need a full size luxury car or, if you are on a tight budget, a compact or subcompact car. SkyCar is your one-stop car rental offering you or your company the best price in the industry.

SkyCar Rental has over 4,000 locations worldwide including 700 locations in airports in more than 100 countries.

For reservations, call your travel agent or call SkyCar at 1-800-SKY-CARS.

Flights

From Page 1

will make you feel relaxed after a long day of business or sightseeing. Just mention you are a member of the Wings Club and receive a 10% discount on your stay.

Why is New World Airlines rated best in customer satisfaction for flights over 500 miles? Because New World Airlines has one of the best on-time records, more legroom than any other carrier, and some of the friendliest service in the skies!

Long transcontinental flights, such as the ones on special, offer first-run films with digital stereo sound and big screens.

Our frequent flyer program was one of the first of its kind giving both business and pleasure travelers the ability to earn free flights to any city in the continental United States.

Round-trip purchase is required. For reservations and information, call your travel agent, or call New World Airlines at 1-800-FLY-AWAY.

A Letter From The President

On behalf of the 2,000 New World Airlines employees world-wide, I would like to thank you for choosing our airline to be your means of flying to your destinations. We would like to thank those who travel our airline with free airline tickets.

Most of you know about the many benefits to joining the Eagle Club, the New World Airlines frequent flyer club. I would like to briefly review how easy it is to receive a free bonus flight.

If you want to earn free travel fast, the New World Airlines frequent flyer program is your best choice. Members earn a free round-trip ticket on New World Airlines starting at just 25,000 miles. For every flight you will receive a minimum of 800 frequent flyer miles. We fly to every major city in the United States, as well as some of the most important cities in the world including London, Dublin, Frankfurt, Paris, Munich, Berlin, Rome, Madrid, and Athens.

No other major airline offers a free ticket for less mileage. Your free flights can take you exciting destinations in North America.

Besides free flights, our frequent flyers receive the best treatment. You can earn free upgrades to first class, automatic seat reservations, and some of the finest meals at our Eagle Clubs located throughout the world.

We also offer many great discounts with our partner corporations. You can receive discount or upgrade service in many hotels, car rentals agencies, and food restaurants as well as major attractions. No other frequent flyer program treats their customers better.

We are an employee-owned, and every customer is important to us. If you should ever have any questions about our service you can call me directly at 1-800-NEW-AIRL. Thank you for your participation and we ask you to pass the word about New World Airlines to colleagues and friends.

Design Workshop, continued

Pages 2 and 3 of Joe's newsletter are shown in Figure 5-22. Let's continue critiquing the design.

STEPS

5 **Was the spread designed effectively?**
Joe used the spread on pages 2 and 3 to write a large headline that spans both pages. Although there are separate stories on each of the pages, Joe's large headline acts as a main title relating to both stories. Page 2 deals with the Caribbean while page 3 concerns Europe, but both pages together stress the New World Airlines' commitment for flying nonstop to most of its destinations. The large pop-out graphic of Big Ben on page 3 shows quality design. A photo reproduced this large on a page needs the benefit of a spread to "give it room" on the page.

6 **If a photo splits the page, is it still considered a spread design?**
The key to successful design of page spreads is the theme being shared among all items on the page. If the contents contain no overriding theme, then the pages should not be designed as a spread, but separately. In this case, nonstop service is the theme, and all materials relate to it. The space between the towers helps to provide a bold graphic on one of the pages and acts as a border for the Europe story.

7 **Are the headlines an appropriate size and do they encourage the audience to read the story?**
The headline should reach out and encourage the audience to read the story. Joe created a headline that went across pages 2 and 3 announcing New World Airlines' new non-stop service, then he added subheadlines describing the new locations for this service.

8 **Does the use of graphics enhance the text?**
Joe included large graphics and white space to break up the text. The large photo also draws the reader's eye to the story about flying to Europe. Joe wanted the photo of Big Ben to be large enough to act as a division between the two stories. The tower physically splits the space devoted to the Caribbean and Europe stories.

FIGURE 5-22: Pages 2 and 3 of the newsletter

Page 2

September 25, 1996

WINGS

New World Airlines Goes Nonstop

Fly To The Caribbean

Why not give yourself a vacation from the rat race and fly one of New World Airlines's newest Caribbean destinations: San Juan, Puerto Rico, or St. Thomas in the Virgin Islands. If getting away from your hectic work schedule is not enough motivation, what about double frequent flyer miles? Yes, from now until Feb. 21, you can receive double frequent flyer miles on all round trips to the Caribbean destinations.

The Virgin Islands offer some of the most beautiful beaches in the entire world. You can relax on the powder-soft, white, sandy beaches or snorkel through a coral reef. St. Thomas also offers duty-free shopping. Walk through the narrow streets of Charlotte Amalie, and marvel at the fine displays of jewelry, perfumes and crystal.

And then there's San Juan, the Las Vegas of the Caribbean. Try your luck at one of the elaborate casinos or enjoy one of the stunning floor shows. Enjoy yourself throughout the night in the city that never goes to sleep.

By flying on New World Airlines, you can plan a romantic cruise throughout the Caribbean. Sunset Tours, will be more than happy to help you customize a cruise on any of the major cruise lines servicing the Caribbean.

Surveying the Caribbean, its cobalt-blue waters, and scenery encapsulates a fantastic vacation destination. We hope you will take some time to get away and visit the Caribbean. Remember, between now and Feb. 21, you will receive double frequent flyer miles.

The famous beaches of St. John Island are just a 20-minute ferry ride from St. Thomas. Most of the island's shoreline is protected by the National Park Service, so you can revel in the beauty of inlets like Trunk Bay, rated as one of the top five beaches in the world. White sand and crystal-clear waters make snorkeling and sunbathing unforgettable.

NEW WORLD AIRLINES

You Don't Have To Be Royalty To Fly To Europe

By Michelle Snow

Are you planning a business or pleasure trip to Europe? If you are, why not fly New World Airlines and receive triple frequent flyers miles on all flights between the U.S. and Europe, Sept.15 to Dec. 23.

Fly to any of your favorite European cities, London, Dublin, Frankfurt, Paris, Munich, Berlin, Rome, Madrid, or Athens, and receive triple frequent flyer miles.

In addition to receiving triple freqeuent flyer miles, all members of our Eagles Flight Program may dine at any of the fine Eagle Club restaurants.

Also next month New World Airlines will be adding two new nonstop flights to Lisbon, Monaco, and Barcelona.

If you want to see all the sights of Europe, why not plan a tour with New World Airlines' official travel agency, Sunset Tours? When you tour with Sunset, you will see Europe in a special way. Sunset will do the planning, and all you have to do is enjoy the beauty and history of Europe.

For flight or tour information and reservations, call your travel agent, or call New World Airlines at 1-800- FLY-AWAY.

CONCEPTS REVIEW

Label each of the publication window elements shown in Figure 5-23.

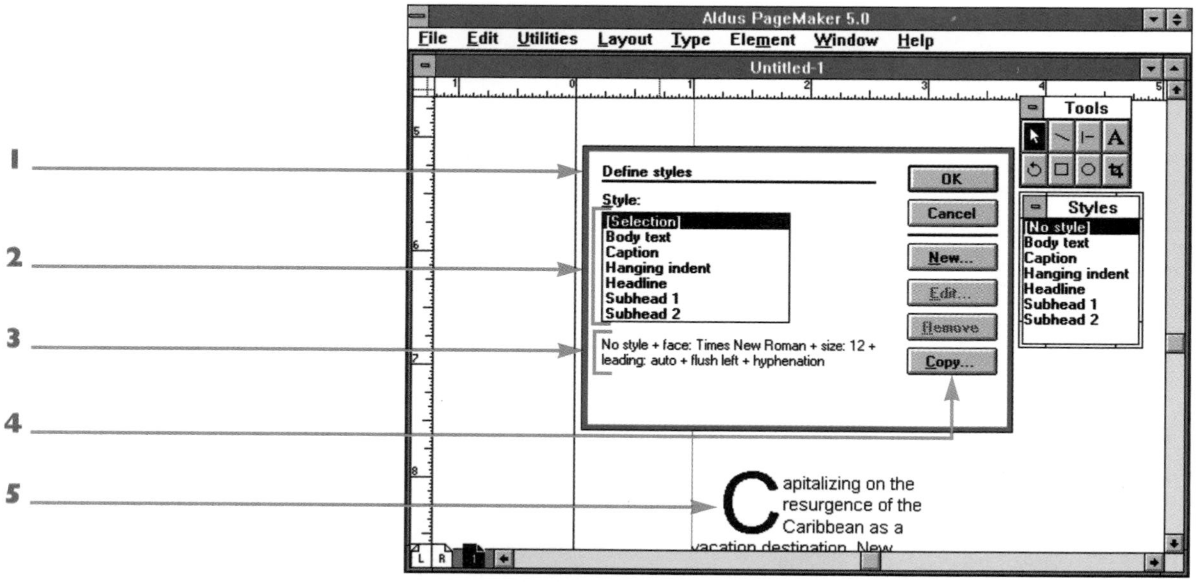

FIGURE 5-23

Match each of the terms with the statement that describes its function.

7 Flag
8 Cutline
9 Master page
10 Style
11 Aldus Additions

a. Text attributes
b. Elements placed here appear on all pages
c. Place where the title, date, and other identification information appears in a newsletter
d. The description of photos or graphics
e. Customized features to automate repetitive or complex publishing tasks

12 Which of the following is NOT a guideline for creating a design:
- a. The overall layout should focus the reader's attention
- b. Use many fonts for variety
- c. Use space, shading, or lines to break up sections of text
- d. Design headlines to draw the reader's attention

13 Which of the following is true about master pages?
- a. They are a template for the entire publication
- b. They allow you to add page numbers
- c. They are the best page to place graphics
- d. Both a and b

14 Ruler and column guides set on master pages
- a. Appear on all pages
- b. Appear only on pages you define
- c. Appear only on the master pages
- d. Cannot be set on the master pages

15 Cutlines are
- a. Preview areas in a newsletter
- b. Text describing photos or graphics
- c. Subheadlines
- d. Both a and b

16 All of the following are true about styles, except
- a. Styles can be applied to all text
- b. Styles can be edited at any stage in the page production process
- c. Creating and setting styles can slow overall page production
- d. Once you edit a style, PageMaker automatically updates all uses of that style in the text

17 Which of the following can be marked to be included in the table of contents?

a. Styles

b. Graphical elements

c. Photos

d. All of the above

18 All of the following are true about balancing columns, except

a. You select text blocks to be balanced by highlighting them with the text tool

b. The balance columns Aldus Addition saves time from manually balancing the columns

c. The balance columns Aldus Addition only balances columns in a threaded story

d. All of the above are true

APPLICATIONS REVIEW

1 Use the master pages to add page numbers.

a. Start PageMaker and open the file UNIT_5-3.PM5 from your Student Disk.

b. Go to the master pages.

c. Change the view to Actual size, then scroll to see the lower-left corner of the right master page.

d. Place the insertion point inside the column and create a text block.

e. Type "Holistic Health News" followed by three spaces, then type a hyphen (-) followed by one space.

f. Insert the page number marker.

g. Change the alignment to center.

h. Add a 4-point line across the bottom margin and above the page number text.

i. Go to page 1 and check to see if the page number appears.

j. Turn off the Display of the master page items option on page 1.

2 Define styles.

a. Open the Define styles dialog box.

b. Create a new style called "Headline."

c. The Headline style is based on No style, and the Next style is based on the Same style.

d. Change the Type specifications to Arial, 24 points, bold.

e. Close the dialog boxes.

3 Apply the style Headline to the newsletter headlines.

a. Display the Style palette.

b. Go to page 2.

d. Apply the Headline style to the headline that reads "Plants Process...."

e. Apply the Headline style to the headline that reads "Organically Grown...."

f. Go to page 3.

g. Apply the Headline style to the headline that reads "Going Mainstream...."

4 Create a table of contents.

a. Open the Define styles dialog box.

b. Edit the Headline style.

c. Open the Paragraph specifications dialog box and select the Include in table of contents option.

d. Close the dialog boxes.

e. Open the Create table of contents dialog box from the Utilities menu.

f. Choose the Page number after entry option, and insert a tab (^T) in the Between entry and page number text box.

g. Place the TOC in the box on page 1.

5 Edit a style.

a. Open the Define styles dialog box.

b. Edit the Body text style.

c. Change the paragraph alignment to Justify.

d. Edit the Headline style.

e. Change the size of the type to 26 points. (Hint: You can manually enter a font size if the list box doesn't have the size you're looking for.)

f. Close the dialog boxes.

6 Balance the columns on page 2.

a. Go to page 2.

b. Select the text blocks that make up the story under the headline "Organically Grown Controversy."

c. Open the Balance columns dialog box and align top.

d. Add the lines of text that cannot be divided equally among the selected text blocks to the left column.

e. Close the dialog box.

f. Place the story CHALL1.DOC, located on your Student Disk, at the bottom of page 3.

g. Balance the columns of the story you just placed.

7 Create a drop cap.
   a. Go to page 1.
   b. Scroll to center the first paragraph of the story in the publication window.
   c. Click I anywhere within the first paragraph.
   d. Open the Drop cap dialog box.
   e. Descend the drop cap three lines into the paragraph.
   f. Close the dialog box.
   g. Save your work, then exit PageMaker.

INDEPENDENT CHALLENGE 1

As the marketing agent for BioLabs, Inc, it's your job to create a newsletter for the health research company. Your budget is small, but the expectation is great. You decide the newsletter will only be two pages—the front and back of a letter-size page.

To complete this independent challenge:

1 Create a new double-sided publication with two letter-size pages and save it to your Student Disk as BIOLAB.PM5.

2 Add column guides to the master pages that divide each page into three columns.

3 Name the newsletter. Type the name of the newsletter on page 1. Use the Line and Shape tools to add interest to the flag. Use shading and text formatting to make the flag interesting. Add a line for the date and company name.

4 Place four stories into the newsletter: CHALL1.DOC, CHALL2.DOC, CHALL3.DOC, and CHALL4.DOC (all located on your Student Disk).

5 Add lines, boxes, and shading as necessary to separate stories in the page layout.

6 Create any styles necessary to complete the newsletter. Create a style for headlines, body text, cutlines, and subheadlines.

7 Make sure the columns are evenly balanced to give the newsletter a professional appearance.

8 Evaluate the final design. Does the newsletter's flag stand out? Are the pages too congested? Did you use a sans serif font for the body text and a serif font for the headline styles? Does the use of graphics enhance the overall layout of the newsletter?

9 Save and print the publication.

INDEPENDENT CHALLENGE 2

Millions of groups and organizations publish newsletters. It's one of the most effective ways of informing a targeted group of people of whatever you're doing. Find several newsletters and critique their designs. Design a model newsletter, then create it using dummy text and graphics.

To complete this independent challenge:

1 Find at least two editions of three separate newsletters from organizations in your area. Finding two editions will help you survey and evaluate the newsletter's consistency from publication to publication.

2 Critique the newsletters you collected using the guidelines from the first lesson, the Design Workshop, and criteria you establish. Answer the following questions: Do they communicate their information effectively? How?

3 Take the best aspects from each of the newsletters you collect and develop a model newsletter that incorporates these aspects.

4 Draw thumbnail sketches of your model newsletter, including the length of stories, number of pages, size of graphics, type styles, use of white space, etc.

5 Create a new publication and save it as NEWS.PM5 to your Student Disk.

6 As you create the master pages of the newsletters, add column guides, page numbers, and any other elements that would be helpful.

7 Create a flag on page 1.

8 Place the files TEXTHLD.DOC and PLACEHLD.TIF (located on your Student Disk) on the pages as many times as necessary to illustrate what the final newsletter will look like. Add dummy headlines and format them, making sure to show an example of a short (two- or three-word) headline, a longer headline that takes two lines, and a subheadline. Add cutlines to the graphics.

9 Evaluate your final design. Is it cluttered? Do individual stories stand out on the page? Does the first page of your newsletter invite your audience to continue reading?

10 Save the publication and print it.

UNIT 6

OBJECTIVES

- Plan an advertisement
- Change line weights and styles
- Crop a graphic
- Rotate an object
- Stack objects
- Wrap text around a graphic
- Add a custom text wrap
- Design Workshop: Advertisements

Working WITH GRAPHICS

Working with graphics in PageMaker is much like working with text. You can resize, manipulate, and rotate graphics in similar ways as text blocks. In this unit, you will learn to draw rectangles, to manipulate the stacking order of objects, crop and rotate graphics, and add text that wraps around graphics. ► Joe Martin needs to create a quarter-page advertisement for the local newspaper. He began placing graphics on the page, but he needs to finish the design. ►

Planning an advertisement

Most advertisements try to initiate an immediate response from the reader. Some ads help build awareness of a specific product or company. It is important that you consider the ultimate purpose or goal of your advertisement when planning and creating it. ▶ New World Airlines advertising director, Carlos Bruno, wants to create an ad to be placed in the business section of a local St. Louis newspaper, promoting nonstop flights from St. Louis to Toronto. ▶ Working with Carlos, Joe starts to plan the quarter-page ad, as shown in Figure 6-1. Joe decides to use photos from a stock photography catalog to act as the ad's foundation and to write the small amount of text in the ad himself. The advertisement will be black and white because the business section requires that all ads be black and white. The following guidelines will help Joe produce an effective ad.

STEPS

1 **Build the ad around strong visual elements**
Large headlines or graphics should attract the readers' attention. Once caught, their attention focuses to other aspects of the ad, such as the text or a way to respond. Joe sets the page size according to the newspaper's specifications for a quarter-page ad. The ad is 6.25 inches wide and 10.5 inches tall. Joe uses photos of monuments in St. Louis and Toronto rather than text in his ad. He thinks the design will have more impact by using photos. The headline type is also large and bold.

2 **Organize the ad's layout**
Because print advertising is expensive, there is a tendency to put as much information as possible into an advertisement to justify the cost. However, too much information or a poor design confuses the reader. A good ad is designed to be read top to bottom with a simple message at the top and specific details at the bottom. Joe's design literally moves the reader down the ad with his use of arrows and a continuing headline.

3 **Visually separate the ad from other items on the page where it will appear**
With all the information included in newspapers and magazines, it is important to make your ad stand out on the page. Increasing the thickness of the border is one solution. Another solution is to use white space around the ad to separate it from the other page items. Joe uses white space to set off his ad.

4 **Encourage a quick response**
Similar to a flyer, an ad's main goal is to elicit a response from the reader. The reader should be given a clear course of action, such as an address or phone number for more information. For some advertisements, this would include the price of the product or service. Because the ad is for the airline and not a specific travel agency, Joe's design calls for placing the New World Airlines logo and 800 number in the ad.

FIGURE 6-1: Joe's sketch of the ad

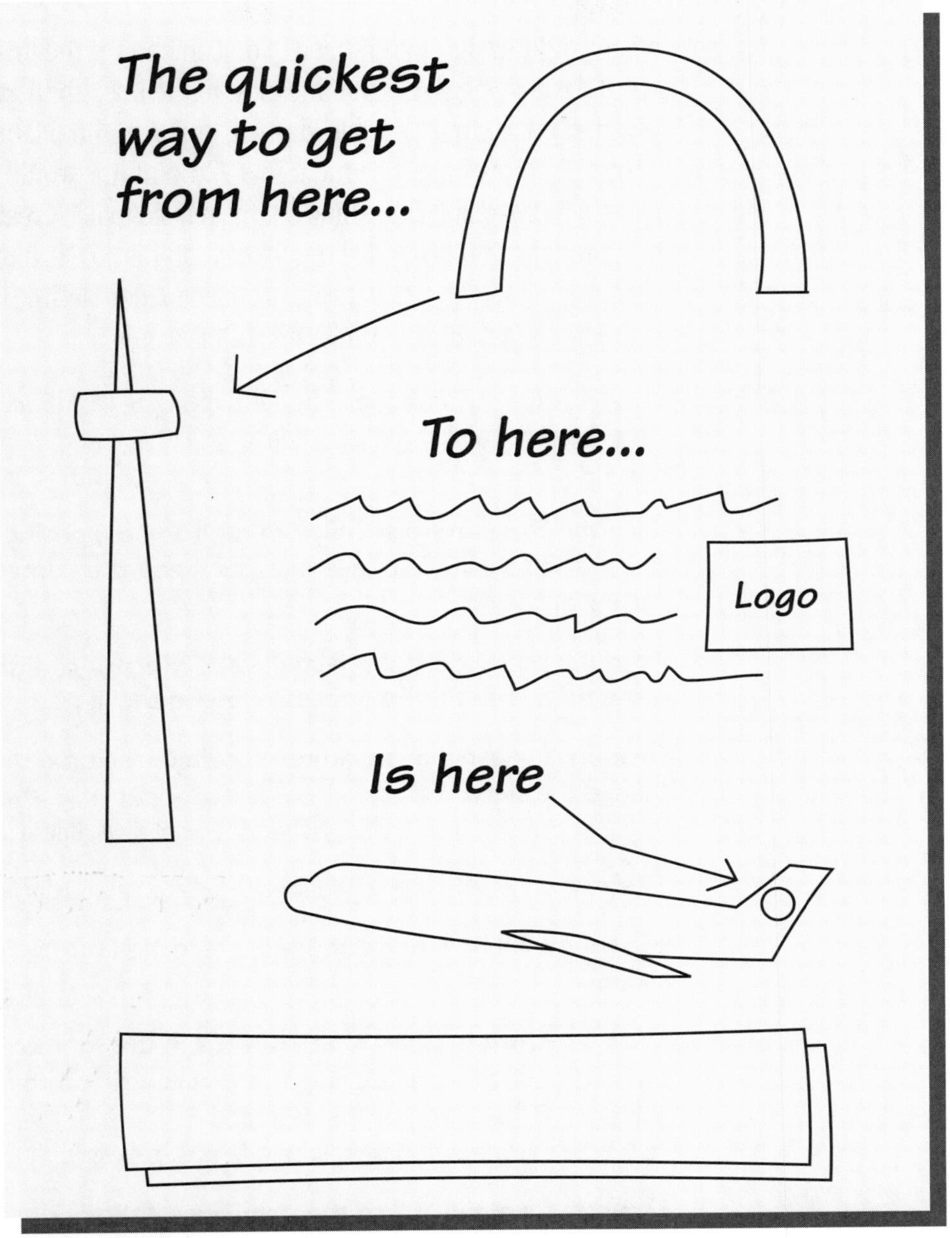

Changing line weights and styles

When you draw lines and shapes, you can change the line weight and the line style. **Line weight** is the thickness of the line, and **line style** is the line's design, such as single, double, dashed, or reverse line. Lines are measured in points; 72 points equal one inch, so a 72-point line would be 1" thick. The default line style is a 1-point single line. See the related topic "Creating custom line weights" for more information. ▶ Joe has worked on his ad. He has already placed the graphics and the text. Now he wants to add a double-line box around his ad for a border and a thick line under one of the words.

STEPS

1 **Start PageMaker and open the file UNIT_6-1.PM5 from your Student Disk**
The ad Joe started working on appears in the publication window. First, Joe draws a box around the entire ad.

2 **Click the Rectangle tool ▢ in the toolbox, position + over the corner where the top and left page margins meet, then drag to the lower-right corner of the ad**

3 **With the rectangle still selected, click Element on the menu bar, click Line, then click the 4pt double line in the list**

4 **Position + near the left center handle of the box, then right-click to change the view**
See Figure 6-2. The line has changed from a 1-point single line to a 4-point double line.

Next, Joe wants to add a line under the word "here" in the headline "Is here."

5 **Use the scroll bars to position the headline Is here in the publication window**

6 **Click the Constrained-line tool ⊢ in the toolbox, then position + under the word here aligning the vertical bar on the pointer with the bottom left-hand serif in the letter "h"**
Make sure you leave a small amount of white space between the word and the pointer.

7 **Drag + from the "h" to the right side of the period**
A 1-point line appears under the word. Joe wants to make this line thicker because the type is so big.

8 **With the line still selected, click Element on the menu bar, then click Line**
Notice the checkmark next to 1pt. If a different line weight is selected on your screen, someone changed the default line weight; just continue with the next step.

9 **Click the 4pt single line**
See Figure 6-3. The line changes to a 4-point line.

10 **Click File on the menu bar, then click Save**

FIGURE 6-2: 4-point double line

Box around outside edge of ad

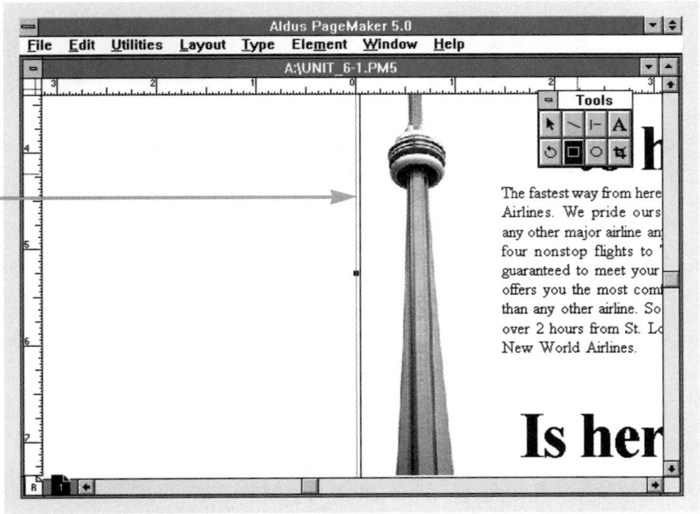

FIGURE 6-3: 4-point single line added

Thicker line added to balance heavy text

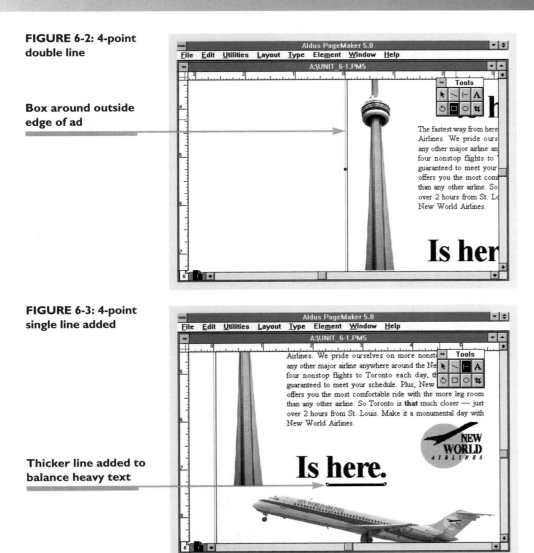

Creating custom line weights

PageMaker lets you create custom line weights from 0 to 800 points. To create a custom line weight, click Custom on the Line submenu to open the Custom line dialog box shown in Figure 6-4. You can choose a style from the Line style list box, then enter a point size in the Line weight text box. Click to check the Transparent background check box if you want to see through a pattern-style line with blank spaces, such as the space between the two lines on a double line.

Enter point size from 0 to 800

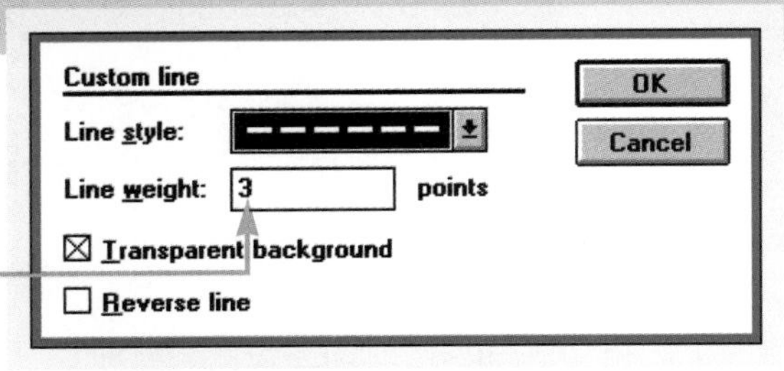

FIGURE 6-4: Custom line dialog box

DESIGN TIP

Extra white space will help an ad stand out more than overuse of shading or lines.■

QUICK TIP

To create a white line on a dark background shade or color, select the line, click Element on the menu bar, click Line, then click Reverse.■

Cropping a graphic

PageMaker's Cropping tool lets you remove a portion of a graphic you don't want. Cropping changes how the graphic looks but it does not permanently delete any portion of the graphic. ▶ The only photo of St. Louis in the stock photography catalog included the words "Saint Louis" beneath the photo. Using PageMaker's cropping tool, Joe easily crops the photo so the words are no longer visible.

STEPS

1 Scroll the publication window so that the Arch graphic is centered in it

2 Click the **Cropping tool** in the toolbox
The pointer changes to .

3 Click the **Arch graphic** to select it
The graphic's handles appear.

4 Position over the bottom middle handle, then press and hold the **mouse button**
The pointer changes to . See Figure 6-5.

5 Drag the pointer up to the white space just above the words "Saint Louis"
Portions of the graphic disappear as you move the pointer up. Once a graphic is cropped, you can move it around inside its boundaries.

6 Position on top of the Arch graphic, then press and hold the **mouse button**
A box appears around the graphic and the pointer changes to .

7 Move up, *but do not release the mouse button*
The words you cropped reappear at the bottom of the graphic, but now the top of the Arch is cropped off. See Figure 6-6. The extent to which the graphic scrolls around inside the boundaries is limited to how much you cropped the graphic.

8 Move down until the graphic has scrolled down as far as it will go, then release the mouse button
The graphic should now look like Figure 6-7.

9 Click **File** on the menu bar, then click **Save**

FIGURE 6-5: Cropping a graphic

Graphic boundaries

Mouse pointer

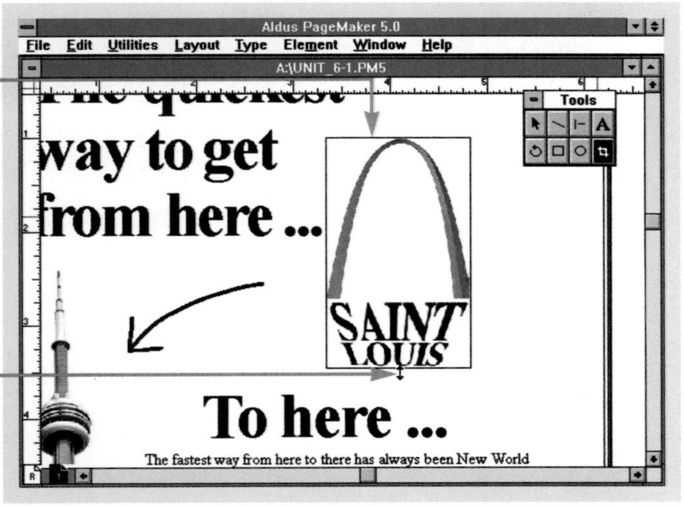

FIGURE 6-6: Moving a graphic inside its boundaries

Mouse pointer

FIGURE 6-7: Graphic after cropping

Final cropped arch

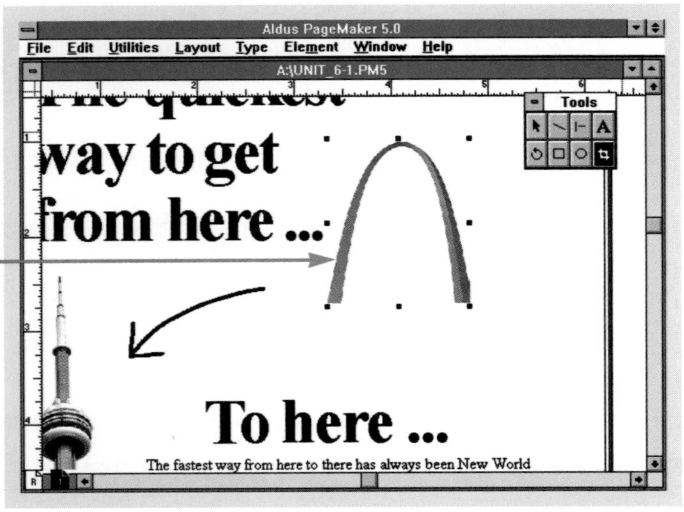

DESIGN TIP

If you resize a graphic after cropping it, it will remain cropped.

QUICK TIP

Cropped graphics take longer to print than graphics that aren't cropped.

Rotating an object

The Rotating tool in the toolbox lets you rotate graphics by 360 degrees at increments of .01 degrees. ▶ Joe created the arrow in a drawing application and placed it in the ad. Now he wants to add another arrow to the ad but one that points in the opposite direction. The arrow will extend from the "Is here" headline to the logo on the tail of the plane. He decides to copy the existing arrow and rotate it.

STEPS

1 Click the **Pointer tool** in the toolbox
First Joe will copy the graphic. You copy graphics the same way you copy text.

2 Click the **arrow graphic** to select it, click **Edit** on the menu bar, then click **Copy**
PageMaker copies the graphic to the Clipboard.

3 Click **Edit** on the menu bar, then click **Paste**
PageMaker pastes the arrow on top of the original arrow, offset to the bottom right. The pasted arrow is selected. This graphic is considered line art. **Line art** consists of graphics drawn as outlines of objects. Black and white cartoons are examples of line art.

4 Drag the selected arrow to the right of the "Is here" text block
PageMaker scrolls the page view as you drag the element down the page. See Figure 6-8. The precise location of the graphic isn't crucial because you can move it into position later.

5 Position over the top right handle, press and hold **[Shift]**, drag the pointer to the left to reduce the graphic to about 50% of the original size, then release [Shift]
See Figure 6-9. The space you need to fill with the arrow is much smaller than the corresponding space at the top of the ad.

6 Click the **Rotating tool** in the toolbox
The pointer changes to ✣.

7 Position ✣ at the center of the selected arrow graphic, then drag the pointer counter-clockwise from approximately the 4 o'clock position to the 10 o'clock position
See Figure 6-10. As you dragged, a rotation lever followed the pointer from the starting point to the ending position. You rotate lines, text blocks, and other objects the same way you rotated the graphic.

8 Click the **Pointer tool** in the toolbox, then, if necessary, move the rotated graphic so the arrow points from the "Is here" text block to the New World Airlines logo on the airplane's tail
You might need to reduce the graphic further so the tips of the arrow don't cover parts of the text block or the airplane's tail. Joe uses this arrow to create a visual link between the words of the headline and the logo.

9 Click **File** on the menu bar, then click **Save**

FIGURE 6-8: Moving a duplicated graphic into position

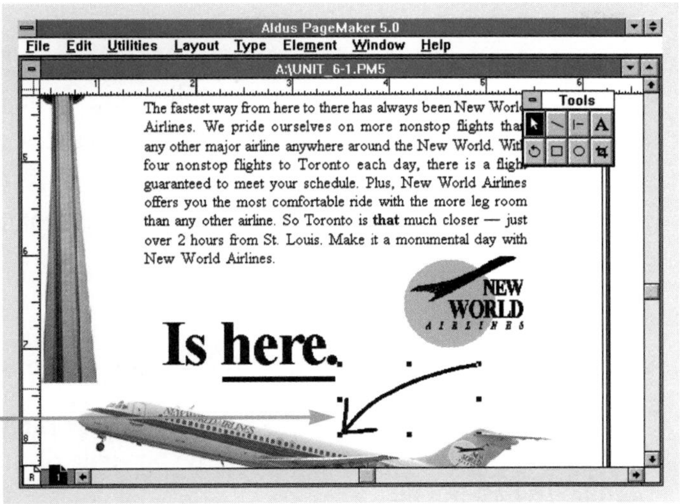

Duplicated arrow

FIGURE 6-9: Resized graphic

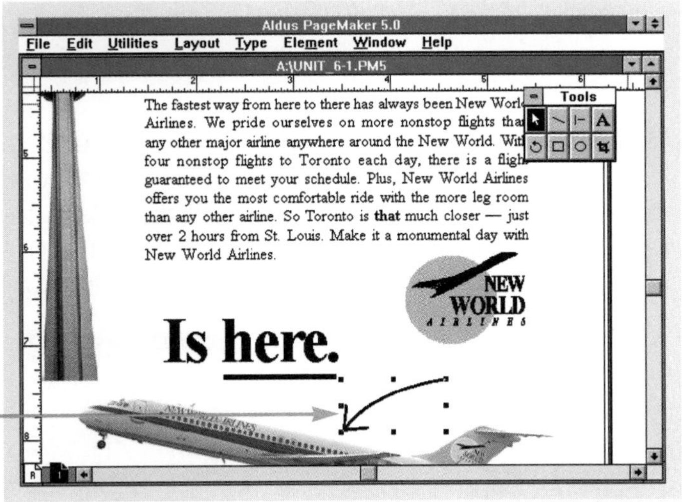

Resized arrow

FIGURE 6-10: Rotated graphic

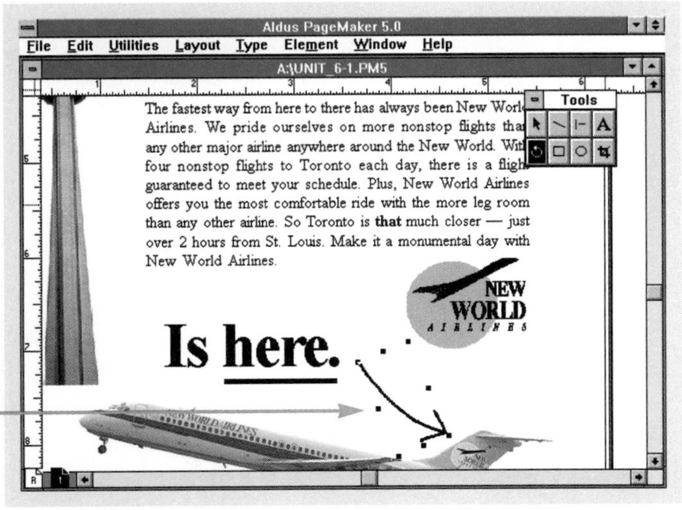

Rotated arrow pointing to logo

DESIGN TIP

To rotate an object at 45-degree angles, press [Shift] while you are rotating the object.

TROUBLE?

Rotated objects, especially TIFF images, can slow overall printing times.

Stacking objects

Graphics in a publication are not always imported from one file. They can consist of several objects imported from other applications or created in PageMaker all stacked on top of each other. When objects are **stacked**, they overlap each other as shown in Figure 6-11. ▶ Joe wants to increase the size of the Arch. He will resize it, then check to make sure that the larger also will create **a shadow box**, a box with a drop shadow on two sides, to make the point of response stand out.

STEPS

1 **Scroll to the top of the page until the Arch is centered in the window**

2 **Click the Arch graphic to select it, click the top right handle, press and hold [Shift], then drag ↗ toward the top right of the ad's border without touching the ad border**
See Figure 6-12. The top left portion of the Arch graphic now covers the end of the text block to the left, so the "t" in the word "quickest" seems to have disappeared. PageMaker imports photos with a solid white background. For more information about backgrounds in imported graphics, see the related topic "Graphic backgrounds." Joe needs to fix this by sending the Arch to the back of the layout.

3 **Click Element on the menu bar, then click Send to back**
All of the text block's characters appear because the Arch now lies behind the text. If you move the graphic, PageMaker makes it the top object in the stacking order. You would again need to use the Send to back command to place it behind the other elements.
Joe also needs to add a shadow box around the point of response and adjust the stacking order.

4 **Use the scroll bars to center the bottom third of the ad in the publication window**
See the continuation of this lesson to create this shadow box.

FIGURE 6-11: Two objects stacked to create a shadow box

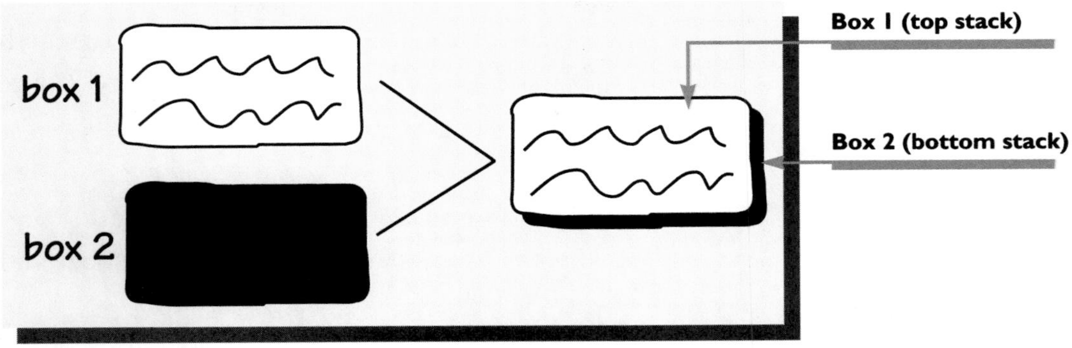

FIGURE 6-12: Graphic covers text

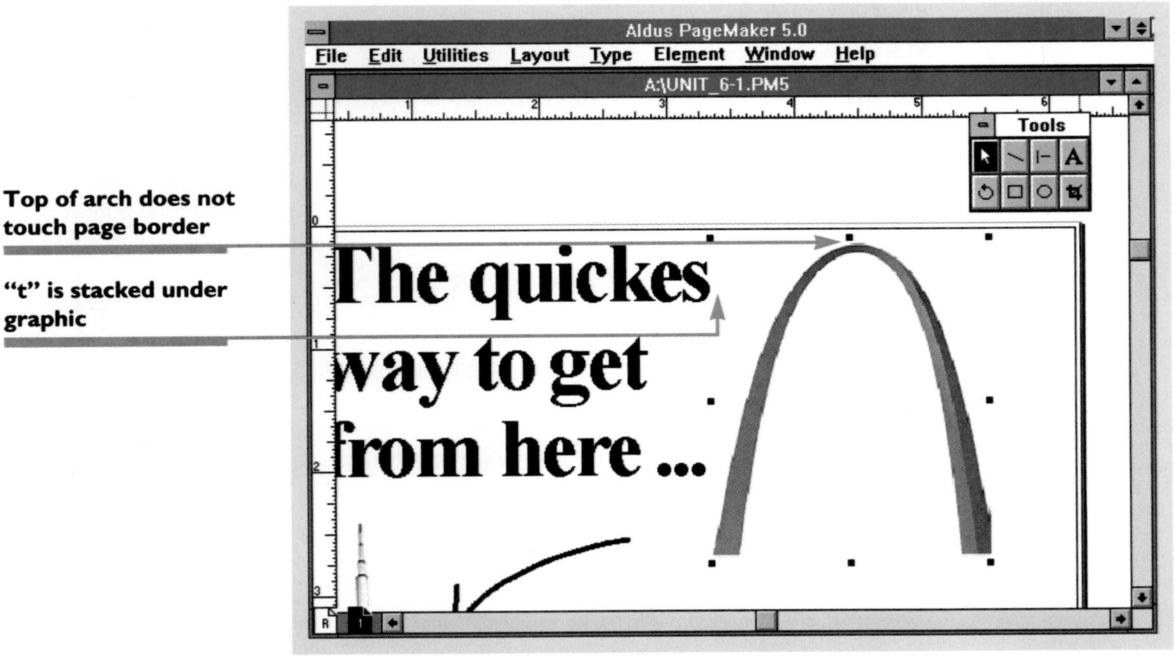

Graphic backgrounds

The area surrounding an imported graphic is either transparent or filled with solid white. PageMaker imports line art images with transparent backgrounds; it imports **grayscale images**, like the Arch, Needle, or the jet in this publication with shades of gray and a white background. In grayscale TIFF images, any space not occupied by shades of gray contains white.

Stacking objects, continued

Now Joe needs to create a shadow box. First he will copy the box, then fill the copied box with a shade of gray, and lastly send it to the back of the stacking order.

STEPS

5 Click the **box** that surrounds the phone number with to select it, click **Edit** on the menu bar, then click **Copy**

6 Click **Edit** on the menu bar, click **Paste**, then click **Element** on the menu bar, click **Fill**, then click **20%**
PageMaker pastes a copy of the box on top of the phone number and box and offsets it to the lower right. Changing the Fill to 20% shades the box gray. Next, Joe needs to change the stacking order to make this look like a shadow box.

7 Click **Element** on the menu bar, then click **Send to back**
See Figure 6-13. PageMaker sends the gray box behind the phone number text block and the original box, but now you can't see the phone number clearly because the original box is transparent so the gray box shows through it. You need to fill the original box with solid white, or what PageMaker calls "Paper."

8 Click the **box** you originally copied, click **Element**, click **Fill**, then click **Paper**
PageMaker fills the box with white, and the box now covers the phone number.

9 Click **Element** on the menu bar, then click **Send to back**
PageMaker sends the white box to the back of the stacking order. Joe needs to use the Send to back command again on the gray box to set the stacking order correctly.

10 Click the **box** filled with 20% gray, click **Element** on the menu bar, then click **Send to back**
See Figure 6-14. The gray box is now behind both the white box and the phone number. The white box sits between the phone number and the gray box.

11 Click **File** on the menu bar, then click **Save**

FIGURE 6-13: Gray box sent to back

FIGURE 6-14: Shadow box with proper stacking order

QUICK TIP

Whenever you move an object, PageMaker places it at the top of the stacking order.

Wrapping text around a graphic

When you wrap text around a graphic, you make text flow around the graphic object at a specific distance. Unit 5 contained a text wrap on page 3 of the newsletter where the story about England wrapped around the photo of Big Ben. Wrapping text offers a unique way of blending text and graphics in a layout. ▶ Joe wants text to wrap around the logo he places on top of the descriptive text.

STEPS

1. **Use the scroll bars to center the New World Airlines logo in the publication window**
2. **Click the logo with ↖ to select it, then drag the logo and place it toward the right side of the ad on top of the body text**
3. **Click Element on the menu bar, then click Text wrap**
   The Text wrap dialog box opens. See Figure 6-15. See Table 6-1 for a description of the icons in the Text wrap dialog box.
4. **Click the Rectangular Wrap option icon to turn on text wrapping**
   The Wrap-all-sides Text flow icon is automatically selected. This means that PageMaker will flow the text around all four sides of the graphic. PageMaker sets the **standoff**, or the amount of space between the graphic being wrapped and the text, to .167 inches.
5. **Click OK**
   Your screen should match Figure 6-16. You might need to move the logo slightly to better match the results. The standoff is indicated by the non-printing dotted-line barrier around the logo. You can move any of the standoff lines by dragging them when the graphic is selected.
6. **Click File on the menu bar, then click Save**

TABLE: 6-1: Text wrap dialog box icons

ICON	OPTION	DESCRIPTION
	No Boundary Wrap option	Text flows on top of the graphic object
	Rectangular Wrap option	Text flows around a graphic object in a rectangular fashion, and you can control the amount of white space between the graphic and the text
	Custom Wrap option	Text flow around an irregularly shaped graphic; you will learn about this option in the next lesson
	Column-break Text flow	Text wraps to the top of the graphic, then continues to flow in the next column or page
	Jump-over Text flow	Text wraps to the top of the graphic, then continues below the graphic's bottom boundary
	Wrap-all-sides Text flow	Text wraps the graphic on all four sides

FIGURE 6-15: Text wrap dialog box

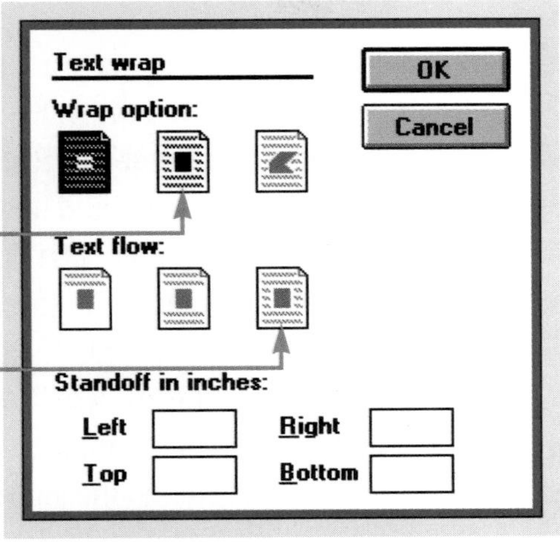

Click to wrap text around default borders

Click to wrap text on all four sides of graphic

FIGURE 6-16: Wrapped graphic

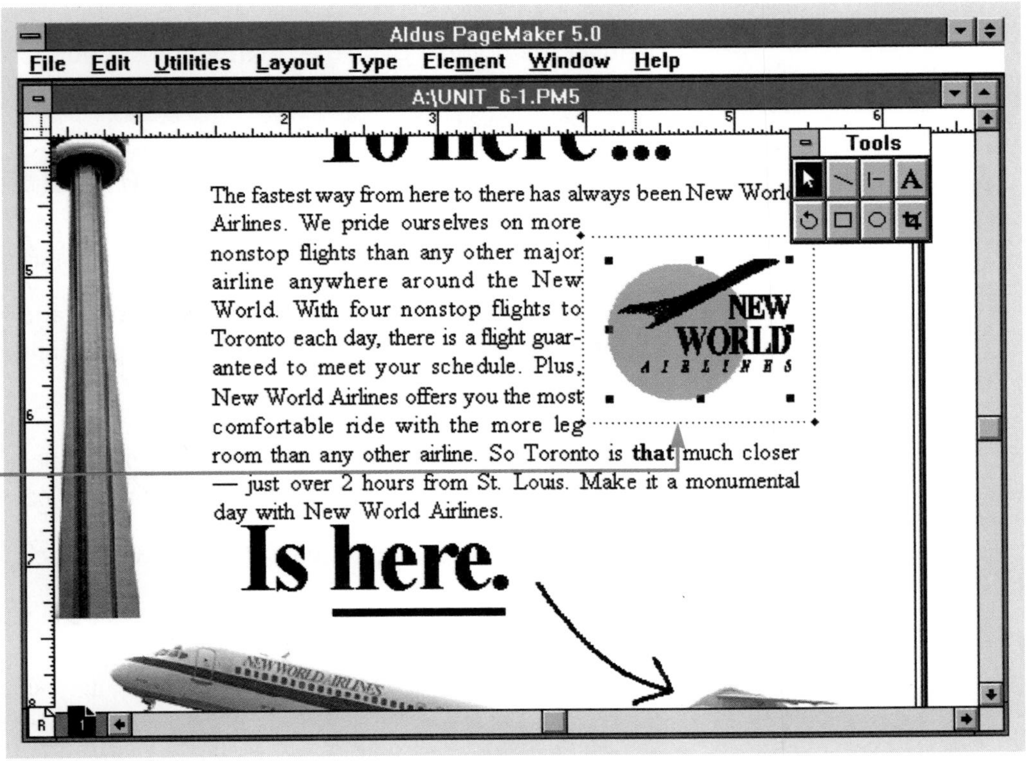

Standoff is .167 inches

TROUBLE?

You cannot wrap text around a text block, only around graphic objects.

Adding a custom text wrap

When graphics are placed in a publication, they have an invisible rectangular border. If you want to custom-wrap text around the shape of the graphic, you can change the standoff to match the shape of the graphic. To custom-wrap the graphic, you first need to apply the Rectangular text option and then change the standoff by dragging the standoff lines using definition points. **Definition points** define the shape of the standoff. You add definition points to the standoff line by clicking the standoff. By default, four definition points are placed at the corners of a rectangular text wrap. ▶ Joe wants to customize the text wrap so it follows the curve of the New World Airlines logo. By curving the text wrap, Joe fits the ad copy as tightly around the logo as possible, making the text and the logo act as one graphic unit.

STEPS

1. **With the logo still selected, click on the left side standoff line near the upper-left corner, as shown in Figure 6-17**
   This adds a definition point to the standoff line.
2. **Position the pointer over the point you just added, then press and hold the mouse button**
   The pointer changes to +.
3. **Drag to a location closer to the curved surface of the logo, as shown in Figure 6-18**
   Keep some white space between the logo and the text so they don't run together.
4. **Add about eight more definition points to the standoff line around the left, bottom, and top curved portions of the graphic, and drag each point to the logo after you add it**
   You should not allow more than a quarter-inch of space between the text and logo. Your screen should look similar to Figure 6-19—it's okay to have more definition points. With each point you add and move into position, PageMaker rewraps the text block around the graphic.
5. **Click Layout on the menu bar, click View, then click Fit in window**
6. **Click anywhere on the pasteboard to deselect the graphic, then evaluate the text wrap**
   Make any adjustments necessary to the size of the logo or the position of the text block to achieve the proper amount of space between the logo and the text. Satisfied with the final ad, Joe saves and prints it, then closes PageMaker.
7. **Save and print your publication, then exit PageMaker**

FIGURE 6-17: Adding a definition point to a standoff line

Added definition point

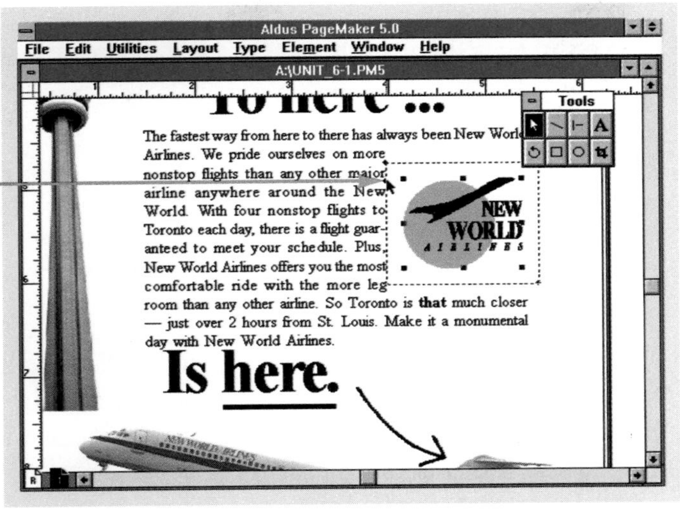

FIGURE 6-18: Custom-wrapping a graphic

Dragged definition point

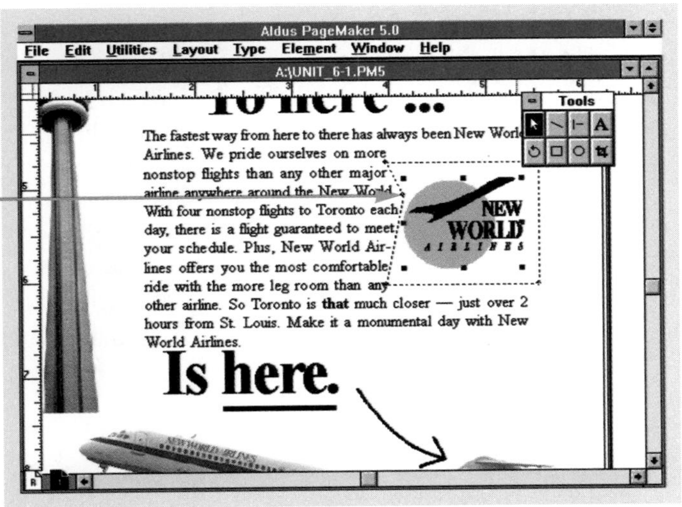

FIGURE 6-19: Custom text wrap applied

Standoff is curved around circle

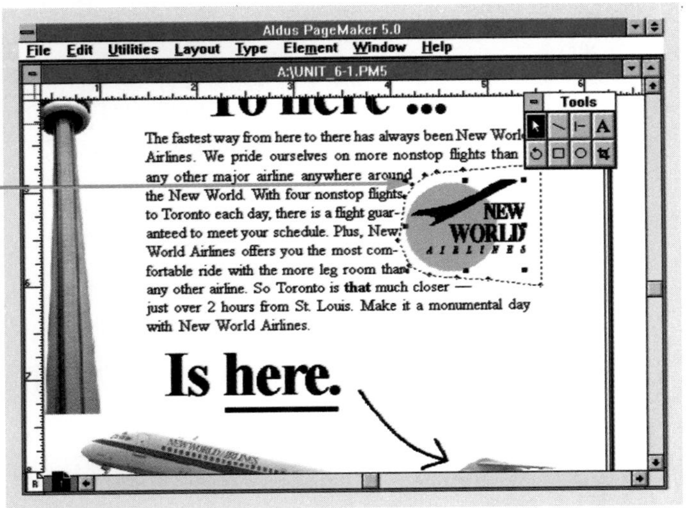

DESIGN TIP

To prevent text from being redrawn each time you adjust a text wrap boundary, press and hold [Spacebar] as you create and move definition points.

TROUBLE?

A custom text wrap's definition points will be deleted if you later convert the text wrap to its default rectangular standoff.

Design Workshop: Advertisements

A successful advertisement should provide a clear course of action or form a positive image of a company or product. ▶ Let's evaluate the Joe's design, as shown in Figure 6-20.

STEPS

1. **Does the ad achieve its goal?**
   Graphics are the first things people see when looking at a page, followed by the text. Joe's design of blending text and graphics makes the ad's goal clear: New World Airlines offers service from St. Louis to Toronto. Joe used well-known symbols of each city to inform people about the service. The monuments in each of these cities form a better visual picture for the reader than simply typing the names of the cities in the ad.

2. **Is the ad well organized?**
   The three photos in Joe's ad break up separate blocks of text in the ad. The short headlines in a large, bold typeface and the arrow graphics help smooth the transition between the photos. Although Joe made the graphics the central focus of the ad, he still needed text to elaborate on the services being offered. He placed the first and largest headline on the top left so it would be read first. The rest of the information flows from left to right and top to bottom.

3. **Will the ad stand out on the newspaper page?**
   Unless it is a full-page ad, an ad in a newspaper can get lost in the crowd of other ads and news stories. Joe realized his ad would lose impact in the crowded travel section of the local newspaper, so he used simple graphics and plenty of white space to help his ad be seen. He achieved a crisp-looking image ad that is free from crowded text blocks and discount prices common to the rest of the business section.

4. **How will the color of the ad affect the impact?**
   Although studies show a reader is more apt to view color areas on a page before black and white ones, this doesn't detract from the successful design of this ad. In the end, an ad's success is determined by its response, not by the amount of color used. Sometimes, using a single color ink, in this case black, can be a greater challenge to designers because creativity is seemingly limited. Together, black and white form the best contrast to one another. More often than not, you will be forced to work using black as your only color so it's important to have a good design. Joe used black and white to his advantage by using quality photographs and large, bold graphics. He blended those with a generous use of white space to help each graphic element stand on its own.

FIGURE 6-20: Joe's quarter-page advertisement

CONCEPTSREVIEW

Label each of the publication window elements as shown in Figure 6-21.

1 ____
2 ____
3 ____
4 ____
5 ____

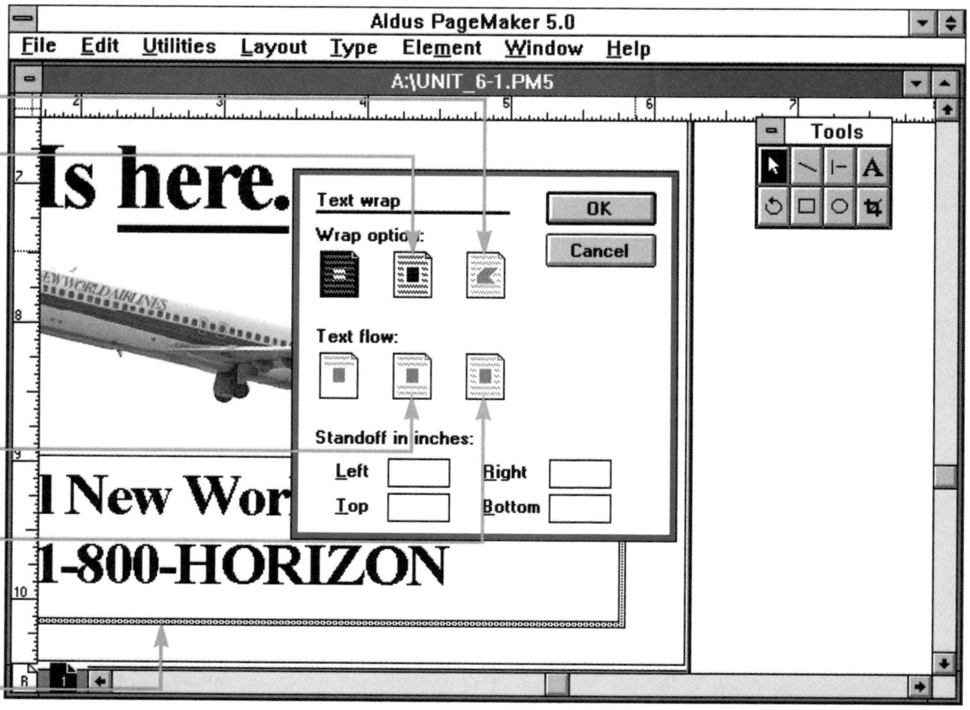

FIGURE 6-21

Match each of the terms with the statement that best describes its function.

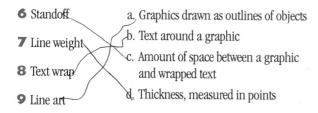

6 Standoff
7 Line weight
8 Text wrap
9 Line art

a. Graphics drawn as outlines of objects
b. Text around a graphic
c. Amount of space between a graphic and wrapped text
d. Thickness, measured in points

10 How many points equal an inch?

a. 24
b. 36
c. 60
d. 72

11 All of the following statements about cropping are true, except

a. Cropping permanently deletes a portion of the graphic
b. Cropping changes only the view of the graphic
c. You can crop a graphic as many times as you wish
d. All of the above

12 You can rotate a graphic:

a. At 45-degree increments
b. At increments of .01 degree
c. Only at 90-degree increments
d. Both a and b

13 When you move a layered object, it

a. Can never be sent to its original layer
b. Moves all of the layered objects
c. Always moves to the top layer
d. Both a and b

14 Rectangular wrap option allows you to

a. Wrap text only around boxes

b. Wrap text around graphic objects in rectangular fashion

c. Wraps text only on top of the graphic

d. All of the above

15 When using text wraps you can control the space between the graphic and the text by

a. Adjusting the standoff measurement

b. Creating a custom wrap

c. Both a and b

c. None of the above

16 You can only change the line style on

a. Rectangles

b. Lines

c. Circles

d. All of the above

APPLICATIONS REVIEW

1 Draw a border around an advertisement.

a. Start PageMaker and open UNIT_6-2.PM5 from your Student Disk.

b. Draw a single-line border around the entire ad just outside the page margin/border.

c. Change the line weight to 4pt.

d. Draw a second box around the headline and body text describing Sunset Travel Tours.

e. Change the single line weight to 2pt.

2 Crop a graphic.

a. Place the file UNIT_6-3.TIF, located on your Student Disk, in the advertisement.

b. Using the Cropping tool, crop the graphic until you can no longer see the plane on the left.

c. Drag the graphic to the white area to the left of the text.

3 Rotate an object.

a. Make sure the plane is selected.

b. Rotate the graphic so the front of the plane angles toward the sky, similar to rotation of the plane in the New World Airlines logo.

c. Enlarge the plane graphic to about 25% of its original size.

4 Stack objects.

a. Now add a second border box. Refer to Figure 6-22 for placement. Click the Rectangle tool in the toolbox, create a second box on top of the type that is larger than the black box vertically, but smaller horizontally.

b. Change the Fill to 20% gray.

c. Send the object to the back as shown in Figure 6-22. Make sure your layered boxes match. If you have to move the gray box more to the center, use the Pointer tool to select it, then drag it to be more centered. The gray box will move to the front once you let go of the mouse, then Send to back once again.

d. Fill the original box with Paper.

e. Restack the objects by using the Send to back and Bring to front commands.

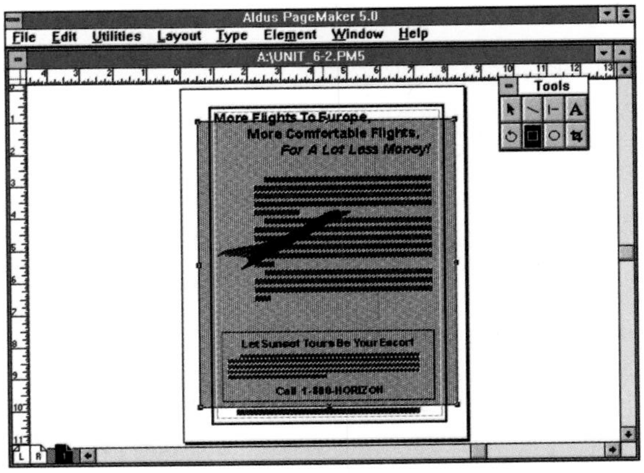

FIGURE 6-22

5 Wrap text around graphic.

a. Select the plane graphic, and open the Text wrap dialog box.

b. Select the Rectangular Wrap option, then select the Wrap-all-sides Text flow icon. Use the default standoff settings.

c. Select the text to the right of the graphic.

d. Position the pointer on the top left handle of the text block, then drag it toward the left margin, but do not go as far as the left margin.

6 Add a custom text wrap.

a. Select the plane graphic.

b. Select the plane's right standoff line, then add definition points.

c. Use the definition points to reshape the plane's standoff to create a custom wrap.

d. Save, then print the publication.

e. Exit PageMaker.

INDEPENDENT CHALLENGE 1

Create a black and white advertisement for the Board of Tourism for Paris, France. Make the advertisement 7" tall by 5" wide.

To complete this independent challenge:

1 Open the file UNIT_6-4.PM5 from your Student Disk.

2 Place the text called UNIT_6-5.DOC, located on your Student Disk.

3 Place the graphic called PARIS.TIF, located on your Student Disk.

4 Crop the graphic so that only the tower is visible.

5 Double the size of Paris graphic.

6 Create a custom text wrap so that the text almost touches the right border of the tower.

7 Include a headline.

8 Add a circle behind the partial New World Airlines logo. The circle should be 20% gray. Then send the circle to the back.

9 Create a shadow box around the entire advertisement.

10 Save your work as PARISAD.PM5 to your Student Disk.

11 Print the publication, then submit the printout.

INDEPENDENT CHALLENGE 2

Pick three black and white advertisements from a newspaper. Try to find advertisements that include the following features: varied borders, rotated graphics, layered objects, and text wraps. Evaluate the advertisements, then be prepared to share your findings with others.

To complete this independent challenge:

1 Critique the advertisements using the guidelines from the first lesson in this unit. Do the graphical features, such as a rotated graphic, enhance the overall design of the advertisement? Or do they detract? Why?

2 Take the best aspects from each advertisement and sketch a new advertisement design.

3 Try to include rotated graphics and text wraps. Think of a creative headline and use a unique border around your advertisement.

4 Assess whether the designer(s) used black and white creatively. Would these ads look better if multiple colors were used?

5 Submit your evaluation and sketches.

UNIT 7

OBJECTIVES

- Plan a menu
- Set Preferences
- Define the Control palette
- Apply small capitals
- Adjust the baseline
- Adjust text spacing
- Set character widths
- Set tabs
- Set indents
- Use the Bullets and numbering Addition
- Design Workshop: Menus

Formatting TEXT

This unit introduces you to more complex text manipulation features in PageMaker that can enhance the appearance of text in your publication. You will use the Control palette, which contains buttons and options to format text and paragraph attributes quickly. Using the Control palette, you will adjust type specifications options and spacing between characters. You will once again work with styles to modify the width of characters in headings and modify tab and indent settings. ▶ Joe Martin needs to finish a menu he created for the Eagle Club, a comfortable restaurant and lounge reserved for Gold Club Members of the Eagle Flight Program for frequent flyer passengers. ▶

Planning a menu

Creating a menu means more than copying a chef's recipes onto a piece of paper. No matter how simple or complex a menu's design, the menu is responsible for being the final point of sale for a restaurant. Menus offer a "smorgasbord" of design opportunities. Menus usually include a lot text, so you will need to use PageMaker's character manipulation features to enhance the overall appearance of the menu. A poorly planned and designed menu actually detracts from the profitability of a foodservice facility by confusing the customer. ▶ Joe Martin received a handwritten list and description of items for the new Eagle Club menu from Executive Chef Tamara Roche. Tamara carefully selected items for the menu and told Joe that the Surf & Turf special was an item that could bring the most profit because its perceived value is much greater than what it costs to make. This fact helps Joe determine where he places items as he designs the menu.

STEPS

1 **Determine the menu items of importance**
Where you place items on the page directly affects how customers order from the menu. Certain areas of a page or spread of pages are read before others. Areas read first are called **power points** because of their potential impact on the reader. Because the Surf & Turf is the most profitable item for the Eagle Club, Joe makes sure to place the menu item on the top in the center column. He will also place the Chocolate Cake Special as the top entry in the third column.

2 **Create an organized and easy to read layout design**
Menus tend to include a large amount of information. By adjusting the character spacing, you can "loosen" the text and make it easier to read. You can use PageMaker's text manipulation features such as indents and tabs to help organize overall layout design. Joe will use three columns and will use PageMaker's kerning, character width, and type options commands to enhance the appearance of the text. See Figure 7-1 for Joe's and Tamara's rough sketch of the menu.

3 **Organize menu items into categories**
The Eagle Club's menu items allow Joe to create logical categories, such as appetizers and entrées. The menu items will be organized according to category and flow from first course to beverages.

4 **Produce menus on durable paper**
Because menus are constantly in use, it is important to print them on durable card stock paper. **Lamination**, which is a permanent plastic coating, will also preserve the menu. The Eagle Club menus will remain at the tables, but they will receive a lot of use from the shear volume of passengers stopping at the restaurant to eat each day. Joe will use an 80-pound light tan card stock paper. He will also have his commercial printer laminate the menus.

FIGURE 7-1: Joe's and Tamara's sketch of the menu

Menu banner

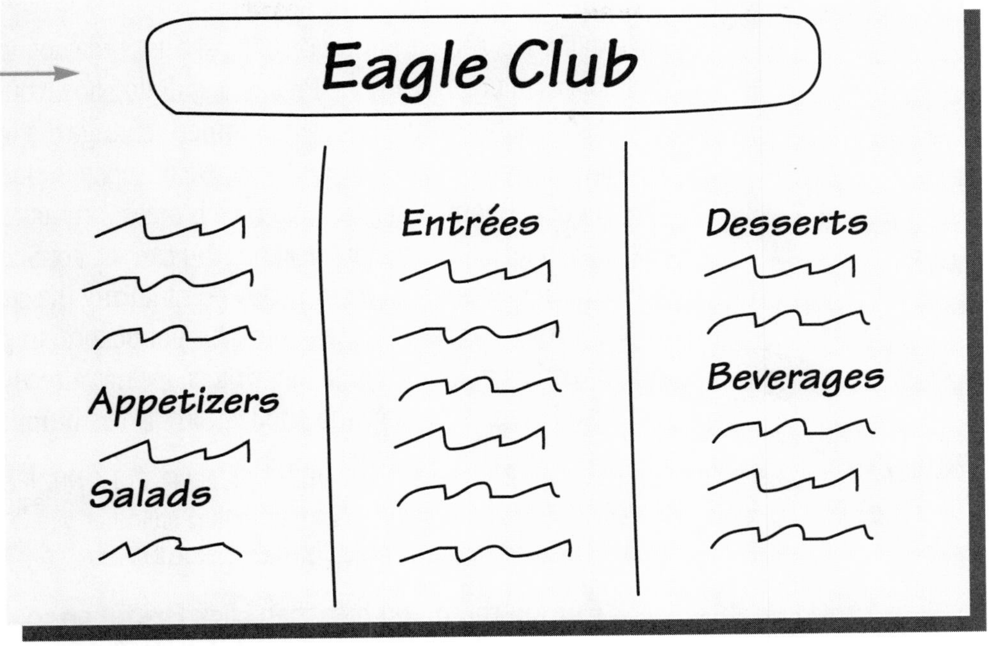

Setting Preferences

PageMaker lets you customize certain aspects of the application through the Preferences dialog box. In the Preferences dialog box, you can set a measurement system for the horizontal and vertical rulers, change the way text displays in the layout and story editor views, and improve the appearance of quotation marks and apostrophes, among other options. The changes you make in the Preferences dialog box apply only to the open publication. You can set a publication's preferences when you begin a new publication or at any point during the creation of the publication. ▶ The printer has asked Joe to submit his publication in **picas**, a measurement system used by many commercial printers. Joe has already begun his Eagle Club menu and needs to change the publication's rulers from inches to picas.

STEPS

1 **Start PageMaker and open the file UNIT_7-1.PM5 from your Student Disk**
The menu Joe started working on appears in the publication window. Joe uses the Preferences dialog box to change the publication's measurement system.

2 Click **File** on the menu bar, then click **Preferences**
The Preferences dialog box opens as shown in Figure 7-2.

3 Click the **Measurement system list arrow**, then click **Picas**
This changes the unit of measure PageMaker uses in the horizontal ruler in layout view. Six picas equal 1", and 12 points equal one pica. In PageMaker, pica measurement is denoted as 0p1, where the zero is picas and the one is points.

PageMaker allows you to set the unit of measure for the vertical ruler to be different from the overall measuring system. Joe wants to set his vertical ruler to picas also.

4 Click the **Vertical ruler list arrow**, then click **Picas**
Joe has noticed that his PageMaker publications have been taking large amounts of disk space. Joe wants to use the Save Smaller option in the Preferences dialog box to help decrease publication file sizes.

5 Click the **Smaller radio button** in the Save option section
This forces PageMaker to save the publication file as small as possible when you use the Save command. The Save Faster option saves the document more quickly, but gradually increases the file's size on disk. See the related topic "Increasing PageMaker's performance" for more ideas on improving your efficiency with PageMaker. You can select more preference settings by clicking Other. See the continuation of this lesson to finish making changes to the preferences settings.

FIGURE 7-2: Preferences dialog box

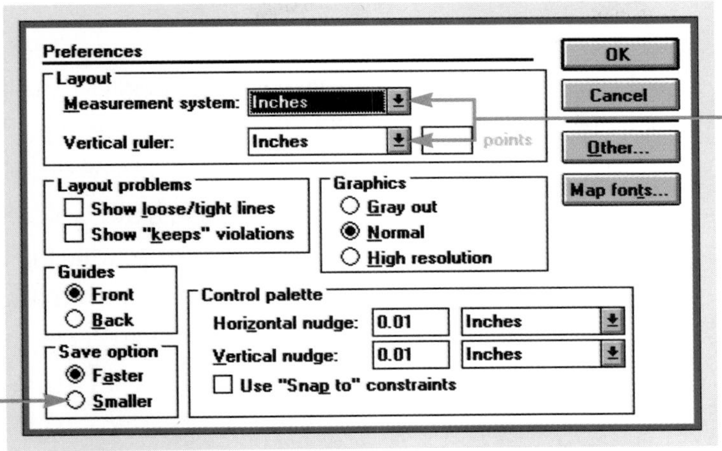

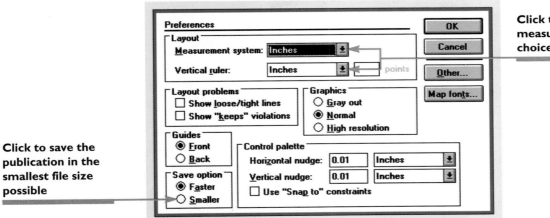

Click to display measurement system choices

Click to save the publication in the smallest file size possible

Increasing PageMaker's performance

You might have noticed some delay time for PageMaker to completely redraw the screen after performing certain commands. These delays usually occur when you work with publications that are large files. Publications that contain many graphics take up a great amount of disk space. One way to speed up PageMaker's performance when your publications contain many graphics is to select the Gray out option in the Graphics section of the Preferences dialog box. The Gray out option replaces the graphic with a gray box in the publication window and redraws the screen quickly. See Figure 7-3. Another method to increase the speed of screen redraw is the Greek text below option. You specify the size below which PageMaker will display text as gray bars. Displaying gray bars instead of text allows PageMaker to speed up the screen redraw in layout view.

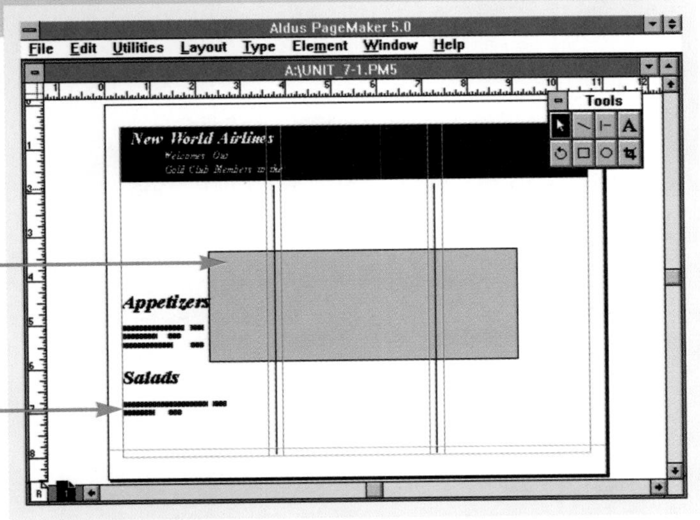

Grayed out airplane graphic

Greeked text

FIGURE 7-3: Gray out setting with greeked text

QUICK TIP

It is best to use only one unit of measurement throughout a publication.

Setting Preferences, continued

You might have noticed PageMaker uses tick marks (" and ') for quotation marks and apostrophes. PageMaker gives you the option to convert the appearance of these tick marks to curly marks, or typographer's quotes. **Typographer** refers to someone who designs or sets type in the commercial printing industry. You can use PageMaker's keystroke combinations each time you wish to use a typographer's quote (as described in Table 7-1), or you can activate the Use typographer's quotes option in the Preferences dialog box to use the curly marks automatically when you type quotation marks or apostrophes. ▶Joe decides to use the Preferences dialog box to improve the appearance of quotation marks and apostrophes.

STEPS

6 Click **Other**

The Other preferences dialog box opens as shown in Figure 7-4. See the related topic "Other preferences options" for additional information.

7 In the Text section, click the **Use typographer's quotes check box**

Typographer's quotes are represented as " " (quotation marks) or ' ' (apostrophes). Using typographer's quotes improves the appearance of quotations and apostrophes especially when used with san serif fonts, but you should still use tick marks when referring to measurements in feet or inches.

8 Click **OK** twice

This change affects only new text you type so you'll need to check your pub for tick marks.

9 Click the Text tool [A] in the toolbox, click I in the second line of the text block in the first column

10 Click **Layout** on the menu bar, click **View**, then click **200%**

Your view changes to 200% size as shown in Figure 7-5. Joe notices the tick mark quotation marks around the words "den-like." He wants to change the appearance of the tick marks to typographer quotes.

11 Select the text **"den-like"**, then retype **"den-like"**

Notice the tick marks have now changed to typographer's quotes.

12 Right-click twice to return the publication to Fit in window view

13 Click **File** on the menu bar, then click **Save**

TABLE 7-1: PageMaker's keystroke combinations for typographer's quotes

CHARACTER	KEY COMBINATION
‘	[Ctrl][[]
“	[Ctrl][Shift][[]
’	[Ctrl][]]
”	[Ctrl][Shift][]]

FIGURE 7-4: Other preferences dialog box

Click to turn on typographer's quotes

Use this section to change the story editor view

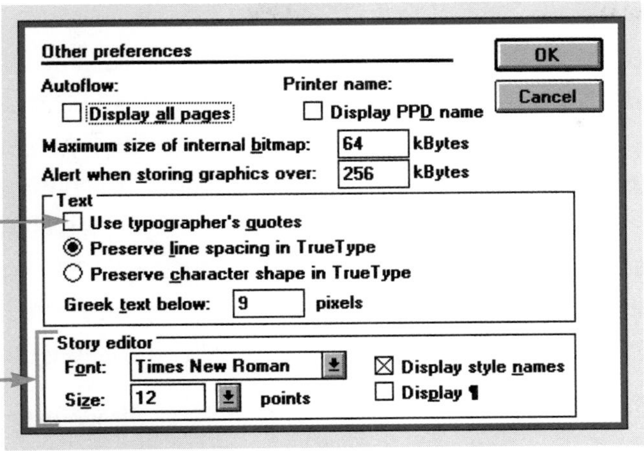

FIGURE 7-5: Tick marks as quotation marks

Tick marks need to be replaced by typographer's quotes

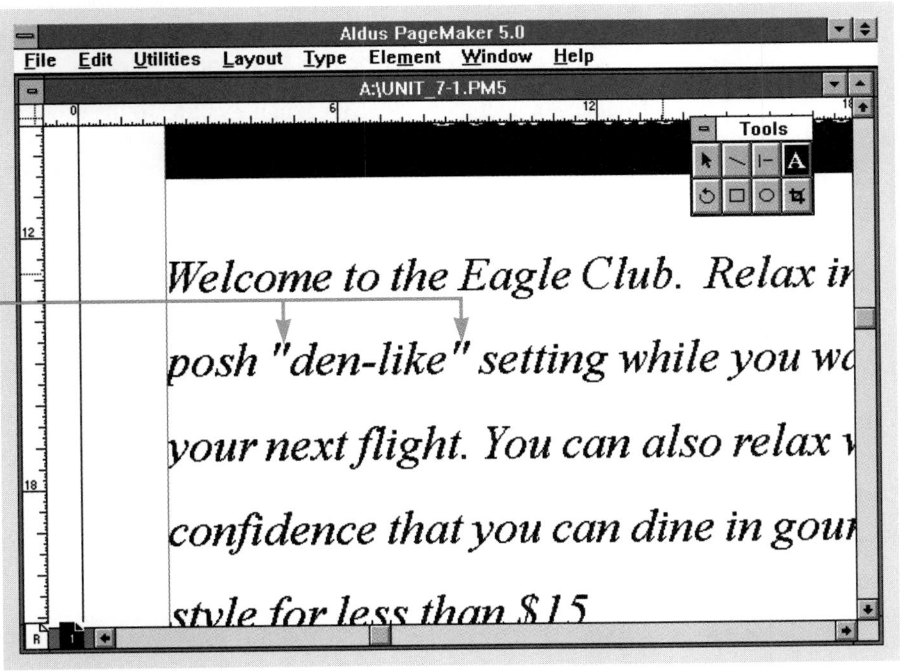

Other preferences options

Using Story editor can improve your ability to create text or edit long bodies of text in a multiple-page publication. Story editor displays all text using the same font and point size. If you use Story editor for any period of time, you might want to change font and size of the text display in story view. The story view display font is set inside the Other preferences dialog box. See Figure 7-4. Certain fonts are used for screen display, such as Geneva, New York, or even Arial because they are easier to read. You can also set Display ¶ to display non-printing characters each time you create or edit text in the Story editor view. Finally you can display style names in the left side of the story view. This is helpful because the story view is not WYSIWYG (What You See Is What You Get).

QUICK TIP

You can set default settings for all new publications by changing preferences settings when there are no documents open.

Defining the Control palette

As you already know, PageMaker gives you several different methods to accomplish the same task. To format text, you can use the Type specifications and Paragraph specifications dialog boxes, or commands on the Type menu. Another method is to use the Control palette, which lets you quickly apply text formats. The Control palette allows you to change text by switching between two views: **character view** for setting type formats and **paragraph view** for setting paragraph formats. You apply format settings by selecting the desired text and clicking one of the format buttons or by changing the edit box options on the Control palette.

Below are some of the benefits of using the Control palette:

- **Format character text quickly and easily**
  Clicking a Control palette button is faster than using the menus. See Table 7-2 for a description of the character view formatting buttons. Compare the Type specifications dialog box in Figure 7-6 and the Control palette's character view in Figure 7-7. Notice the character view allows you to format text by changing type styles, font attributes, word and character spacing.

- **Flexibility to move the Control palette anywhere in the layout or story view windows**
  You activate or hide the Control palette by selecting it from the Window menu. You can move the Control palette anywhere in the publication window by clicking its left border below its control menu box and dragging the palette to the desired location.

- **Easily switch between character and paragraph view**
  You can quickly change the view of your Control palette by clicking the Character view button A or the Paragraph view button ¶.

FIGURE 7-6: Type specifications dialog box

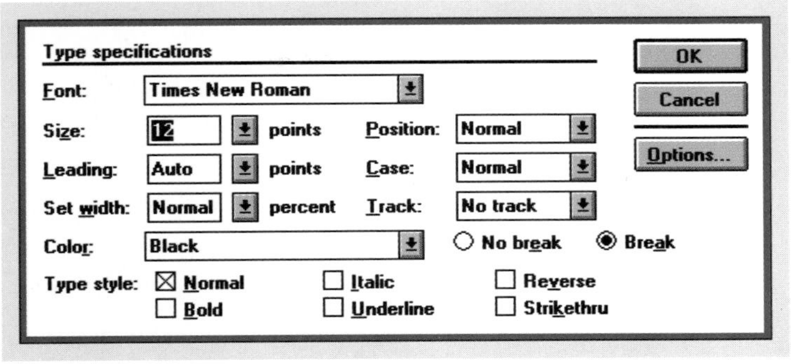

FIGURE 7-7: Control palette in character view

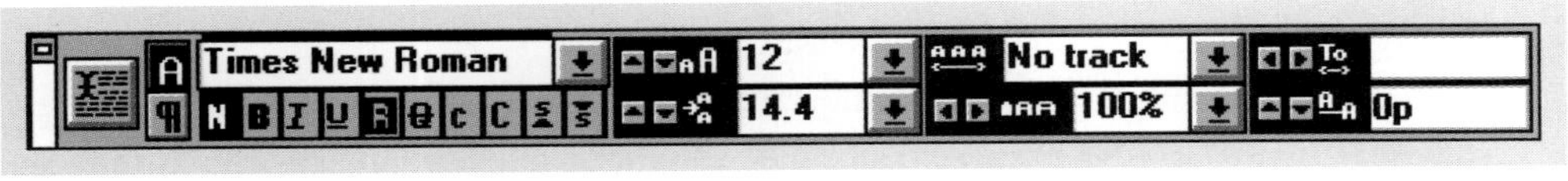

QUICK TIP

Press [Ctrl]['] to quickly open the Control palette in the publication window.

TABLE 7-2: Control palette's character view buttons and options

BUTTON/BOX	OPTION	DESCRIPTION
	Apply button	Applies changes made on the Control palette
	Paragraph view button	Changes Control palette to paragraph view
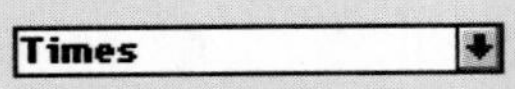	Font option	Applies typeface from list of available system fonts to selected text
	Type style buttons	Apply special type styles to selected text: Normal, Bold, Italic, Underline, Reverse, Strikethru
	Case buttons	Change the case of text; the left button sets lowercase text in small capital letters, and the right button sets the text in all capitals
	Superscript/subscript buttons	Change the size and position of text
	Type size option	Sets the point size; type a value in the edit box or use the list arrow to display available sizes
	Leading option	Sets the leading—type a value in the edit box or use the list arrow to display available sizes of leading; the list includes an auto setting that sets the type to the default leading
	Track option	Sets the tracking or the spacing between characters
	Set width option	Sets the width of characters—100% is the default; you increase the width of the letters by choosing a value greater than 100% and decrease the width with a value less than 100%
	Kerning option	Sets the width between characters
	Baseline shift option	Raises or lowers the baseline for the selected text

Defining the Control palette, continued

Additional benefits of using the Control palette include:

- **Format paragraph text quickly and easily**
  Clicking a Control palette button is faster than using the menus. See Table 7-3 for a description of the paragraph view formatting buttons. Compare the Paragraph specifications dialog box in Figure 7-8 and Control palette's paragraph view in Figure 7-9. The paragraph view allows you to set alignments, indents, styles, and other settings for one or more paragraphs.

- **Change options by precise measurements**
  Next to most Control palette options are little arrows called **nudge buttons** that allow you to make changes by a preset measurement. When you click a nudge button PageMaker immediately makes the change. The amount by which the setting changes depends on the default units of measurement setting. The default nudge amount for inches is 0.01 inches. This default nudge can be changed using the Preferences dialog box. You can also make changes by a mathematical factor. See the related topic "Performing arithmetic adjustments" for more information.

TABLE 7-3: Control palette's paragraph view buttons and options

BUTTON/BOX	OPTION	DESCRIPTION
	Apply button	Applies changes made on the Control palette
	Character view button	Changes Control palette to character view
	Paragraph style option	Applies preset styles to selected text
	Alignment buttons	Align text to the left or right, centers it, or justifies it on the publication page
	Cursor position indicator	Tracks the position of cursor on public action page
	Left indent options	Set the indent from left margin
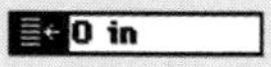	Right indent options	Set the indent from the right margin
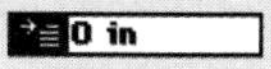	First-line indent options	Set the indent for the first line of the paragraph
	Space-before option	Sets the space above the beginning of a paragraph
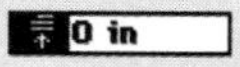	Space-after option	Sets the space below the last line of a paragraph
	Grid-size option	Sets the size of the text grid you want to use when the align-to-grid option is on
	Align-to-grid buttons	Automatically align vertically the baselines of adjacent column (the right button turns the option on and the left button turns it off)

FIGURE 7-8: Paragraph specifications dialog box

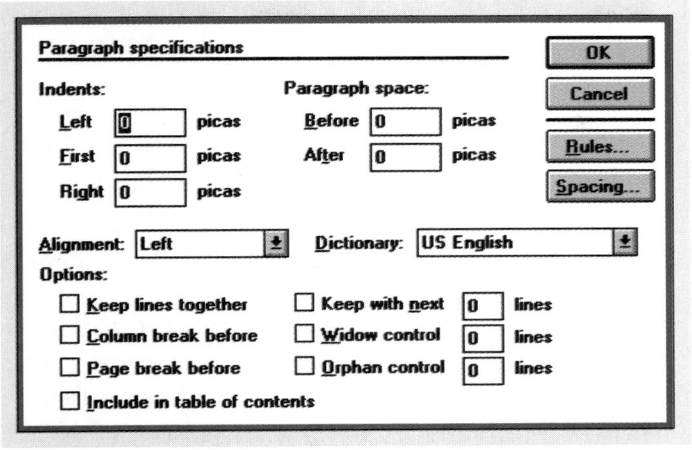

FIGURE 7-9: Control palette in paragraph view

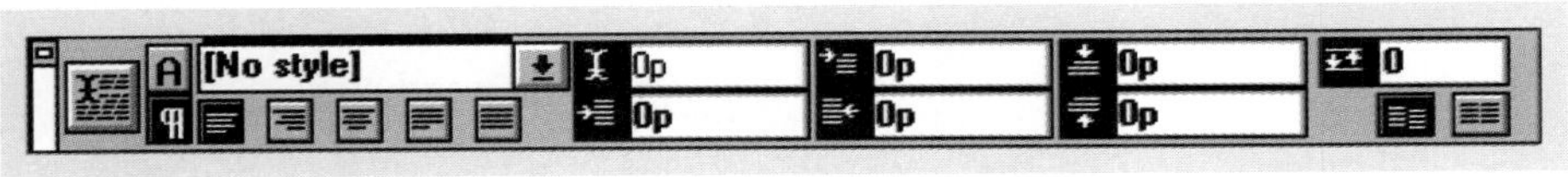

Performing arithmetic adjustments

You can use the Control palette to perform simple arithmetic in any active numeric option by typing the numeric expression into the option's text box. For example, to scale a text headline to three times its size, you would first select the text. Then, the right of the value in the Type size text box, type $\times 3$ and click apply. The text headline automatically scales to three times its original size.

QUICK TIP

A Power Nudge allows you to increase a nudge setting by a factor of 10 by pressing [Ctrl] as you click a nudge button.■

Applying small capitals

PageMaker lets you create special effects using the Control palette or the Type options dialog box. You can choose the settings for position (Superscript or Subscript) and size (All caps, Small caps, or None), and you can also adjust the size of the baseline shift. You will learn about adjusting the baseline in the next lesson. ▶ Joe wants to add the restaurant's name in reverse type to the menu banner across the top of the page. Then he will apply the small capital feature for an innovative look.

STEPS

1. **Click Window on the menu bar, click Control palette, then click the Character view button on the Control palette, if necessary**
   The Control palette appears in character view, as shown in Figure 7-10. If the Control palette does not appear in either character or paragraph view, click the Text tool in the toolbox to switch to character view. Joe wants to define the size of the text block for the restaurant's name.
2. Position at the 30-pica marker on the horizontal ruler and at the 4-pica marker on the vertical ruler, then drag to the lower-right corner of the black box
   After you release the mouse button, the insertion point appears in the black box. Joe is ready to use the Control palette to set the type specifications for the restaurant's name.
3. Click the **Reverse button** on the Control palette, then click the **Font list arrow** on the Control palette
   The font list appears in the Control palette as shown in Figure 7-11. Joe decides to use the sans serif font Arial for the menu banner.
4. Click **Arial**
5. Double-click inside the **Type size text box**, type **72**, then click the **Apply button** on the Control palette
   Joe also needs to set the leading for the text block.
6. Click the **Leading list arrow** on the Control palette, click **Auto**, then type **Eagle Club**
7. Select the name **Eagle Club**, then click the **Small caps button** on the Control palette
   See Figure 7-12. This changes the lowercase text to capital letters smaller than regular capital letters. Joe wants to decrease the size of the small caps in relation to the first letter of each word. This option is not available on the Control palette, so Joe opens the Type options dialog box.
8. Click **Type** on the menu bar, click **Type specs**, then click **Options**
   The Type options dialog box opens as shown in Figure 7-13.
9. Type **50** in the Small caps size text box, then click **OK** twice
   This changes the lowercase letters to capital letters that are 50% of the size of the corresponding full sized capital letters.
10. Deselect the text by clicking anywhere outside the text area, click **File** on the menu bar, then click **Save**

FIGURE 7-10: Control palette in character view

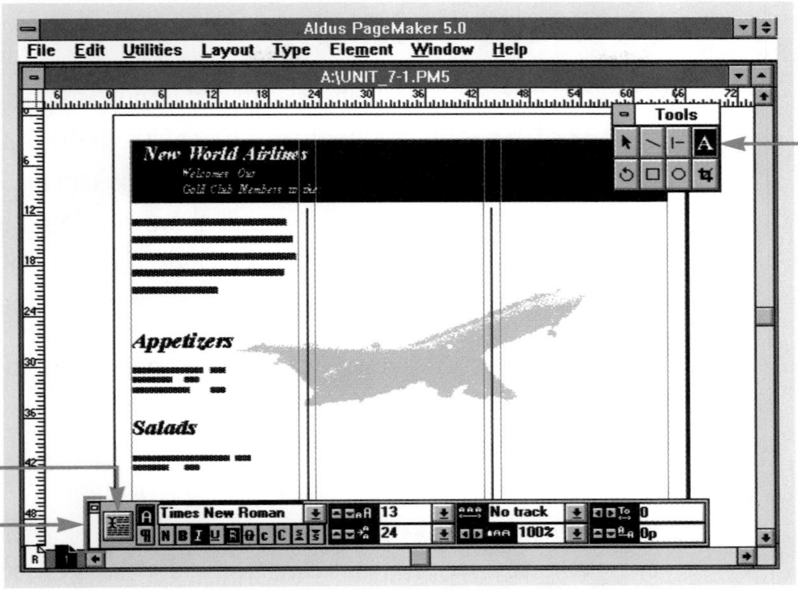

Text tool needs to be selected to display the Control palette in character view

Character view button

Control palette

FIGURE 7-11: Font list

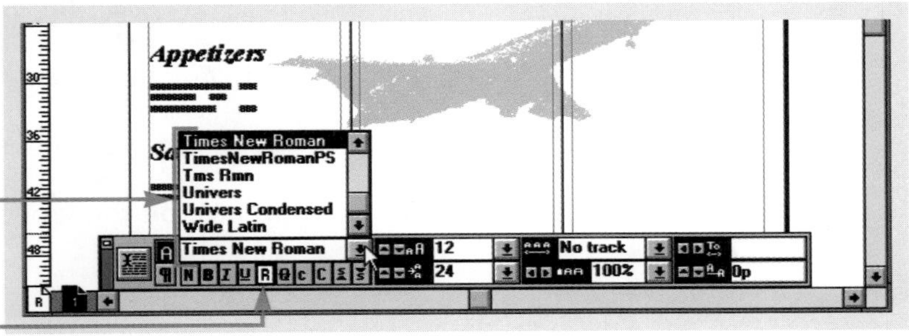

Your font list might be different

Click to turn on reverse text

FIGURE 7-12: Small caps applied to name

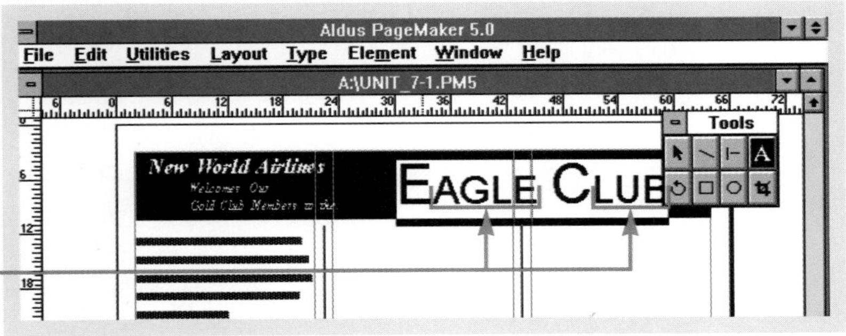

Lowercase letters are now small caps

FIGURE 7-13: Type options dialog box

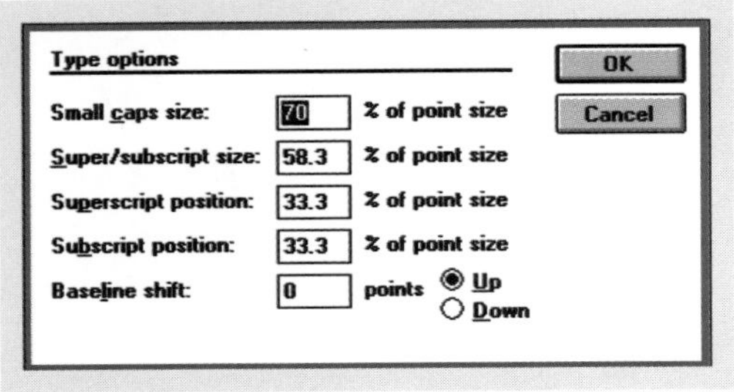

DESIGN TIP

To use it effectively, apply the small caps option only to text that is 14 points or larger.

Adjusting the baseline

You can also create special effects with text by adjusting its position on the baseline. The **baseline** is an imaginary line that text rests on as shown in Figure 7-14. Text can be moved above or below a baseline. You can use the Control palette or the Type options dialog box to shift the text above or below the baseline in increments as little as a tenth of a point. ▶ Joe decides to use the Control palette to shift the baseline of the small capital letters in the restaurant name.

STEPS

1. Select "**agle**" of the word "eagle," then right-click to change view to Actual size
2. Type **0p6** in the Baseline shift text box on the Control palette, then click the **Apply button** on the Control palette
   See Figure 7-15. Joe decides that a baseline shift of a half a pica is not enough. He is not sure how much more to increase the baseline shift so he decides to increment the shift using the nudge buttons.
3. Click the **Baseline shift nudge up arrow** on the Control palette six times
   Notice that the setting in the Baseline shift text box changes each time you click. Joe decides that a baseline shift of 1p looks the best so he decides to do the same with the word "club."
4. Deselect the text, then select "**lub**" of the word "club"
5. Type **1p** in the Baseline shift option box on the Control palette, then click **Apply**
   See Figure 7-16.
6. Click **File** on the menu bar, then click **Save**

FIGURE 7-14: The baseline

Imaginary line on which text rests

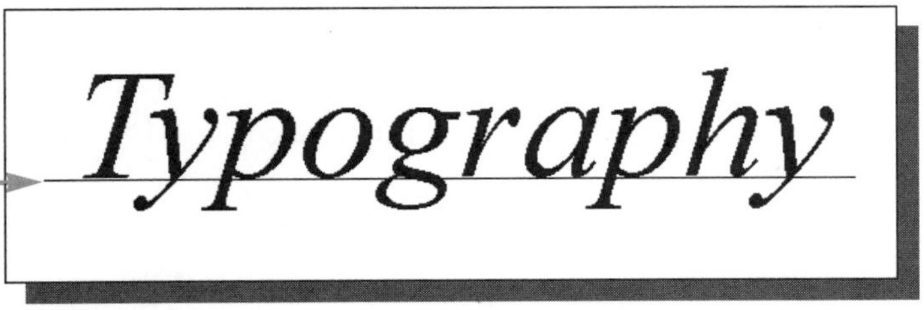

FIGURE 7-15: "AGLE" with a 6 point pica baseline shift applied

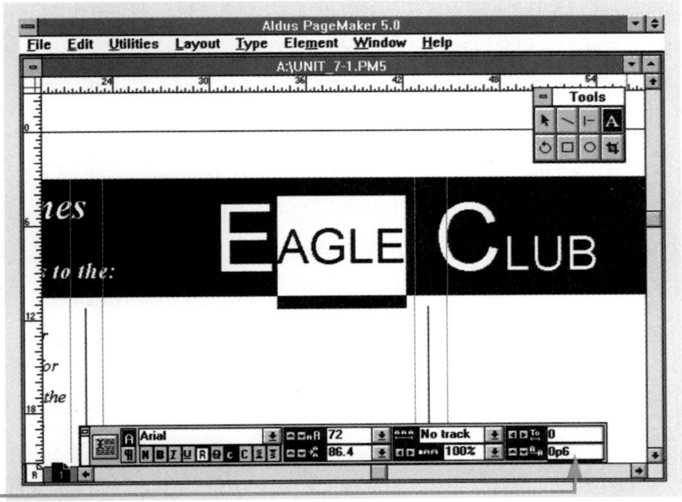

Baseline shift text box

FIGURE 7-16: "Eagle Club" with baseline shift applied

Small caps centered after initial cap

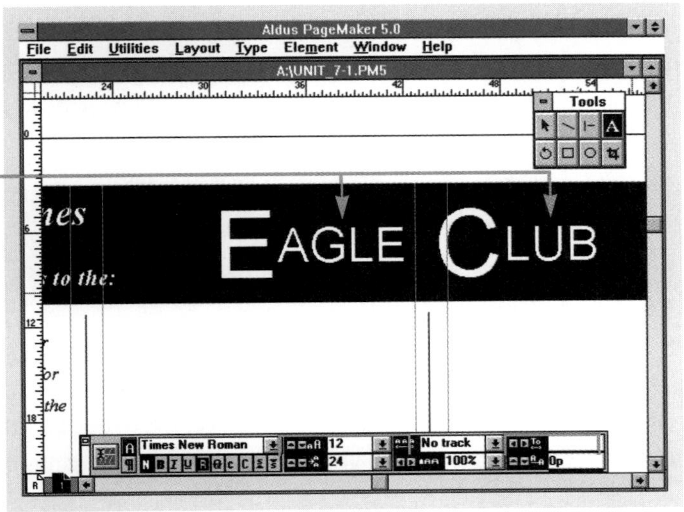

Adjusting text spacing

Adjusting word and letter spacing is a powerful PageMaker feature for improving the overall appearance of your publication. You have full control of the space between each character and the amount of space between each word. You can tighten spacing between characters to fit text in a defined area or make headlines and small text easier to read by increasing the spacing. ▶ You can modify word or character spacing using one of three methods. First, you can adjust spacing of both words and letters in a paragraph or selected paragraphs by percentages using the Spacing option in the Paragraph dialog box. Secondly, you can use the Kerning option on the Control palette to specify the exact measurement of space between characters in the selected text. **Kerning** by definition is adjusting space between a pair or range of characters. Finally, you can also adjust spacing quickly by choosing one of six predefined spacing defaults using the Tracking command. Tracking can be set using the Track option on the Control palette or in the Type Specifications dialog box. ▶ Joe wants to "loosen" the text in the first column to make it easier to read. He also adjusts the kerning of the Categories heading in the menu to make the categories more eye-catching.

STEPS

1. **Use the scroll bars to position the first paragraph in the first column in the center of the publication window**
2. **Select the entire paragraph, then click the Track list arrow on the Control palette**
   See Figure 7-17. The Track submenu appears, offering six tracking options. See Table 7-4 for examples of the tracking options.
3. **Click Very loose**
   Spacing increases between characters. Joe now wants to reduce the space between characters for the category dividers. He will use the kerning option because it gives him more control over spacing than tracking does.
4. **Use the scroll bars to position the word "Appetizers" in the publication window, then select the word Appetizers**
5. **Double-click inside the Kerning text box, type .25, then click the Apply button on the Control palette**
   See Figure 7-18. The space between characters is measured in ems. A unit **em** is equal to the width of a lowercase m of the same size and font. Values greater than 0 increase the space between characters and values under 0 decrease the space. Joe is satisfied with the special effect that is created by the kerning adjustment and will now apply the same setting to the next category.
6. **Scroll down the publication, select the word Salads, type .25 in the Kerning text box on the Control palette, then click**
   You will open a more complete menu in the next lesson, so you can close and save this file.
7. **Click the control menu box in the Control palette to close it, click File on the menu bar, click Close, then click Yes when you are asked if you want to save your publication**

FIGURE 7-17: Track submenu

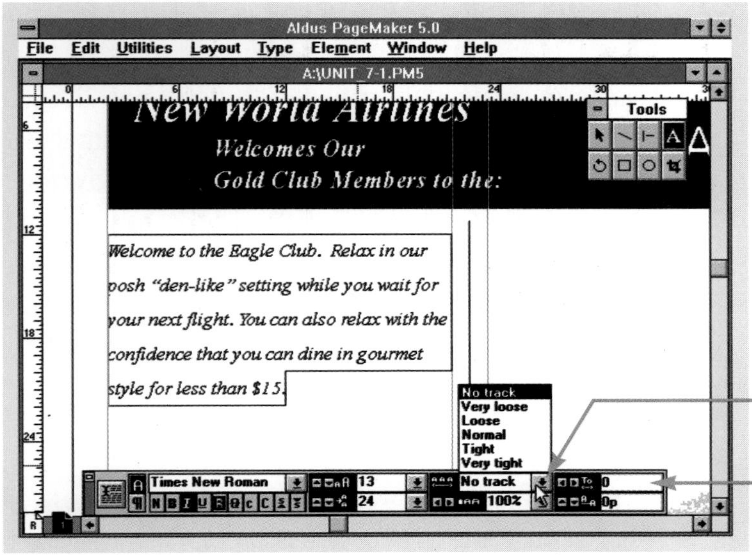

FIGURE 7-18: Reduced kerning applied to category divider

TABLE 7-4: Examples of tracking

EXAMPLE	SETTING
This is an example of Tracking	No track
This is an example of Tracking	Very loose
This is an example of Tracking	Loose
This is an example of Tracking	Normal
This is an example of Tracking	Tight
This is an example of Tracking	Very tight

DESIGN TIP

If you are using styles, make sure you apply spacing attributes for the entire style and not just for individual paragraphs.

QUICK TIP

To remove all manual kerning from selected text, press [Shift][Ctrl][0] (not on the numeric keypad).

Setting character widths

PageMaker gives you the option to change the width of an individual character using the Set width command. You can set the character width by using either the Control palette or the Type specifications dialog box. You can scale character width by any percentage from 5% to 250%. The default percentage is 100%. ▶ Joe would like to widen each character in the category headings. Joe could use the Control palette to adjust the width of the categories, but he decides to adjust all of the category headings at once using the defined Categories style.

STEPS

1 **Open the file Unit_7-2.PM5** from your Student Disk
This menu is nearly complete.

2 Click **Window** on the menu bar, then click **Style palette**
Joe has set up separate styles for the category headings, item names, and the descriptions.

3 Click the **Text tool** [A] in the toolbox, click I inside **Appetizers**, then **right-click** to change the view to actual size
The Categories style is selected in the Style palette. Joe wants to create a special effect and widen the characters' size. See Table 7-5 for examples of styles with applied set widths. Joe decides to widen the category heading's character size to 130% of its actual width. He will modify the widths of all the category headings at once by changing the categories style. You could use the Control palette to change the width one heading at a time.

4 Click **Type** on the menu bar, then click **Define styles**
The Define style dialog box opens.

5 Click **Categories** in the Style list box, click **Edit**, then click **Type**
The Type specifications dialog box opens. Notice the current width of the characters is Normal.

6 Click the **Set width list arrow**
See Figure 7-19. You can choose one of the predefined widths or type the desired percentage that you wish to scale the text. Joe wants to draw attention to the category names, so he chooses the largest predefined width setting.

7 Click **130**, then click **OK** three times
See Figure 7-20. Notice the character width for all of the text in Categories style has increased in size.

Joe, upon viewing the entire publication, is satisfied with the effect of the widened category headings so he saves his publication.

8 Click **File** on the menu bar, then click **Save**

FIGURE 7-19: Set width list options

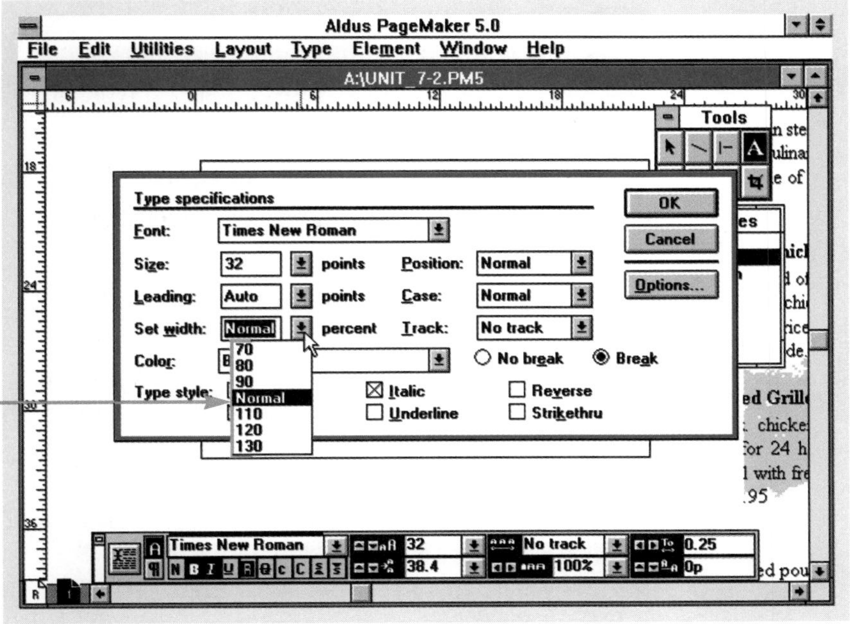

Predefined widths

FIGURE 7-20: Set width applied to the Categories style

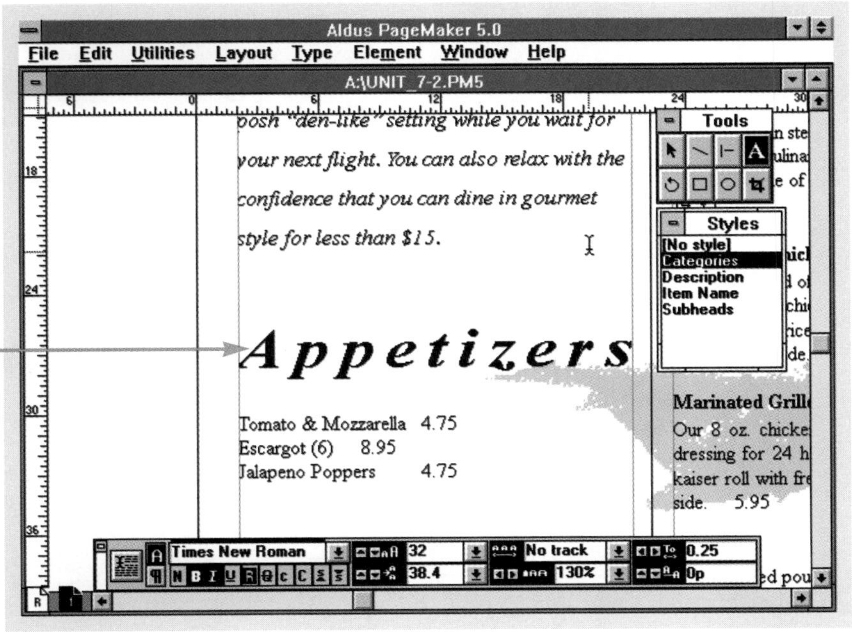

Width of characters increased to fill entire column

TABLE 7-5: Examples of character widths

WIDTH SETTING	EXAMPLE
80% set width	New World Airlines
Normal width	New World Airlines
130% set width	New World Airlines

TROUBLE?

Print your publication to make sure the printed character widths match your screen's character widths.

Setting tabs

Tabs, which are nonprinting characters, allow you to position text at specific locations within a text block. Tabs can help you create columns of text within a text block. You can set left, center, right, and decimal tabs. See Table 7-6 for a description of the tab icons in the Indents/tabs dialog box. Tab settings can also include a leader. **Leaders** are repeat patterns between tabbed items. Examples of leaders include repeated dots or dashes. ▶ Joe wants to add dot leaders to create a visual link between the item description and the price.

STEPS

1. **Move I over the text in column 2, then right-click twice**
   Joe could change the tabs for each description individually using the Indents/tabs dialog box found on the Type menu. However, by editing the description style, Joe changes all of the description tabs and leaders at once.
2. **Click Type on the menu bar, then click Define styles**
   The Define styles dialog box opens.
3. **Click Description in the Style list box, click Edit, then click Tabs**
   The Indents/tabs dialog box opens. A small section of the ruler shows the default tabs and the indent markers reflect the width of the text block. Joe wants to use a right tab to align the prices near the right margin.
4. **Click the Right tab icon**
   Now, if you click in the tab area located above the ruler, you will set a right-aligned tab.
5. **Click the tab area around 18 picas**
   See Figure 7-21. The exact position of the tab you placed appears in the Position text box. See the related topic "Using the Indents/tabs Position button" for more information. Joe decides to drag the tab closer to the right margin.
6. **Drag the right tab marker to the 19-pica mark**
   The Position text box verifies the location of the tab.
7. **Click Leader**
   A menu displays options for tab leaders as shown in Figure 7-22. You choose one of the options from this list, or you can type any character in the Leader text box. The character in the text box then repeats between tabs as a leader.
8. **Click the dotted lines option, then click OK three times**
   Dotted lines now fill the space between the last word in the menu item description and the price, as shown in Figure 7-23.

TABLE 7-6: Tab icons in the Indents/tab dialog box

TAB ICONS	NAME	DESCRIPTION
	Left tab	Sets a left-aligned tab
	Right tab	Sets a right-aligned tab
	Center tab	Sets a tab that centers text over it
	Decimal tab	Sets a tab aligned to a decimal point

FIGURE 7-21: Right tab at the 18-pica mark

Tab area for setting tabs

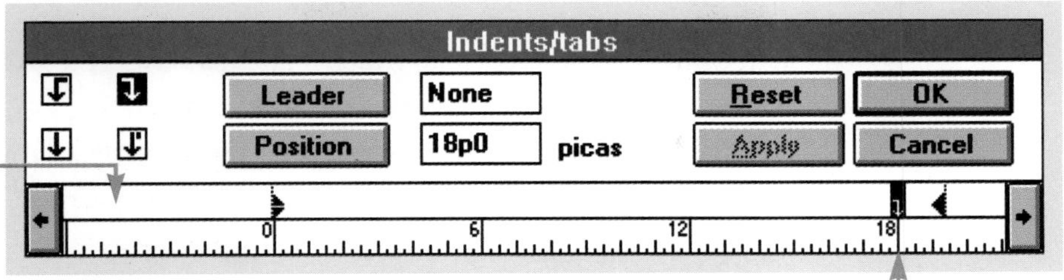

18-pica mark

FIGURE 7-22: Leader options

Click to choose this leader

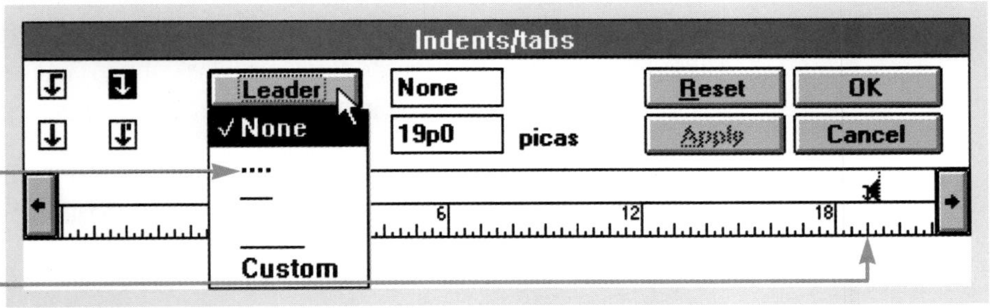

19-pica mark

FIGURE 7-23: Tabs and leaders applied to text block

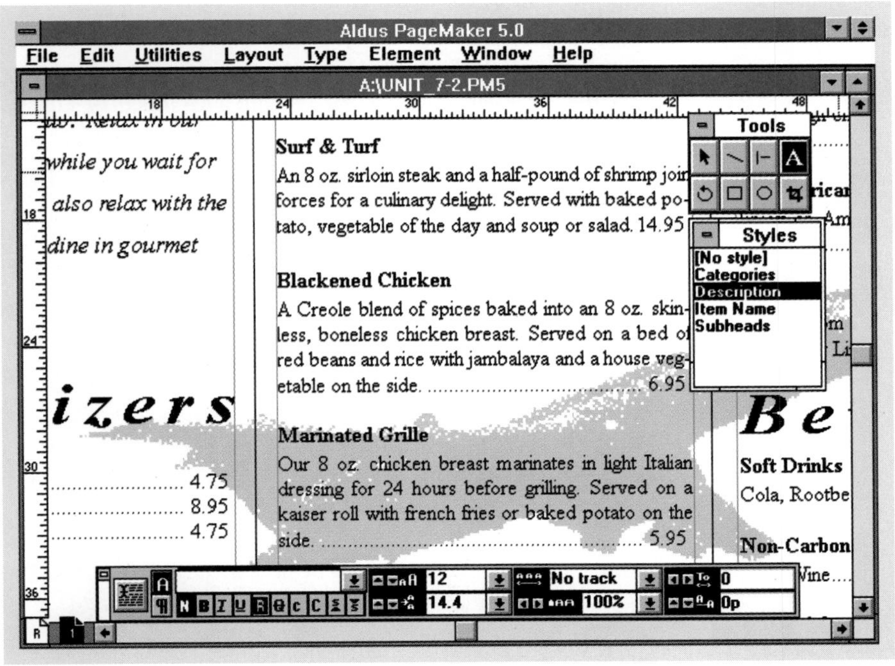

Using the Indents/tabs Position button

When you work with small monitors, it can be difficult to drag a tab to a specific position on the ruler. The Position button in the Indents/tabs dialog box allows you to set tabs at smaller increments than your ruler displays. To set a tab using the Position button, type the position of the tab in the text box, click Position, then click Add tab. You can also set tabs in increments by clicking Position, then clicking Repeat tab.

Setting indents

PageMaker lets you set both indents and tabs within a text block. Indents allow you move text inward from either the right or left margin without changing the original margin settings. ▶ You can change indents many different ways. You can use the Control palette, the Paragraph specifications dialog box or the Indents/tabs dialog box. See Table 7-7 for a description of the indent icons in the Indents/tabs dialog box. ▶ Joe wants to indent each of the menu description paragraphs to create a layered effect that will make the menu items stand out from their descriptions.

STEPS

1 Click **Type** on the menu bar, then click **Define styles**
The Define styles dialog box opens. Once again Joe wants to change the indents for all the descriptions at once so he will edit the indent settings for the Description style.

2 Click **Description** in the Style list box, click **Edit**, then click **Tabs**
The Indents/tabs dialog box opens. Joe decides to indent the descriptions 4 picas from the left column guide.

3 Drag the **left indent icon** ▸ until **4p0** appears in the Position text box
See Figure 7-24. Make sure you click the lower triangle of ▸. The top triangle moves independently from the bottom, so you need to drag the bottom triangle to set the left indent.

4 Click **OK** three times
All the menu item descriptions now contain a left indent of 4 picas along with their dotted leaders as shown in Figure 7-25. Joe would now like to set a first line indent for the welcome paragraph in the first column. He didn't set a style for this body of text so he will use the paragraph view of the Control palette to set the indent independently.

5 Scroll to display the paragraph of text in the first column, then click I inside the paragraph
You need to place the insertion point inside the paragraph to which you wish to apply the first line indent. Joe needs to display the control palette before he can use it to set the indent.

6 If the Control palette is not already displayed, click **Window**, click **Control palette**, then click the **Paragraph-view button** ¶ on the Control palette

7 Double-click **0** inside the First line indent text box, type **4p**, then click the **Apply button** on the Control palette
See Figure 7-26. Joe decides 4 picas is too much space for a first line indent, so he changes the indent to 2 picas.

8 Select the **4** in the First line indent text box, type **2**, then click
Joe is satisfied with the indents and saves his publication.

9 Click **File** on the menu bar, then click **Save**

FIGURE 7-24: Indents/tabs dialog box

Left indent icon at 4 picas

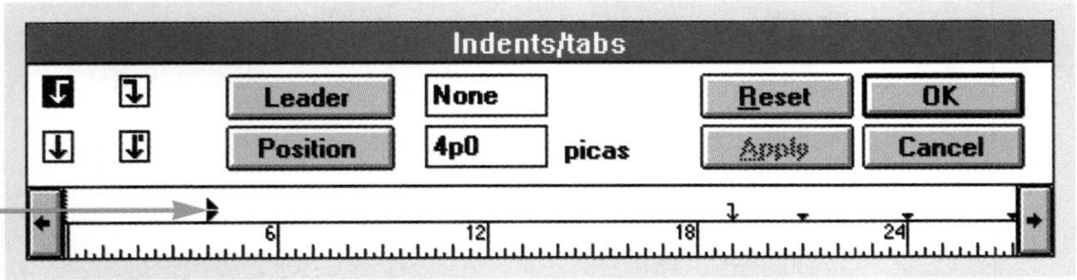

FIGURE 7-25: Indents applied to text

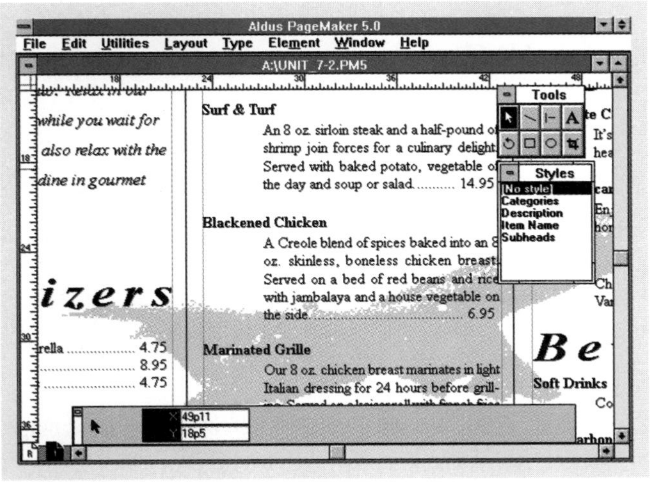

FIGURE 7-26: First line indented 4 picas

First-line indent text box

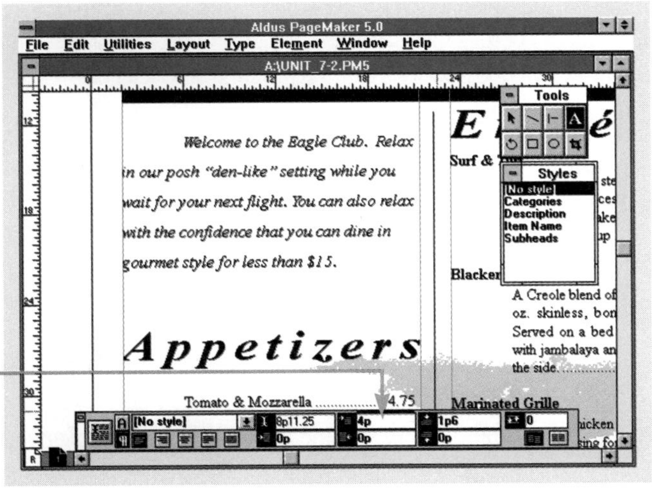

TABLE 7-7: Indent icons in the Indents/tabs dialog box

INDENT ICONS	DESCRIPTION
	First-line indent
	Left indent
	Right indent

TROUBLE?

You cannot directly access the Indents/tabs dialog box when you are using Story editor—you have to place the story first.

Using the Bullets and numbering Addition

The Bullets and numbering Addition allows you to use bullets, numbers, or special characters with a tab in front of each selected paragraph. You can use this feature to add bullets or numbers to consecutive paragraphs, to all paragraphs with a specific style, to every paragraph in a story, or to only selected paragraphs. ▶ Joe would like to add a special airplane character in front of each menu item.

STEPS

1. **Click I inside the menu item Surf & Turf in the second column**
   In order to use the Bullets and numbering Addition, the insertion point must be placed inside the text block where the feature will be applied.
2. Click **Utilities** on the menu bar, click **Aldus Additions**, then click **Bullets and numbering**
   The Bullets and numbering dialog box opens as shown in Figure 7-27. You can pick any bullet under the Bullet style or click Edit to see a list of all the optional characters that can be used instead of a bullet.
3. Click **Edit**
   The Edit bullet dialog box opens as shown in Figure 7-28. All of the characters for the selected font appear in the dialog box. Joe needs to choose the Wingdings font, which contains a special airplane character.
4. Click the **Font list arrow**, then click **Wingdings**
   Notice that all of the characters from the previous font change to the characters for the Wingdings font. Joe now looks for the airplane character.
5. Click the **Airplane character** in the second row from the top near the middle
   The Example box changes to display the airplane character.
6. Click **OK**
   The Edit bullet dialog box closes and returns to the Bullets and numbering dialog box.
7. In the Range section, click the **All those with style radio button**
   This will apply the airplane character to the beginning of each paragraph in the selected style. Notice that Description appears in the list box. Joe needs to change the style to Item Name.
8. Click the **style list arrow**, click **Item Name**, then click **OK**
   The airplane character is automatically applied to the front of each paragraph in the Item name style, as shown in Figure 7-29.
9. Close the Control palette, save the publication, then exit PageMaker

FIGURE 7-27: Bullets and numbering dialog box

Style list arrow

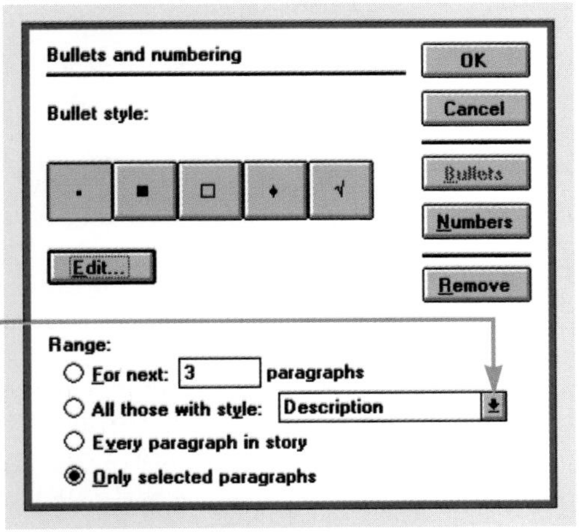

FIGURE 7-28: Edit bullet dialog box

Font list arrow

Shows selected bullet character

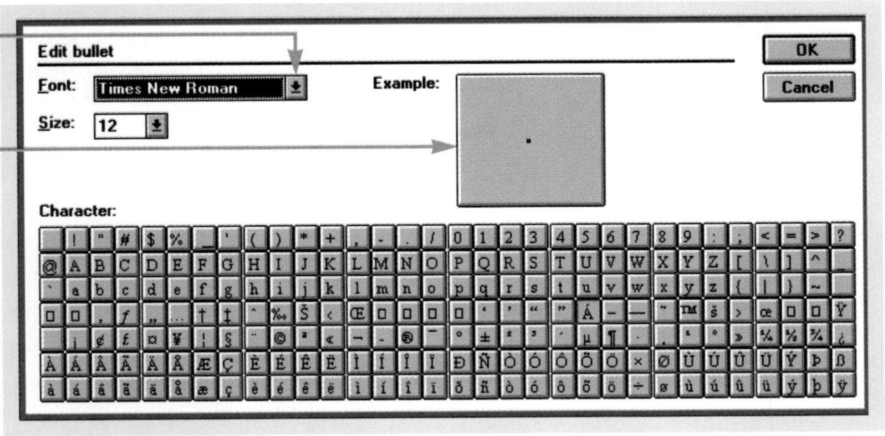

FIGURE 7-29: Airplane character applied to Item Name style

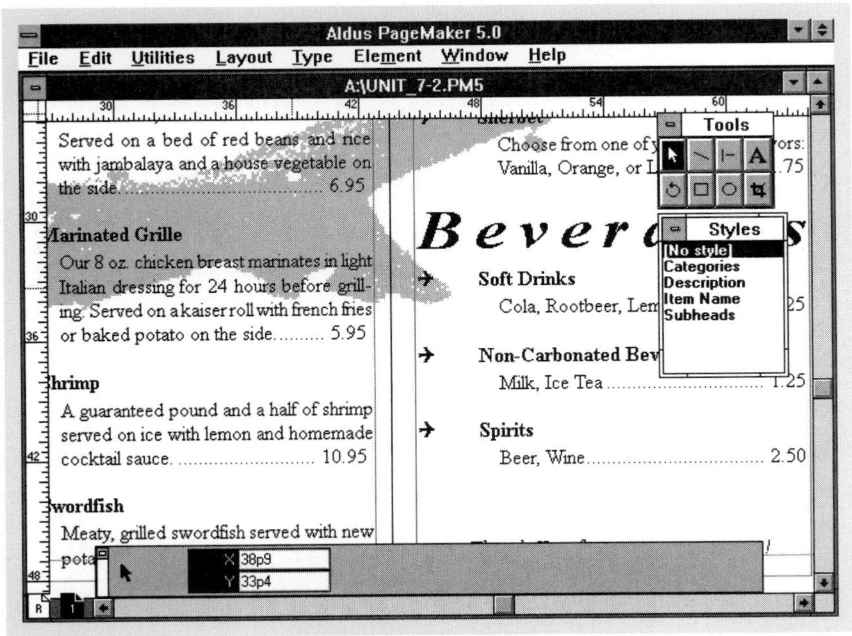

TROUBLE?

Use the Revert command on the File menu if you make a mistake while using the Bullets and numbering Addition.

Design Workshop: Menus

A menu needs to provide a creative, concise listing of a restaurant's fare. The menu needs to feature certain selections and give an overall impression of the restaurant. ▶ After creating the menu, Joe critiques his work, as shown in Figure 7-30.

STEPS

1 **Does the menu highlight the items it should?**
According to Joe's information, the Surf & Turf needed to be featured prominently to help sell it. He placed the menu item at the top of the center column of the menu. Other ways to highlight the menu item could be to reverse the text, place a bullet or other icon next to the menu item to give it special treatment, or change the font to something much bolder. No one way is the correct way. Usually, a few different techniques can work well together to produce the desired result.

2 **Is the menu well organized?**
Joe separated the menu into main sections to help customers select items quickly. He also placed all of the entrées in one column so customers wouldn't have to search the menu for more selections.

3 **What other improvements can Joe make?**
By making the menu one color (black), Joe keeps costs down. He plans to take the menu to a local copy center and copy the entire menu on a cream-colored stock paper. The color scheme matches that of the Eagle Club. Joe can easily change menu items to meet the needs of the chef or change the menu to meet the season. For example, during Thanksgiving, a turkey dinner could replace the Surf & Turf. To add variety or to add more menu items, Joe could change the size of the menu or possibly rotate the orientation so the menu is tall instead of wide.

FIGURE 7-30: The completed menu

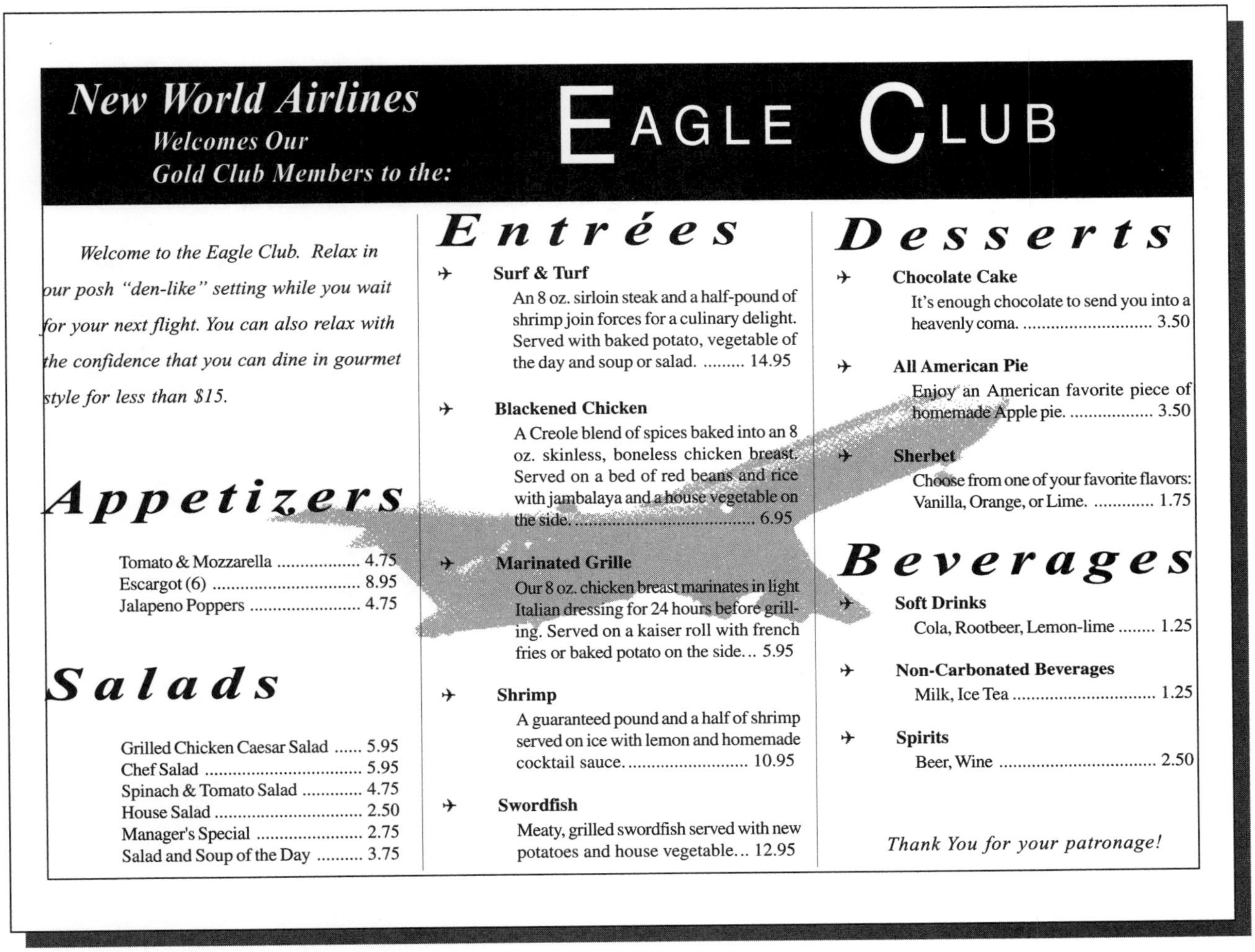

New World Airlines
Welcomes Our
Gold Club Members to the:

EAGLE CLUB

Welcome to the Eagle Club. Relax in our posh "den-like" setting while you wait for your next flight. You can also relax with the confidence that you can dine in gourmet style for less than $15.

Appetizers

Tomato & Mozzarella 4.75
Escargot (6) 8.95
Jalapeno Poppers 4.75

Salads

Grilled Chicken Caesar Salad 5.95
Chef Salad 5.95
Spinach & Tomato Salad 4.75
House Salad 2.50
Manager's Special 2.75
Salad and Soup of the Day 3.75

Entrées

Surf & Turf
An 8 oz. sirloin steak and a half-pound of shrimp join forces for a culinary delight. Served with baked potato, vegetable of the day and soup or salad. 14.95

Blackened Chicken
A Creole blend of spices baked into an 8 oz. skinless, boneless chicken breast. Served on a bed of red beans and rice with jambalaya and a house vegetable on the side. 6.95

Marinated Grille
Our 8 oz. chicken breast marinates in light Italian dressing for 24 hours before grill-ing. Served on a kaiser roll with french fries or baked potato on the side... 5.95

Shrimp
A guaranteed pound and a half of shrimp served on ice with lemon and homemade cocktail sauce. 10.95

Swordfish
Meaty, grilled swordfish served with new potatoes and house vegetable... 12.95

Desserts

Chocolate Cake
It's enough chocolate to send you into a heavenly coma. 3.50

All American Pie
Enjoy an American favorite piece of homemade Apple pie. 3.50

Sherbet
Choose from one of your favorite flavors: Vanilla, Orange, or Lime. 1.75

Beverages

Soft Drinks
Cola, Rootbeer, Lemon-lime 1.25

Non-Carbonated Beverages
Milk, Ice Tea 1.25

Spirits
Beer, Wine 2.50

Thank You for your patronage!

CONCEPTS REVIEW

Label each of the publication window elements shown in Figure 7-31.

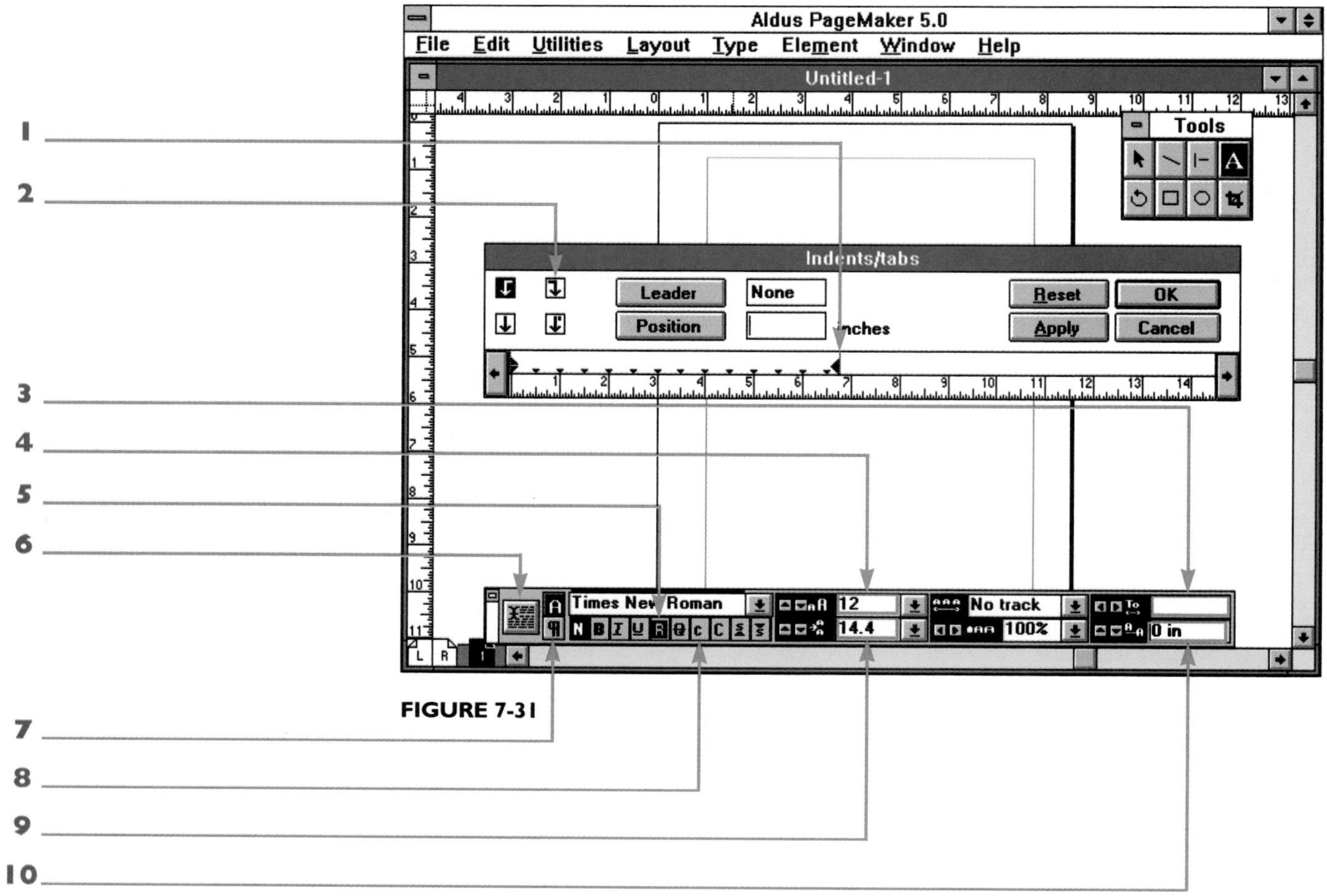

FIGURE 7-31

Match each of the statements with the term it describes.

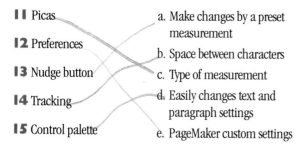

11 Picas
12 Preferences
13 Nudge button
14 Tracking
15 Control palette

a. Make changes by a preset measurement
b. Space between characters
c. Type of measurement
d. Easily changes text and paragraph settings
e. PageMaker custom settings

Select the best answer from the list of choices.

16 When you create your page layout, what are the power points?

a. The four corners where the margins intersect
b. The most read sections of the publication
c. The graphics in the lower-left corner
d. None of the above

17 Using the Preferences dialog box, you can customize the following

a. Measurement system
b. Quotation marks
c. Save file size options
d. All of the above

18 The imaginary line on which characters of type reside is the

a. Margin line
b. Bar
c. Baseline
d. Either b or c

19 The Track command on the Type menu allows you to

a. Choose one of six predefined spacing defaults
b. Manually set the space between characters
c. Track the amount of space taken up on a page
d. Track the letter size of a paragraph

20 The Kerning option on the Control palette allows you to

a. Set the tracking for paragraphs
b. Choose a predefined spacing default
c. Change the text size
d. Manually set the space between characters

21 PageMaker's default setting for tabs is

a. Every .25"
b. Every .5"
c. Every 1"
d. There is no default setting

22 Leaders refer to

a. Repeated patterns between tabs
b. Default tab setting
c. Decimal tab setting
d. Both b and c

23 Indents allow you to

a. Set tabs within text
b. Move text up or down within a column
c. Move text inward from either the right or left margin
d. Both a and b

24 Using the Control palette in character view, you can modify the following, except

a. Font size
b. Type style
c. Rotate text
d. None of the above

25 Using the Control palette in paragraph view, you can modify the following, except

a. Indents
b. Tabs
c. Widows and orphans
d. None of the above

26 Character width can be set using

a. Font menu
b. Control palette
c. Type specifications dialog box
d. Both b and c

APPLICATIONS REVIEW

1 Set the preferences.

a. Start PageMaker and open the file UNIT_7-3.PM5 from your Student Disk.
b. Open the Preferences dialog box.
c. Select Picas from the Measurement system list box.
d. Select Picas from the Vertical ruler list box.
e. Move the guides to the back.
f. Select the Save Smaller option to decrease the size of the saved publication file.
g. Open the Other preferences dialog box.
h. In the Text section, select the Use typographer's quotes option.
i. Close the dialog boxes.

2 Apply small capitals and adjust baseline.

a. Select the headline.
b. Open the Type specifications dialog box.
c. Select the Small caps option from the Case list box.
d. Open the Type options dialog box.
e. Type "50" in the Small caps size text box, then click OK twice.
f. Apply a baseline shift to the headline.

3 Adjust text spacing.

a. Select the entire menu text. **Hint:** Do not include headline.
b. Select the Very loose track option from the Control palette.
c. Select the headline.
d. Adjust the Kerning option to add space between the characters.

4 Set character widths.
   a. Select the menu category Appetizers.
   b. Widen the character width for the style.
   c. Apply the same width to all of the menu category items.

5 Set indents.
   a. Select the entire text block.
   b. Open the Indents/tabs dialog box.
   c. Move the first-line indent to the 3p0 mark.

6 Set tabs.
   a. Select the entire text block.
   b. Open the Indents/tabs dialog box.
   c. Click the Right tab icon.
   d. Click the ruler at the 18p0 mark.
   e. Select the dotted line Leader option.
   f. Click OK.

7 Use the Bullets and numbering Addition.
   a. Place the pointer next to category Appetizers.
   b. Use the Bullets and numbering Addition to place an appropriate character in front of the category item. Apply the same character to each of the other category items.
   c. Save your publication, then exit PageMaker.

INDEPENDENT CHALLENGE 1

You are a cook at a New York pizza shop called Tainted's Basement Pizza Parlor. The owner, Avis Figlioni, asks you to create a new menu. Avis wants the menu to be one page with two columns in a page size smaller than 8½" x 11". He wants to list his appetizers and salads in the left column and the pizzas and different toppings in the upper-right corner of the menu. Below the pizzas Avis wants to list the beverages and the Friday night happy hour pizza and drink specials.

The clientele at the pizza parlor is mostly college students and young adults, so the design needs to be creative but legible.

To complete this independent challenge:

1 Create a rough sketch of the menu indicating the different categories of foods and the different graphics you want to use.

2 Create a new document 5" wide by 9" tall, then save it as PIZZA.PM5 on your Student Disk. Use the Page setup dialog box for the margins and the size of the menu. Use the Preferences dialog boxes to set typographer's quotes and greeked text. Use pica measurement and choose the Save Faster option.

3 Place the file UNIT_7-4.TIF, then place the menu text called UNIT_7-5.DOC. These files are located on your Student Disk.

4 Use small caps for the headlines and subheadlines.

5 Adjust the tracking for the fonts you choose to enhance their appearance.

6 Set tab leaders between the menu items and their prices.

7 Save your publication, then print it and submit the printout and your sketch.

INDEPENDENT CHALLENGE 2

Collect three menus from local restaurants. Critique the menus using the design guidelines from this unit by answering the following questions:

- Does the menu adequately use the power points? What is the first thing you see when you open the menu?
- Does the overall design organize the categories of food in a simple, easily understood format?
- Does the menu contain too much text? Is there too much text because of the number of items in the menu or is it because of extensive explanations of the menu items.
- Does the menu offer too many choices? Studies show restaurant guests look at a menu for 1.5 minutes. Can you make your choices easily in this time frame?

Now try to recreate one of the menus using the techniques learned in this unit. Use the Control palette as much as possible for both text and paragraph formatting modifications. Before creating the new menu in PageMaker, draw a rough sketch of the menu.

To complete this independent challenge:

1 Modify the following Preferences: use the metric measuring system, choose the Save Smaller option, set greeked text at 8 points, and set typographer's quotes.

2 Adjust tracking and letter spacing to give the type the correct look.

3 Use tab leaders between menu items and prices.

4 Save your publication as MENU2.PM5 to your Student Disk.

5 Print the new menu, then submit the printout and your sketch.

UNIT 8

OBJECTIVES

- Plan a poster
- Use the Control palette in object view
- Minimize PageMaker file sizes
- Scale a graphic
- Place an inline graphic
- Modify an inline graphic
- Skew and reflect
- Change links
- Use Image control
- Design Workshop: Posters

Using ADVANCED GRAPHICS

You can use PageMaker's advanced graphics capabilities to improve the overall appearance of your publication. In this unit, you will use the object view of the Control palette to modify text blocks and graphics quickly and precisely. To manage your files better, you will also learn how to minimize a PageMaker publication file size. You will learn how to place a graphic in a line of text. Using the Control palette options and Image control dialog box, you will learn to manipulate graphics to create special effects, such as skewing and reflecting. ▶ Joe Martin needs to develop several advertising posters for New World Airlines flights to New York City. ▶

Planning a poster

Posters follow many of the same rules as other advertising publications but on a larger scale (see the planning lesson in Unit 6). Posters usually contain large, color graphics and bold type. Although full-color posters can be expensive, they are often worth the expense because they can create an instant and lasting impact on viewers. ▶ Joe's next task is to plan a series of posters advertising New World Airlines destinations. His first poster will advertise new flights to New York City and will target the person who will be flying to New York for a vacation.

STEPS

1 **Create a proof version of poster**
A **proof version** is a smaller scaled, less costly version of the final poster. You can use a proof version for editing purposes and for previewing the final output. Because posters are costly to produce, Joe wants to be sure of a successful design in a less costly form before he proceeds. The proof version will be an 8" × 14" page size. After Joe is satisfied with his proof version of the poster, he will send his PageMaker publication file to the commercial printer. The printer will create another proof to make sure the printing equipment can produce the correct color output. Once Joe approves this version, the commercial printer will then print the poster scaled to the final size dimensions at 24" × 42" poster size.

2 **Use colorful, striking graphics**
Posters are meant to be on display. Whether tacked up on a wall or placed in a frame, posters have a longer life span than most other forms of advertising. For a successful design, you need to use graphics or photography that is pleasing and memorable. Joe uses a photo of a New York City street scene from a stock photography catalog. This photo dominates Joe's sketch of the poster. See Figure 8-1.

3 **Use bold text in a unique way**
If you plan to use text on your poster, it should be large and bold so it jumps out at the viewer. Joe will use the words "New York" in bold blue type, then he will add a clip art graphic of the Statue of Liberty to help make the words "New York" stand out.

4 **Use paper stock that is durable**
Picking out the type of paper your poster will be printed on depends on the amount of money you have budgeted for your project. Poster paper can be expensive, especially when a thicker card stock paper is chosen. The thicker the paper, the longer the poster will last. Joe decides to use a 60-pound glossy paper so the poster can be rolled into a mailing tube and sent to travel agencies across the country.

FIGURE 8-1: Joe's sketch of the poster

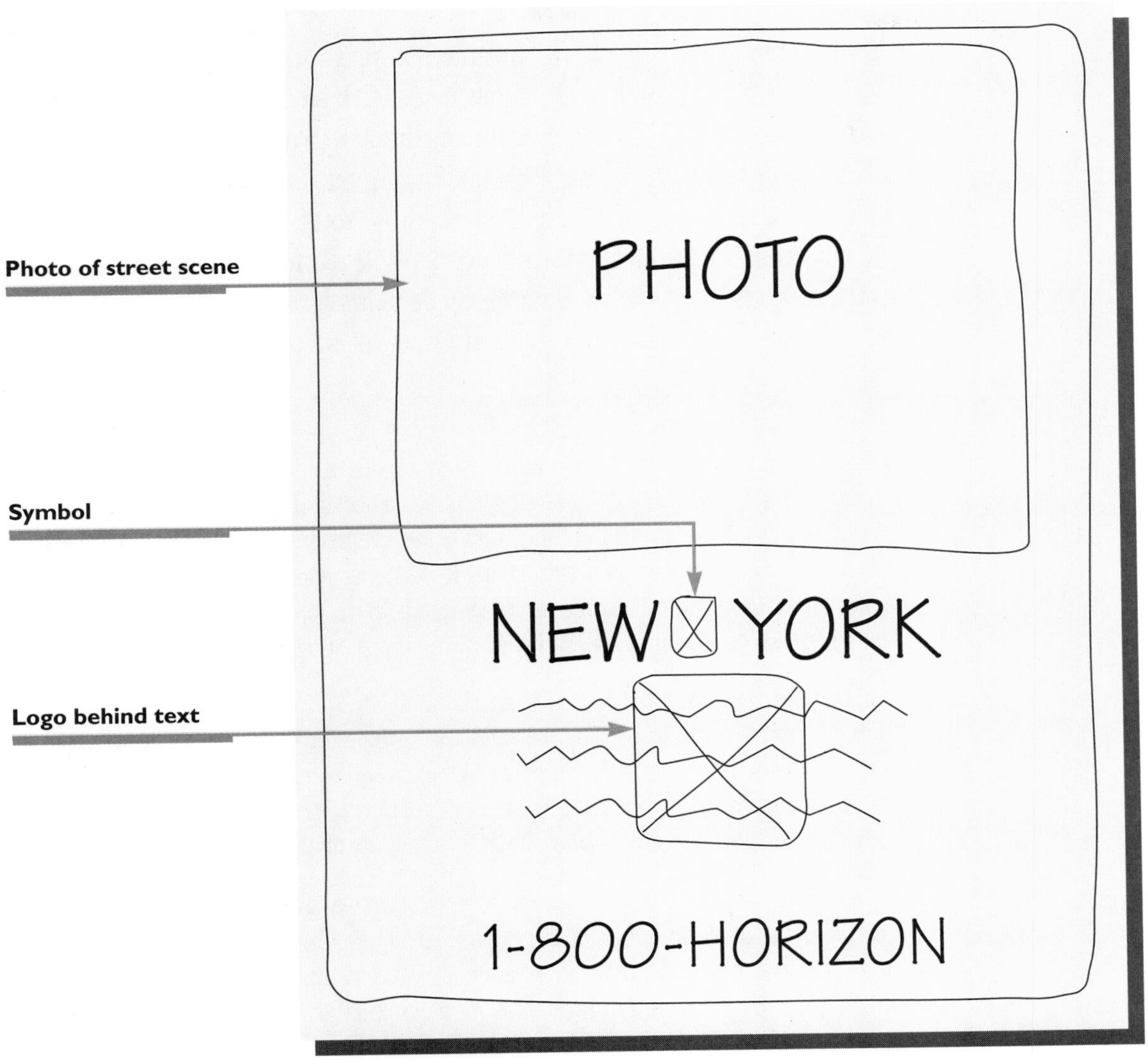

Using the Control palette in object view

As you learned in Unit 7, the Control palette can appear in character view and paragraph view. It can also appear in object view. **Object view** gives you the ability to create unique effects with graphic images and to modify or transform them easily and uniformly. To **transform** an object means to change its appearance by sizing, rotating, skewing, reflecting, or cropping. You have complete control of graphic objects in the publication window. See Table 8-1 for a description of the object view options. ▶ Joe uses the Control palette in object view as he develops the poster. He understands, and hopes to take advantage of, all of its features and benefits.

The Control palette offers:

- **Additional graphics capabilities**
  The Control palette in object view gives you the ability to reflect and skew graphic objects. **Reflecting** means flipping an object either from top to bottom or from right to left. **Skewing** allows you to stretch the object at an angle, giving it a distorted appearance. Joe wants to use both of these features to create a box positioned behind both the top and bottom headlines on his poster. These two new features are available only on the Control palette. See Figure 8-2.

- **Precise measurement transformations**
  In the previous units, you relied on the rulers and your own judgment to size, rotate, or move graphics using the mouse. Using the object view of the Control palette, you can enter exact measurement values for sizing, rotating, and moving graphic objects. Joe will use the Control palette to determine the exact dimensions of the New York City photo.

- **Transform objects from a specific reference point proxy**
  The proxy represents a selected object on the Control palette. You must choose one reference point (the edge, corner, or center of the graphic) to serve as base that remains stationary as you transform your graphic, as shown in Figure 8-3. Joe will select the proxy reference point before he sizes, skews, and reflects the graphic objects in his poster.

- **Transform multiple objects at once**
  You can rotate, reflect, or move multiple objects at one time using the Control palette. This method allows for a quick and easy way to transform graphics. However, you cannot scale or skew multiple objects at one time. Remember to select multiple objects you can use the selection marquee or the shift-click method. Joe will not be using this feature in this lesson but will remember to use it if he formats multiple objects in his other posters.

FIGURE 8-2: Control palette in object view

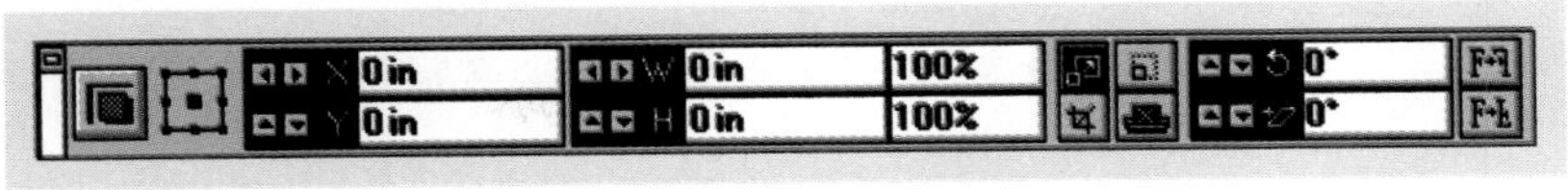

FIGURE 8-3: The proxy reference point

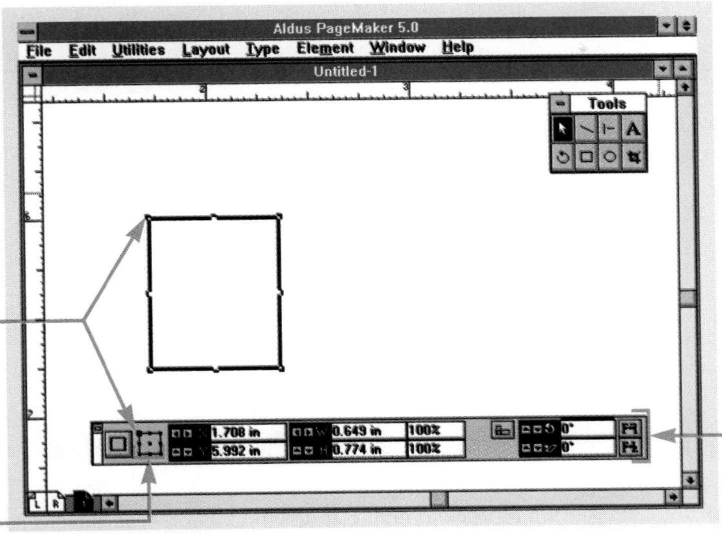

Selected reference point on graphic represented on proxy

Control palette in object view

Proxy

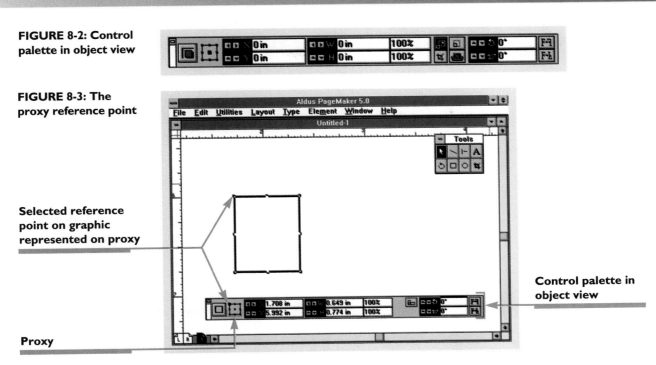

TABLE 8-1: Control palette's object view buttons and options

BUTTON/BOX	OPTION	DESCRIPTION
X 0 in	Position X button	Coordinate for the reference point on the horizontal ruler
Y 0 in	Position Y button	Coordinate for the reference point on the vertical ruler
W 0 in 100%	Width sizing	Sets the horizontal measurement value of the selected object
H 0 in 100%	Height sizing option	Sets the vertical measurement value of the selected object
	Scaling button	Sizes a graphic proportionally or non-proportionally
	Cropping button	Conceals part of the graphic
	Proportional Scaling button	Sizes an image to any percentage of its original dimensions
	Printer Resolution Scaling button	Scales a placed graphic image to match the resolution of the target printer
0°	Rotating	Changes the rotation position of an object; you can adjust the rotation by 1% increments using the proxy reference point
0°	Skewing	Changes the skew position of an object; you can adjust the skew by 1% increments from the proxy reference point
	Horizontal reflecting button	Flips a selected object horizontally
	Vertical reflecting button	Flips a selected object vertically

Minimizing PageMaker file sizes

Each time you place a graphic, your publication's file size increases by the original size of the placed graphic. You can minimize the size of your PageMaker publication by turning off the option for storing a copy of a graphic in the publication. When you no longer store a copy of the placed image in the publication, it is important to keep the original source graphic file on the same disk as your PageMaker publication file. PageMaker needs to link the publication file to the source file to display the placed graphic at the highest resolution on your screen and in the final printed output. ▶ Joe has a limited amount of space on his disk; therefore, he decides to minimize the size of his PageMaker publication file by turning off the Store copy within publication option.

STEPS

1. **Start PageMaker and open the file UNIT_8-1.PM5 from your Student Disk**
   The poster Joe started working on earlier appears in the publication window. Joe needs to place the New York City photo in the poster. Before he does this, he first wants to change the link option defaults for graphic objects that will minimize his publication's file size.
2. Click **Element** on the menu bar, then click **Link options**
   The Link options Defaults dialog box opens. See Figure 8-4. Under Graphics, the Store copy in publication check box is selected; the Update automatically check box is not.
3. Click the **Store copy in publication check box** to deselect this option
   Turning off this option turns on the Update automatically option. This ensures that the placed graphics will be linked to their original source files, so that PageMaker will have the necessary information to display the graphics at the highest quality on the screen and in printed output. Note that turning off the Store copy in publication option only affects all future placed objects; it does not affect graphic objects previously placed in a publication.
4. Click **OK**
   The Link options Defaults dialog box closes. Now that Joe has turned off the Store copy in publication option he can place the photo in the poster.
5. Click **Window** on the menu bar, then click **Control palette**
   The Control palette appears in object view. Notice as you drag your mouse pointer across the pasteboard, the values in both the Position X and Y text boxes change to reflect the exact position of the pointer. Instead of using the publication window's rulers, Joe will use the Control palette to determine the precise position where he would like to place the photo. The photo is in the file UNIT_8-2.TIF on your Student Disk.
6. Click **File** on the menu bar, click **Place**, then select the file **UNIT_8-2.TIF** from your Student Disk
   The pointer changes to ⊠. Joe uses the Control palette to specify the reference point for the exact placement.
7. Move ⊠ to display "1 in" in the Position X text box, and "1 in" in the Position Y text box, as shown in Figure 8-5
8. Click the **mouse button**
   The graphic appears in the layout at the position specified in Step 7. In the next lesson Joe will enlarge the photo.
9. Click **File** on the menu bar, then click **Save**
   If you had not turned off the Store copy in publication option, your PageMaker publication file would have been 475,000 kilobytes in size as compared to its present size of 115,000 kilobytes.

FIGURE 8-4: The Link options Defaults dialog box

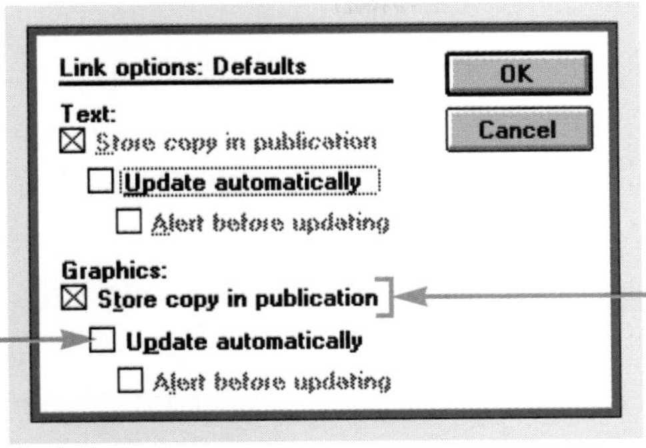

FIGURE 8-5: Using the Control palette to place a graphic precisely

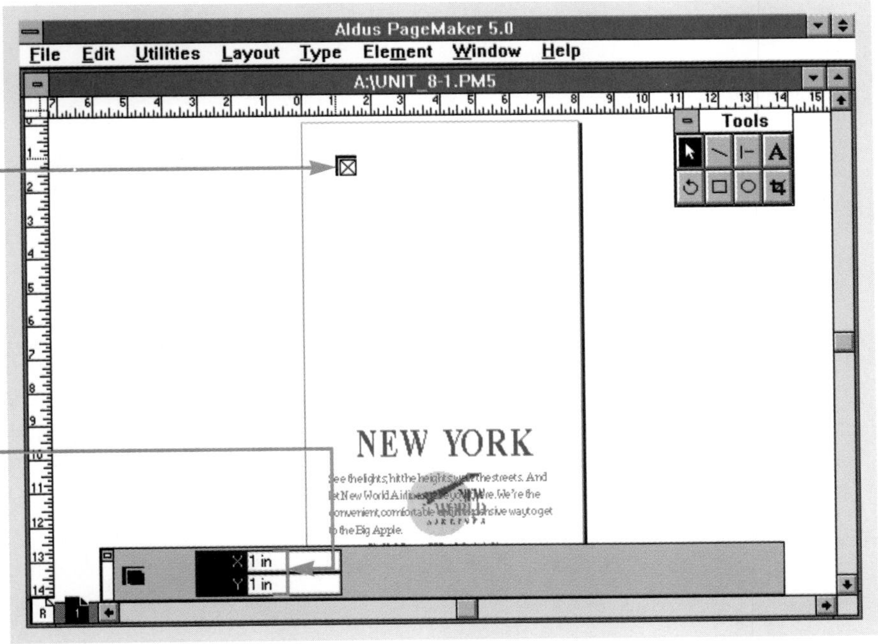

QUICK TIP

To change the linking default settings for all new publications, open the Link options Defaults dialog box when no publications are open.

Scaling a graphic

When a graphic is selected, the Control palette displays its coordinates on the page, its dimensions, and the percentage its size has been increased or decreased. The Control palette allows you to **scale** an object by decreasing or increasing the dimensions of its size either proportionally or nonproportionally. The advantage of manipulating an object with the Control palette is the precision of entering figures for the exact measurements for the object. You can use a proxy reference point on the Control palette as a base from which PageMaker transforms the selected object. You can also crop objects. See the related topic "Using the Control palette to crop a graphic" for more information. ▶ Joe wants to proportionally resize the street scene photo of New York City to make it more prominent on the page. He will use the Control palette to do this.

STEPS

1 **If the New York City photo is not selected, click the Pointer tool in the toolbox, then click the graphic to select it**
Eight handles appear to indicate the graphic is selected as shown in Figure 8-6. Notice on the Control palette that the top left proxy reference point is also selected. The dimensions displayed in the Position X and Y text boxes apply only to the upper-left corner of the selected graphic, which is represented by the top left reference point on the proxy.

Joe is satisfied with the placement of the upper-left corner of the graphic, but he would like to resize his photo proportionally to give a 1 in margin to each side of the photo. He needs to reselect the top left proxy reference point. Then, he will change the width of the photo to be 6 in wide and let PageMaker automatically determine the final proportional length.

2 **Make sure the top left reference point on the proxy on the Control palette is selected; if it isn't, click to select it**
This reference point will be the base point that will remain constant as Joe resizes the photo.

3 **Make sure the Control palette displays the Proportional-scaling option , if not, click**
This is a toggle button, which toggles between the two options.

4 **Double-click the Width sizing text box, type 6 (be sure to include a space), then click the Apply button**
See Figure 8-7. With the Proportional Scaling option selected, Joe was able to enter 6 in for the width size. PageMaker automatically scaled the height size dimension to 8.154 in, maintaining the size of the graphic proportionally.

5 **Click in the pasteboard to deselect the graphic**

6 **Click File on the menu bar, then click Save**

FIGURE 8-6: Graphic coordinates on the Control palette

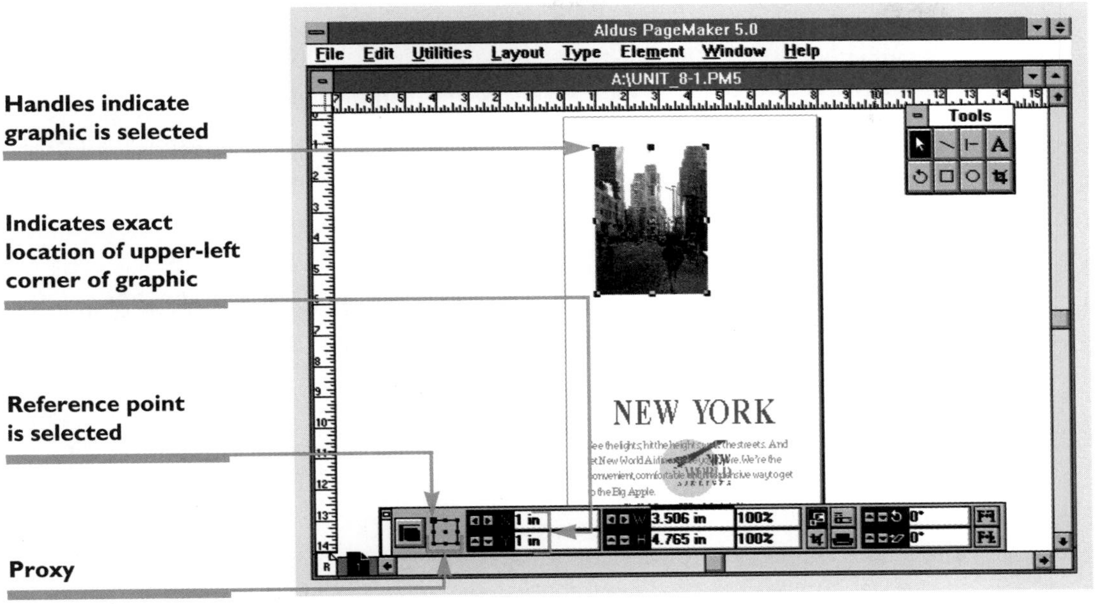

FIGURE 8-7: PageMaker proportionally sized photo

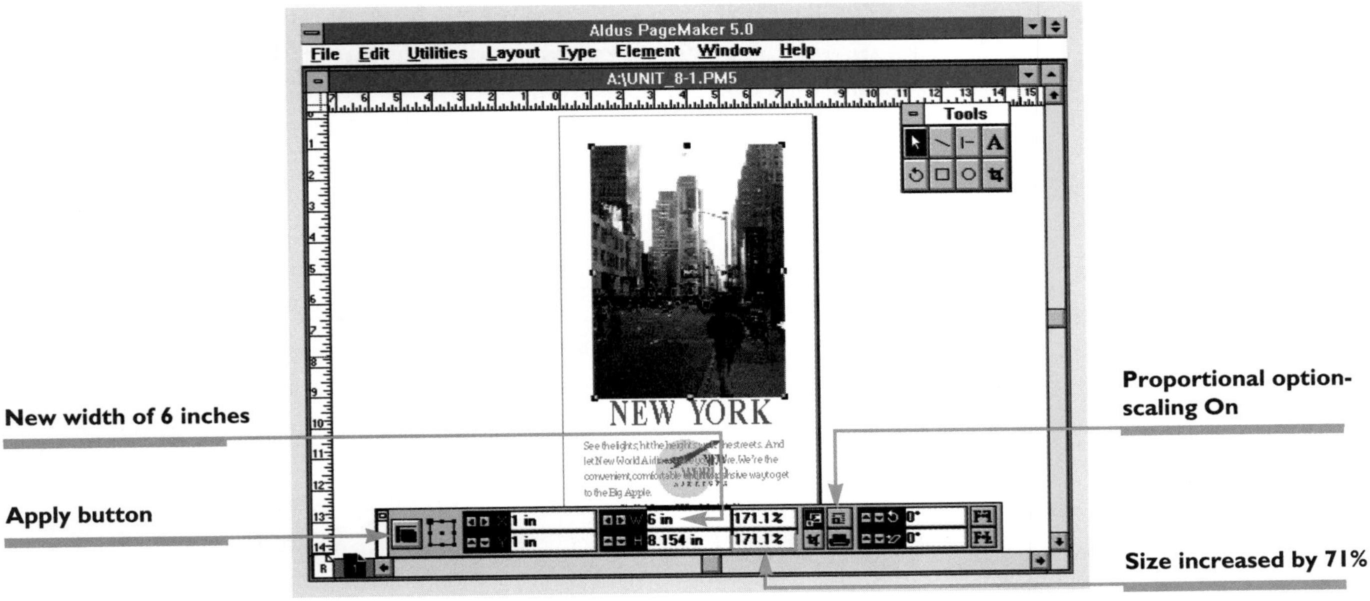

Using the Control palette to crop a graphic

You can use the Control palette in object view to crop a graphic precisely. With the graphic selected, click the Cropping button on the Control palette. Select your base reference point on the proxy, then enter values in the Position X and Position Y text boxes or in the Height and Width text boxes. Then click the Apply button to accept your modifications.

TROUBLE?

Any sizing changes you make to a graphic can be undone by using the Control palette and typing "100" in the size text boxes. ■

Placing an inline graphic

PageMaker allows you to place graphics within text blocks. This feature is commonly referred to as **inline graphics**. In the previous unit, the graphics you placed were "independent," meaning that you move them freely within the layout view. Inline graphics remain within the text block. The inline graphic moves when the text block or the text in the text block moves. See the related topic "Advantages and disadvantages of using inline graphics" for more information. ▶ Joe wants to personalize the headline "New York" by adding an inline graphic of the Statue of Liberty. Joe feels that the inline graphic will give the word "New York" a strong identity and enhance his poster.

STEPS

1. Click the **Text tool** in the toolbox, position I before the letter "Y" between the words "New" and "York," then click again to position the insertion point
   The Control palette changes to character view because you chose the Text tool. The inline graphic will be placed at the exact position of the insertion point in the text block.
2. Click **File** on the menu bar, then click **Place**
   The Place document dialog box opens.
3. Select the file **UNIT_8-3.TIF** from your Student Disk
4. Make sure the **As inline graphic radio button** to the right of the Directories list box is selected
   Because you selected the Text tool before you opened the Place document dialog box, PageMaker automatically determined that you are going to place a graphic in text. If this is not the case, you can select the As an independent graphic radio button.
5. Click **OK**
   The Statue of Liberty graphic appears between "New" and "York," as shown in Figure 8-8. If you select the Pointer tool to move or resize the text block, PageMaker adjusts the graphic as if it were a word in the text block. Joe decides the headline would look better at the top of the poster.
6. Click the **Pointer tool** in the toolbox, position the pointer on top of the word **New**, then click the **mouse button**
   The text block with the inline graphic is selected. The Control palette switches to object view. Joe enters the exact coordinates of where he wants the text block positioned.
7. Make sure the top left proxy reference point is selected, double-click the **Position X text box**, type **0** (be sure to include a space), double-click the **Position Y text box**, type **0** , then click the **Apply button**
   See Figure 8-9. The text block moves to the zero point on the page. The text block with the inline graphic appears below the top page border, but the photo covers the text block slightly. Joe decides to move the photo below the New York text block by changing the coordinate for the photo's reference point on the vertical ruler to 2 inches.
8. Position the pointer over the New York City photo, click to select it, make sure the top left proxy reference point is selected, double-click the **Position Y text box**, type **2**, then click the **Apply button**
   The photo moves below the text block; the object is brought to the front.
9. Click **File** on the menu bar, then click **Save**

FIGURE 8-8: Statue of Liberty graphic placed in text

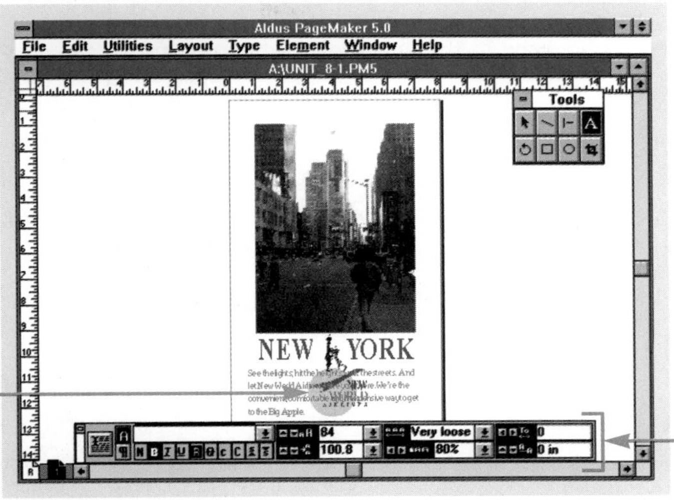

In line graphic

Control palette in character view

FIGURE 8-9: Text block moved to the top of the page

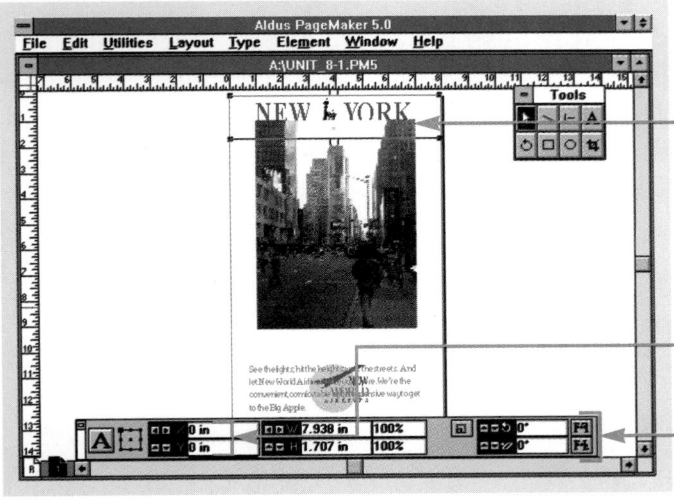

Photo covers text block

New position of the text block

Control palette in object view

Advantages and disadvantages of using inline graphics

One advantage of using an inline graphic is the ability to keep related text and graphics together. When you move the text block, the graphic moves with text. This is particularly useful for figures with captions. You can align an inline graphic using the same commands you use to align text. One disadvantage of using inline graphics is that when you enter or delete text, the graphic moves. Therefore the graphic continuously moves during editing. Another disadvantage is the inability to move the graphic independently of the text. You can move the graphic only when you move the entire block of text. Finally, you cannot use the text wrap option on a selected inline graphic. To wrap text around an inline graphic, you need to use a tabs, spacing, indents, and line spacing.

QUICK TIP

You can import graphics as inline graphics using story editor.

Modifying an inline graphic

As you learned in the last lesson, when you move a text block, the inline graphic moves with it. If you had rotated the text block, the inline graphic would have rotated the same degree as the text block. In this lesson you will learn how to transform an inline graphic independently from its text block. You can size and rotate an inline graphic within its position in the line of text. You can also adjust the inline graphic's baseline position. When you place an inline graphic, PageMaker automatically places the graphic two-thirds above the baseline, independent of the paragraph's leading. Depending on your desired layout, you can edit the vertical baseline position of an inline graphic manually or adjust the space before and after the inline graphic. See the related topic "Spacing around inline graphics" for more information. ▶Joe decides to resize the Statue of Liberty graphic to make it smaller. After reducing the size, Joe wants to adjust the graphic's baseline position to center it vertically in the text block.

STEPS

1 **Position the Pointer tool over the Statue of Liberty inline graphic, click the left mouse button to select it, then right-click to change the view**
See Figure 8-10. Notice on the Control palette the Baseline shift option has replaced the proxy and Position X and Y options. The Control palette includes only the features that can be used to transform inline graphics such as skewing and rotating. Joe first needs to decrease the width size of the inline graphic to exactly 80% of the original size.

2 **Make sure the Proportional-scaling On option is selected, double-click the Width sizing percentage box, type 80, then click the Apply button**
The inline graphic is resized to 80% of its original size, as shown in Figure 8-11. If you get an error message, check that you typed 80 in the percentage box and not in the text box (in). Joe then decides to adjust the graphic's baseline shift so the bottom of the inline graphic lies on the imaginary baseline.

3 **Position over the inline graphic, then press and hold the mouse button**
See Figure 8-12. The pointer changes to , allowing you to move the graphic either up or down in relationship to the baseline.

4 **Drag until the graphic's baseline shift reads 0 in in the Baseline shift text box on the Control palette**
Joe is satisfied with the baseline position of the graphic; however, he thinks the graphic is too close to the letter "Y" in York. He wants to insert a space before the letter "Y."

5 **Click the Text tool A in the toolbox, click between the graphic and the letter "Y" in York, then press [Spacebar]**
The inline graphic is now centered between the headline text. Joe is pleased with the effect of placing the Statue of Liberty graphic with the words "New York."

6 **Click File on the menu bar, then click Save**

FIGURE 8-10: Inline graphic

FIGURE 8-11: Inline graphic at 80% of its original size

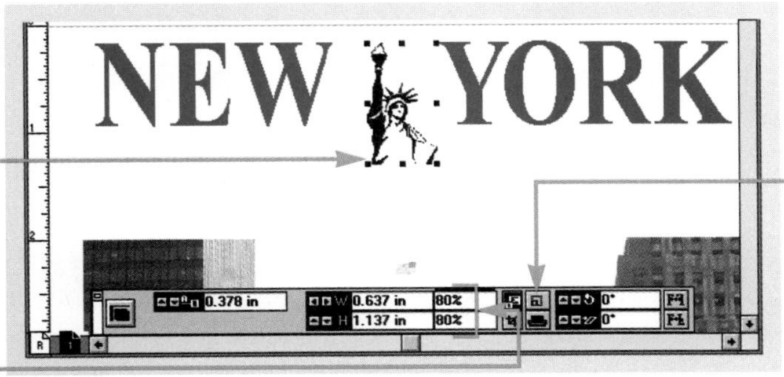

FIGURE 8-12: Adjusting the graphic's baseline position

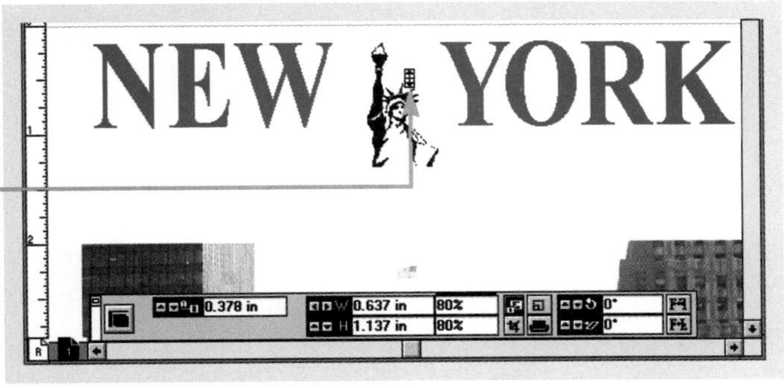

Spacing around inline graphics

By simply using the Spacebar, you can add space between the text and an inline graphic. You can also use indents and tabs to set space between one or more inline graphics. Using indents and tabs is especially helpful when creating a table with inserted inline graphics. Whenever you place a inline graphic, PageMaker assigns it to be autoleading independent of the paragraph's leading. This might create odd line spacing in a particular paragraph of text. You can resize your inline graphic and increase the paragraphs leading to accommodate the inline graphic.

DESIGN TIP

Try to size or adjust inline graphics to fit within the paragraph's leading value.■

QUICK TIP

Inline graphics can be aligned within a text block by making the inline graphic its own paragraph, then selecting either right, left, or center alignment.■

Skewing and reflecting

PageMaker lets you **skew**, or distort, an object's dimensions horizontally only. Skewing stretches the selected object at an angle, giving it a distorted appearance. Using the Control palette, you can skew a graphic horizontally only by plus or minus 85 degrees at .01 degree increments. The Control palette also allows you to **reflect** an object to its mirror image, either vertically or horizontally. ▶ Joe wants to create a visual link between the top and bottom headlines in the poster. By adding a skewed box positioned behind the New York headline, he will create a unique shadow effect. He will then duplicate the skewed box, reflect it, and place it behind the bottom phone number headline. This will create the desired visual link.

STEPS

1 **Click Layout** on the menu bar, click **View**, then click **50%**
Joe can now view the top half of the poster in greater detail. Before Joe draws his box, he sets up vertical ruler guides and turns on the Snap to guides option. This will make it easier to draw the box to the exact measurements. Joe uses the Control palette once again for the precise placement of the ruler guides.

2 Drag a **vertical ruler guide** to the **.75 in** mark on the horizontal ruler
Joe wants his box to be 6" long, so he will need a second vertical ruler guide at the 6.75 in mark on the horizontal ruler.

3 Drag a second **vertical ruler guide** to the **6.75 in** mark on the horizontal ruler
Now Joe needs to activate the Snap to guides option.

4 Click **Layout** on the menu bar, click **Guides and rulers**, then click **Snap to guides**
This option gives the ruler guides a "magnetic" effect, making it easy to align items to the guides. It allows you to measure and size graphics precisely. Joe is now ready to draw his box.

5 Click the **Rectangle tool** in the toolbox; using the ruler guides and the Control palette as a reference point for the exact measurements, move + to display the **.75 in mark** in the Position X text box and the **.75 in mark** in the Position Y text box

6 Drag + until the **Width sizing text box** displays **6 in** and the **Height sizing text box** is **.5 in**, then release the mouse button
See Figure 8-13. Notice the box's size dimensions in the Control palette. Joe now wants to add a gray shade fill and to eliminate the line border on the box.

7 Click **Element** on the menu bar, click **Fill and line**, click the **Fill list arrow**, click **20%**, click the **Line list arrow**, click **None**, then click **OK**
Joe will use the Control palette to skew the box to create a unique shadow effect for the New York headline.

8 Double-click the **Skew text box** 55°, type **55**, then click the **Apply** button
See Figure 8-14. The box now is skewed horizontally.

9 Click **Element** on the menu bar, then click **Send to back**
The gray box moves behind the New York text and inline graphic. Before deselecting the box, Joe wants to copy the skewed box and paste a reflected copy behind the bottom headline.

FIGURE 8-13: The box's dimensions in the Control palette

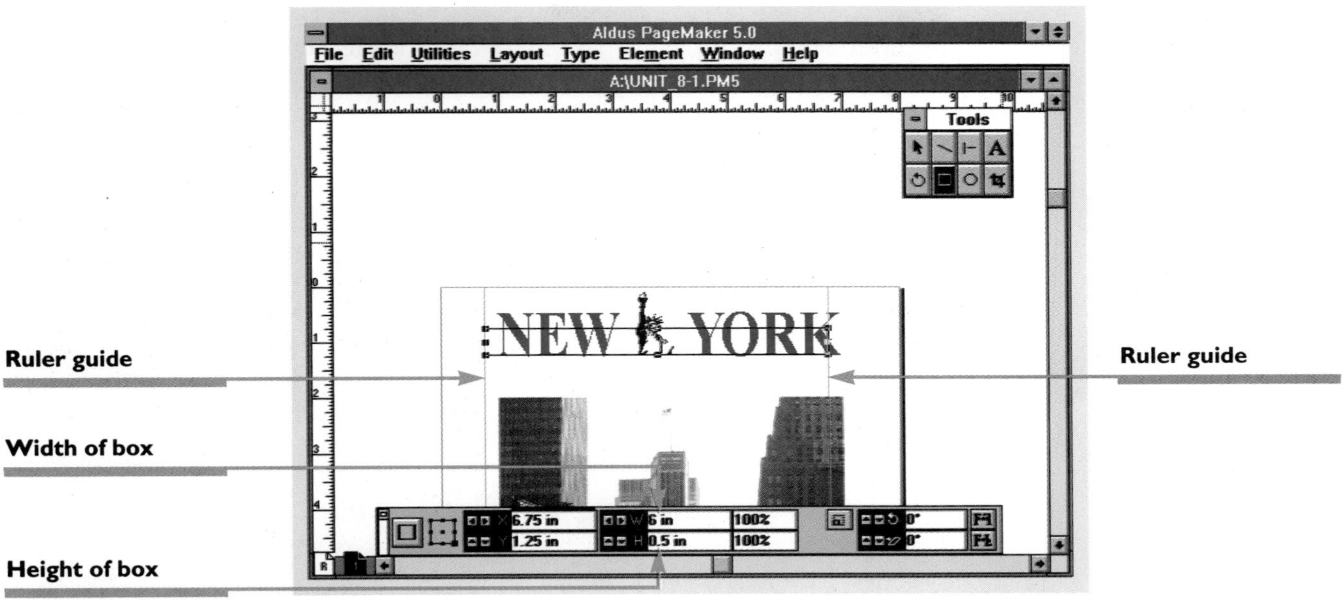

FIGURE 8-14: The box skewed horizontally

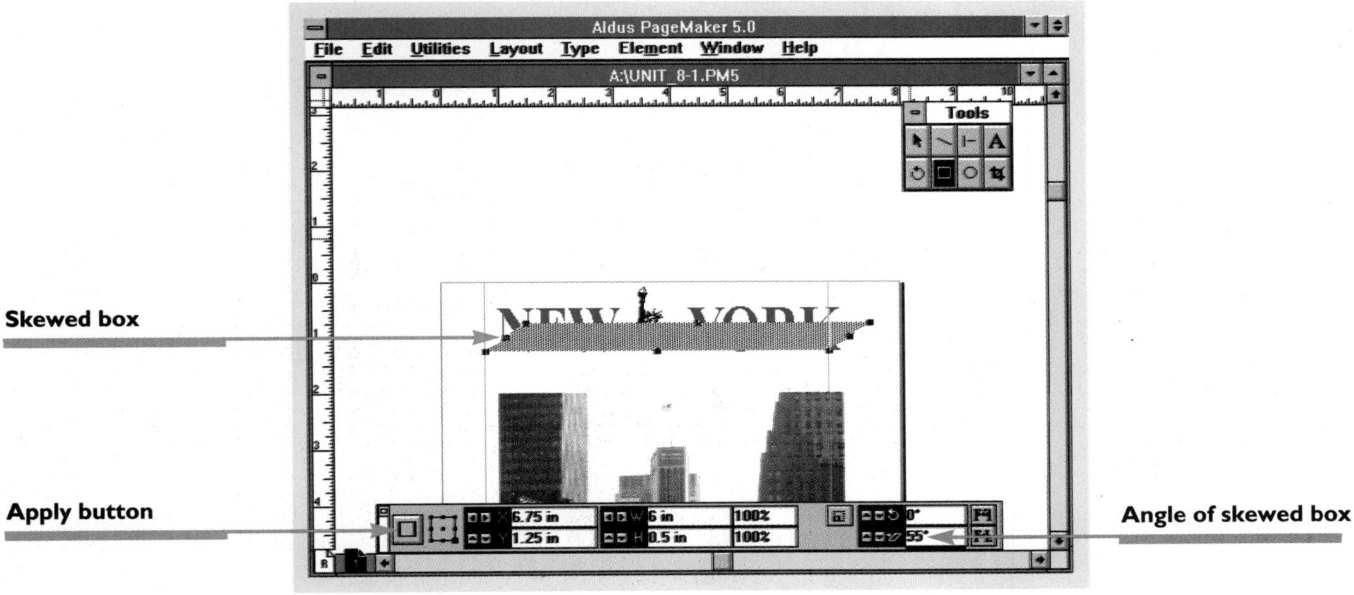

DESIGN TIP

Skewing can create an unique effect with headlines as long as you do not overuse it on a page.

Skewing and reflecting an object, continued

Joe continues by copying and pasting the box, then reflecting the box and placing it behind the headline at the bottom of the page.

STEPS

10 **Make sure the box behind the headline is still selected; if not, click the text block, press and hold [Ctrl], then click the gray box**
You can select layered objects by holding down [Ctrl] and clicking the objects.

11 **Click Edit on the menu bar, click Copy, then press [Ctrl][V] to paste a copy of the gray box**
PageMaker pastes a copy on top of the headline. Before Joe moves the new skewed box, he wants to create a vertical reflection.

12 **Click the Vertical reflecting button on the Control palette**
The box instantly reflects vertically, as shown in Figure 8-15. Joe would like to change the publication view so he can easily move the graphic to the point of response at the bottom of page.

13 **Right-click twice in the publication window**
The view returns to Fit to window. Joe notices that the Control palette covers the bottom of the page, so he decides to move it to the middle of the page before he moves the box.

14 **Position the pointer on the vertical title bar on the Control palette, press and hold the mouse button, and drag the Control palette to the middle of the page**
See Figure 8-16. Now Joe can see the bottom of the page, and he is ready to move the box.

15 **Drag the reflected box to the bottom of the page on top of the New World Airlines phone number**
See Figure 8-17. Joe needs to send the reflected box behind the text.

16 **Press [Ctrl][B]**
The box moves behind the text, and Joe is satisfied with the placement of the skewed box. Joe decides to move the Control palette back to the bottom of the publication window.

17 **Drag the Control palette back to the bottom of the publication window above the horizontal scroll bars**
Joe no longer needs the ruler guides, so he drags them off the pasteboard to remove them.

18 **Click the vertical ruler guide at the .75" mark, drag it to the left of the pasteboard over the vertical ruler, then drag the second ruler guide off the pasteboard to remove it**
This removes the ruler guides.

19 **Save your changes**
There is now a visual link between the New York headline at the top of the poster and the New World Airlines phone number at the bottom of the poster.

FIGURE 8-15: The reflected skewed box

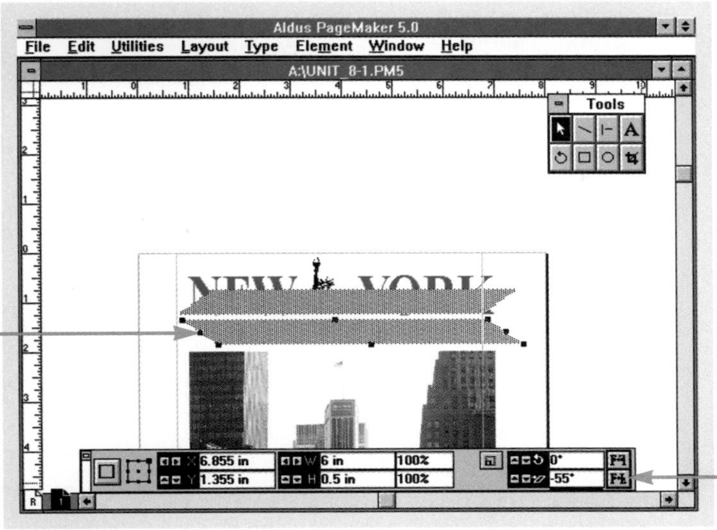

Reflected box

Vertical reflecting button

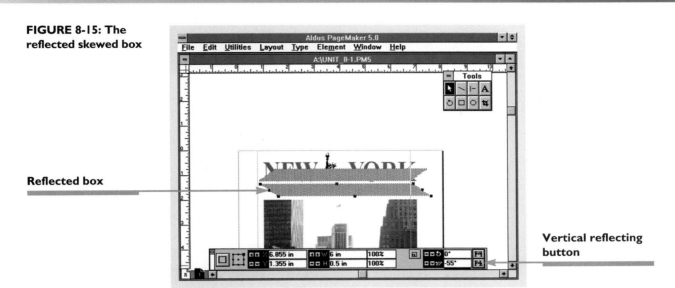

FIGURE 8-16: Control palette moved to the middle of the publication window

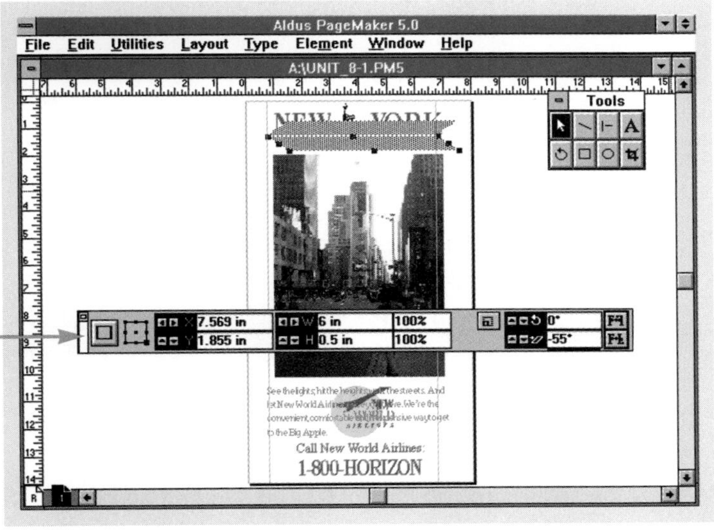

Vertical title bar

FIGURE 8-17: The reflected skewed box placed on top of the phone number

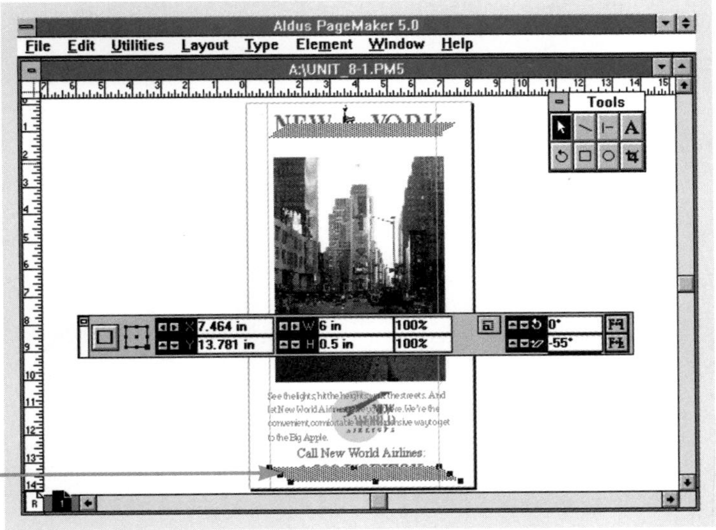

Box positioned over phone number

QUICK TIP

To remove skewing or reflecting from an object, select the object, click Element on the menu bar, then click Remove transformations.

Changing an object's links

Using the Links dialog box in PageMaker, you can monitor and control object linking in your publication. When you place graphics in your publication, PageMaker automatically creates a link to the graphic's source file. The opened Links dialog box lists the source files of every graphic placed in your publication. See the related topic "Object linking and embedding in PageMaker files" for more information about linking. ▶ Because the text on top of the New World Airlines logo is hard to read, Joe decides to lighten the graphic. Only black and white graphics can be lightened however. Joe will change the link to a black-and-white version of the New World Airlines logo.

STEPS

1. **Click Layout on the menu bar, click View, click 50% size, then scroll to view the bottom half of the poster**
2. **Click File on the menu bar, then click Links**
   The Links dialog box opens, as shown in Figure 8-18. The Info command tells you the filename of the linked object, the file type, and the page on which the linked object appears. If the placed graphic's source file has been changed, a plus sign (+) appears in front of the filename. You must click the Update button to update the placed graphic with the new changes made to the source file. Table 8-2 shows the symbols that can appear before a filename in the dialog box. Joe will use the Links Info dialog box to establish a different link file for the New World Airlines logo.
3. **Click LOGO.TIF, then click Info**
   The Link info dialog box opens, in which you can unlink a file or establish a link with another file. Joe wants to select the black and white version of the logo, which is called LOGO_BW.TIF.
4. **In the Filename list box, click LOGO_BW.TIF, then click Link**
   The Link info dialog box closes and you are returned to the Links dialog box. Notice the document name has changed from LOGO.TIF to LOGO_BW.TIF.
5. **Click OK**
   Now the New World Airlines logo is the black-and-white version, as shown in Figure 8-19. Joe still has to lighten its appearance to make the text more readable.
6. **Click File on the menu bar, then click Save**

TABLE 8-2: Symbols in the Links dialog box

SYMBOL	DEFINITION
NA	The object was pasted into the document but is not linked or is an OLE-embedded object
?	PageMaker cannot find the linked file
+	The linked file has been modified since importing it; to update the linked file when changes have been made to the external file, click the Update button
!	The external file and the imported image have both been altered; if you update the link, the external copy will replace the changes made to the imported image
X	The external file has been modified, click Update to update the linked image

FIGURE 8-18: Links dialog box

Color version of graphic

Click to open Link info dialog box

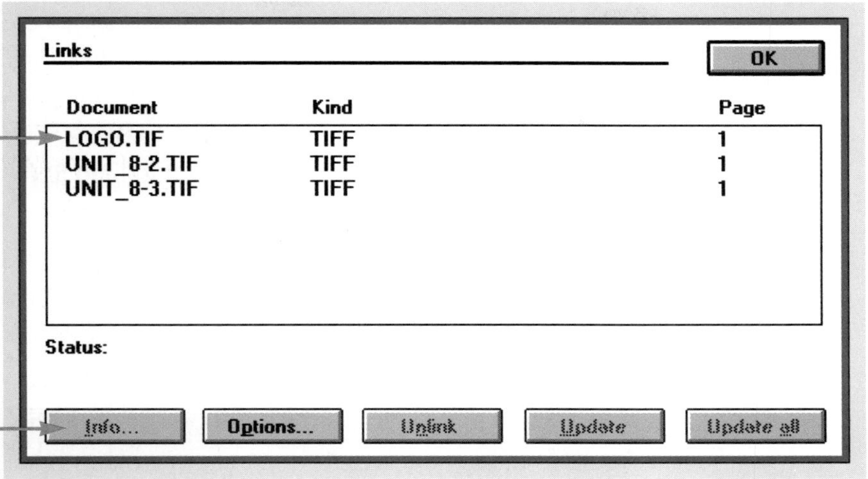

FIGURE 8-19: The newly linked logo

Newly linked graphic

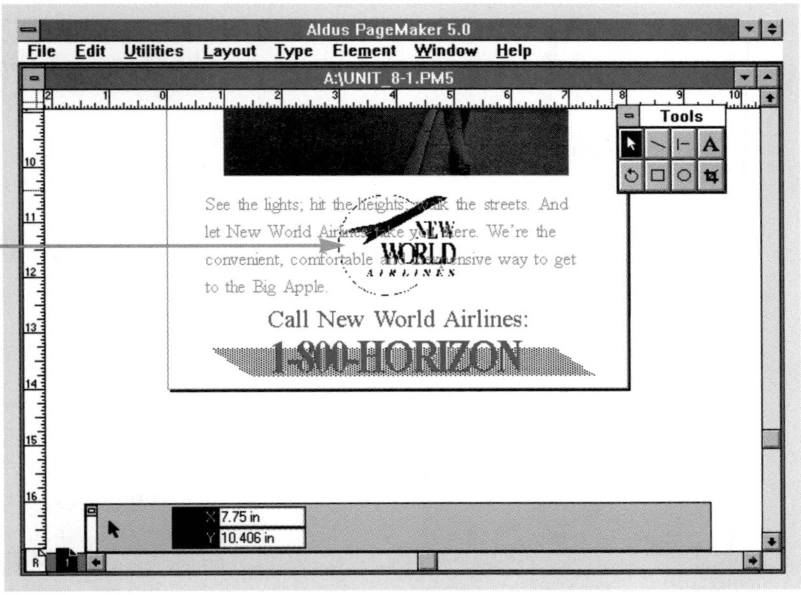

Object linking and embedding in PageMaker files

Object Linking and Embedding (OLE) allows you share information between application programs. OLE gives you two distinct options for sharing information. Using Object Linking (OL), you can create an object link to place text or graphics and automatically update the objects after they have been changed in the source file. In contrast, Object Embedding (OE) allows you to embed an object and update it without linking to a separate source file. Object Linking is performed by choosing the Place command and choosing a text or graphic file to place. Object Embedding is performed by choosing the Insert Object command and choosing a text or graphic to insert.

Using Image control

PageMaker lets you alter or enhance the appearance of grayscale and line art TIFF and PICT images using the Image control dialog box. However, you cannot change color TIFF images. Using **Image control** is like having access to a photographic darkroom in which you can lighten and adjust the contrast of black-and-white photographs and images. Image control helps you to improve the appearance of images you place in your publication. You can lighten images so they can be printed behind text or graphics. Or you can adjust the image's contrast to increase or decrease the gray levels of the image. See Table 8-3 for a description of options and commands. The text on top of the New World Airlines logo is still hard to read, so Joe will adjust the lightness of the logo to appear faded. To do this, Joe wants to lighten the logo so he can keep it behind the text.

STEPS

1. **Click the text block on top of the New World Airlines logo**
   The text is selected.
2. **Position on the graphic, press and hold [Ctrl], then click the logo to select it**
3. **Click Element on the menu bar, then click Image control**
   The Image control dialog box opens, as shown in Figure 8-20.
4. **Change the Lightness to 80% using the scroll box and scroll arrows to the right of the text box**
   Notice that the Apply button in the Image control dialog box becomes active. Joe can click the Apply button to preview his changes before he clicks OK to accept his changes.
5. **Click Apply**
   PageMaker redraws the graphic in the publication window, but Joe cannot see the applied changes because the dialog box remains open and covers the logo in the publication window.
6. **Drag the dialog box to the bottom of the publication window**
   See Figure 8-21. Joe can now see the logo changes, and he is satisfied with the appearance of the logo.
7. **Click OK**
   The graphic now contains a 20% gray shade. Joe can clearly see the text on top of the logo.
8. **Save then print your publication, and exit PageMaker**

FIGURE 8-20: Image control dialog box

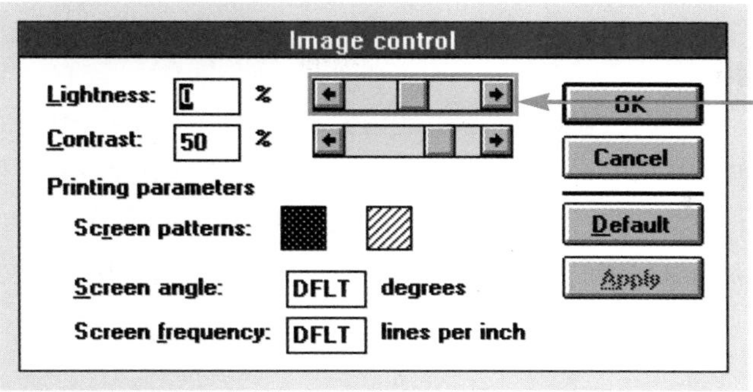

Use scroll box and scroll arrows to adjust lightness

FIGURE 8-21: Image control dialog box moved in the publication window

Lightened logo makes text more readable

Dialog box in new position

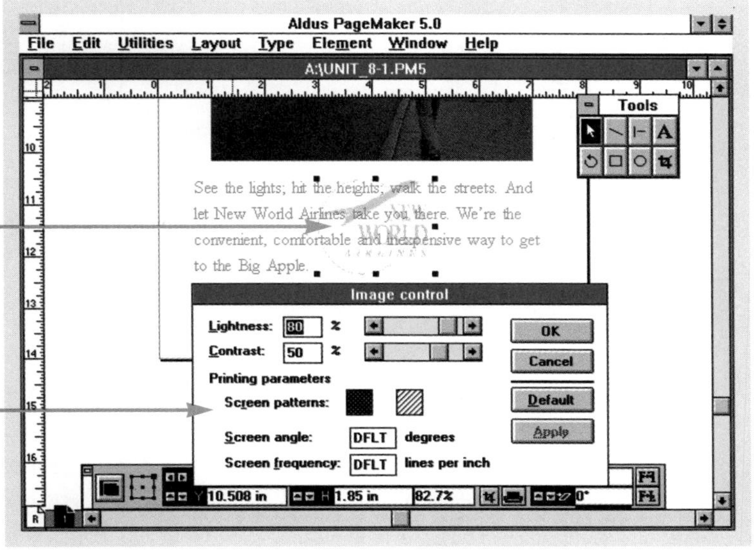

QUICK TIP

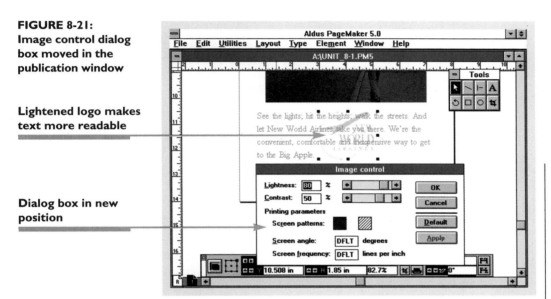

If you click Cancel in the Image control dialog box, the image reverts to a solid black-and-white image.

DESIGN TIP

Graphics placed behind text should be light enough that the text can be read easily.

TABLE 8-3: Image control dialog box options and commands

OPTION/COMMAND	DESCRIPTION
Lightness	Lightens or darkens an image from –100% to 100%; the higher the number, the lighter the image
Contrast	Changes the balance between the dark and light parts of the image; from –100% to 100%; higher numbers will "blacken" the image, lower percentages will add more gray parts to the image; enter –50% to achieve a reverse image
Cancel	Undoes any changes and closes the dialog box
Default	Reverts the dialog box to the default settings
Apply	Lets you see the changes you make to an image's lightness and contrast without closing the dialog box

Design Workshop: Posters

Joe's series of posters highlighting the New World Airlines destinations requires large graphics that make the viewer want to plan a trip to one of those destinations. Each poster needs to make a positive statement and to attract attention. Joe reviews his work to see if his design meets his original plan.

STEPS

1 **Do the graphics add to the overall effect of the poster?**
Joe used a street scene from Times Square to showcase life in New York. Covering about 75% of the surface area with text and graphics enhances the quality of the poster. The Statue of Liberty inline graphic helps make the top headline jump out at the viewer. The inline graphic is sized and evenly spaced in between the two words, New York. Joe could have added color to enhance the inline graphic.

2 **Is the message clear?**
A poster can handle any amount of text; however, people need to be able to read information from a distance. You must choose the font and point size carefully. When Joe reproduces this poster at full size, the body copy will be nearly 30 points, which is almost ½". That is perfect for Joe's needs.

3 **Does the headline's shadow effect enhance the poster?**
Joe uses skewed and reflected boxes to link the top and bottom headlines in his poster. The skewed box creates a unique effect. Joe could have improved their overall appearance by adding color to the shaded, skewed box.

4 **Does the poster lend itself to additional posters in a series?**
Joe hopes to use this same basic layout for posters advertising other New World Airlines destinations. The large photo and top headline can easily be changed to accommodate other cities. For the top headline inline graphic, Joe will need to identify a well-known icon that will represent each city as well as be easily identifiable by potential travelers. For example, for Miami Florida, he could use a sunshine logo; for St. Louis, Missouri, he could use an arch graphic; or for San Francisco, he could use a graphic of the Golden Gate Bridge. For the photo, he will select a representative picture from each place.

FIGURE 8-22: Joe's completed poster

CONCEPTS REVIEW

Label each of the publication window elements shown in Figure 8-23.

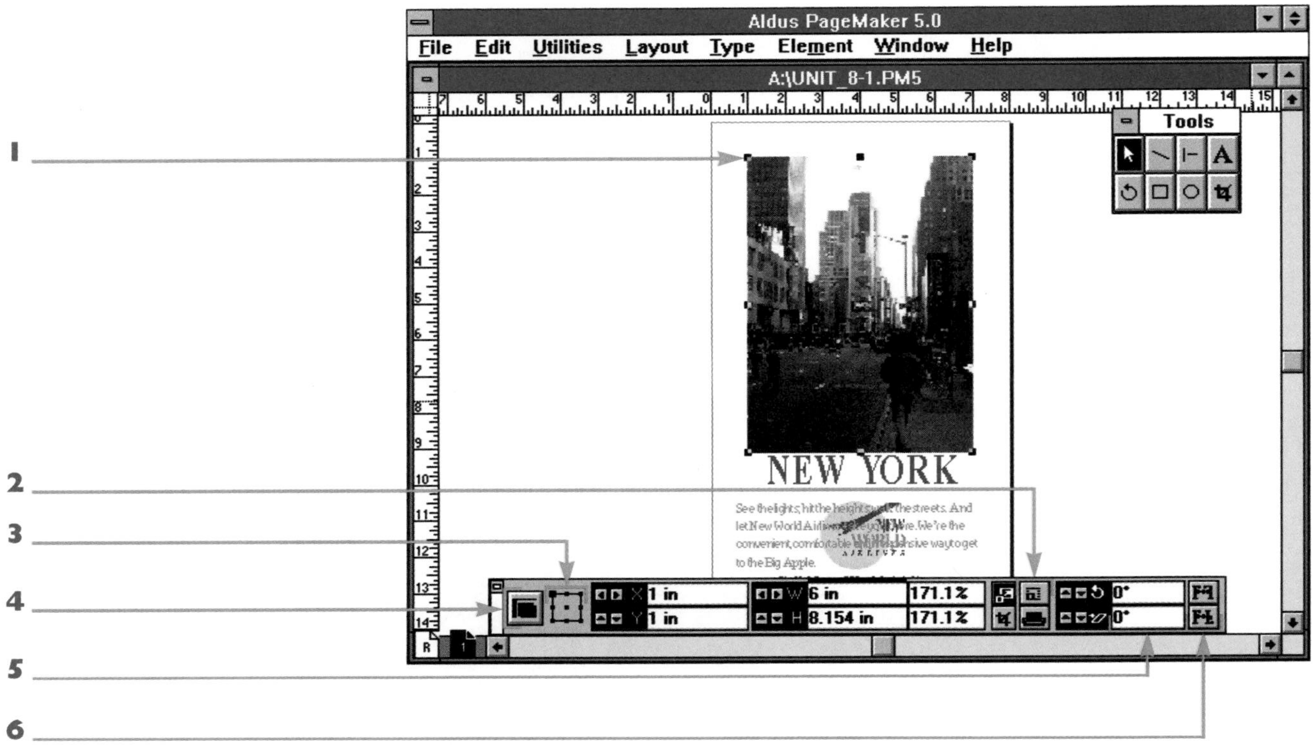

FIGURE 8-23

Match the term with the description that best fits:

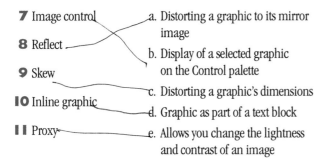

7 Image control

8 Reflect

9 Skew

10 Inline graphic

11 Proxy

a. Distorting a graphic to its mirror image

b. Display of a selected graphic on the Control palette

c. Distorting a graphic's dimensions

d. Graphic as part of a text block

e. Allows you change the lightness and contrast of an image

12 Image control works with all the following graphic types, except

a. Line art or monochrome TIFF

b. Grayscale TIFF

c. Color TIFF

d. PICT

13 Skewing

a. Changes a graphic's size

b. Changes a graphic's dimensions

c. Distorts a graphic

d. All of the above

14 Which of the following transformations can be made to multiple selected objects?

a. Skewing

b. Scaling

c. Rotating

d. All of the above

15 All the following transformations can be made to inline graphics, except

a. Resize

b. Adjust its baseline position

c. Rotate

d. All of the above

16 To edit an inline graphic

a. Select the graphic with I then make the changes on the Control palette

b. Select the graphic with ↖ then make the changes on the Control palette

c. Replace the graphic using the Place document dialog box

d. PageMaker doesn't allow edits to an inline graphic

17 To lighten a black-and-white line art TIFF image in PageMaker, you would use

a. Image control

b. Fill and Line

c. Either a or b

d. TIFF images cannot be lightened in PageMaker

18 Each time you place a graphic, PageMaker

a. Stores a copy of the placed file's information in the PageMaker publication

b. Creates a link to the source file

c. Only a

d. Both a and b

APPLICATIONS REVIEW

1 Minimize a PageMaker file size.

a. Start PageMaker and open the publication UNIT_8-4.PM5 from your Student Disk.

b. Turn off the Store copy in publication option in the Link options Default dialog box.

2 Scale a graphic.

a. Activate the Control palette.

b. Place the photo stored in the file UNIT_8-5.TIF at the 1" intersection on the horizontal and vertical rulers.

c. Change the graphic's width to 7" and its height to 10". Make sure the Proportional-scaling On option is turned off.

3 Place an inline graphic.

a. Position the insertion point in the bottom headline between the words "World" and "You."

b. Place the file UNIT_8-6.TIF as an inline graphic.

4 Modify an inline graphic.

a. Select the inline graphic.

b. Make sure Proportional-scaling On option is turned on.

c. Size the graphic to 50% of its original size.

d. Adjust the baseline shift to roughly .125".

e. Select the headline, then select the bottom left reference point on the proxy, then change the Position Y text box to 14 in.

5 Skew and reflect an object.

a. Select the inline graphic.

b. Select the Horizontal reflecting button on the Control palette.

c. Place vertical ruler guides at the .5" and 8.5" marks on the horizontal ruler.

d. Turn on the Snap to guides option.

e. Draw a box to be placed behind the bottom headline. The dimensions should be 8" wide.

f. Add a 30% gray fill to the box, then remove the line border around the box.

g. Change the skew to 35° on the Control palette.

h. Send the object to the back.

6 Change an object's link.

a. Select the Sunset Tours logo behind the text block.

b. Open the Links dialog box.

c. Select the ST_LOGO.TIF, then open the Link info dialog box.

d. In the filename list click the ST_B&W.TIF, click Link, then click OK.

7 Use Image control.

a. Select the Sunset Tour logo.

b. Open the Image control dialog box.

c. Change the Contrast control to 60.

d. Click the Apply button, then click OK.

e. Save your changes, then print your publication.

f. Exit PageMaker.

INDEPENDENT CHALLENGE 1

You volunteered to help your theater department promote its fall play. Your job is to design material to help promote the production. This includes posters that students will hang around campus in various locations. Your budget is small, but you discover you can inexpensively produce tabloid-size (11 × 17) posters at your local copying store. You can work only in black and white, but color paper stock is available. You need to create three different posters for variety.

To complete this independent challenge:

1 Create a three-page document with tabloid-sized pages.

2 Use any type and graphics you choose to create headlines and complementary graphics. Use graphics from various units in this book to help your design.

3 Determine the play's name, running dates, location, and times of each performance.

4 Use reflected, rotated, or skewed graphics or text in each of the three posters, but do not overuse these effects.

5 Use Image control on appropriate graphics to create unique effects with the Lightness and Contrast controls.

6 Do not use text in the publication smaller than 72 points. Headlines should be at least 150 points.

7 Save and print your work, then submit your posters.

INDEPENDENT CHALLENGE 2

Posters surround your world. Even billboards are sometimes considered posters. Posters can hang inside frames or on walls with staples or tape. But what makes a poster attractive?

To complete this independent challenge:

Make a list of the next 10 posters you see and critique them using what you learned in this unit.

1 Answer the following questions?
- What is the quality of the photography?
- Are graphics used at all?
- How large is the text, and does the size help the design of the poster?
- Is the poster selling or promoting something? Is it successful in its sales or promotional pitch?
- Why?

2 Submit your findings and evaluation.

UNIT 9

OBJECTIVES

- Plan a brochure
- Apply color to text and graphics
- Use color in PageMaker
- Use a color library
- Create a new color
- Edit a color
- Create a tint
- Create color separations
- Design Workshop: Brochures

Adding COLOR TO PUBLICATIONS

Color adds impact to your publications. In this unit you will learn how to create colors and apply those colors to graphical elements and text. Then you will learn how to edit colors and produce tints. You will learn to use PageMaker's color libraries to give you an expanded variety of colors that can be applied to your publications. Finally you will create color separations from your publication that could be used by a commercial printer to print your publication. ▶ Joe needs to create a color brochure to be mailed to frequent flyer members with their next mileage summary. This brochure describes travel through Rome, Italy, which is one of the New World Airlines and Sunset Tours joint vacation destinations. ▶

Planning a brochure

Brochures come in all sizes and styles depending on the type of information and the audience for which they are designed. Some brochures include most if not all of the details of a product or service, such as a 10-page color brochure that you would receive at a car dealership. This brochure has large, colorful pictures of cars and a detailed explanation of the car's features. A "teaser" brochure, in contrast, wants you to respond to receive more information (usually in the form of another brochure) about a product or service. **Teaser** brochures do not have a lot of text—they depend on graphics and color to make the viewer want to find out more. ▶ Joe wants to create a teaser brochure announcing new guided tours through Rome, sponsored by New World Airlines and Sunset Tours travel agency. It will be mailed to New World Airlines frequent flyers. To design the color brochure, Joe considers the following guidelines:

STEPS

1. **Determine the purpose of your brochure**
   If your brochure is going to be a teaser brochure, you don't want to include too much information. You will rely more on pictures and other graphics. If your brochure is going to be an informational brochure you want to consider unique ways of presenting the information, including page size, paper quality, photo quality, and the layout of graphics and supporting amount of text. Joe decides that this will be a teaser brochure for two reasons. First, respondents will give him a database of people who are interested enough in New World Airlines to fill out a card and mail it back. Second, Joe's follow-up brochure is large and expensive to produce. If he knows exactly who to send the follow-up brochure to, his audience is already a targeted, interested group.

2. **Be creative with the brochure's size**
   Most designers experiment with paper size and the way the paper folds when they begin the design process. One of the most popular brochure sizes is a vertical three-panel, two-fold brochure based on a letter-size (8.5" × 11") page. You can be creative and try horizontal folds, varied paper sizes, or even a folder-type brochure with one-page handouts. Joe decides to make a four-panel, three-fold brochure based on a legal page size of 8.5" by 14".

3. **Be consistent with other marketing materials**
   Brochures describing a single product or service should maintain consistency with other corporate brochures. The New World Airlines logo placed in the brochure will help provide a consistent corporate identity. Joe develops a layout for his brochure that could be replicated easily for future brochures highlighting any of New World Airlines tours.

4. **Include point of response**
   Like all publications you have created so far, it is important to give the reader a point of response. Include a phone number where those people who are interested can call. Some brochures include a reply card that can be mailed for more information. Because Joe is creating a teaser brochure, he includes a perforated cutoff self-mailer, a portion of the brochure for people to fill out and mail back for more information.

Figures 9-1 and 9-2 show Joe's sketches of the teaser brochure.

FIGURE 9-1: Joe's sketch of the outside panels (page 2)

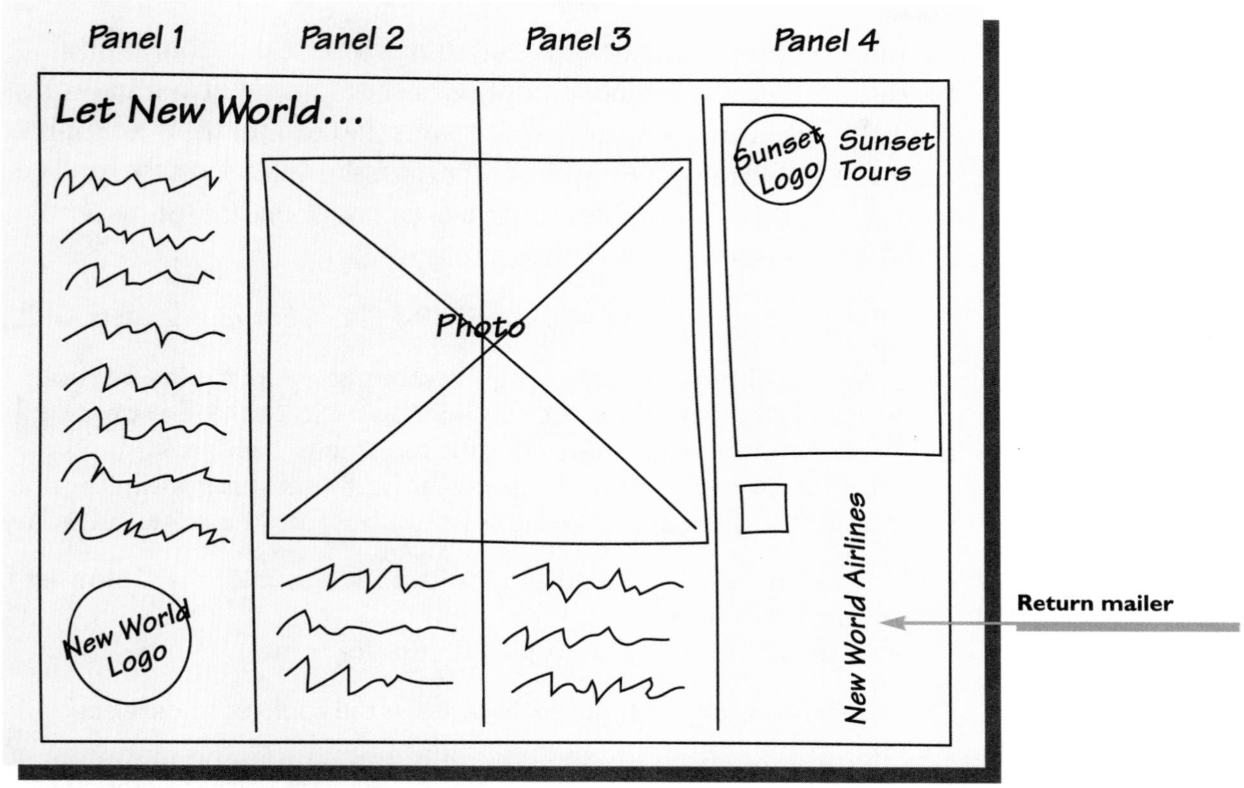

FIGURE 9-2: Joe's sketch of the inside panels (page 3)

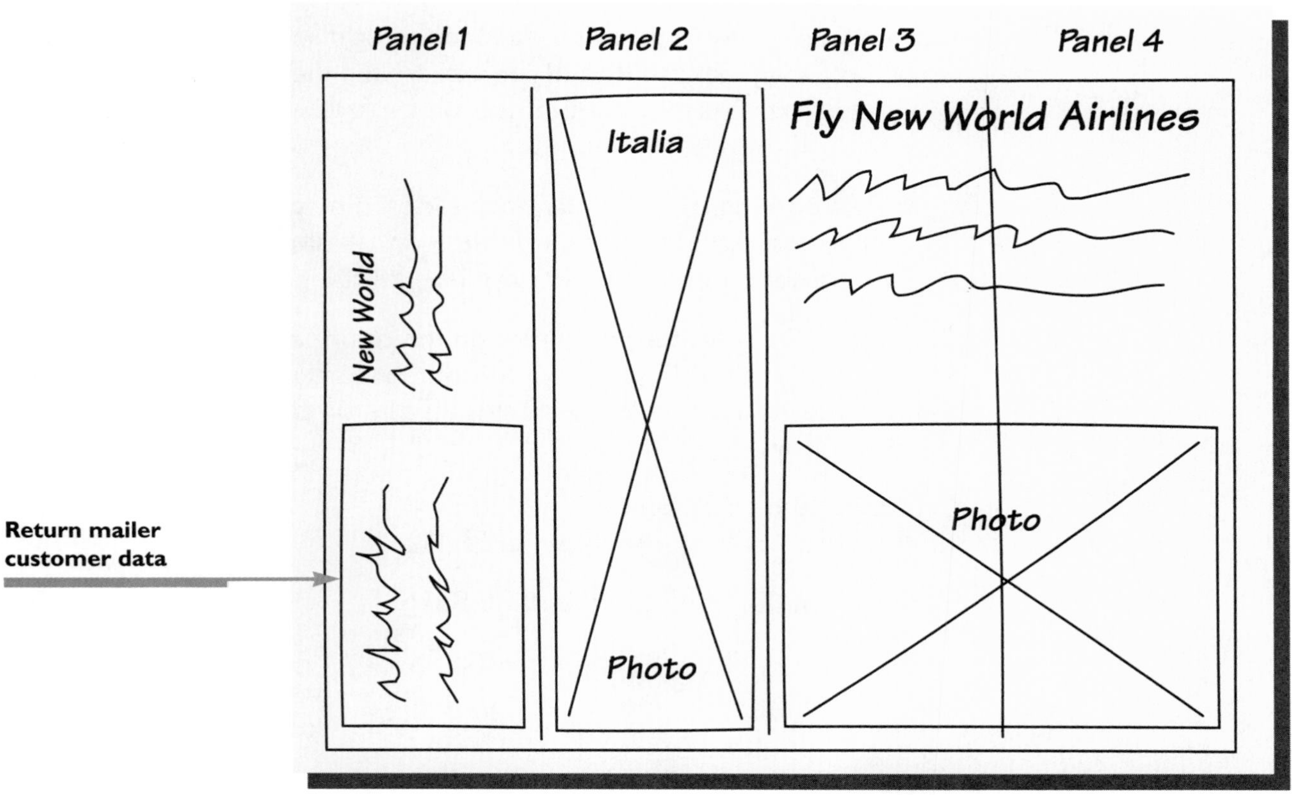

Applying color to text and graphics

You can apply color to graphical elements such as boxes and lines. In addition, you can apply colors to headlines, body type, or other types of text. You apply colors to text using the Type specifications dialog box or the Color palette. ▶ Joe wants to add red color to the headline on page 2 to be consistent with color of the headlines on page 3. Then he wants to add blue color to the box around the self-mailer included in the brochure to make it stand out.

STEPS

1 **Start PageMaker and open the file UNIT_9-1.PM5 from your Student Disk**

2 **Click the headline at the top of page 2 with ↖ to select it, click Layout on the menu bar, click View, then click 50% size, click the Text tool [A] on the toolbox, then drag the I over the headline to highlight it**
Joe changed the view to see the headline better. He must highlight the desired text in order to apply color to it. Joe will use the Type specifications dialog box to apply red color to the headline.

3 **Click Type on the menu bar, then click Type specs, click the Color list arrow, then click Red**
The color black is the default. You can replace it with red, blue, or green.

4 **Click OK, then click the Pointer tool [↖] in the toolbox to deselect the text**
The headline text is now red, as shown in Figure 9-3. Next Joe needs to change the color of the box around the self-mailer to help set it off from the rest of the brochure, drawing the reader's attention to the publication's point of response.

5 **Use the scroll bars to move down and to the right so you can see the self-mailer box, then click the dashed line box around the self-mailer information**
Joe wants to apply the blue color only to the dashes that make the box. He will leave the color inside the box white.

6 **Click Window on the menu bar, then click Color palette**
The Color palette appears on the right side of the publication window as shown in Figure 9-4. For a description of all the options in the Color palettes, see Table 9-1.

7 **Click the Color palette list arrow on the color palette**
See Figure 9-5. The Line, Fill, and Both options appear. You need to select one of these options to apply a color to an object. Since Joe wants to apply the color only to the dashed line box, he chooses the Line option.

8 **Click Line, then click Blue**
The dashes change to blue. Joe is satisfied with the color.

9 **Click File on the menu bar, then click Save**

FIGURE 9-3: Applying color to text

Headline with red color applied

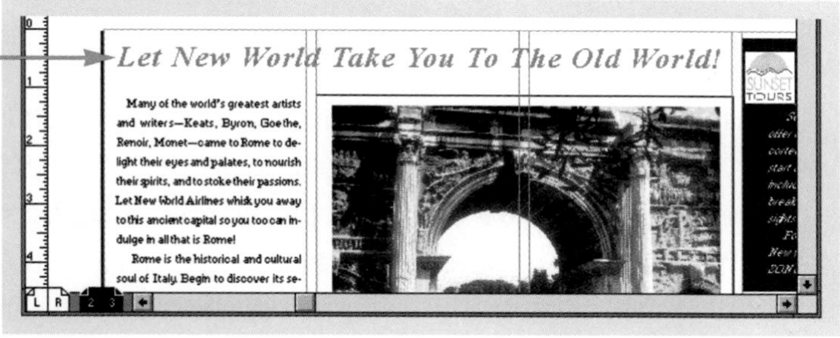

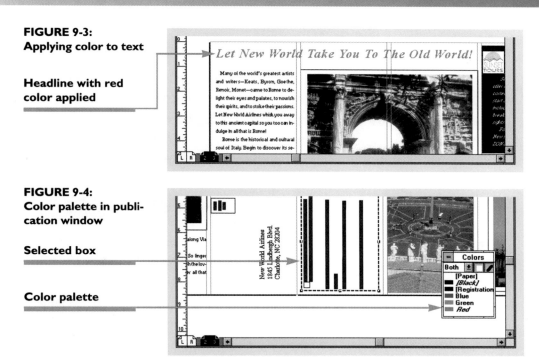

FIGURE 9-4: Color palette in publication window

Selected box

Color palette

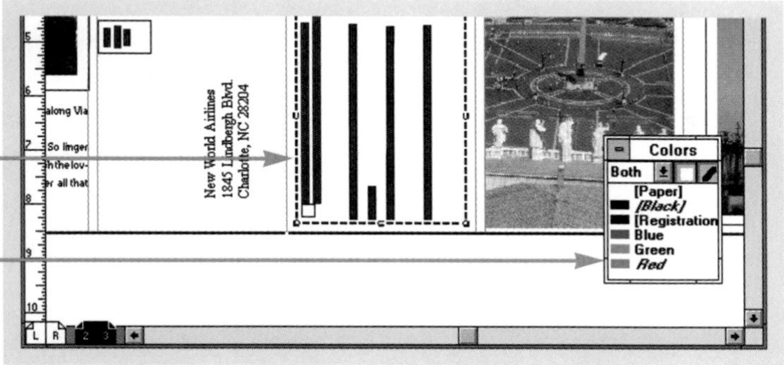

FIGURE 9-5: Color palette list options

Color palette list arrow

Color options

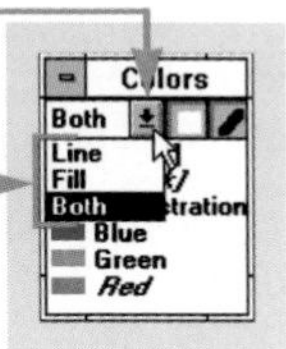

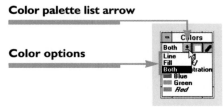

TABLE 9-1: Color palette options

OPTION	DESCRIPTION
Both	Indicates to which object(s) you want to apply a color
(fill icon)	Indicates the color you want to apply as as fill
(line icon)	Indicates the color you want for a line
[Paper]	Indicates the color of the paper on which you are currently printing
[Black]	Indicates one of the process colors (black prints over all other colors)
[Registration	Indicates the percentage of each of the colors in your publication
Blue	Indicates choice of Blue, Green, and Red
% 50% Blue	Indicates if the color is a tint by showing the percentage of color
Purple	Indicates a color that is part of an imported EPS image

Using color in PageMaker

When you create a PageMaker publication that will eventually be sent to a commercial printing press, you need to consider the two types of color that you can use in the publication: spot colors and process colors. **Spot color** is one specific ink used to create a color. For example, to create green using spot colors, you use one of PageMaker's on-line color libraries to specify the green that suits your publication. **Color libraries** are "industry standards" for creating specific colors. **Process colors** are made from four basic colors combined in percentages to create other colors. The four basic colors are **cyan** (C) (a shade of blue), **magenta** (M) (a shade of red), **yellow** (Y), and **black** (K). This process is commonly referred to as **CMYK**. Most color publications you see, including this book, are printed using process colors. To create green using process colors, you mix 100% of cyan and 100% of yellow for a one to one ratio. See the related topic "Using commercial printers" for information on how a color publication is printed. ▶ Joe needs to create color separations that will be given to a commercial printer to create the brochure as shown in Figure 9-6. Joe uses the following guidelines when deciding to use spot or process colors or both methods.

- **Use spot colors to keep production costs low**
  Each time you use a different color, you add to the overall cost of producing your publication. If you are on a limited budget for producing a publication, adding one spot color will add the extra impact needed to make your publication stand out without adding excessive costs. Printing a publication with three or fewer colors should be produced using spot colors. Spot colors are sometimes needed to match an exact color. Joe's budget will allow him to use process color for this brochure; however, he will still need to use a spot color to match exactly the yellow color in the New World Airlines logo.

- **Use process colors to produce a greater variety of colors and reproduce photographs**
  When using process colors, you pay for four inks, CMYK, but you can create a wide variety of colors. Process colors must be used to produce color photographs. Process colors should also be used if you need to create a publication with four or more spot colors. The process colors can be used to create the specified spot color; however, it is important to note, most commercial printers don't guarantee that process colors will create an exact match to an "industry standard" predefined library color. Joe needs to use process colors in his brochure because he will be using color photographs.

- **Use both spot and process colors to give you the most flexibility**
  Using spot and process colors together in a publication is the most expensive method for printing a publication. However, using both color methods will give you the most flexibility in producing a publication with colors you want. You can print color photographs and also specify an exact spot library color for a graphical element such as a company logo. In order to create the most attractive and stunning brochure possible, Joe will use both spot and process colors in his publication.

FIGURE 9-6: Color separations of a publication page

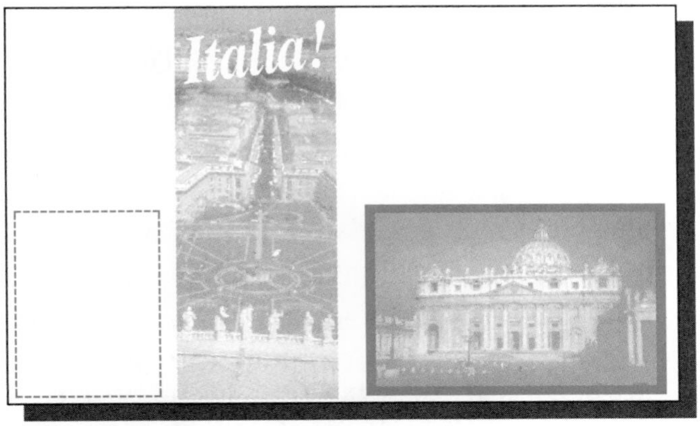

Cyan

Magenta

Yellow

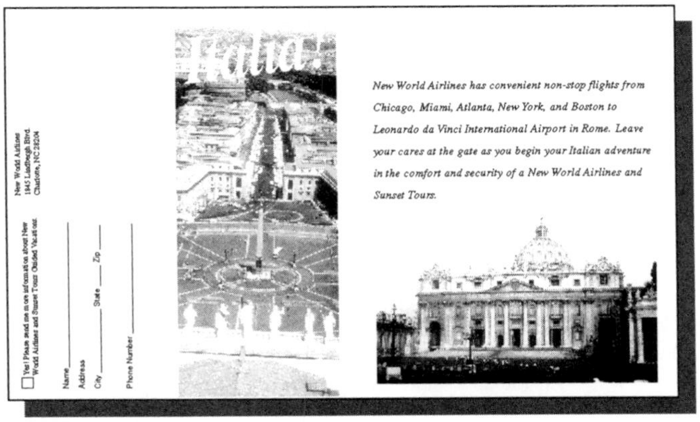

Black

Using commercial printers

Because printing a color publication is costly, make sure you discuss with a printing representative the colors you plan to use and whether the printing company has the appropriate equipment and time to handle the job. After you give your PageMaker publications to the printing company, the printing company creates a film copy for each spot color used in your publication. These are known as **separations**. Each film separation is then used to make printing plates. The plates are placed directly onto the printing press to make impressions on the paper in the publication. In color printing, each color ink has its own set of plates and the paper passes through each plate once. For four-color process printing, four plates are created and each paper receives four passes of color. Each ink is an additional cost: therefore, four-color printing is more complex and more costly than one- or two-color printing. However, the commercial printer can create a wide variety of different colors using a four-color process.

QUICK TIP

If you wish to print a color photograph in your publication, you must use CMYK process colors to create the wide variety of colors in the photograph. If you use process colors in your publication, you can also use process colors to create your own specific spot colors.

Using a color library

One of the greatest challenges in printing is matching colors in your PageMaker publication with the color of the final output from a commercial printer. Color representation can vary between monitors and even vary on different days using the same monitor. Several companies have developed color matching systems that are used by designers and printing companies as standards to print consistent colors. PageMaker supports several color matching systems which are stored as color libraries in the Define colors dialog box. See Table 9-2 for a list of PageMaker color libraries. ▶ Joe recreated the New World Airlines logo in PageMaker so he could have more control over the colors in the logo. The circle behind the New World Airlines text is a specific color in the Pantone Matching System (PMS). It is a color known as Pantone color 123. Joe wants to add this color to the Color palette. When this publication is sent to the commercial printer, it will require a separate ink to print the Pantone color 123.

STEPS

1. **Click Element on the menu bar, then click Define colors**
   The Define colors dialog box opens.
2. **Click New then click the Libraries list arrow**
   A list of PageMaker's color libraries appears.
3. **Click PANTONE® Coated**
   The PANTONE® Coated dialog box opens, as shown in Figure 9-7. To choose a Pantone color, you can scroll through the list or type a specific Pantone number in the text box. The designer who originally created the New World Airlines logo used the spot color Pantone color 123 for the golden sun behind the text and airplane. Joe wants use the exact color for his logo in this brochure.
4. **Drag I over the text in the PANTONE CVC text box, then type 123**
   A golden color appears in the color window. The color on your monitor might not match the color presented in this book.
5. **Click OK**
   See Figure 9-8. Notice PANTONE 123 CVC automatically appears in the text box. Joe closes the dialog box so he can apply the color to the logo.
6. **Click OK twice**
7. **Use the scroll bars to move to the far left to display the New World Airlines logo on page 2, click the circle in the logo with ↖, click the list arrow on the Color palette, then click Both**
   Joe wants to add Pantone color 123 to both the line and fill of the circle. It is important that the logo match the exact color specifications for the company logo.
8. **Click PANTONE 123 CVC (yellow box) on the Color palette**
   PageMaker changes the circle's color from white to the spot color Pantone 123, as shown in Figure 9-9.
9. **Click File on the menu bar, then click Save**

FIGURE 9-7: PANTONE® Coated color dialog box

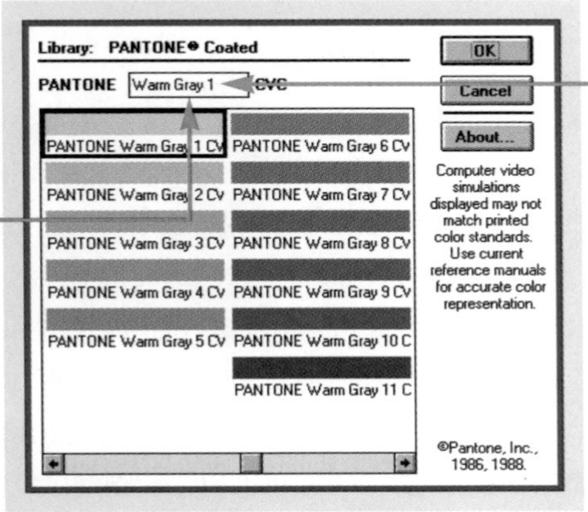

PANTONE CVC text box

Your available PANTONE colors will vary

FIGURE 9-8: The new color

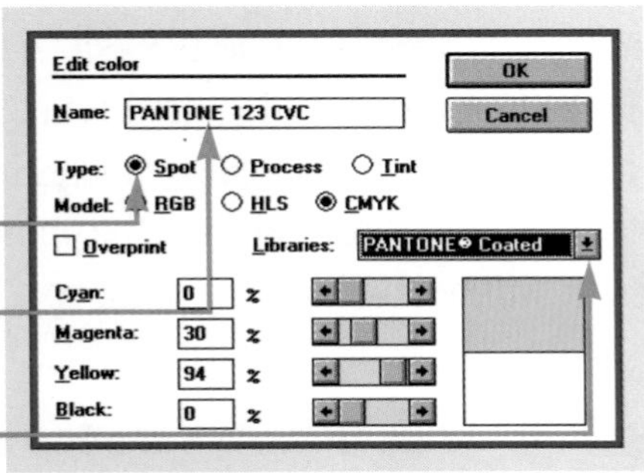

Spot color

Color name

Library selection

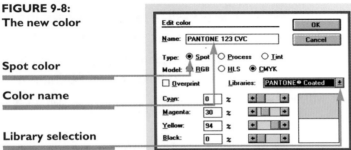

FIGURE 9-9: Logo with new color applied

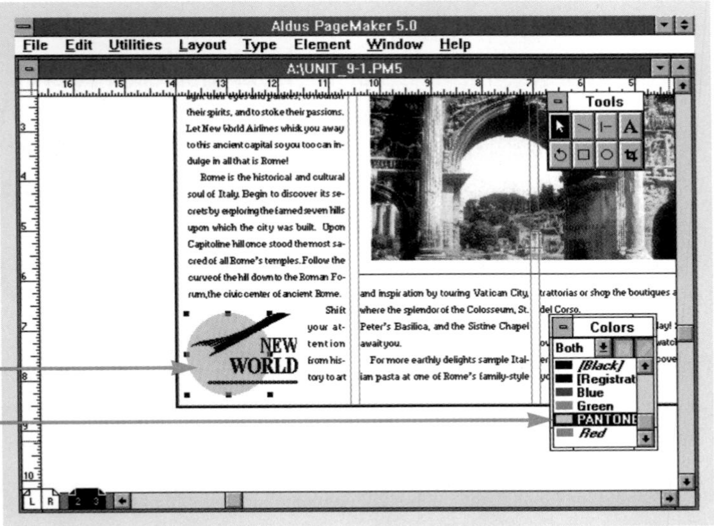

Pantone 123 CVC applied to circle

Pantone 123 CVC

QUICK TIP

Before selecting a library color, make sure your commercial printer can print your publication using the specified matching system color.■

TROUBLE?

To see the complete names of the colors in the Color palette, you can resize the palette by dragging the outside border.■

TABLE 9-2: A sample of PageMaker's color matching libraries

LIBRARY NAME	TYPE	NUMBER OF COLORS	LIBRARY NAME	TYPE	NUMBER OF COLORS
Dainippon	Spot	1280	PANTONE	Process	3006
Focoltone	Process	763	TOYO	Spot	1050
PANTONE	Spot	736	Trumatch	Process	2093

Creating a new color

When using process colors, you can mix the four CMYK colors to create any color you want. To create a new color, use the Define colors dialog box. See the related topic "Using process colors to create Pantone colors" for more information on creating colors. ▶ In addition to the spot color used in the last unit, Joe needs to use process colors so the commercial printer can print color photographs in his publication. He wants to create an additional spot color to use for text and airplane graphic in the company logo in his publication. This time he will use process colors to create the new spot color. In the previous lesson, you used a specific spot color for the New World Airlines logo. When the brochure is printed by the commercial printer, a separate ink called Pantone 123 will be used to print color in the brochure in addition to the four process colors (cyan, magenta, yellow, and black), which will be used to create all of the other color images in the brochure. He will also apply the new spot color to the boxes around the photos. Joe will be charged for five colors; however, he will not be charged for the spot color created using the process colors.

STEPS

1. **Click Element on the menu bar, then click Define colors**
   The Define colors dialog box opens. Notice the Pantone color is selected in the list box. Joe needs to click Paper to clear the previously selected color settings in order to create a new color.

2. **Click Paper in the Color list box, then click New**
   The Edit color dialog box opens. Joe wants to create a blue color to apply to the text in the logo and to the boxes around the photos. Joe will give the color a name. You can customize the name to your preference. Using any number of characters. However, the new color name must be unique—do not use an existing name.

3. **Type Royal Blue in the name text box**
   This is the name that will identify the new color that Joe is creating by using process colors.

4. **Click the Process radio button in the Type section of the dialog box, then make sure the CMYK radio button is selected in the Model section**
   With CMYK selected, PageMaker bases your new color on the four components of process colors: cyan, magenta, yellow, and black.

5. **Type 100 in the Cyan text box, then press [Tab] twice**
   See Figure 9-10. PageMaker displays an example of the color you are creating. The cursor is in the Magenta text box. Joe decides to add magenta to darken the cyan color.

6. **Type 75 in the Magenta text box, then press [Tab] once**
   See Figure 9-11. The color changes from cyan to a darker blue.

7. **Click OK**
   The Edit color dialog box closes and the Define colors dialog box reopens. Notice that the color you just created is in the Color list box.

8. **Click OK**
   The Define colors dialog box closes. Royal Blue is added to the Color palette.

FIGURE 9-10: Cyan added to the new color

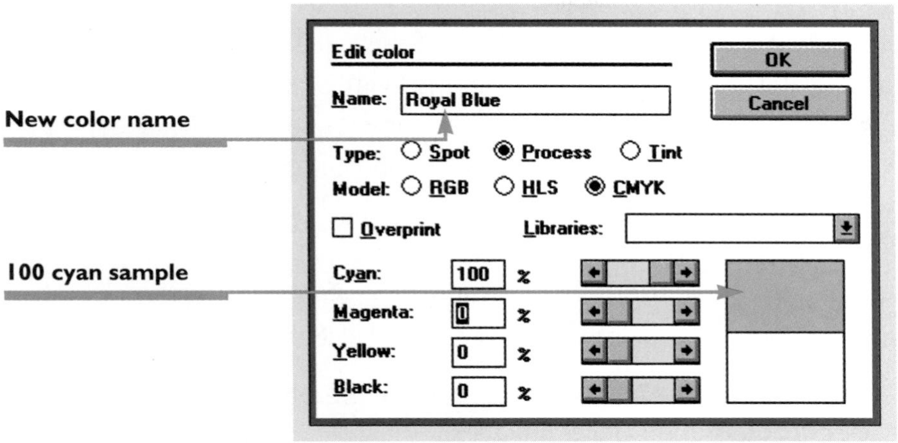

FIGURE 9-11: Cyan and magenta combined to create the new color

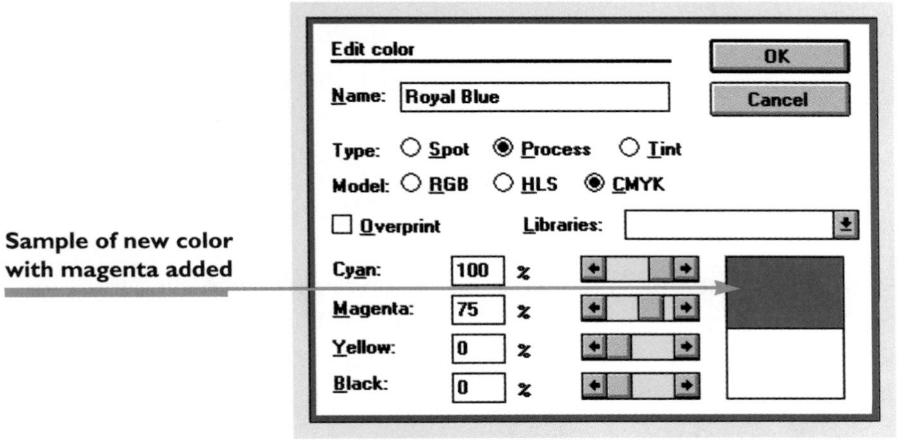

Using process colors to create Pantone colors

You can mix process colors to create Pantone colors. If you have a Pantone swatch book, you can determine the percentage of the process colors needed to create a Pantone color. The only disadvantage is that some commercial printers won't guarantee that mixing process colors will exactly match the Pantone color.

DESIGN TIP

Publications stand out when color is used selectively and not excessively.

Creating a new color, continued

Joe would now like to apply the colors to both the text and graphics in his brochure. See the related topic "Applying colors to imported graphics" for more information on how colors can be applied in your PageMaker publication. First Joe would like to add the new color to the New World Airlines logo.

STEPS

9 Click the **Text tool** [A], drag I over the word **New**, right-click to change the view, click **Royal Blue** on the Color palette, then click outside of the highlighted area
See Figure 9-12. The word is now in the newly created Royal Blue color.

10 Drag I over the word **Airlines**, click **Royal Blue** on the Color palette, then click outside of the highlighted area
The word "Airlines" is now Royal Blue. Next, Joe wants to apply PageMaker's default Red color to the word "World" in the logo.

11 Highlight the word **World**, click **Red** on the Color palette, then click outside of the highlighted area
Joe is satisfied with the color of text. Now Joe wants to add the Royal Blue color to the airplane graphic.

12 Click the **Pointer tool** in the toolbox, click the **airplane graphic**, then click **Royal Blue** on the Color palette
Joe's PageMaker version of the logo is now complete and the colors match his ongoing identity plan for the logo's use. Next Joe wants to apply the new Royal Blue color to the boxes that surround the photos.

13 Right-click, select the box around the photo on page 2, then click the **Line button** on the color palette, then click **Royal Blue**
Notice that just the line has the Royal Blue color. Joe then decides a solid color fill will help make the photos stand out.

14 Click the Fill button on the Color palette, then click **Royal Blue**
See Figure 9-13. Now both the line and fill change to Royal Blue.

15 Click to select the box around the photo of the church on page 3, click the **Control palette list arrow**, click **Both**, then click **Royal Blue** on the Color palette
Once again the box behind the photo turns to the new color Royal Blue. Joe would like to finish applying red color to the brochure's headlines on page 3.

16 Click [A] in the toolbox, drag I over the rotated headline **Italia!** on page 3, click **Red** on the Color palette, highlight the headline on page 3 beginning with the words "Fly New World...," then click **Red** on the Color palette

17 Click to deselect the text
Joe reviews his brochure and determines that the royal blue color is not quite "royal" enough. He would like to darken it. He wants to save his work before he edits the color.

18 Click **File** on the menu bar, then click **Save**

FIGURE 9-12: Working on Joe's PageMaker version of the logo

Royal Blue applied to text

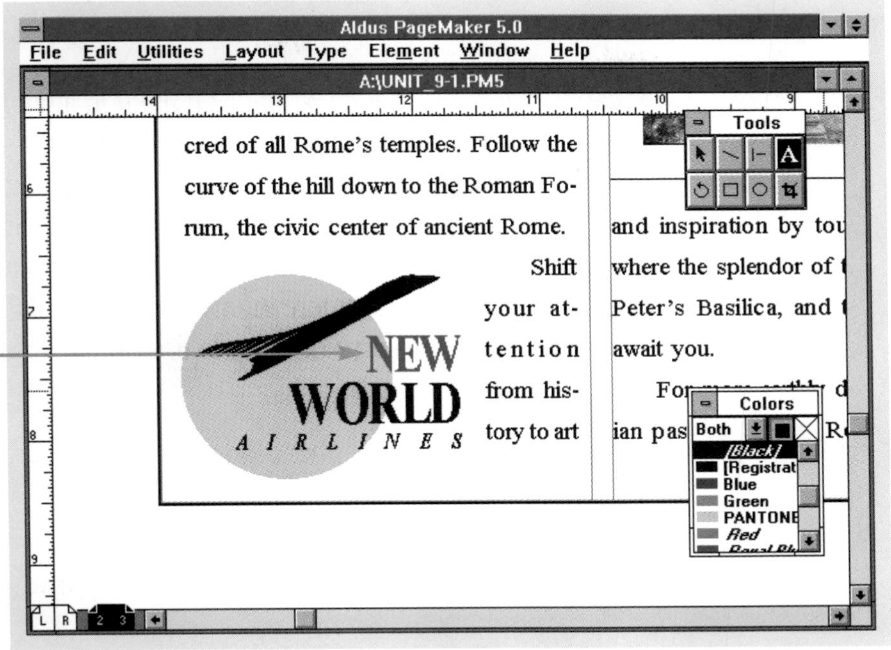

FIGURE 9-13: Box with Royal Blue applied

Royal Blue line

Selected box

Completed logo

Royal Blue fill

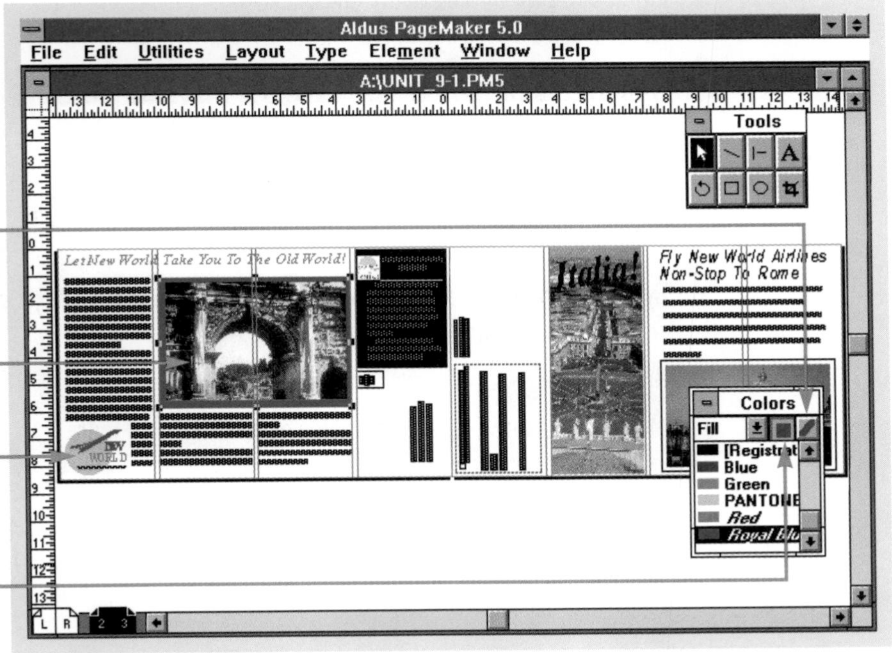

Applying colors to imported graphics

You can apply a color to imported grayscale TIFF, EPS, or PIC file formats. Color TIFF files imported in a PageMaker publication will print in their original colors, even if you apply a color to the image. To apply a color to an imported graphic, select the image and then choose the color from the color palette. If you decide to return the graphic image to its original colors, select Restore original color from the Element menu.

Editing a color

You can edit any color before or after you use it in a publication. Use the Define colors dialog box to edit a color. After the color is edited, PageMaker automatically changes the color wherever you applied it in the publication. When you import an EPS image in your publication, PageMaker automatically adds the image spot colors to PageMaker's Color palette. See the related topic "Editing color in an EPS image" for more information. ▶ Joe doesn't think the shade of blue is the color he wants, so he plans to deepen the Royal Blue color by increasing the amount of magenta.

STEPS

1. **Click the box around the photo on page 2 to select it, then right-click**
   Joe would like to darken the color around this box. He needs to open the Define colors dialog box to edit his color.
2. **Click Element on the menu bar, then click Define colors**
   The Define colors dialog box opens.
3. **Click Royal Blue, then click Edit**
   The Edit color dialog box opens.
4. **Use the scroll bars to increase the Magenta percentage to 100**
   See Figure 9-14. Joe notices the color in the top half of the preview box has changed. The bottom half of the preview box remains the original color. Joe is still not satisfied with the appearance of the color. He refers to a color chart that gives formulas for mixing colors to create new colors. He determines that he needs to add yellow to make the color a "royal" blue.
5. **Type 25 in the Yellow text box, then press [Tab] once**
   Joe likes the new color.
6. **Click OK twice**
   The Edit color and Define color dialog boxes close. See Figure 9-15. PageMaker automatically updates the color boxes behind the photos.
7. **Right-click to return the view to Fit in window, notice that the color text in the New World Airlines logo is updated as well, click File on the menu bar, then click Save**

FIGURE 9-14: Edit color dialog box

Magenta increased to 100%

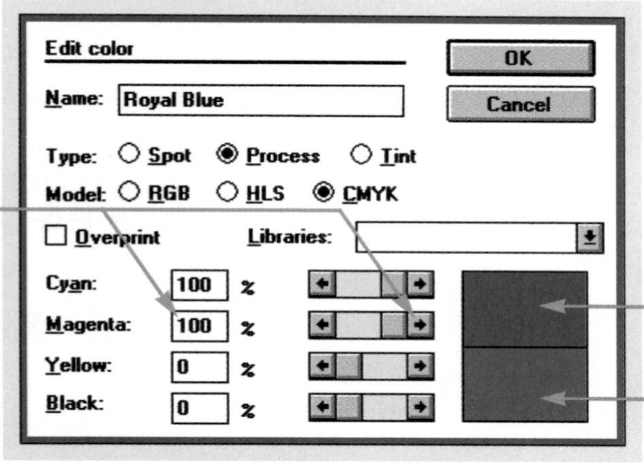

Sample of modification

Color prior to modification

FIGURE 9-15: Edited color applied in the publication

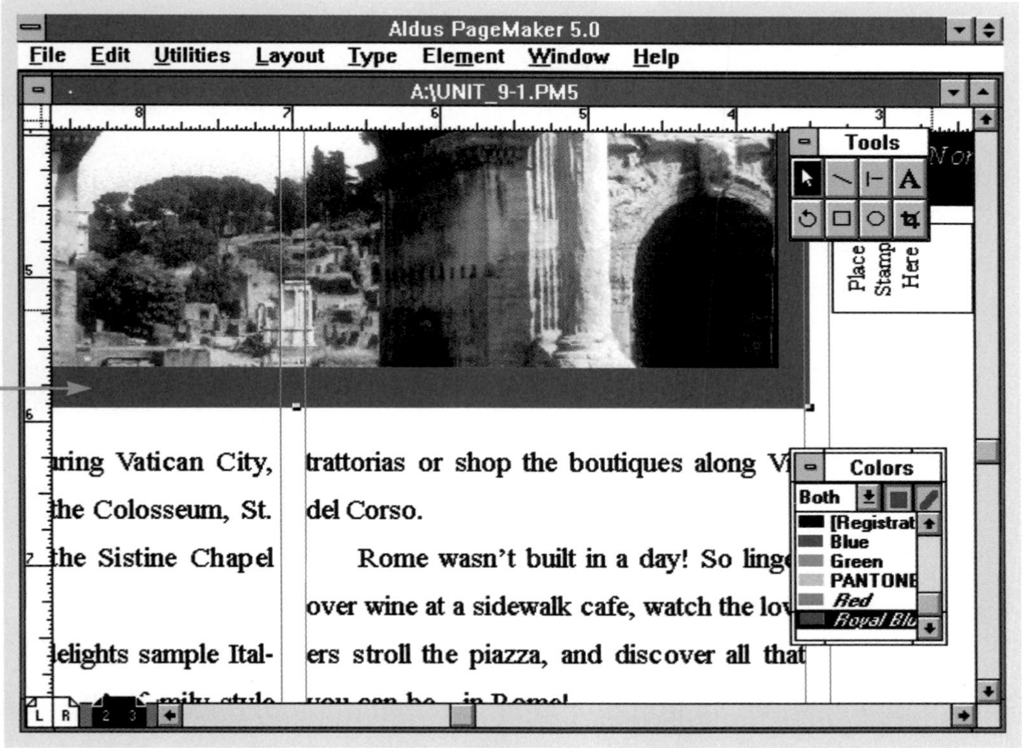

Darker "Royal" Blue

Editing color in an EPS image

When you place a color EPS file in a publication, PageMaker imports all colors stored in the image into the Color palette. The colors appear in the color palette with an EPS graphic place icon PS symbol placed in front of the newly imported color. Imported colors can be converted from spot colors to process colors, or you can modify a spot color. Process colors that are part of an EPS file cannot be edited in PageMaker.

QUICK TIP

To remove a fill color from an object, click Element on the menu bar, click Fill, then select None.

Creating a tint

A **tint** is a new color based on a percentage of a color you created or based on one of PageMaker's default colors. When you use only spot colors in your publication, tints can save money because the commercial printer uses only one ink to create original color as well as the tint. Tints appear on the Color palette with a percent sign (%) in front of the color's name. ▶ Joe wants to lighten the red color box behind the text in the fourth panel on page 2. He creates a new red tint.

STEPS

1. **Click Element on the menu bar, click Define colors, click Paper in the color list box, then click New**
   The Edit color dialog box opens.
2. **Type 75% red in the Name text box**
   It is best to begin the name of your tint color with the percentage of the original color.
3. **Click the Tint radio button**
   See Figure 9-16. The bottom half of the dialog box changes to display only the color selected in Base Color list box. Joe wants to create a tint of the red, so he will select red as his base color.
4. **Click the Base Color list arrow, then click Red**
5. **Type 75 in the Tint text box, press [Tab], then click OK twice**
   The Edit color dialog box closes, and the 75% tint of red appears in the Color list palette with in front of the name. Joe wants to use the new tint color in the reversed text box on page 2 in the fourth panel.
6. **Click the black box surrounding the text box in the fourth panel on page 2, then click 75% red in the Color palette**
   The box fills with the tint and the line changes from black to 75% red, as shown in Figure 9-17. Joe is pleased with the new color. The 75% red provides a clear background for the text, and the tint unites the red headlines in the brochure.
7. **Click File on the menu bar, then click Save**

FIGURE 9-16: Edit color dialog box

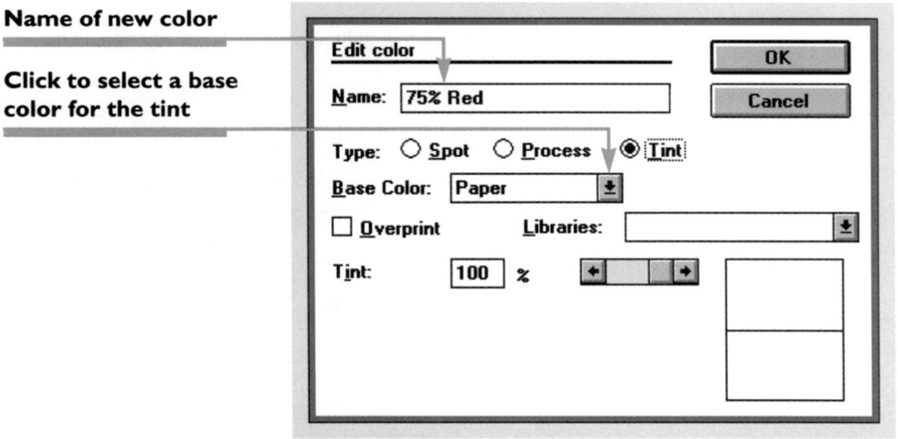

FIGURE 9-17: 75% red tint applied

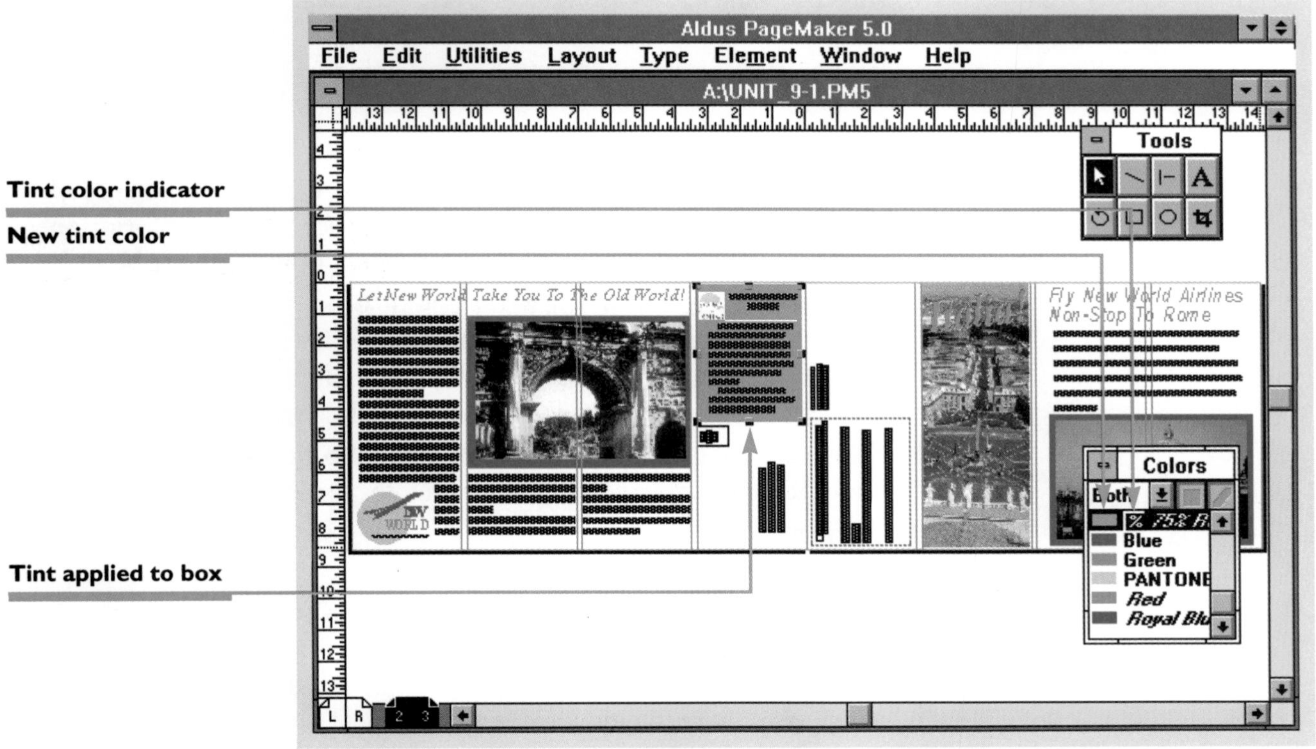

QUICK TIP

You can use the default values listed on the Fill submenu on the Element menu to create quick tints for objects.

Creating color separations

Separations are printouts on paper or film, one for each of the four process colors. If you used spot colors, PageMaker prints out a separation for each spot color applied to your publication. When you create color publications, PageMaker lets you print separations from the Print document dialog box that your commercial printer uses to apply color to your publication. ▶ Joe wants to print separations of his brochure to proof it before sending it the commercial printer. By printing the separations, Joe can make sure the graphic objects and text blocks have been assigned the correct spot or process colors.

STEPS

1. **Click File on the menu bar, then click Print**
   The Print document dialog box opens. First Joe needs to change the orientation of his publication from portrait to landscape.
2. **Make sure the Landscape orientation icon at the bottom of the dialog box is selected**
   Joe needs to open the Paper dialog box to switch to legal size paper.
3. **Click Paper**
   The Paper dialog box opens as shown in Figure 9-18.
4. **If you have a printer capable of printing on legal-size paper, make sure US Legal appears in the Size list box in the Paper section; if you can print only on letter-size paper, make sure US Letter appears in the Size list box**
5. **Click the Center page in print area check box**
   This centers the information on the page. This option is helpful if you can print only on letter-size paper and your publication is based on legal-sized pages. PageMaker can reduce the legal-size pages to fit on smaller paper and will center the information on the page you print.
6. **In the Scale section, click the Reduce to fit radio button**
   The Reduce to fit command reduces the brochure to fit on whatever paper size you chose in Step 4.
7. **Click Options**
   The Options dialog box opens.
8. **In the Markings section, click the Printer's marks and Page information check boxes**
   Printer's marks are the cropping and registration marks used by commercial printers to line up separations on the printing press and then trim the print job to the final size after it's printed. **Page information** adds the file name, date, and separation name to the bottom of each separation page.
9. **Click the Separations radio button, then click Color**
   The Color dialog box opens as shown in Figure 9-19. Notice the small "x" next to each of the four process colors.
10. **Scroll down the Separations color list box to display PANTONE 123 CVC, click PANTONE 123 CVC, click the Print this ink check box, then click Print**
    PageMaker sends the file to the specified printer one separation at a time, starting with the cyan plate and ending with the Pantone 123 plate. A total of five separations should be printed.
11. **Save the publication, then exit PageMaker**

FIGURE 9-18: Paper dialog box

Click to center page

Click to fit all information on the page

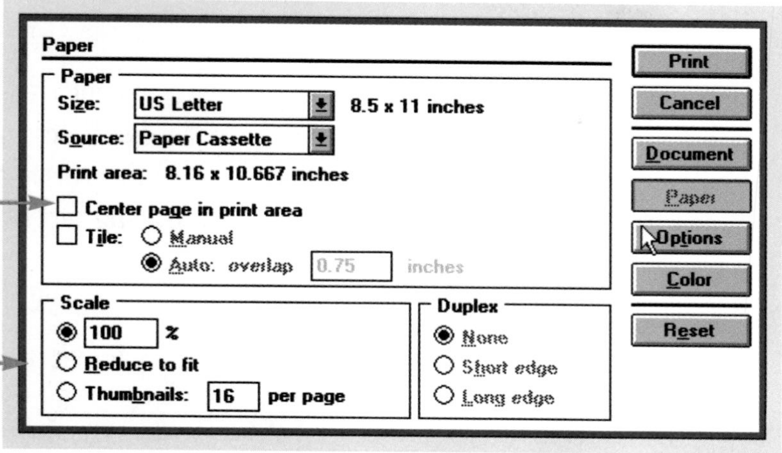

FIGURE 9-19: Color dialog box

Click to print each color separation

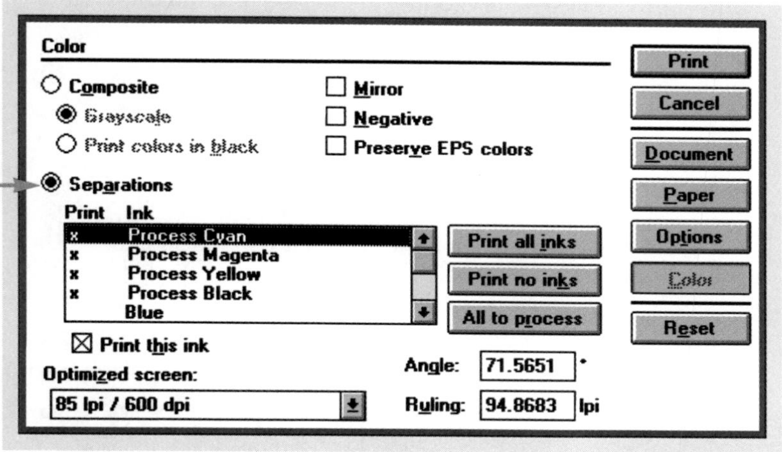

TROUBLE?

If you do not have a postscript printer connected to your computer, you cannot print color separations.■

Design Workshop: Brochures

Brochures are one of the most common ways for people to learn more about a company's products or services. A brochure is meant to educate. By using color in a brochure effectively, you can help get the message across to the reader. Color should be used to enhance the information or help distinguish the differences or unite the commonalities of the information being presented. ▶ Let's review Joe's brochure design.

STEPS

1 **Does the brochure educate the reader?**
Although Joe plans on using this as a teaser, the brochure educates as it entices. In the brochure, a customer learns about the special deals being offered by New World Airlines and Sunset Tours. Customers also discover that there is more information on the subject available to them if they send away for it.

2 **How does color add to the brochure's design?**
Although Joe could have designed the brochure using just black ink, the effect of the photos of Rome would not be the same. If members of Joe's target audience have been to Italy, color photos will spur their memories of past vacations better than black and white photos. Besides the photos, Joe used color conservatively, not splashing it onto every text block or every part of white space.

3 **Does the paper size and folding technique help or hinder the design?**
Joe's design using standard legal-size paper is relatively common in the printing industry. He will have no problems finding an economical way to print the brochure. The brochure's folds are also simple, folding the longest measurement in half, then in half again.

4 **Does the brochure make it easy for potential customers to respond?**
Potential response is where Joe's design really pays off. By using just one flap for both addressing the piece to customers and a reply card on the reverse side Joe saves money and makes responding easier for customers. How? Joe can have the printing company add a perforation along the fold line to separate the card easily from the rest of the brochure. The bulk of the brochure stays intact for the customer, and the response card is mailed back to New World Airlines.

FIGURE 9-20: Joe's completed brochure

Let New World Take You To The Old World!

Many of the world's greatest artists and writers—Keats, Byron, Goethe, Renoir, Monet—came to Rome to delight their eyes and palates, to nourish their spirits, and to stoke their passions. Let New World Airlines whisk you away to this ancient capital so you too can indulge in all that is Rome!

Rome is the historical and cultural soul of Italy. Begin to discover its secrets by exploring the famed seven hills upon which the city was built. Upon Capitoline hill once stood the most sacred of all Rome's temples. Follow the curve of the hill down to the Roman Forum, the civic center of ancient Rome. Shift your attention from history to art and inspiration by touring Vatican City, where the splendor of the Colosseum, St. Peter's Basilica, and the Sistine Chapel await you.

For more earthly delights sample Italian pasta at one of Rome's family-style trattorias or shop the boutiques along Via del Corso.

Rome wasn't built in a day! So linger over wine at a sidewalk cafe, watch the lovers stroll the piazza, and discover all that you can be—in Rome!

NEW WORLD AIRLINES

SUNSET TOURS

Take A Sunset Tour To Rome

See the best that Rome has to offer on Sunset Tours fully escorted 8 day/7night tour. Prices start at $1,000 per person. This includes first class hotels, daily breakfast, 6 dinners and full sightseeing.

For more information, call your travel agent or New World Airlines at 1-800-HORIZON .

Place Stamp Here

New World Airlines
1845 Lindbergh Blvd.
Charlotte, NC 28204

New World Airlines
1845 Lindbergh Blvd.
Charlotte, NC 28204

☐ Yes! Please send me more information about New World Airlines and Sunset Tours Guided Vacations.

Name ____________

Address ____________

City ________ State ______ Zip ______

Phone Number ____________

Fly New World Airlines Non-Stop To Rome

New World Airlines has convenient non-stop flights from Chicago, Miami, Atlanta, New York, and Boston to Leonardo da Vinci International Airport in Rome. Leave your cares at the gate as you begin your Italian adventure in the comfort and security of a New World Airlines and Sunset Tours.

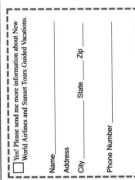

CONCEPTS REVIEW

Label each of the publication window elements shown in Figure 9-21.

1 ____
2 ____
3 ____
4 ____
5 ____
6 ____
7 ____
8 ____
9 ____
10 ____
11 ____

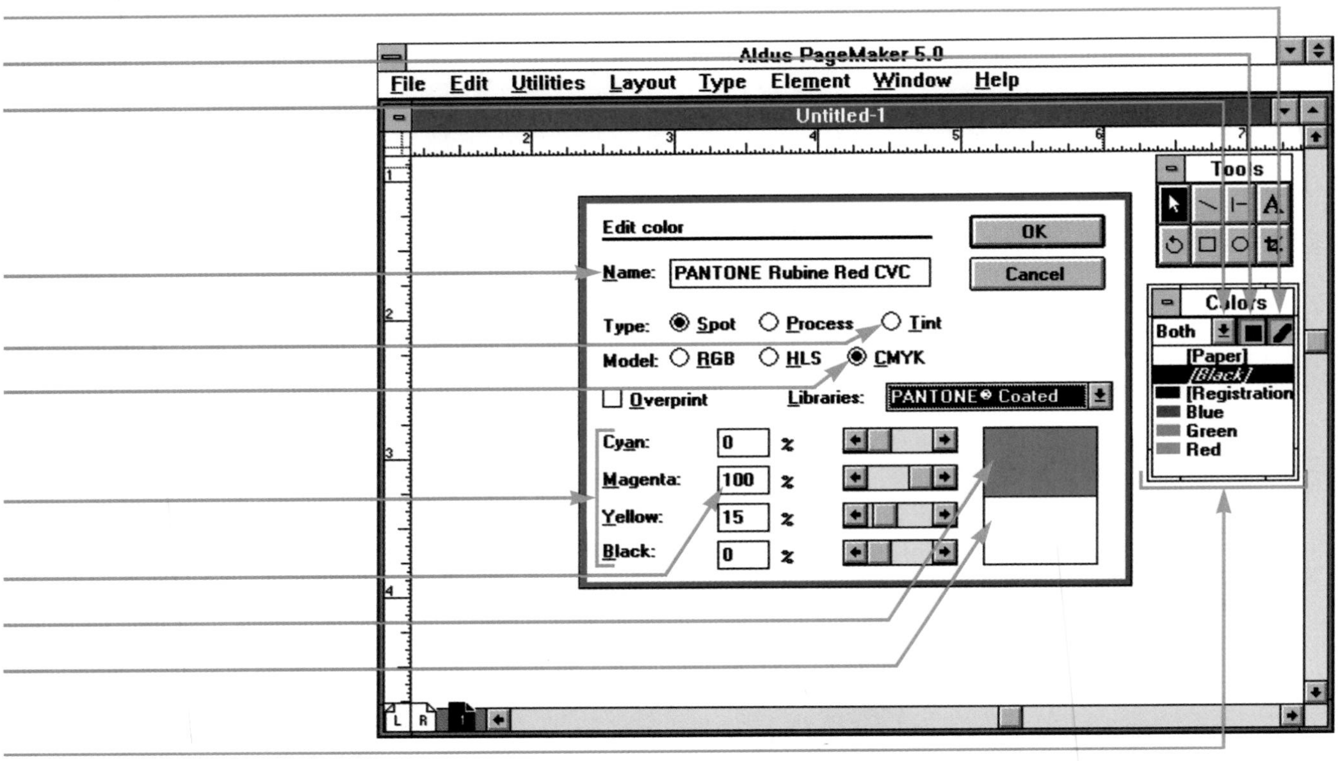

FIGURE 9-21

Match each of the terms with the statement that describes its function.

12 Process color
13 Spot color
14 Tint
15 Color library
16 Separations

a. Based on a specific color ink
b. Printouts on paper or film of each color used for commercial printing of publications
c. PageMaker's storage for color matching systems
d. The four main colors used in combinations to create many other colors
e. A new color based on a percentage of another color

17 Which of the following is true about brochures?

a. Brochures can be used as teasers to entice the reader to find out more information
b. Brochures should be distinctive in design from other corporate brochures
c. Brochures come in all different sizes
d. Both a and c
e. All of the above

18 The four process colors are

a. Cyan, magenta, yellow, red
b. Cyan, magenta, green, yellow
c. Cyan magenta, yellow, black
d. Red, yellow, blue, black

19 Spot colors are not
- a. Percentages of another color
- b. Created using a color matching system
- c. Based on a specific color ink used in printing
- d. All of the above

20 Colors can be applied to
- a. Text
- b. Graphical elements
- c. Lines
- d. All of the above

21 Tints are based on
- a. Color matching systems
- b. Process colors
- c. Black
- d. All of the above

22 The purpose of a color matching system is to create
- a. Colors that display vibrantly on a color monitor
- b. Color separations
- c. Process colors
- d. Consistent color representation between monitors and print output

23 Color separations are
- a. Previews of final color composite output
- b. Printouts on paper or film of process colors
- c. Printouts on paper or film of spot colors
- d. Both b and c

APPLICATIONS REVIEW

1 Create a new color.
- a. Start PageMaker and open the publication UNIT_9-2.PM5 from your Student Disk.
- b. Use the Define colors dialog box to create a new color.
- c. Select the Process color and CMYK options.
- d. Set the process color settings to 100% Cyan and Yellow, and 50% for Magenta.
- e. Name the color Forest Green.

2 Apply color to a graphic and remove a color.
- a. Display the Color palette in the publication window.
- b. Apply the Forest Green color to both the fill and line of the horizontal box in the upper-left corner on page 2.
- c. Apply the Forest Green color to both the fill and line of the vertical box intersecting the box on the far left side of page 2.
- d. Select the vertical box you just applied the color to and return the color to black.
- e. Apply the Forest Green color to the fill and line of all horizontal boxes on page 2 and the left two panels on page 3.

3 Edit a color.
- a. Use the Color dialog box to edit the Forest Green color.
- b. Use the scroll bars to increase the Magenta percentage to 75%.
- c. Close the Color dialog box and make sure your new color is automatically applied to all objects set to that color.

4 Use a color library.
- a. Use the Color dialog box to create a new color using a color library.
- b. Select the PANTONE® Coated library.
- c. Scroll to the right, then select the Rubine Red color.
- d. Create a second PANTONE® Coated color, select color PANTONE 3955.

5 Apply color to text.
- a. Select, then highlight, the headline text inside the Forest Green box in the upper-left corner on page 2.
- b. Apply the Rubine Red color.
- c. Repeat the steps above to apply the Rubine Red color to all headline text inside of Forest Green boxes.

6 Create a tint.
- a. Use the Define color dialog box to create a new tint color.
- b. Select the PANTONE 3955 color in the Color list box, then open the Edit color dialog box.
- c. Select the Tint option.
- d. Use the scroll bars to select 60% in Tint text box.

7 Create color separations.
- a. Use the Print dialog box to create color separations.
- b. Open the Paper dialog box.
- c. Open the Color dialog box.
- d. Print the color separations.
- e. Save your publication, then exit PageMaker.

INDEPENDENT CHALLENGE 1

You work for Sunset Tours in the Young Audience Tours division. You have decided to create a brochure that can be sent to all New World Airlines customers who are between the ages of 18 and 24 announcing new spring break trips to the Caribbean Islands. This brochure will serve as a teaser with the purpose of encouraging the reader to send back an attached mailer for more information. This brochure will be printed using four-color process inks. Include photos and color elements to enhance the overall message of the brochure.

To complete this independent challenge

1 Plan and sketch the brochure design.

2 Open a new publication and determine the size, shape, and possible ways to incorporate a reply card. Use a size other than letter or legal, and a format other than three- or four-panel.

3 Place Caribbean-related photos in the brochure. The photos are called PHOTO1.TIF and PHOTO2.TIF and are located on your Student Disk.

4 Add headlines and copy for the brochure, then apply color to the sections you think are appropriate. If necessary, you can use the Word document, PROPOSAL.DOC located on your Student Disk, for text describing the Caribbean.

5 Create a spot color using the process colors. Apply the color to the headlines.

6 Create an additional spot color using one of PageMaker's color libraries. Apply the color to appropriate graphical elements included in your brochure.

7 Create color separations for each of the process colors. Be sure to include a separation for each additional spot color.

8 Save the brochure as BROCHURE.PM5.

9 Submit your sketch and final brochure.

INDEPENDENT CHALLENGE 2

Visit a local bank or financial planner and find brochures about investment opportunities. Try to find brochures that include full color. Review the examples, then redesign one of the brochures to improve its appeal. Answer the following questions as you plan your design:

1 What is the purpose of the brochure? Is it meant to be informational or serve as a teaser to encourage the reader to inquire for more information?

2 Do the different brochures from a single company present a single corporate identity?

3 Does the brochure give the reader the opportunity to inquire for more information?

4 Does the size of the brochure seem appropriate? Does the information presented seem to fit the dimensions proportionately?

To complete this independent challenge:

1 Sketch your version of the brochure.

2 Open a new publication and save it as NEWBROC.PM5 on your Student Disk.

3 Create columns in your publication if necessary.

4 Place the Word document TEXTHLD.DOC and the graphic file PLACEHLD.TIF to serve as dummy text and graphics.

5 Add boxes and lines to enhance the overall design of the brochure.

6 Create new colors that can be applied to headline and other appropriate text blocks.

7 Create a new color from a PANTONE® Coated library. Use this color and apply it to graphical elements in your publication.

8 Create a new tint color and apply it to either text or graphics.

9 Include a point of response. This could be a mailer or simply be a address and phone number depending on your brochure.

10 Create color separations for the each of the process colors. Be sure to include a separation for each additional spot color.

11 Save the publication then print it.

12 Submit your sketch and final brochure.

UNIT 10

OBJECTIVES

- Create a letterhead
- Create a fax cover page
- Create an advertisement
- Create a flyer
- Create a fact sheet
- Create a brochure
- Create a newsletter

Additional PROJECTS

This unit provides seven additional projects for you to practice the skills you learned in the lessons of this book. Begin each project by organizing how you want the information to flow on the page, using the planning techniques you learned in this book. The layout and design of your publications should be simple and easy to understand, yet creative enough to involve the reader totally in each publication's message. ▶ Sunset Tours, an independent travel agency, provides quality self-guided and packaged tours in the United States and around the world. Matt Candela, of Sunset Tours, needs to finish some projects he has been working on over the last couple of weeks. ▶

Creating a letterhead

Matt's first project is to create a new Sunset Tours letterhead using a different business address and a newly designed logo. The information on Sunset Tours' previous company letterhead was poorly organized and difficult to read. ▶ Corporate letterhead should contain a slogan statement, name, address, phone number, and fax number. In addition to containing this valuable information, it should be well designed and should effectively project the company's image. To help complete this project, open a new PageMaker document, set page dimensions, then create and import the information needed to design a professional-looking letterhead. Use the sample letterhead Matt sketched, shown in Figure 10-1, to create the new letterhead.

STEPS

1 **Start PageMaker and open a new publication, then set page specifications for the letterhead in the Page setup dialog box**
This publication should be single-sided because it is a one-page publication. Set the left and bottom margins with the same setting and top and right margins with the same setting. All of the margins should be less than 1". Be sure to compose your letterhead to your specific printer.

2 **Save the letterhead with a meaningful name to your Student Disk**
Since you have only eight characters to use for a name, give the letterhead a name that you can easily recognize.

3 **Place the logo, SUNSET.TIF, located on your Student Disk, in the publication**
The Sunset Tours' logo appears, as shown in Figure 10-2. Matt waits to experiment with the placement of the logo until he creates the letterhead text.

4 **Use the Text tool [A] to enter the company address, phone number, fax number and a company slogan**
Matt creates two text objects independent of each other, so he can move each object around the page. Matt formats the text before he experiments with its position on the page.

5 **Use the Font, Size, and Type style commands on the Type menu to format the letterhead text**
Before deciding on the best look for your letterhead text, try a number of different font types, sizes, and styles.

6 **Move the logo and the text objects into their final positions**
Use the design guidelines you learned in this book to place the logo and text. As you experiment with different logo and text positions, print the letterhead designs you favor to see how they look on paper. Printing the letterhead at different stages of development provides good clues on how the document needs to change. Remember, your letterhead needs to be simple and visually pleasing.

7 **Finish the project by checking for spelling errors, then save and print your publication**

8 **Be able to explain the design of your letterhead**

FIGURE 10-1: Sketch of Sunset Tours' letterhead

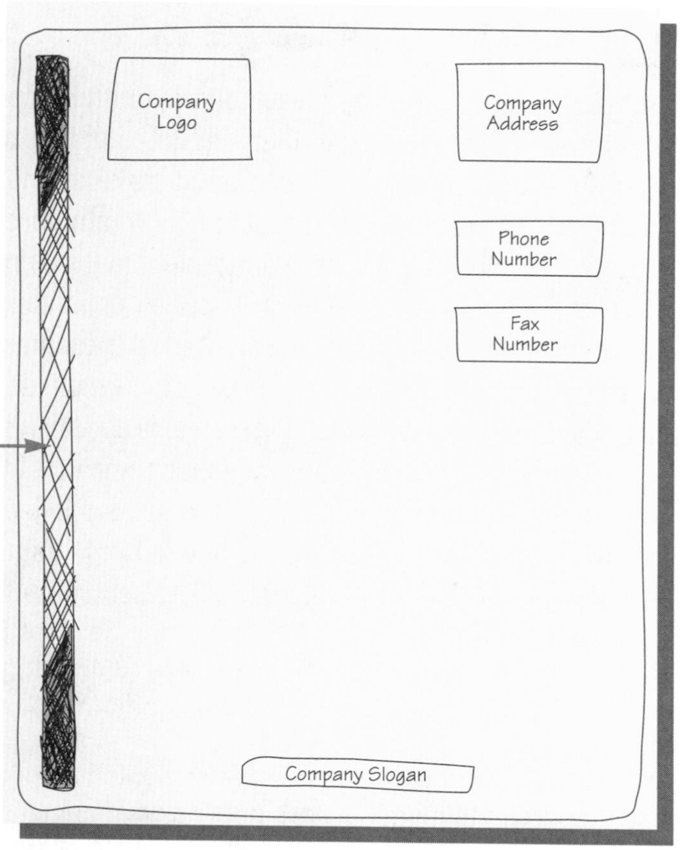

Shaded bar

FIGURE 10-2: Sunset Tours' logo

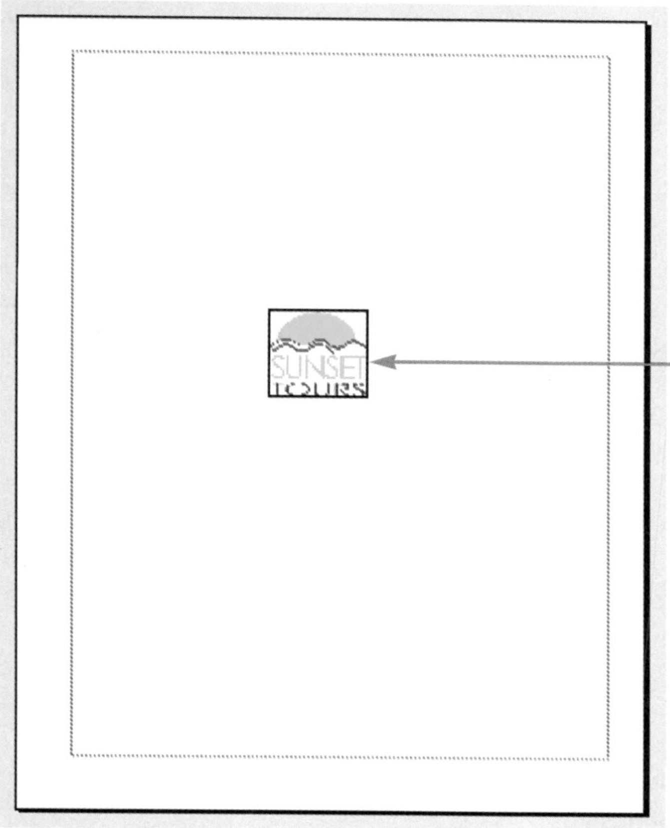

You might place this in a different location

QUICK **TIP**

See Unit 2 for help designing a letterhead and other office stationery.

Creating a fax cover page

Use your drawing skills to help Matt Candela finish the fax cover page he started working on earlier today. Sunset Tours' old fax cover page was not designed well and could not easily accommodate new information. Because faxing documents to potential clients is becoming an important form of communication at Sunset Tours, the fax cover page needs to be concise and professional looking. A fax cover page that is too detailed or that includes intricate designs or photographs, does not print well on the majority of facsimile printers and slows the transmission of the fax. ▶ As with corporate letterhead, a fax cover page needs to include some basic information such as the date, sender and recipient names, phone and fax numbers, number of pages, and a subject area. It should also project the company's identity by containing the company logo and address. Finally, it needs to be well designed so it instantly identifies the intended party and the pages that follow. ▶ Use the sample fax cover page Matt sketched, shown in Figure 10-3, to help you design your fax cover page.

STEPS

1. **Open the publication FAX.PM5 from your Student Disk**
   The fax cover page appears. So far, Matt has entered the text and placed the Sunset Tours' logo on the fax cover page. Take this information and organize it into a simple but effective fax cover page.
2. **Use the Rectangle tool [▭] to draw an unfilled box (use a line larger than 1 point) over the margin guides of the document**
   Use the box resize handles to move the box lines over the margin guides, if necessary. Placing the box over the margin guides gives your fax cover sheet boundaries to follow when you place text or other elements on the page. Next, create some unfilled boxes where you can place the fax cover text. Putting boundaries around the text provides defined areas to write the necessary sending and receiving information.
3. **Choose a position on the vertical ruler, then draw a ¼" box from the left vertical margin guide to the right vertical margin guide**
   You might need to turn on the Snap to guides option. The sides of the box should snap to the vertical margin guides. Drag the box resize handles to stretch the box to fit between the vertical margin guides, if necessary. While the box is selected, experiment with different line widths and styles. Keep in mind, as you experiment with line widths and styles, that the purpose of this box is to surround text.
4. **Duplicate the box four times, then drag the boxes into logical positions on the page**
   Use a horizontal ruler guide to help position the boxes relative to each other, if necessary. Once you place the boxes on the page, move the fax cover page text inside the boxes.
5. **Drag the text objects inside the boxes, then group the text objects together**
   Before you drag the objects inside the boxes, plan how you want the text organized. You have the width of the page to work with, so make use of all the space.
6. **Use the Line tool [╲] to draw a vertical line to separate the text objects**
   Be sure to print the fax cover page at different stages of development, so you can see exactly how all the elements fit together.
7. **Finish the project by checking for spelling errors, then save and print your publication**
8. **Be able to explain the design of your fax cover page**

FIGURE 10-3: Sketch of Sunset Tours' fax cover page

Unfilled box over margin guides sets boundaries

Unfilled boxes contain text objects

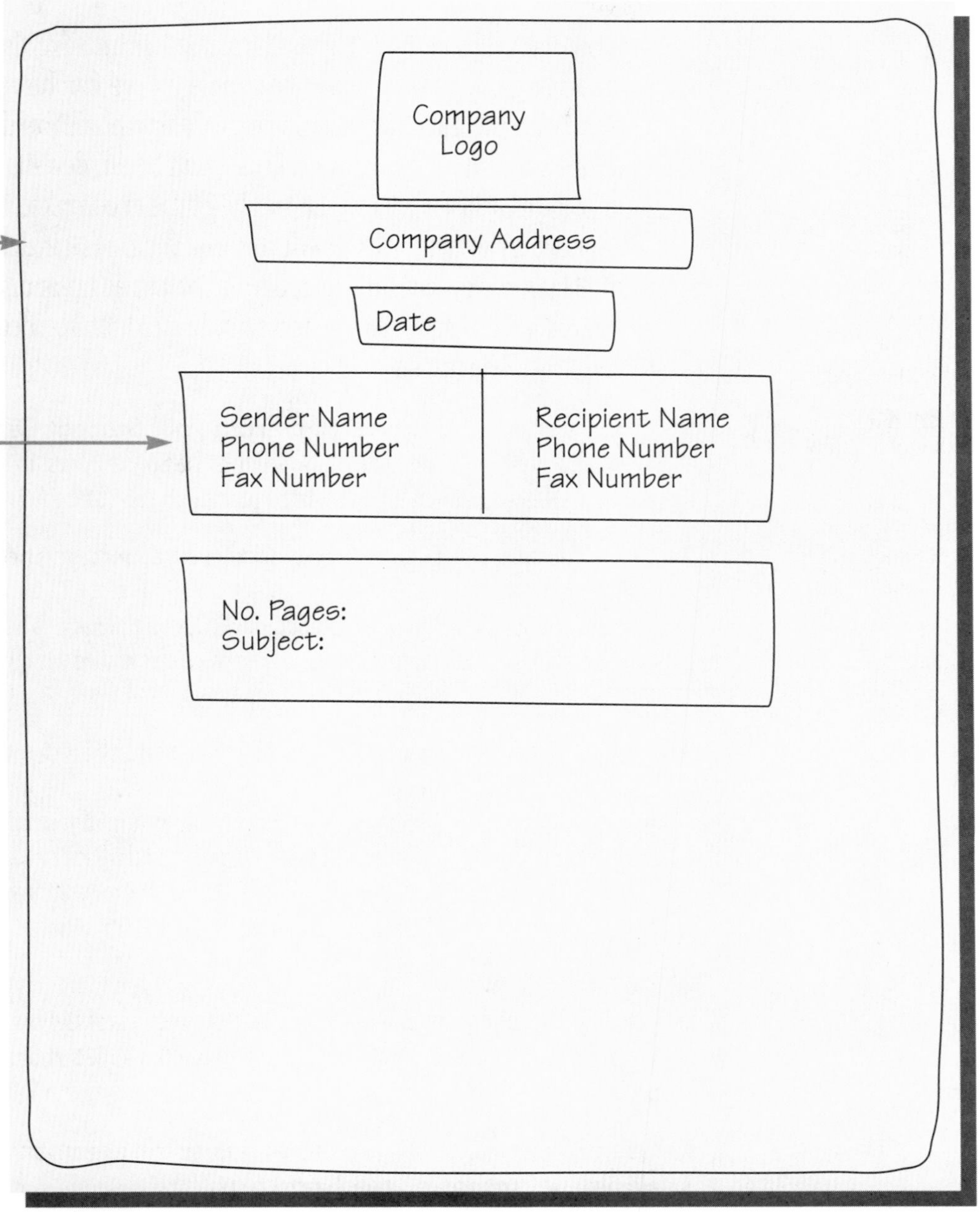

QUICK **TIP**

See Unit 3 for help designing a fax cover page.

Creating an advertisement

One of Matt's jobs at Sunset Tours is to create print advertisements for trade magazines and newspapers. Ads must be simple yet eye-catching. They should pique the readers' interest and make them want to learn more. You do this by incorporating graphics and text in a meaningful way. Matt began developing an advertisement on tours to Europe last week but has not had time to complete it. He needs to finish this 1-color advertisement, which will run in a national travel magazine on European tours. The magazine publisher will only accept ads that are one-color and submitted on 8½" × 11" paper. ▶ Use the sample ad Matt sketched, shown in Figure 10-4, to help complete the ad.

STEPS

1 **Open the publication AD.PM5 from your Student Disk**
The partially complete ad appears. Notice that the Sunset Tours' logo is imported but not positioned on the page. You need to begin by placing the text and the logo in better positions.

2 **Place the Sunset Tours' logo and the title text on the page, then place the ad text**
Remember that the ad and logo need to stand out on the page. When you think you have a good layout design, print and review the page. After you are satisfied with the design, you need to format the text.

3 **Use the Control Palette to change the font type, font size, and text tracking to achieve the desired look**
Be careful not to rush through the text formatting portion of your ad. You want to ensure that the main points of the ad are clear and easily absorbed. You might need to adjust the text position again because of the formatting you choose. Remember to be simple and clear in your layout design and to include plenty of white space.

4 **Add bullets to the text list**
The bullets should draw attention to the features being highlighted in the list but not away from the rest of the ad. Adjust the spacing between the bullets and the text to achieve a professional look.

5 **Use the alignment commands to adjust the alignment of text or use the alignment buttons on the Control palette**
The default alignment of text is left, which is appropriate for most text objects; however, some text lines look better with a different alignment. Experiment with text alignment in the ad.

6 **Finish the project by checking for spelling errors, then save and print your publication**

7 **Be able to explain the design of your advertisement**

FIGURE 10-4: Sketch of Sunset Tours' advertisement

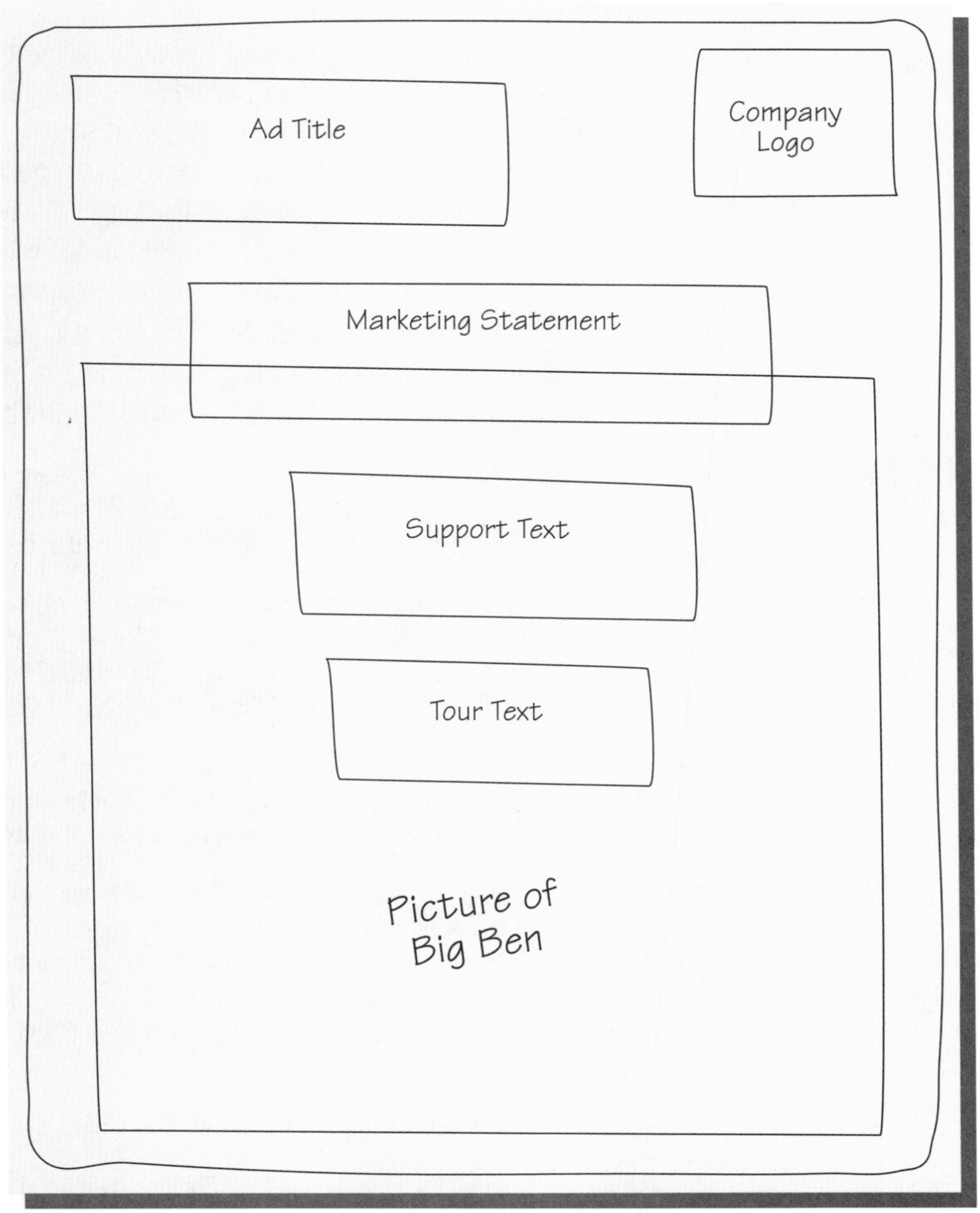

QUICK **TIP**

See Unit 6 for help designing a print advertisement.

Creating a flyer

Every month Sunset Tours produces a flyer that highlights special package tours to its "country of the month." Sunset Tours decided to highlight four full-package tours to Russia for next month. As with an advertisement, a flyer needs to have a simple, eye-catching design. The flyer must direct the reader to the important information on the page by using color, shading, or different text style attributes, such as bold or italic. Flyers might not provide readers with all the information they need, so be sure to provide a way for readers to contact the company for more information. ▶ Matt can finish the flyer by resizing a graphic, rotating and recoloring text, and adjusting text tracking and leading. Use the sample flyer Matt sketched, shown in Figure 10-5, to help finish designing the flyer.

STEPS

1. **Open the publication FLYER.PM5 from your Student Disk**
   The partially completed flyer appears. Notice that the graphic of Russia does not fill the page. You will need to resize the graphic to fit the width of the page (within the vertical margin guides).

2. **Use the Control palette to resize the Russia graphic proportionally to the width of the page, then rotate the word "Russia!" inside the graphic**
   Be careful how much you rotate the text; it needs to be readable. Print the page to check the size of the object and the rotation position of the text in the object. Now change the color of the text in the graphic so it stands out.

3. **Use the Type specifications dialog box to change the text color of the word "Russia!" to contrast with the Russia graphic color**

4. **Use the Type specifications dialog box to format the font, font style, leading, and tracking of the two lists on the page**
   The tabs Matt set between the cities and the day and prices in the lower list need to be reformatted using the Tab command. Matt just set a normal tab, using the Tab key, between the cities and the days and prices. Because each text line is a different length, using the Tab key does not align the text properly.

5. **Set and adjust a tab in the lower list to line up all the days and prices in two clearly separate columns**
   The position of a tab is dependent on the size of the text object and the formatting of the text. You might need to experiment with the tab or the size of the text object to achieve just the right look. If possible, make sure that you are finished formatting the text before you set the tabs, because later text formatting can change a tab's position.

6. **Finish the project by checking for spelling errors, then save and print your publication**

7. **Be able to explain the design of your flyer**

FIGURE 10-5: Sketch of Sunset Tours' flyer

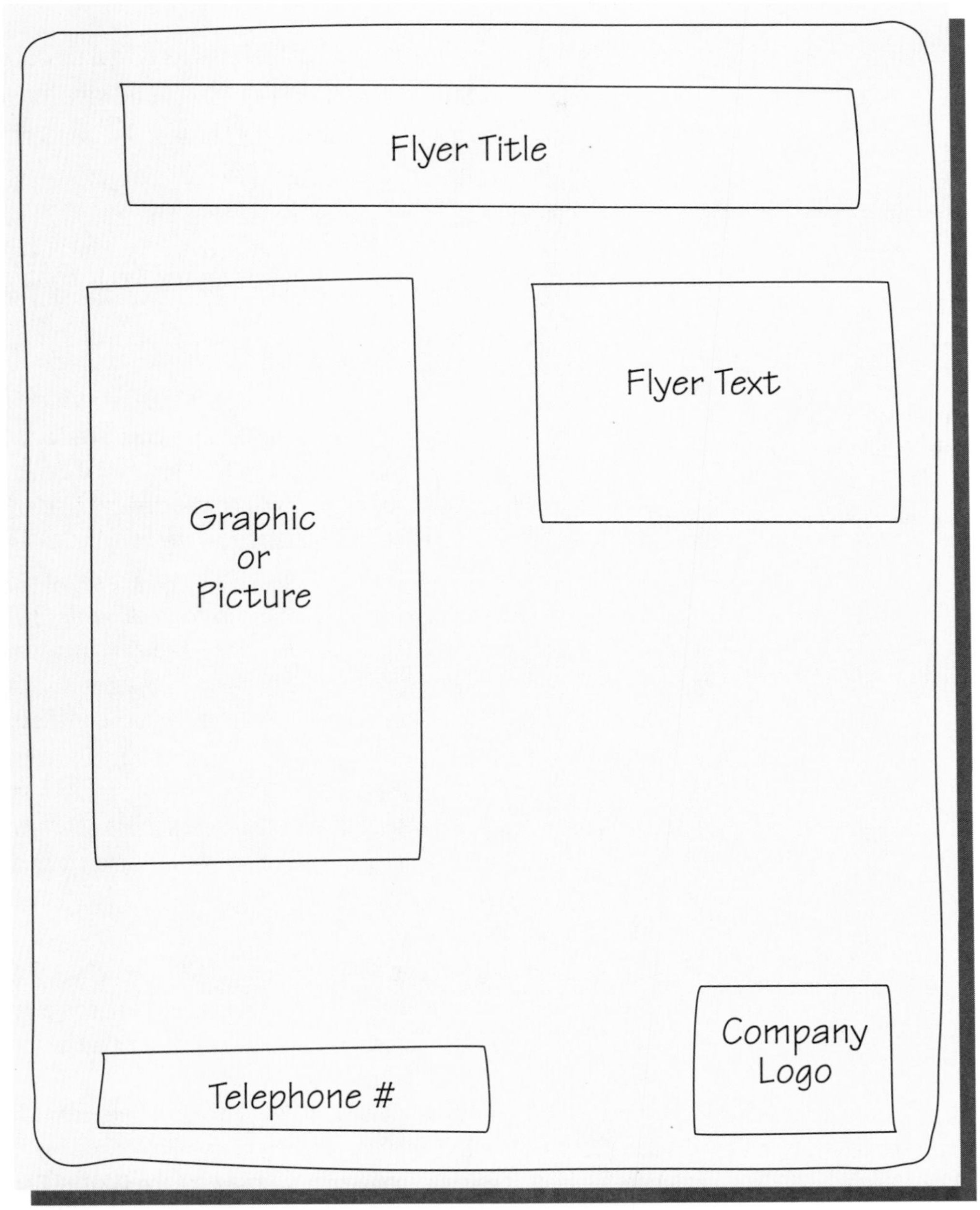

QUICK **TIP**

See Unit 7 for help designing a flyer.

Creating a fact sheet

Matt is responsible for creating color fact sheets that describe all the U.S. domestic tours offered by Sunset Tours. Fact sheets should give the reader all necessary information and also provide a point of response so the reader can act on the information. ▶ Matt is currently working on the New York City fact sheet, updating it with a new layout, color, and information. The information that he wants to add is in the form of a Microsoft Excel worksheet. He will need to import this file into PageMaker. To complete this project, draw upon the skills you learned in Unit 4, and use the sample fact sheet Matt sketched, shown in Figure 10-6.

STEPS

1. **Open the publication FACT.PM5 from your Student Disk.**
   The unfinished fact sheet opens. Notice that Matt has moved the Sunset Tours logo and the New York picture off the page so he can easily work with the text objects. To help align the header with the text and other objects on the page, Matt uses the margin Guides to determine the outside edges of the document. Matt changes the page layout to a two-column format.
2. **Change the page layout to 2-column format with .25" between columns**
   The column guides appear in the middle of the page. Now move the Sunset Tours' logo into the top left text object and custom wrap the text around the graphic. Matt moves this graphic first because he wants to make sure that all the information fits in the left column.
3. **Move the Sunset Tours' logo into the top left text object, then custom wrap the text around the logo**
   Add as many definition points to the standoff line as you need to achieve the look you want. Move the Sunset Tours' logo to different positions in the text object to find the best location. Now, before you place the picture of New York, import the Excel worksheet (as a graphic) so you can determine how wide the right column needs to be.
4. **Import the worksheet file FACTSOL.XLS from your Student Disk into your publication as a graphic, type the cell coordinates a1:d20 in the Place Excel range dialog box, then move the worksheet to the bottom of the right column inside the right margin guide**
   You need to identify the worksheet range in order for PageMaker to place the graphic. Once the worksheet is moved into position, it becomes an inline graphic so be sure you move it to the right location. If you have problems importing, see the TROUBLE? on the next page.
5. **Move the column guides so that they fit between the text on the left and the worksheet on the right**
   If necessary, adjust the text boxes so the two columns fit inside the page margins. Remember to use the width of the worksheet as your guide to determine the width of the right column.
6. **Move the picture of New York City into place, then use the Cropping tool in the toolbox to crop the picture so it fits inside the column**
7. **Change the style and color of the border line and the color of the header box**
8. **Check for spelling errors, then save and print your fact sheet**
9. **Be able to explain the design of your fact sheet**

FIGURE 10-6: Sketch of Sunset Tours' fact sheet

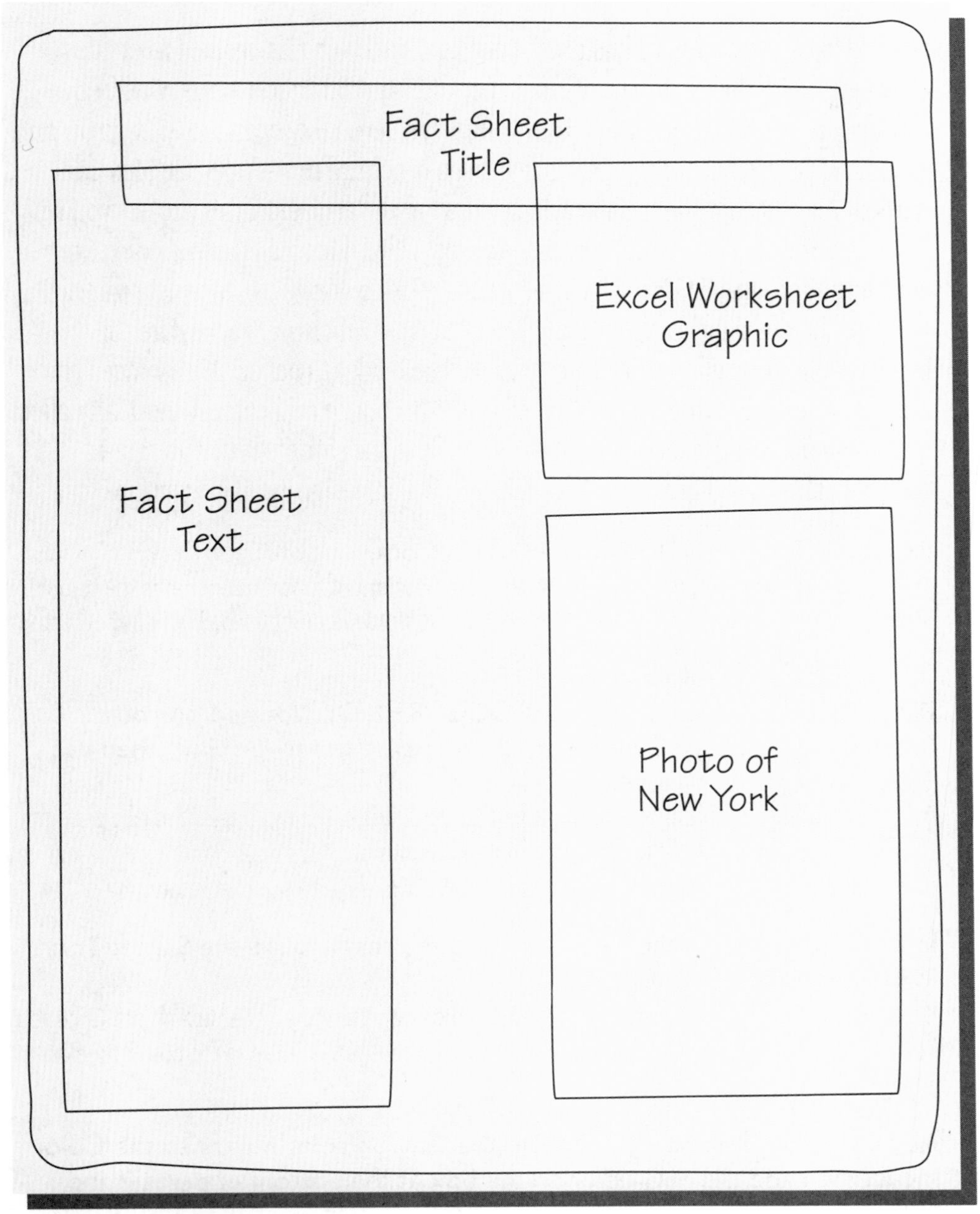

TROUBLE?

You must have an installed version of Microsoft Excel 4 or higher to place the worksheet as a graphic in the publication.

QUICK TIP

See Unit 8 for help designing a fact sheet.

Creating a brochure

In order to attract a larger customer base, Sunset Tours has decided to create full-color 8½" × 11" brochures on its most popular and profitable tours. One of the most popular tours that Sunset Tours offers is a seven day cruise to Mexico on an American Cruise Lines ship. Matt's two-page brochure introduces the Mexican ports of interest that the traveler will see during the cruise. In this project you will place text into the brochure from a Microsoft Word document, add a color from a color library to the Color menu, then create a tint color. ▶ To complete this project, use the design ideas from Unit 9 to plan your brochure. Make sure the brochure provides enough information for the reader to act on. Well-placed color and graphics add to the overall appeal of the brochure and can dramatically affect how the reader responds to the information. Use the sample brochure Matt sketched, shown in Figure 10-7, to help you finish designing the brochure.

STEPS

1 **Open the publication BROCHURE.PM5 from your Student Disk**
The first thing you need to do is place the text in the document so you can arrange the layout for both pages. The text for the brochure is in a Microsoft Word document, which you import using the Place command.

2 **Place the Word document file, BROCHURE.DOC, located on your Student Disk on page 2 of the brochure, resize the text object, then use to move text to page 3**
Be sure to leave white space around the picture in the center of the two pages. You can use the ruler guides to help place the text object. Before you continue, you might want resize the text objects on both pages so they match each other, then print the pages to check your work.

3 **In the text object on the left page, wrap the text around the Sunset Tours' logo**
Experiment with the logo's position to determine the best place for it in the text object. Once you finish adjusting the logo, add a new color to the menu that you will use in the box at the bottom of pages 2 and 3.

4 **Add the Orange Yellow color from the Crayon color library to the Color menu, then add the new color to the box at the bottom of pages 2 and 3**
Make sure the Orange Yellow color is a Process CMYK color. Matt uses the Orange Yellow color because it matches the color used in the Sunset Tours' logo. Now, Matt moves to the last page of the brochure and creates a tint from the Orange Yellow color to apply to the turquoise-colored box.

5 **Move to page 4 of the publication, create a tint from the Orange Yellow color, name the new color "Tint #1," then apply the color to the turquoise colored box**
Remember to use Orange Yellow as your base color when you create the tint.

6 **Finish the project by checking for spelling errors, then save and print your brochure**

7 **Be able to explain the design of your brochure**

FIGURE 10-7: Sketch of Sunset Tours' brochure

Shaded band

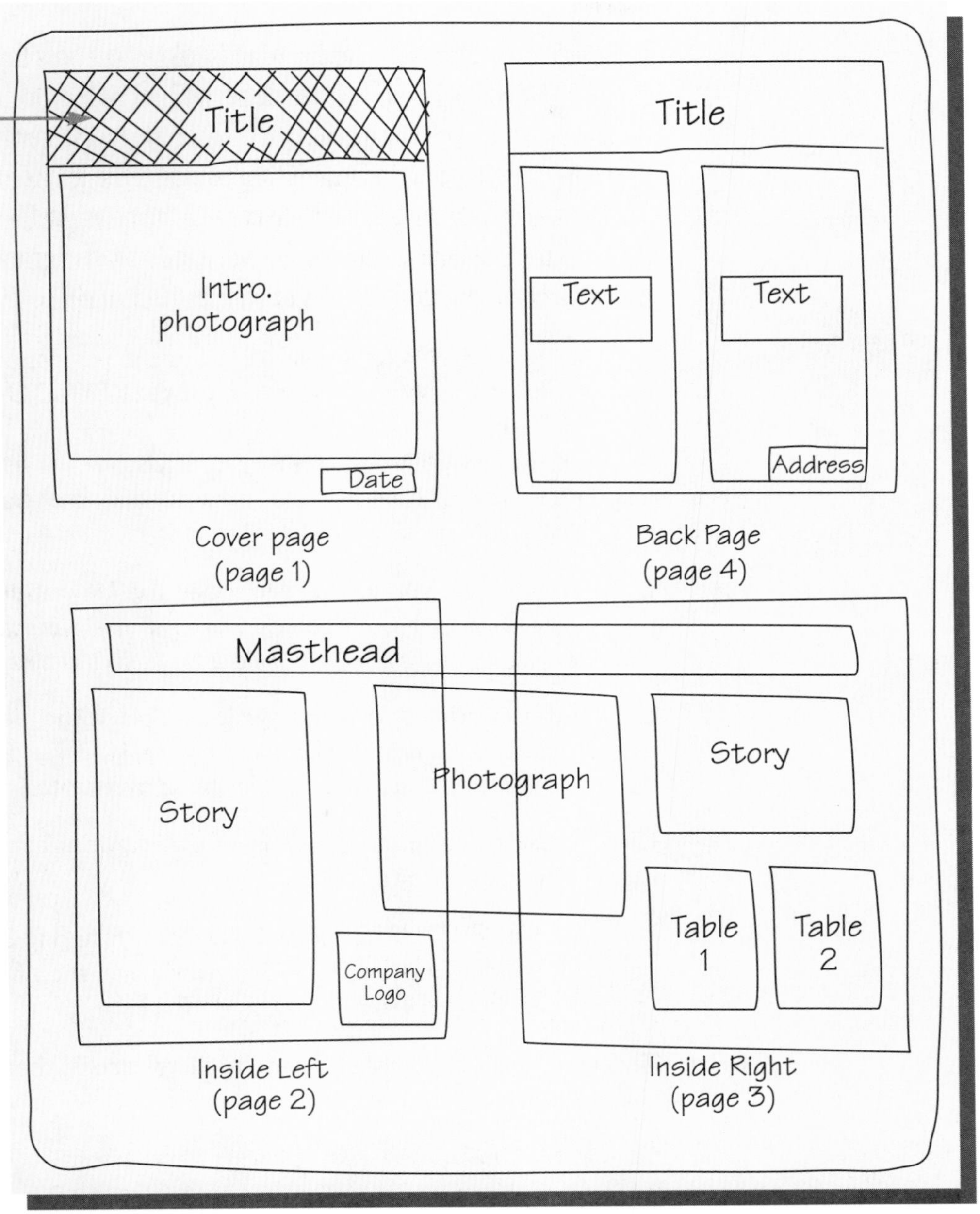

QUICK **TIP**

See Unit 9 for help designing a brochure.

Creating a newsletter

Upon arriving at his office today, Matt is told by his boss that he misplaced the disk that contained the company newsletter he had been working on. The only thing Matt has left to work from is a hard copy of the newsletter he printed the day before and a Microsoft Word document that contains the text for the publication. Recreate Matt's work by referring to his hard copy of the newsletter. ▶ Set the page specifications for the publication first, then place the text and graphics. Make your publication look like the page examples in Figures 10-8, 10-9, 10-10, and 10-11.

STEPS

1. **Open a new PageMaker publication, set the page specifications, then place the text from the Word document NEWSLTTR.DOC, located on your Student Disk**
   Don't spend too much time designing the page at this stage, just get the information in place. Now check the Link options dialog box to make sure that placed graphics are not stored in the newsletter.
2. **Deselect the text you just placed, open the Link options dialog box, then make sure there are no graphics stored in the publication**
   Storing graphic files in the newsletter would dramatically increase its file size.
3. **Create the masthead for the newsletter, place the file PICTURE1.TIF, then format the information as shown in Figure 10-8**
   Use the ruler guides to help you place the information on the page.
4. **Create text styles for the body text, the caption text, and the header text, then apply the styles to the text**
5. **Place the files PICTURE2.TIF, PICTURE3.TIF, and PICTURE4.TIF located on your Student Disk on the publication page, then format the information as shown in Figures 10-9, 10-10, and 10-11**
6. **Finish the project by checking for spelling errors, then save and print your newsletter**
7. **Be able to explain the design of your newsletter**

FIGURE 10-8: Newsletter page 1

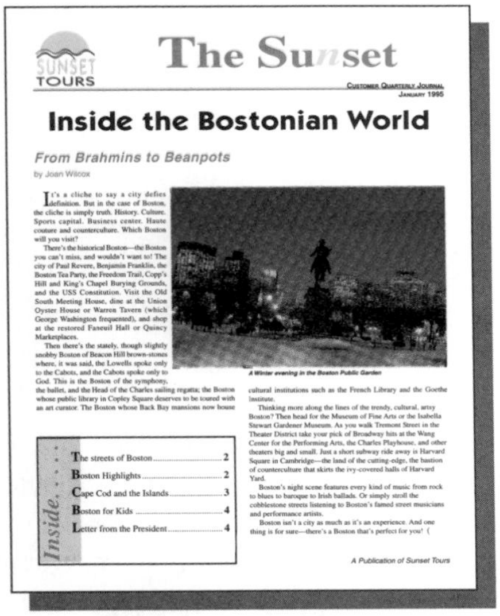

FIGURE 10-9: Newsletter page 2

FIGURE 10-10: Newsletter page 3

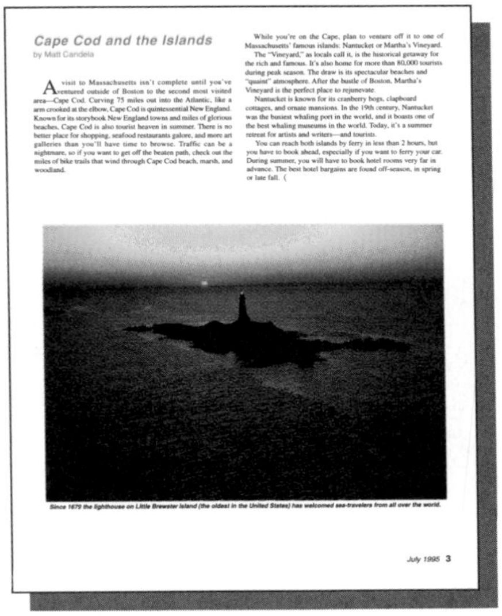

FIGURE 10-11: Newsletter page 4

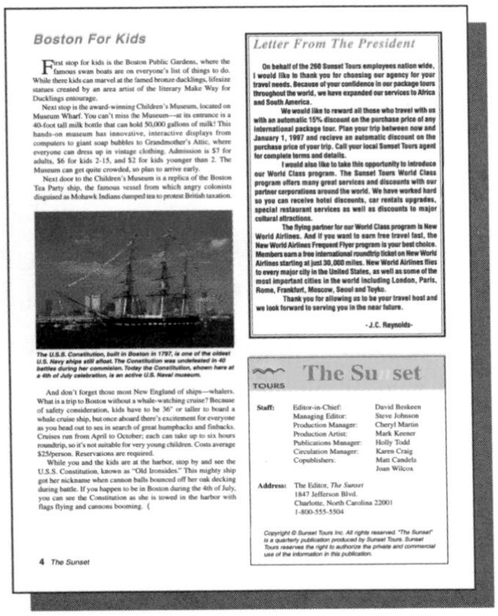

QUICK TIP

See Unit 5 for help designing a newsletter.

Glossary

Active application The application or program that is running. See also *Task List*.

Active window A window that you are currently using. If a window is active, its title bar changes color to differentiate it from other windows.

Alignment The horizontal position of text within a page or column. PageMaker aligns text left, right, centered, or justified.

Autoflow Automatically places text flowing from one column to the next, filling up as many columns and pages necessary.

Application A task-oriented software program that you use for a particular kind of work, such as word processing or database management. Microsoft Access, Microsoft Excel, and Microsoft Word are all applications.

Balance columns An addition which lets you align the top or bottom of text blocks threaded in a story on a single page or facing pages.

Baseline An imaginary line that text rests on.

Baseline leading Measures the leading from the baseline of the line of text.

Bitmapped Windows Paint File An image created by dot resolution.

Bullet A small graphic, usually a round or square dot, often used to identify items in a list.

Camera-ready A paper publication that can be sent directly to a printing company to be printed.

Character view Refers to the view on the Control palette in which you can change character related commands such as font, type style, leading, baseline shift, and other settings.

Clip art Graphic images or photography stored as electronic files, usually saved on compact disks.

Click To press and release the mouse button quickly.

Clipboard A temporary storage area for cut or copied text or graphics.

CMYK The four process colors: cyan (C), magenta (M), yellow (Y), black (K).

Color Matching System A method used by commercial printers to make sure the color used in your publication matches the color of the final output.

Color palette A moveable panel that lets you apply color to both text and graphics. Color can be applied to a graphic element's outside border line, inside fill, or both the line and fill.

Column guides Vertical, dotted, nonprinting lines that mark the right and left side of defined columns in publication page.

Command button In a dialog box, a button that carries out an action. A command button usually has a label that describes it action, such as Cancel or Help. If the label is followed by an ellipsis, clicking the button displays a dialog box.

Command prompt Symbol used to represent the drive and directory at which you can launch a program (usually C:\> is called the DOS command prompt).

Constrained-line tool Draws a straight line at 45-degree angles.

Crop To cut down a graphic to improve the image by eliminating unnecessary portions.

Cropping tool Allows you to crop graphic elements.

Cursor A blinking vertical line that shows you where you are on the screen. Often called the insertion point, it can also indicate the place where text will be inserted when you type.

Cut A command that removes selected text or a graphic from a document and places it on the Clipboard so you can paste it to another place in the document or to another document.

Cutlines Text that describes photos or graphics in a newsletter.

Cyan One of the four basic process colors. A shade of blue.

Default settings Predefined settings such as page margins, page size, and number of pages among other settings.

Definition points Adjustable points that define shape of the text wrap.

Desktop An electronic version of a desk that provides a workspace for different computing task on a computer screen.

Desktop publishing The ability to integrate text, graphics, spreadsheets, and charts created in different programs into one document on a personal computer, condensing into hours what used to take days in traditional publishing.

Dialog box A window that appears temporarily to request information. Many dialog boxes have options you must choose before Windows can carry out a command.

Directory Part of a structure for organizing your files on a disk. A directory can contain files and other directories (called subdirectories).

Dots per inch (dpi) A measure of the dots in a line that create an image. The higher the DPI number, the better the quality of the printout.

Double-click To press and release the mouse button twice quickly.

Drag To point at an item, press and hold the left mouse button, move the mouse to a new location, then release the mouse button.

Drag Placing Defining the size of a text block at the same time you import text.

Drop cap The first letter in a story that is enlarged and lowered so the top of the letter is even with the first line of text and the base of the letter drops next to the rest of the paragraph.

Ellipse Tool A tool used to draw circles or ovals in PageMaker.

Element Individual or grouped items in the publication window are called elements or objects.

Encapsulated PostScript A file created using Postscript code to create an image.

Export To create a new text file out of PageMaker's story editor.

Fact sheet An informational publication.

Fill The area within a drawn graphic element.

Fit in window command Adjusts page(s) to fill publication window so you see all of the page(s) and some of the surrounding pasteboard.

Flag The graphical element that serves as your identification and gives a purpose to your newsletter.

Floating palette A moveable window within the publication window.

Font The specific design of the characters.

Format The appearance of text or paragraph settings.

Grabber hand An icon that acts like a hand on a piece of paper and lets you move the page in any direction in the publication window.

Graphics Images created in a drawing or painting program or photographs or art scanned into the computer using a scanner.

Graphic elements An umbrella term that describes anything on a page other than the text.

Graphical user interface (GUI) A software program that works hand in hand with the MS-DOS operating system to control the basic operation of a computer and the programs that run on it.

Greeked text Text on page that cannot be read but represents text on the screen.

Group A collection of applications and accessories within Program Manager.

Guides PageMaker has three nonprinting lines: ruler, column, and margin. These guides are used to help align text on the page.

Gutter Space between columns.

Handles Square marks that appear on text and graphics when selected.

Highlight Dragging the cursor over text in order to change its appearance.

Hyphenate Inserting hyphens into words in order to separate the word between from the end of one line and the beginning of the next line.

I-Beam The shape of the icon pointer when the text tool is selected from the toolbox.

Icon A picture or symbol used to represent a command.

Image control This dialog box gives you the ability to lighten and adjust the contrast of black and white photographs and images.

Indent The distance between the text boundaries and page or column guides.

Inline graphic An object placed within a text block that moves with the text block or text in the text block moves.

Insertion point A blinking vertical line that shows your current location and where text graphics are inserted.

Kerning Adjusting the space between characters in the selected text.

Kilobyte Approximately 1,000 characters.

Landscape A term used to refer to horizontal page orientation; opposite of portrait, or vertical orientation.

Launch To start a program or application so you can use it.

Leaders Repeated pattern between tabbed items. Example of leaders include repeated dots or dashes.

Leading The vertical space between lines of text. Leading is the total height of a line from the top of the tallest character in the line to the top of the tallest characters in the line below.

Line tool Draws a straight line at any angle.

Line style A lines design, such as a single, double, dashed, or reverse line.

Line weight The thickness of the line.

Linked file A text or graphic file links to a PageMaker publication.

Magenta One of the four process colors. A shade of red.

Margin guides A magenta-colored box inside the page border indicates the margin guides.

Master Page A nonprinting page used for placing text and/or graphics that will appear on all pages of the publication.

Maximize To enlarge a window so it takes up the entire screen. There is usually a Maximize button in the upper-right comer of a window.

Menu A list of available commands in an application window.

Menu bar A horizontal bar containing the names of the application's menus. It appears below the title bar.

Minimize To reduce the size of a window. There is usually a Minimize button in the upper-right comer of a window. Double-clicking the Minimize button shrinks the window to an icon.

Mouse A hand-held input device that you roll on your desk to position the mouse pointer on the Windows desktop. See also *Mouse pointer*.

Mouse pointer The arrow-shaped cursor on the screen that follows the movement of the mouse as you roll the mouse on your desk. You use the mouse pointer to select items, choose commands, start application, and word in applications. The shape of the mouse pointer changes depending on the application and the task being executed.

Notepad A simple text editor that lets you create memos, record notes, or edit text files. It is a Microsoft Windows accessory.

Nudge buttons Small arrow buttons on the Control palette that let you make changes by a preset measurement.

Object An imported or a drawn graphic that you can select and transform.

Object view Refers to the view on the Control palette in which you can transform a graphic by changing size, position, rotation, or reflection.

Orphan A short line at the bottom of a column or page.

Orientation A page position either portrait (vertical) or landscape (horizontal).

PageMaker Additions Customized features to automate repetitive or complex publishing tasks. PageMaker ships with 24 different additions.

Page icons Miniature icons that represent pages in the publication. To move to a different page, click the desired page icon at the lower-left corner of the screen. In a single-page document, only one page icon appears.

Paragraph rule A line that can appear above or below a paragraph of text.

Paragraph view Refers to the view on the Control palette in which you can change Paragraph related commands such as indents, alignment, styles as well as other settings.

Pasteboard The white area surrounding and including the publication page. You can use the pasteboard as a work area to hold text or graphics until you place them in your publication. Any area beyond the pasteboard is represented by yellow or a color other than white.

Picas A measurement system used by many commercial printers. Six picas equal one inch.

Place The ability in PageMaker to import text or graphics.

Point $\frac{1}{72}$ of an inch.

Pointer tool Selects, moves and resizes objects.

Point of response The phone number or the address where the reader can respond to information in the publication.

Portrait A term used to refer to vertical page orientation, opposite of landscape or horizontal view.

Power points Areas in a publication that are read first by the viewer.

Picture/Draw Generally geometric drawings or charts and graphs (.PIC).

Proof A smaller scaled version of the final publication used by the creator for editing.

Process color Colors made from four basic colors (cyan, magenta, yellow, and black) combined in percentages to create many colors.

Proportional leading The default setting that allows for proportional amounts of space above the tallest character and the lowest character in a line.

Publications Using a desktop publishing program such as PageMaker, you can create brochures, newsletters, reports, advertisements, flyers, letterhead, forms, simple one-page letters, magazines and even books.

Publication page The solid-lined, boxed area where you create and modify text and graphics to build a publication. The maximum size allowed in PageMaker is 42" × 42." The publication can be displayed as a single page or with two facing pages. The publication is shadowed on the bottom and outer page borders so that you can see if you are working on a right or a left page.

Publication window The area that includes the page where the publication will be created.

RAM (Random Access Memory) The memory that can be used by applications to perform necessary tasks while the computer is on. When you turn the computer off, all information in RAM is lost.

Resize To change the size graphics by dragging the handles of the graphic to the size you want.

Reflecting Flipping an object either from top to bottom or from right to left.

Resolution Print quality, measured in dots per inch

Reverse text White or lightly shaded text or lines on black or dark background.

RGB A color system composed red (R), green (G) and blue (B). These colors are predefined in each new PageMaker publication.

Rotating Tool The ability to move graphic or text block at any angle.

Rulers Located on the top and left of the window, you use rulers to size the and align your text and graphics precisely and accurately.

Run To operate a program.

San Serif font A font whose characters do not include serifs, the small strokes at the ends of the characters. Arial is a San Serif font. These fonts are usually used for headlines or large text.

Scale Increase or decrease an object's size dimensions either proportionally or nonproportionally.

Scanner A device that allows you to convert text or graphics to files that be imported into PageMaker.

Screen elements The basic components of all PageMaker publications.

Scroll bar A bar that appears at the bottom and/or right edge of a window whose contents are not entirely visible. Each scroll bar contains a scroll box and two scroll arrows. You click the arrows or drag the box in the direction you want the window to move.

Select To highlight, or mark, an item so that a subsequent action can be carried out on the item.

Selection handles The small black squares at the corners and sides of the graphic, indicate that the graphic is selected.

Serif font A font that has small strokes at the ends of the characters. Times New Roman is a Serif font. These fonts are best used for small text, making it easier to read.

Scroll bars Located on the right and bottom edges of the window. You use them too display portions of the pasteboard that are not visible in the current view.

Selection marquee You can select several objects at once in PageMaker by drawing a selection marquee around the group of objects you want to move or edit.

Semi-Automatic flow The ability to place text which flows to the bottom of a column or page and then waits for you to place text in the next column or page.

Separations Printouts on paper or film, one for each of the four process colors.

Size The dimensions of characters is usually measured in points.

Skewing Lets you stretch the object at an angle, giving it a distorted appearance.

Snap to guides A feature that causes graphic elements to "magnetically" align to a PageMaker guide.

Spot color One specific ink used to create a color.

Stacked Objects overlapped each other.

Standoff Measurement in a text wrap of text from the wrapped graphic.

Story editor A word processor program within PageMaker.

Style How the type is displayed, for example, in italics or bold.

Task List A window that displays the active applications and programs. You can use the Task List to switch between active applications and programs.

Text file A document file containing words, letters, or numbers, but no special computer instructions, such as formatting.

Thumbnail A small sketch that shows only the large elements of the page.

Tabs Nonprinting characters, that allow you to position text at specific locations within a text block.

Tagged Image File Format (TIFF) A file format used for storing graphics or photographs that can be used in PageMaker or other software programs.

Teaser A publication that wants you to respond to receive more information about the a product or service.

Template Predesigned page layouts which have dummy text and graphics and can be replaced with your own text and graphic objects.

Text block Text selected with the pointer tool from the toolbox.

Text tool Tool used for entered or deleted text.

Text wrap Flowing text around a graphic object at a specified distance.

Threaded text Text block that is connected or linked to another text block flowing from a column or page to another column or page.

Tint A new color based on a percentage of a color you created or based on one of PageMaker's default colors.

Toolbox Contains eight tool icons for creating and modifying text and graphics. The toolbox is a floating palette, which is a moveable window within the publication window.

Title bar Displays the open publication's filename.

Tracking Six predefined character spacing options that can be quickly applied to text.

Typographer Refers to someone who designs or sets type in the commercial printing industry.

Widow A line of text that begins a paragraph at the bottom of a column or page.

Window A rectangle space on a screen in which a program or application runs.

Windowshade handles Circles that define the size of a selected text block.

Zero point marker The intersection of the horizontal and vertical rulers

Zero point The point at which the zero marks on the rulers intersect.

Index

Special Characters

A

B

N

O

P

S

U

V

W

Y

Z